✧ SO-ADK-989

Forbes

TRAVEL GUIDE

Formerly Mobil Travel Guide

NEW ENGLAND

3-19-2010
535 160092

ACKNOWLEDGMENTS

We gratefully acknowledge the help of our representatives for their efficient and perceptive inspections of the lodgings listed. Forbes Travel Guide is also grateful to the talented writers who contributed to this book.

NEW ENGLAND
★★★★

ISBN: 9-780841-61419-2   Manufactured in the USA

10 9 8 7 6 5 4 3 2 1

TABLE OF CONTENTS

STAR ATTRACTIONS   4

THE STAR RATINGS   5-7

NEW ENGLAND
    CONNECTICUT   8-35
    MAINE   36-78
    MASSACHUSETTS   79-209
    NEW HAMPSHIRE   210-230
    RHODE ISLAND   231-248
    VERMONT   249-280

INDEX   281-302

STATE MAPS   303-314
    CONNECTICUT   303
        HARTFORD   304
    MAINE   305
        AUGUSTA AND PORTLAND   306
    MASSACHUSETTS   308-309
        BOSTON AND THE CAPE   307
    NEW HAMPSHIRE   310
        CONCORD   311
    RHODE ISLAND   312
    VERMONT   313
        MONTPELIER   314

STAR ATTRACTIONS

If you've been a reader of Mobil Travel Guide, you will have heard that this historic brand partnered with another storied media name, Forbes, in 2009 to create a new entity, Forbes Travel Guide. For more than 50 years, Mobil Travel Guide assisted travelers in making smart decisions about where to stay and dine when traveling. With this new partnership, our mission has not changed: We're committed to the same rigorous inspections of hotels, restaurants and spas—the most comprehensive in the industry with more than 500 standards tested at each property we visit—to help you cut through the clutter and make easy and informed decisions on where to spend your time and travel budget. Our team of anonymous inspectors are constantly on the road, sleeping in hotels, eating in restaurants and making spa appointments, evaluating those exacting standards to determine a property's rating.

What kind of standards are we looking for when we visit a proprety? We're looking for more than just high-thread count sheets, pristine spa treatment rooms and white linen-topped tables. We look for service that's attentive, in-dividualized and unforgettable. We note how long it takes to be greeted when you sit down at your table, or to be served when you order room service, or whether the hotel staff can confidently help you when you've forgotten that one essential item that will make or break your trip. Unlike other travel ratings entities, we visit the places we rate, testing hundreds of attributes to compile our ratings, and our ratings cannot be bought or influenced. The Forbes Five Star rating is the most prestigious achievement in hospitality—while we rate more than 8,000 properties in the U.S., Canada, Hong Kong, Macau and Beijing, for 2010, we have awarded Five Star designations to only 53 hotels, 21 restaurants and 18 spas. When you travel with Forbes, you can travel with confidence, knowing that you'll get the very best experience, no matter who you are.

We understand the importance of making the most of your time. That's why the most trusted name in travel is now Forbes Travel Guide.

STAR RATED HOTELS

Whether you're looking for the ultimate in luxury or the best value for your travel budget, we have a hotel recommendation for you. To help you pinpoint properties that meet your needs, Forbes Travel Guide classifies each lodging by type according to the following characteristics:

★★★★★These exceptional properties provide a memorable experience through virtually flawless service and the finest of amenities. Staff are intuitive, engaging and passionate, and eagerly deliver service above and beyond the guests' expectations. The hotel was designed with the guest's comfort in mind, with particular attention paid to craftsmanship and quality of product. A Five Star property is a destination unto itself.

★★★★These properties provide a distinctive setting, and a guest will find many interesting and inviting elements to enjoy throughout the property. Attention to detail is prominent throughout the property, from design concept to quality of products provided. Staff are accommodating and take pride in catering to the guest's specific needs throughout their stay.

★★★These well-appointed establishments have enhanced amenities that provide travelers with a strong sense of location, whether for style or function. They may have a distinguishing style and ambience in both the public spaces and guest rooms; or they may be more focused on functionality, providing guests with easy access to local events, meetings or tourism highlights.

★★The Two Star hotel is considered a clean, comfortable and reliable establishment that has expanded amenities, such as a full-service restaurant.

★The One Star lodging is a limited-service hotel or inn that is considered a clean, comfortable and reliable establishment.

For every property, we also provide pricing information. All prices quoted are accurate at the time of publication; however, prices cannot be guaranteed.

STAR RATED RESTAURANTS

Every restaurant in this book comes highly recommended as an outstanding dining experience.

★★★★★Forbes Five Star restaurants deliver a truly unique and distinctive dining experience. A Five Star restaurant consistently provides exceptional food, superlative service and elegant décor. An emphasis is placed on originality and personalized, attentive and discreet service. Every detail that surrounds the experience is attended to by a warm and gracious dining room team.

★★★★These are exciting restaurants with often well-known chefs that feature creative and complex foods and emphasize various culinary techniques and a focus on seasonality. A highly-trained dining room staff provides refined personal service and attention.

★★★Three Star restaurants offer skillfully-prepared food with a focus on a specific style or cuisine. The dining room staff provides warm and professional service in a comfortable atmosphere. The décor is well-coordinated with quality fixtures and decorative items, and promotes a comfortable ambience.

★★The Two Star restaurant serves fresh food in a clean setting with efficient service. Value is considered in this category, as is family friendliness.

★The One Star restaurant provides a distinctive experience through culinary specialty, local flair or individual atmosphere.

Because menu prices can fluctuate, we list a pricing range rather than specific prices. The pricing ranges are per diner, and assume that you order an appetizer or dessert, an entrée and one drink.

STAR RATED SPAS

Forbes Travel Guide's spa ratings are based on objective evaluations of more than 450 attributes. About half of these criteria assess basic expectations, such as staff courtesy, the technical proficiency and skill of the employees and whether the facility is clean and maintained properly. Several standards address issues that impact a guest's physical comfort and convenience, as well as the staff's ability to impart a sense of personalized service. Additional criteria measure the spa's ability to create a completely calming ambience.

★★★★★Stepping foot in a Five Star spa will result in an exceptional experience with no detail overlooked. These properties wow their guests with extraordinary design and facilities, and uncompromising service. Expert staff cater to your every whim and pamper you with the most advanced treatments and skin care lines available. These spas often offer exclusive treatments and may emphasize local elements.

★★★★Four Star spas provide a wonderful experience in an inviting and serene environment. A sense of personalized service is evident from the moment you check in and receive your robe and slippers. The guest's comfort is always of utmost concern to the well-trained staff.

★★★These spas offer well-appointed facilities with a full complement of staff to ensure that guests' needs are met. The spa facilities include clean and appealing treatment rooms, changing areas and a welcoming reception desk.

CONNECTICUT

WHEN SOME PEOPLE THINK OF CONNECTICUT, THEY ENVISION KHAKI-CLAD MILLIONAIRES sipping martinis on manicured Greenwich lawns. Others call to mind the state's manageable capital city, Hartford, home to insurance companies and the country's first newspaper. Still others think of charming Mystic and the southeastern coastal area that has been wildly popular ever since Julia Roberts' performance in *Mystic Pizza*. And some will picture the state's quiet northwestern and northeastern corners, full of rambling old farmhouses and hilly country roads. All would be correct.

A region of around 3 ½ million residents, Connecticut has much diversity and much to offer discerning travelers. For starters, the Constitution State has the mildest climate in New England and many historic tree-lined towns. It also has an entire southern border on Long Island Sound and an eponymous river. Adriaen Block sailed into the latter in 1614; Connecticut's first colonists soon followed, settling Hartford, Windsor and Wethersfield. The state hosted a myriad of important Revolutionary and Civil War events, and is home to many famous inventors.

Today, Connecticut's industry revolves around agriculture, manufacturing and insurance. But most travelers will continue to remember it fondly as a beautiful state full of grand old summer homes, endless green pastures, soft sand beaches and the occasional fleet of mega yachts.

AVON

See also Farmington, Hartford

This central town on the Farmington River dates to 1645. The town has historic churches, buildings and even a covered bridge.

WHAT TO SEE

FARMINGTON VALLEY ARTS CENTER

25 Arts Center Lane, Avon, 860-678-1867; www.fvac.net

Located in a historic stone explosives plant, these twenty studios are now occupied by artists. The onsite Fisher Gallery features guest-curated exhibits and handmade crafts, gifts and artwork.

January-October: Wednesday-Saturday, Sunday afternoons; November-December: daily 9 a.m.-5 p.m.

WHERE TO STAY

★★★AVON OLD FARMS HOTEL

279 Avon Mountain, Avon, 860-677-1651, 800-836-4000; www.avonoldfarmshotel.com

Avon has many "authentic," albeit rusty (yes, that's rusty, not rustic) bed and breakfasts. If you're looking for quaint yet comfortable, check into the Avon Old Farms Hotel instead. The 160-room property is low on kitschy charm and high on functionality and service. Twenty landscaped acres, brass chandeliers and white canopied beds save the property from business-retreat banality. A lively outdoor pool scene adds further life to the mountainside hotel.

160 rooms. Complimentary breakfast. Restaurant. Fitness center. Pool. $151-250

WHERE TO EAT
★★★AVON OLD FARMS INN
1 Nod Rd., Avon, 860-677-2818, 860-674-2434; www.avonoldfarmsinn.com
Set in a 1757 stagecoach stop building, this stone-walled eatery is themed accordingly. Old stirrups and bridles hang from the ceiling, and the floors and walls are built from smooth stone. Entrées range from hearty (filet mignon, short ribs) to healthy (spinach salad, tomato-basil linguine); the menu also includes a few kosher options.
American. Lunch, dinner, Sunday brunch. Bar. Children's menu. $16-35

★★DAKOTA
225 W. Main St., Avon, 860-677-4311; www.dakotarestaurant.com
This local steakhouse serves hearty portions of wood-grilled red meat and fresh seafood. Stone fireplaces and Southwestern accents create a cozy atmosphere.
Steak. Dinner. Bar. Children's menu, Sunday brunch. $16-35

DANBURY
See also Ridgefield, Southbury, Woodbury
This western Connecticut town's history is replete with patriotic pride. During the American Revolution, it was a supply depot and the site of a Continental Army hospital. Originally settled by eight Norwalk families seeking fertile land, the city was once the hub of the hat industry. Danbury native Zadoc Benedict is credited with opening the first factory in 1790—it made just three hats a day.

WHAT TO SEE
CANDLEWOOD LAKE
35 E. Hayestown Road, Danbury; www.candlewoodlake.org
Connecticut's largest lake is more than 14 miles long and, with more than 80 miles of shoreline, extends one finger into Danbury. Swimming, fishing, boating as well as picnicking is allowed on the lake. There are concessions available. Fees are required for some activities.

SPECIAL EVENTS
CHARLES IVES CENTER FOR THE ARTS
Mill Plain Road, Danbury, 203-837-9226; www.ivesconcertpark.com
Outdoor classical, country, folk, jazz and pop concerts are held on Western Connecticut State University's Westside campus.
July-early September: Friday-Sunday.

TASTE OF GREATER DANBURY
Danbury Green, Green Ives and White streets, Danbury, 203-792-1711;
www.citycenterdanbury.com
Food vendors, live music and children's games draw crowds together year after year at this outdoor festival.
September.

WHERE TO STAY
★★★DANBURY PLAZA HOTEL
18 Old Ridgebury Road, Danbury, 203-794-0600; www.danburyplaza.com
Conveniently located just three miles from Danbury Airport, this hotel has comfortably outfitted guest rooms, an onsite restaurant and a fitness room. Amenities include nightly turndown service, and if you just can't get away from work, rooms feature large desks.
242 rooms. Restaurant, bar. $61-150

★★ETHAN ALLEN HOTEL
21 Lake Ave., Danbury, 203-744-1776, 800-742-1776; www.ethanallenhotel.com
Owned by the famed furniture maker and located on its Danbury corporate campus, this independent hotel features rooms decorated in Colonial style and stocked with the company's furnishings. The onsite restaurant, Fairfields, serves upscale fare in a French country-style dining room.
200 rooms. Restaurant, bar. $61-150

WHERE TO EAT
★★TWO STEPS DOWNTOWN GRILLE
5 Ives St., Danbury, 203-794-0032; www.ciaocafetwosteps.com
Housed in a historic brick building that was once home to a firehouse, this casual grill serves steaks and chops, as well as hearty burgers. The outdoor patio offers ample space and is a prime spot for fine weather dining.
American, Southwestern. Lunch, dinner, Sunday brunch. Bar. Children's menu. Outdoor seating. $16-35

ESSEX
See also Old Lyme
With its well-preserved, tree-lined Main Street, Essex has been called the "best small town in America." The peaceful Eastern Connecticut village of 6,000 exudes storybook charm in the form of its brick post office, antique shops and 1700s-era ship captain's houses.

WHAT TO SEE
CONNECTICUT RIVER MUSEUM
67 Main St., Essex, 860-767-8269; www.ctrivermuseum.org
Housed in the last remaining steamboat dock building on the Connecticut River, the museum features exhibits that celebrate the rich cultural heritage and natural resources of the River Valley, including the only full-size operating replica of the *Turtle*, America's first successful submarine.
Tuesday-Sunday 10 a.m.-5 p.m.

VALLEY RAILROAD
1 Railroad Ave., Essex, 860-767-0103, 800-377-3987; www.essexsteamtrain.com
A scenic 12-mile steam train excursion along the Connecticut River to Chester, with an optional one-hour Connecticut River cruise.
Early May-late October, days vary; also Christmas trips.

SPECIAL EVENT
DEEP RIVER ANCIENT MUSTER AND PARADE

Devitt's Field, Main Street, Deep River, 860-388-7575
Approximately 60 fife and drum players recall the Revolutionary War period.
Third Saturday in July.

WHERE TO STAY
★★★COPPER BEECH INN

46 Main St., Ivoryton, 860-767-0330, 888-809-2056; www.copperbeechinn.com
Travelers looking for a romantic New England getaway should check into
this charming 1889 Victorian inn. Once the residence of a prominent ivory
importer, the country retreat is set on sprawling wooded grounds.
13 rooms. No children under 16. Complimentary breakfast. Restaurant.
Closed for a week in January. $61-150

★★★GRISWOLD INN

36 Main St., Essex, 860-767-1776; www.griswoldinn.com
Known to locals as "The Gris," this 1776 inn is known for its lavish English-
style Sunday buffet breakfast (order a mimosa). The rooms and suites are full
of fresh flowers and antiques, but feature updated touches such as wireless
access.
31 rooms. Complimentary breakfast. Restaurant. $61-150

WHERE TO EAT
★★★COPPER BEECH INN

46 Main St., Ivoryton, 860-767-0330, 888-809-2056; www.copperbeechinn.com
Much like its namesake inn, the restaurant is all soft elegance and warm romance. Patrons here dine on hearty, French country fare amidst fresh flowers,
sparkling silver and soft candlelight.
American, French. Dinner. Bar. Jacket required. Closed Monday. Reservations recommended. $36-85

★★SAGE AMERICAN BAR & GRILL

129 W. Main St., Chester, 860-526-9898; www.sageamerican.com
Housed in a former saw mill and brush factory, perched on a small water-
fall overlooking the Pattaconk Brook, this casual restaurant serves classic
American recipes such as lobster bisque and roast prime rib. The bar has an
extensive offering of cocktails, including plenty of champagne drinks.
Seafood, steak. Dinner. Children's menu. Outdoor seating. $16-35

FARMINGTON

See also Avon, Hartford, New Britain
Home to the erstwhile "finishing school" Miss Porter's, Farmington is one
of New England's most bucolic towns. During the early 1800s, the small
city bustled with silversmiths, tinsmiths, cabinetmakers, clockmakers and
carriage builders.

WHAT TO SEE
HILL-STEAD MUSEUM
35 Mountain Road, Farmington, 860-677-4787; www.hillstead.org
A Colonial Revival-style country house designed by Theodate Pope in collaboration with McKim, Mead and White contains industrialist Alfred Pope's collection of French Impressionist paintings.
Tuesday-Sunday. May-October 10 a.m.-5 p.m. November-April 11 a.m.-4 p.m.

STANLEY-WHITMAN HOUSE
37 High St., Farmington, 860-677-9222; www.stanleywhitman.org
This 1720 home is one of the finest early 18th-century houses in the United States.
May-October: Wednesday-Sunday noon-4 p.m.; November-April: Saturday-Sunday afternoons, also by appointment.

SPECIAL EVENT
FARMINGTON ANTIQUES WEEKEND
Polo Grounds, Farmington, 860-677-7862; www.farmingtonantiquesweekend.com
More than 600 dealers descend on the town for one of the largest annual antique events in the state.
Mid-June and early September.

WHERE TO STAY
★★★THE FARMINGTON INN OF GREATER HARTFORD
827 Farmington Ave., Farmington, 860-677-2821, 800-648-9804; www.farmingtoninn.com
With its Colonial décor and small touches like complimentary tea and cookies, this hotel has the charm of a quaint country inn. Rooms feature antiques and works by local artists.
72 rooms. Complimentary breakfast. Restaurant, bar. Business center. $61-150

★★★HARTFORD MARRIOTT FARMINGTON
15 Farm Springs Road, Farmington, 860-678-1000, 800-228-9190; www.marriott.com
Close enough to downtown to be convenient, yet far enough away from the city center to be peaceful, this Marriott pampers business travelers and leisure guests alike with a full range of amenities, including two swimming pools and a tennis court. Rooms feature updated decor and flat-screen TVs.
374 rooms. Restaurant, bar. $151-250

WHERE TO EAT
★★APRICOT'S
1593 Farmington Ave., Farmington, 860-673-5405; www. apricotsrestaurant.com
This two-level restaurant features a formal dining room, as well as a casual pub and parlor. Housed in a converted trolley barn, the eatery features an eclectic menu of dishes such as seared scallops with shitake risotto.
American. Lunch, dinner, brunch. Bar. Reservations recommended. Outdoor seating. $16-35

GREENWICH

See also Stamford

Possibly the state's most talked about town, Greenwich has long been home to hedge fund barons, ladies who lunch and other well-moneyed folk. Its proximity to New York City—28 miles from Times Square—and the sea—oceanfront megamansions dot the coastline—has made this settlement of 58,000 one of the most coveted places to live in the entire United States. Visitors will enjoy Greenwich's leafy, photo-friendly 18th-century streets and Manhattan-worthy boutiques.

WHAT TO SEE
AUDUBON CENTER

613 Riversville Road, Greenwich, 203-869-5272; greenwich.audubon.org
This 522-acre sanctuary includes a self-guided nature trail.
Daily.

BRUCE MUSEUM

1 Museum Drive, Greenwich, 203-869-0376; www.brucemuseum.org
The arts and sciences museum features exhibits, lectures, concerts and educational programs.
Tuesday-Saturday 10 a.m.-5 p.m., Sunday 1-5 p.m. Closed Monday and major holidays.

BUSH-HOLLEY HOUSE

39 Strickland Road, Cos Cob, 203-869-6899; www.hstg.org
This former residence of a successful 18th-century farmer became the site of the Cos Cob art colony at the turn of the century. Current exhibits include late 18th-century Connecticut furniture; paintings by Childe Hassam, Elmer Livingston MacRae and John Henry Twachtman; sculptures by John Rogers; and pottery by Leon Volkmar.
Open Tuesday-Sunday afternoons April-December and Saturday-Sunday afternoons January-March.

PUTNAM COTTAGE/KNAPP TAVERN

243 E. Putnam Ave., Greenwich, 203-869-9697; www.putnamcottage.org
Near this tavern, Revolutionary General Israel Putnam made a daring escape from the Redcoats in 1779.
April-November: Sunday 1-4 p.m.; also by appointment December-March.

WHERE TO STAY
★★★THE DELAMAR

500 Steamboat Road, Greenwich, 203-661-9800; www.thedelamar.com
The award-winning Delamar looks more like a Lake Como mansion than an old Connecticut retreat. Its sprawling cream-colored façade hides an interior rich with original artwork, sparkling chandeliers, ornate sconces and a plethora of marble. Overlooking the Greenwich Marina, the property has 82 rooms filled with up-to-date electronics, luxe Italian linens and cast-iron tubs. Even dogs are pampered here with the resort's "Sophisticated Pet" program.
82 rooms. No children under 12. Restaurant, bar. Pets accepted. Spa. $251-350

★★★HOMESTEAD INN

420 Field Point Road, Greenwich, 203-869-7500; www.homesteadinn.com

Owned by Greenwich hoteliers Thomas and Theresa Henkelmann, the inn—and its accompanying three-star restaurant—is a study in old-school sumptuous elegance. The rooms at the Homestead Inn are not called rooms—they are called "chambers." And the lodging at this renovated 1799 inn is anything but average: second and third-floor suites boast imported furniture, Frette linens and original artwork, plus heated bathroom floors.

18 rooms. Closed two weeks in March. No children under 12. Restaurant, bar. $351 and up

★★★HYATT REGENCY GREENWICH

1800 E. Putnam Ave., Old Greenwich, 203-637-1234, 800-633-7313;
www.greenwich.hyatt.com

Before magazine giant Condé Nast moved to Manhattan, the *Vogue* and *Glamour* publisher was headquartered at 1800 E. Putnam. Now a Hyatt, the building has retained much of its early glamour with an elegant atrium-style lobby with ponds, stone walls and an impressive array of trees, plants and flowers. Guest rooms are spacious and feature Internet access, bathrobes and plush pillows.

373 rooms. Restaurant, bar. Business center. $251-350

WHERE TO EAT

★★★JEAN-LOUIS

61 Lewis St., Greenwich, 203-622-8450; www.restaurantjeanlouis.com

Sophisticated and elegant with professional service to match, this cozy restaurant has a menu grounded in the precision of French classicism. The décor is decidedly Parisian as well, as the serving china and candle lamps were all custom-made in France. The chef works directly with local farmers for the freshest ingredients, and in addition to the à la carte menu, the restaurant offers tastings, petit tastings, plus vegetarian and vegan menus.

French. Lunch, dinner. Closed Sunday; also first two weeks of August. Reservations recommended. $36-85

★★★L'ESCALE

500 Steamboat Road, Greenwich, 203-661-4600; www.lescalerestaurant.com

This French-Mediterranean restaurant earns its stars by re-creating the Mediterranean on the North Atlantic shore with a stone fireplace and terra-cotta floors to warm the dining room and light-filtering thatched bamboo to shade the patio. The menu by Francois Kwaku-Dongo includes a salad of caramelized leeks and chanterelles; apple and prune-paired foie gras; and crispy duck breast. The eatery has become a gathering place for locals and travelers alike, and it's no wonder why: L'Escale allows guests to sail to dinner and tie up their yachts at its waterfront dock.

French, Mediterranean. Breakfast, lunch, dinner, Sunday brunch. Bar. Reservations recommended. Outdoor seating. $36-85

★★TERRA RISTORANTE ITALIANO

156 Greenwich Ave., Greenwich, 203-629-5222; www.terraofgreenwich.com

This intimate Italian bistro serves classic pastas, pizzas and entrees in a casual setting. The wine list is extensive and features mostly bottles from the wine-making regions of Italy.

Italian. Lunch, dinner. Bar. Reservations recommended. Outdoor seating. $36-85

★★THAT LITTLE ITALIAN RESTAURANT

228-230 Mill St., Greenwich, 203-531-7500; www.greenwichtlir.com

The walls are painted with murals of Venetian canals, the menu features a solid chicken parmesan and chianti comes both in bottles and rattan-wrapped carafes. When only a classic no-frills Italian bistro will do, this downtown Greenwich eatery fits the bill.

Italian. Lunch, dinner. Closed Monday. Outdoor seating. $16-35

★★★THOMAS HENKELMANN

420 Field Point Road, Greenwich, 203-869-7500; www.thomashenkelmann.com

German-born, French-trained chef Thomas Henkelmann's eatery proffers clever takes on traditional French fare. The formal spot's lobster bisque is Henkelmann's specialty—a rich, creamy concoction full of sweet and savory flavors. Service is discreet and attentive, and well-cared-for gardens are ideal for an after dinner stroll.

French. Breakfast, lunch, dinner. Closed Sunday; also two weeks in March. Bar. Jacket required. Reservations recommended. $86 and up

HARTFORD

See also Avon, Farmington

Connecticut's capital city falls, appropriately enough, in the center of the state. Settled in 1633 on the region's eponymous river, Hartford has deep democratic roots. When Brit Sir Edmund Andros tried to seize the state's own declaration of independence, loyal citizen Joseph Wadsworth hid the charter in a hollow tree. The secret stashing place is known as the Charter Oak, and Hartford still exhibits creative spirit. *The Hartford Courant*, founded in 1764, is the oldest continuously published newspaper in the United States. This daily paper regularly covers the city's booming insurance and education industries.

WHAT TO SEE
BUTLER-MCCOOK HOMESTEAD AND MAIN STREET HISTORY CENTER

396 Main St., Hartford, 860-522-1806; www.ctlandmarks.org

This preserved house, occupied by four generations of one family between 1782 and 1971, showcases possessions dating back 200 years, a collection of Victorian toys, Japanese armor and a Victorian garden.

Wednesday-Sunday.

HARRIET BEECHER STOWE CENTER

77 Forest St., Hartford, 860-522-9258; www.harrietbeecherstowecenter.org

The restored Victorian cottage of the author of *Uncle Tom's Cabin* contains original furniture and memorabilia.

Tours. Monday-Saturday 9:30 a.m.-4:30 p.m., Sunday noon-4:30 p.m.

MARK TWAIN HOUSE

351 Farmington Ave., Hartford, 860-247-0998; www.marktwainhouse.org

Tom Sawyer, *Huckleberry Finn* and other books were published while Samuel Clemens (Mark Twain) lived in this three-story Victorian mansion featuring the decorative work of Charles Comfort Tiffany.

Tours. Monday-Saturday 9:30 a.m.-5:30 p.m., Sunday noon-5:30 p.m. Closed Tuesday January-March.

MUSEUM OF CONNECTICUT HISTORY

Connecticut State Library, 231 Capitol Ave., Hartford, 860-757-6335; www.museumofcthistory.org

Exhibits include the Colt Collection of Firearms; Connecticut artifacts, including the original 1662 Royal Charter; and portraits of Connecticut's governors. The library features law, social sciences, history, genealogy collections and official state archives.

Monday-Friday 9 a.m.-4 p.m. and Saturday 9 a.m.-3p.m.

NOAH WEBSTER FOUNDATION AND HISTORICAL SOCIETY

227 S. Main St., West Hartford, 860-521-5362; www.noahwebsterhouse.org

This 18th-century homestead was the birthplace of America's first lexicographer, writer of the *Blue-Backed Speller* and the *American Dictionary*.

Thursday-Monday 1-4 p.m.

OLD STATE HOUSE

800 Main St., Hartford, 860-522-6766; www.ctoldstatehouse.org

The oldest state house in the nation was designed by Charles Bulfinch. The restored Senate chamber has a Gilbert Stuart portrait of George Washington.

Monday-Friday 9 a.m.-5 p.m. Summer hours begin mid-July Tuesday-Saturday 10 a.m.-5 p.m.

STATE CAPITOL

210 Capitol Ave., Hartford, 860-240-0222; www.cga.ct.gov

Take guided one-hour tours of the restored, gold-domed capitol building and the contemporary legislative office building. Tours leave every hour Monday-Friday, starting at 9:15 a.m., with the last tour leaving at 1:15 p.m. A 2:15 p.m. tour is added July-August. Saturday tours are available April-October 10:15 a.m.-2:15 p.m.

UNIVERSITY OF HARTFORD

200 Bloomfield Ave., West Hartford, 860-768-4100; www.hartford.edu

This independent institution has 6,844 students on a 320-acre campus. The university plays host to many free concerts, operas, lectures and art exhibits.

WADSWORTH ATHENEUM MUSEUM OF ART

600 Main St., Hartford, 860-278-2670; www.wadsworthatheneum.org

This is one of the nation's oldest continuously operating public art museums with more than 40,000 works of art spanning 5,000 years. Exhibits include 15th- to 20th-century paintings; American furniture; sculpture, porcelains; English and American silver, the Amistad Collection of African-American art; and changing contemporary exhibits.

Admission: free. Wednesday-Friday 11 a.m.-5 p.m. and Saturday-Sunday 10 a.m.-5 p.m.; Every first Thursday of the month, the museum is open until 8 p.m.

WHERE TO STAY
★★CROWNE PLAZA HARTFORD-DOWNTOWN
50 Morgan St., Hartford, 860-549-2400, 877-227-6963; www.crowneplaza.com
This downtown hotel caters to business travelers with its ample workspaces, complimentary wireless and updated luxury bedding. The onsite restaurant, Bistro Z, serves Asian-influenced cuisine and features a sushi bar.
350 rooms. Restaurant, bar. $61-150

★★★SHERATON HARTFORD HOTEL
100 E. River Drive, East Hartford, 860-528-9703, 888-530-9703; www.sheraton.com
Located outside downtown Hartford in a corporate office park, this hotel caters to business travelers. Rooms have contemporary décor and sweet sleeper beds.
215 rooms. Restaurant, bar. $151-250

WHERE TO EAT
★★★CARBONE'S
588 Franklin Ave., Hartford, 860-296-9646; www.carbonesct.com
Hearty Italian dishes and friendly service have kept Carbone's a longtime Hartford favorite. Need evidence? Take a look at the entrance walls, plastered with many autographed pictures of politicians, sports figures and other satisfied customers.
Italian. Lunch, dinner. Closed Sunday. Bar. Reservations recommended. $36-85

★★★MAX DOWNTOWN
185 Asylum St., Hartford, 860-522-2530; www.maxrestaurantgroup.com
Lively and central, Max Downtown is a hit with staffers from the nearby Capitol Building. Many other city dwellers make the pilgrimage to the New American spot as well, eager to partake in its upscale atmosphere, extensive wine list and inventive cuisine.
American menu. Lunch, dinner, late-night. Bar. Business casual attire. Reservations recommended. Valet parking. $36-85

★★PEPPERCORN'S GRILL
357 Main St., Hartford, 860-547-1714; www.peppercornsgrill.com
This casual restaurant serves generous portions of classic Italian pastas, grilled seafood and meats. The wine list offers plenty of selections available by the glass or by the bottle.
Italian. Lunch, dinner, late-night. Open Sunday for special events only. Bar. Reservations recommended. Outdoor seating. $36-85

LITCHFIELD

See also Hartford

Home to the country's first law school, Litchfield sits on a plateau above the Naugatuck Valley. For the most part, the industrial revolution bypassed the quiet hamlet; its most famous citizens include the Reverend Henry Ward Beecher and his sister, Harriet Beecher Stowe, author of *Uncle Tom's Cabin*.

WHAT TO SEE
HAIGHT-BROWN VINEYARD AND WINERY

29 Chestnut Hill Road, Litchfield, 800-577-9463

One of the few vineyards to grow vinifera grapes in New England, Haight is Connecticut's first winery.

Tours, tastings. Daily.

LITCHFIELD HISTORY MUSEUM

7 South St., Litchfield, 860-567-4501; www.litchfieldhistoricalsociety.org

Onsite is an outstanding collection of American art and artifacts from the 18th to 21st centuries.

Mid-April-November: Tuesday-Sunday.

TAPPING REEVE HOUSE

82 South St., Litchfield, 860-567-4501

A retrospective of 19th-century Litchfield through the lives of the students who attended the Litchfield Law School and the Litchfield Female Academy; graduates include Aaron Burr and John C. Calhoun.

Mid-April-November: Tuesday-Sunday.

TOPSMEAD STATE FOREST

46 Chase Road, Litchfield, 860-567-5694; www.ct.gov

This 511-acre forest includes an English Tudor mansion overlooking a 40-acre wildlife preserve.

Second and fourth weekends of June-October.

WHERE TO STAY
★★★LITCHFIELD INN

7 Village Green Drive, Litchfield, 860-567-4503, 800-499-3444;
www.litchfieldinnct.com

Rooms are individually decorated with antique furnishings. Their on site restaurant offers family-style dining.

32 rooms. Complimentary breakfast. Restaurant, bar. $61-150

WHERE TO EAT
★★VILLAGE RESTAURANT

25 West St., Litchfield, 860-567-8307 www.village-litchfield.com

This casual restaurant is a favorite with locals who come for its clam chowder and filet mignon with garlic mashed potatoes. The menu includes a number of wines by the glass, plus weekly wine specials.

American. Lunch, dinner, Sunday brunch. Bar. Children's menu. $16-35

MADISON

See also New Haven

This beachfront central Connecticut town has a quaint main street lined with boutiques, coffee shops and bed and breakfasts.

WHAT TO SEE
ALLIS-BUSHNELL HOUSE AND MUSEUM

853 Boston Post Road, Madison, 203-245-4567; www.madisoncthistorical.org

Period rooms with four-corner fireplaces, a doctor's office and equipment, costume exhibits and shipbuilding tools are all located inside this 1785 house.

May-October: Wednesday, Friday-Saturday, limited hours; other times by appointment.

HAMMONASSET BEACH STATE PARK

1288 Boston Post Road, Madison, 203-245-2785; www.ct.gov

This beach covers more than 900 acres and has a two-mile-long stretch on Long Island Sound. Saltwater swimming, scuba diving, fishing, boating, hiking, picnicking and camping are available.

WHERE TO STAY
★★MADISON BEACH HOTEL

94 W. Wharf Road, Madison, 203-245-1404; www.madisonbeachhotel.com

Simple and streamlined rooms fill this beachfront hotel, which dates to the early 1800s. Updated touches include Egyptian cotton sheets and Rusk bath products in each room.

35 rooms. Closed January-February. Complimentary breakfast. Restaurant, bar. $61-150

WHERE TO EAT
★★★CAFÉ ALLEGRE

725 Boston Post Road, Madison, 203-245-7773; www.allegrecafe.com

This upscale restaurant serves Italian favorites in an elegant setting. Menu standouts include Sicilian chicken, tossed in a white wine and hot pepper sauce, served with gnocchi, or linguini with seafood.

Italian. Lunch, dinner. Closed Monday. Bar. Children's menu. Outdoor seating. $16-35

★★FRIENDS AND COMPANY

11 Boston Post Road, Madison, 203-245-0462 www.friendsandcompanyrestaurant.com

A local haunt that serves everything from pasta to Thai beef noodles, this restaurant is known for its fresh baked breads. The bistro menu offers a more casual selection of salads and sandwiches.

Seafood, steak. Lunch, dinner. Sunday brunch. Closed last Monday in June. Bar. Children's menu. $16-35

MYSTIC

See also New London

The town of Mystic, a shipbuilding and whaling center from the 17th-19th centuries, sits on both sides of its eponymous river. Its name is derived from the Pequot, "Mistuket." Today, the town is famous for its world class aquarium and maritime museum.

WHAT TO SEE
DENISON HOMESTEAD

120 Pequotsepos Road, Mystic, 860-536-9248; www.denisonsociety.org

This 1717 home is full of heirlooms from 11 generations of a single family. Guided tours are available.

Late May-mid-October: Friday-Monday afternoons, closed Tuesday-Thursday; all other times, by appointment.

CLASSIC CONNECTICUT

Situated halfway between New York City and Boston, the fabled town of Mystic is one of Connecticut's top tourist destinations. Having read that, you might be imagining swarms of camera-toting day-trippers. And you'd be right, sort of. Mystic in the summer can be tough to navigate, but Mystic in the winter, spring and fall is a charming, uncrowded spot. The ever-popular Seaport Museum and Aquarium are must-visits, as is the nearby Foxwoods Resort, the world's largest gambling casino. But more than anything, Mystic is a great place to start your state exploration. The surrounding seaside, hills, cities and farming communities are, for the most part, picture perfect.

From Mystic, take I-95 to Old Lyme, home of the Florence Griswold Art Museum and Rocky Neck State Park beach. Cross the bridge into Old Saybrook, and follow Highway 9 to Essex, a picturesque village with shops and restaurants. The Connecticut River Museum is located here, as is the departure point for the Valley Railroad, which runs along the river. Follow scenic Highway 154 to Chester, and take the country's oldest continuous ferry—don't worry, it carries cars—across to Gillette Castle in East Haddam. Or continue over the bridge for a great view of the Victorian Goodspeed Opera House, a destination in its own right. You can return via Highway 9 or take the scenic way: Highway 82 to Highway 156 to I-95, back along the eastern side of the river. Continue west on I-95 to Hammonasset Beach State Park in Madison. Then head down Highway 1, past the town's classic historic homes, to Guilford, site of the Henry Whitfield State Museum.

MYSTIC AQUARIUM

55 Coogan Blvd., Mystic, 860-572-5955; www.mysticaquarium.org

The exhibits here feature more than 6,000 live specimens from around the world. Demonstrations with dolphins, sea lions, and the only captive whales in New England delight young and old alike, as does Seal Island, an outdoor exhibit of seals and sea lions in natural settings, and the penguin pavilion. The facility also includes Dr. Robert Ballard's Institute for Exploration, which is dedicated to searching the deep seas for lost ships. The museum's Challenge of the Deep exhibit allows visitors to use state-of-the-art technology to re-create the search for the Titanic or explore the biology of undersea ocean vents.

Daily; hours vary by season.

MYSTIC SEAPORT

75 Greenmanville Ave., Mystic, 860-572-5315; www.mysticseaport.org

This 17-acre complex is the nation's largest maritime museum, dedicated to the preservation of 19th-century oceanic history. Visitors may board the 1841 wooden whale ship *Charles W. Morgan*, the square-rigged ship *Joseph Conrad*, or the fishing schooner *L.A. Dunton*. The collections also include some 400 smaller vessels; a representative seaport community with historic homes and waterfront industries; a working shipyard, children's museum and planetarium.

May-October: daily.

WHERE TO STAY
★★★HILTON MYSTIC

20 Coogan Blvd., Mystic, 860-572-0731, 800-774-1500; www.hilton.com

On a quiet side road near the noisy Olde Mystic Village, and just one block from Interstate 95, this business-oriented hotel is all about location. Shopping outlets, the Seaport Museum and the aquarium are all nearby. Not into fighting through the tourist hoards? Stay inside and mellow out at the hotel pool.

183 rooms. Restaurant, bar. $151-250

★★★INN AT MYSTIC

3 Williams Ave., Mystic, 860-536-9604, 800-237-2415; www.innatmystic.com

This five-building property is the only Connecticut inn that overlooks both Mystic Harbor and Long Island Sound. Its five buildings are spread over 15 manicured acres, in the center of which sits the 1904 Classical Revival mansion where Lauren Bacall and Humphrey Bogart honeymooned. Inside, the rooms come with period furnishings, whirlpools and orchard views.

68 rooms. Restaurant, bar. $151-250

★★★WHALER'S INN

20 E. Main St., Mystic, 860-536-1506, 800-243-2588; www.whalersinnmystic.com

Homey, comfortable and located in the heart of historic Mystic, the Whaler's Inn is ideal for those seeking an upscale New England bed and breakfast experience. The 1865 Colonial clapboard has a wide front porch and rocking chairs. Rooms are outfitted with Waverly wall coverings, four-poster beds and wing-back chairs, and the large bathrooms have pedestal sinks and whirlpool tubs. Each guest room has a view of the scenic Mystic River; lucky guests will snag suites with private verandas.

49 rooms. Complimentary breakfast. Restaurant, bar. $151-250

WHERE TO EAT
★★★BRAVO BRAVO

20 E. Main St., Mystic, 860-536-3228; www.ckrestaurantgroup.com

This local favorite, located at the seaside Whaler's Inn, serves creative gourmet dishes. Thanks to floor-to-ceiling windows, the spacious dining room is bright and inviting.

Italian. Lunch, dinner. Bar. Reservations recommended. $16-35

★★★FLOOD TIDE

3 Williams Avenue, Mystic, 860-536-8140, 800-237-2415; www.mysticinns.com

Complimentary hors d'oeuvres are served in the piano lounge at this waterfront restaurant. The gourmet dishes, Sunday brunch and harbor views are all worth the trip.

American, Continental. Breakfast, lunch, dinner, Sunday brunch. Bar. Children's menu. Reservations recommended. Outdoor seating. $36-85

★★GO FISH

Olde Mistick Village, Mystic, 860-536-2662 www.gofishct.com

Fresh from the nearby ocean, seafood is the specialty at this casual restaurant. Choose from sushi and sashimi, grilled slabs of swordfish, littlenecks on the halfshell and more on the classic New England menu.

Seafood. Lunch, dinner. Bar. Reservations recommended. $16-35

★MYSTIC PIZZA

56 W. Main St., Mystic, 860-536-3700; www.mysticpizza.com

Situated in a prime Main Street location, this family-style pizza parlor was in business before it caught the eye of a vacationing screenwriter, who borrowed its name for the 1988 film starring Julia Roberts. The pies served at Mystic Pizza are simple and satisfying, with a thin, doughy crust and a choice of toppings.

Pizza. Lunch, dinner. $15 and under

★★SEAMEN'S INNE

105 Greenmanville Ave., Mystic, 860-572-5303; www.seamensinne.com

With a location on the Mystic River, this casual pub has indoor and outdoor seating and a menu that's heavy on local seafood. The clam chowder wins raves from locals, but the lobster roll is another menu standout.

American, seafood. Lunch, dinner. Bar. Children's menu. Reservations recommended. Outdoor seating. $16-35

NEW HAVEN

See also Madison

New Haven is an unlikely cultural center. Part gritty metropolis of 130,000, part educational mecca, the city has long struggled with its split personality. Much of the action revolves around Yale University, which hosts some 10,000 students and countless more employees. No doubt every Yalie knows the historical importance of his adopted city: It was here that Eli Whitney worked out the principles of mass production and where Revolutionary War hero Nathan Hale studied. Just 75 miles from New York City, New Haven is a park-filled industrial city on the rise.

WHAT TO SEE
AMISTAD MEMORIAL

165 Church St., New Haven; www.edhamiltonworks.com

Created by Ed Hamilton, this 14-foot bronze relief sculpture is a unique three-sided form that depicts a trio of significant episodes in the life of Joseph Cinque, one of 50 Africans kidnapped in Sierra Leone and slated for sale in Cuba in 1839. His ship was secretly rerouted to Long Island Sound, after which a fierce battle for the would-be slaves' freedom ensued in New Haven. Two years later, their victory was won.

EAST ROCK PARK
Orange and Cold Spring Streets, New Haven, 203-946-6086; www.cityofnewhaven.com
The city's largest park includes the Pardee Rose Gardens, a bird sanctuary, hiking trails, athletic fields, tennis courts and picnic grounds.
April-November: daily; rest of year: Saturday-Sunday and holidays.

FORT NATHAN HALE PARK AND BLACK ROCK FORT
36 Woodward Ave., New Haven, 203-946-8790; www.fort-nathan-hale.org
Federal guns kept British warships out of the harbor in 1812. Since then, Black Rock Fort has been restored and archaeological excavations are in progress. The Civil War-era Fort Nathan Hale has also been reconstructed. Both offer spectacular views of the harbor.
Memorial Day-Labor Day. Daily 10 a.m.-4 p.m.

GROVE STREET CEMETERY
227 Grove St., New Haven, 203-787-1443; www.grovestreetcemetery.org
This was the first cemetery in the United States to be divided into family plots. Noah Webster, Charles Goodyear, Eli Whitney and many early settlers of the area are buried here.

LIGHTHOUSE POINT PARK
2 Lighthouse Point Road, New Haven, 203-946-8005; www.cityofnewhaven.com
The 82-acre park on Long Island Sound is home to an 1840 lighthouse, a restored antique carousel, a bird sanctuary, a bathhouse, a boat ramp and a beach.
Daily.

NEW HAVEN GREEN
Church and Elm Streets, New Haven; www.pps.org
In 1638, these 16 acres were laid out, making New Haven the first planned city in America. On the town common are three churches: United, Trinity Episcopal and Center Congregational. The latter is a masterpiece of American Georgian architecture.

PEABODY MUSEUM OF NATURAL HISTORY
170 Whitney Ave., New Haven, 203-432-5050; www.peabody.yale.edu
The museum has exhibits of mammals, invertebrate life, Plains and Connecticut Native Americans, meteorites, minerals, birds of Connecticut and several life-size dinosaurs, including a 60-foot-long brontosaurus reconstructed from original fossil material.
Monday-Saturday 10 a.m.-5 p.m., Sunday noon-5 p.m.

YALE UNIVERSITY
149 Elm St., New Haven, 203-432-2300; www.yale.edu
Founded by 10 Connecticut ministers and named for Elihu Yale, an early donor to the school, Yale is widely recognized as one of the best universities in

the country. Walking tours are conducted daily by undergraduate students. Monday-Friday 10:30 a.m., 2 p.m.; Saturday-Sunday 1:30 p.m.

SPECIAL EVENTS
NEW HAVEN SYMPHONY ORCHESTRA
Woolsey Hall, College and Grove streets, New Haven, 203-776-1444; www.newhavensymphony.com
A series of concerts by leading artists.
October-May; summer concert series.

YALE REPERTORY THEATER
1120 Chapel St., New Haven, 203-432-1234, 800-833-8134; www.yalerep.org
The Yale Repertory Theater prides itself on creating bold and passionate theatrical productions. The troupe often includes artistic leaders; four of the productions have won the Pulitzer Prize.
Early October-mid-May.

WHERE TO STAY
★★COURTYARD NEW HAVEN AT YALE
30 Whalley Ave., New Haven, 203-777-6221, 800-228-9290; www.courtyardmarriottyale.com
This budget-friendly hotel is located near campus and downtown New Haven. Rooms include free wireless access and CD/MP3 players. Complimentary breakfast is served each morning.
160 rooms. Restaurant, bar. $61-150

★★★OMNI NEW HAVEN HOTEL
155 Temple St., New Haven, 203-772-6664, 800-843-6664; www.omnihotels.com
This hotel is close to Yale University's campus, making it a popular choice for parents helping their kids move to college. After all the heavy lifting, the plush beds and feather pillows are heaven-sent. The hotel also contains a bar and restaurant in which to refuel.
305 rooms. Restaurant, bar. $151-250

NEW LONDON
See also Mystic, Norwich, Old Lyme
New London has one of the finest deep-water ports on the Atlantic coast. From the first days of the republic well into the 21st century, the small city has been a seagoing community. Whalers once amassed fortunes here, and townspeople still welcome ships of all kinds—submarines, cutters, yachts, cruisers—home. Today, the economy has veered somewhat onshore, to steel, medicine and high-tech product manufacturing plants.

WHAT TO SEE
EUGENE O'NEILL THEATER CENTER
305 Great Neck Road, Waterford, 860-443-5378; www.oneilltheatercenter.org
The complex includes the O'Neill Playwrights Conference, the O'Neill Critics Institute, the O'Neill Music Theater Conference, the O'Neill Puppetry Conference and the National Theater Institute. There are staged readings of

new plays and musicals during summer at the Barn Theater, Amphitheater and Instant Theater.

Center open year-round; theater performances run June-August.

JOSHUA HEMPSTEAD HOUSE

11 Hempstead Court, New London, 860-443-7949; www.ctlandmarks.org

This is the oldest house in the city. The Hempstead family diary details life in the house during colonial times.

May-June: Saturday-Sunday noon-4 p.m., July-August: Friday-Sunday noon-4 p.m. and September-October: Saturday-Sunday noon-4 p.m.

LYMAN ALLYN ART MUSEUM

625 Williams St., New London, 860-443-2545; www.lymanallyn.org

More than 15,000 works are on display; the collection includes Contemporary, Modern and Early American fine arts.

Tuesday-Saturday 10 a.m.-5 p.m., Sunday 1-5 p.m. Closed Mondays and major holidays.

MONTE CRISTO COTTAGE

325 Pequot Ave., New London, 860-443-5378; www.oneilltheatercenter.org

The restored boyhood home of playwright and Nobel prize winner Eugene O'Neill.

Late May-Labor Day: Sunday 1-3 p.m. and Thursday-Saturday noon-4p.m; closed Monday-Wednesday.

NATHANIEL HEMPSTEAD HOUSE

11 Hempstead Court, New London, 860-443-7949; www.ctlandmarks.org

One of the state's two surviving examples of mid-18th-century cut-stone architecture.

Mid-May-mid-October: May-June: Saturday-Sunday noon-4 p.m., July-August: Friday-Sunday noon-4 p.m. and September-October: Saturday-Sunday noon-4 p.m.

OCEAN BEACH PARK

1225 Ocean Ave., New London, 800-510-7263; www.ocean-beach-park.com

Swim in the ocean or an Olympic-sized pool (with a waterslide). There's also a boardwalk, amusement arcade and mini-golf.

Saturday before Memorial Day-Labor Day: daily.

SHAW PERKINS MANSION

11 Blinman St., New London, 860-443-1209; www.newlondonhistory.org

The Naval headquarters for the state during the Revolutionary War is now a genealogical and historical library.

Wednesday-Friday 1-4 p.m. and Saturdays (Mid-May-mid-October) 10 a.m.-4 p.m.

US COAST GUARD ACADEMY

31 Mohegan Ave., New London, 860-444-8444; www.cga.edu

The school houses 800 active cadets. The Visitors' Pavilion has a multimedia show (May-October daily); the museum includes the 295-foot-long ship Eagle.

Friday-Sunday, when in port; limited hours.

SPECIAL EVENTS
CONNECTICUT STORYTELLING FESTIVAL

Connecticut College, 270 Mohegan Ave., New London, 860-439-2764;

www.connstorycenter.org

Nationally acclaimed artists lead readings, workshops and concerts.

Late April.

SAILFEST

New London City Pier, Bank St., New London, 860-443-1879; www.sailfest.org

Arts and crafts and food vendors line the streets downtown while people of all ages browse, eat and enjoy the three stages of entertainment. The largest fireworks show on the East Coast takes place on Saturday night.

One weekend in early July.

WHERE TO STAY
★★RADISSON HOTEL NEW LONDON

35 Governor Winthrop Blvd., New London, 860-443-7000, 888-201-1718;

www.radisson.com

Located near New London's historic areas, restaurants and shops, this hotel has basic rooms with wireless access and spacious workspaces. The updated fitness center has new cardio machines and an indoor pool.

120 rooms. Restaurant, bar. $61-150

NORWICH

See also Mystic, New London

Norwich was one of the first chartered cities in Connecticut. Since the end of the 18th century, it has been a leader in area industrial development. The colony's first paper mill was opened here in 1766, and the first cut nails in America were Norwich-made in 1772. The city of nearly 40,000 is divided into three distinct sections: Norwichtown to the northwest; a business section near the Thames docks; and a central residential area that showcases many 19th-century homes.

WHAT TO SEE
INDIAN LEAP

Yantic and Sachem streets, Norwich, 860-886-4683

These falls were a favorite resort and outpost of the Mohegans. Legend has it that a band of Narragansetts, during the 1643 Battle of Great Plains, came upon the falls while fleeing the Mohegans (more popularly known as the Mohicans). Many were forced to jump off the cliffs and into the chasm below.

ROYAL MOHEGAN BURIAL GROUNDS

Sachem and Washington streets, Norwich, 860-862-6390; www.mohegan.nsn.us
The resting place of Uncas, chief of the Mohicans.

TANTAQUIDGEON INDIAN MUSEUM

1819 Norwich-New London Turnpike, Uncasville, 860-848-0594; www.mohegan.nsn.us
Works of Mohegan and other New England tribes, past and present.
May-November: Wednesday-Saturday 10 a.m.-4 p.m.

SPECIAL EVENT
BLUE GRASS FESTIVAL

Strawberry Park, 42 Pierce Road, Preston, 860-886-1944, 888-794-7944;
www.strawberrypark.net
You can either come for the day or make reservations for a campsite and enjoy four days of bluegrass music. Past performers have included Rhonda Vincent, the Tim O'Brien Band and the Waybacks.
Late May-early June.

WHERE TO STAY
★★★THE SPA AT NORWICH INN

607 W. Thames St., Norwich, 860-886-2401, 800-275-4772;
www.thespaatnorwichinn.com
From the outside, this property looks like any other upscale New England country inn. Step across the Norwich Inn's threshold, though, and you'll be transported to a very bucolic retreat. The property has 42 acres of grounds to roam, plus a 32-room treatment spa. Offerings include the requisite massage and facials, but also more cutting-edge treatments like hydrotherapy and energy work.
65 rooms. Restaurant, bar. Golf. Fitness center. Pool. $151-250

WHERE TO EAT
★★KENSINGTON

607 W Thames St., Norwich, 860-886-2401, 866-410-5942;
www.thespaatnorwichinn.com
Located at the Spa at Norwich Inn, this upscale restaurant serves contemporary cuisine with a focus on health-conscious choices. Everything from the vegetable cannoli to the osso bucco comes with its nutritional value listed, and most are safely in a waistline-friendly range.
American. Breakfast, lunch, dinner, Sunday brunch. Bar. Outdoor seating. $36-85

OLD LYME

See also Essex, New London, Old Saybrook
Lore has it that sea captains, flush from their huge hauls, once owned and occupied every Old Lyme house. The town's modern inhabitants are a more sophisticated (though no less monied) lot. The sleepy village, with its restored manors and safe, tree-lined streets, has become a classier mini-Greenwich for summering New Yorkers. Artsy types come here for the local design scene; tourists flock here for the seaside vistas. Only a privileged few get to stay year-round.

WHAT TO SEE
FLORENCE GRISWOLD MUSEUM
96 Lyme St., Old Lyme, 860-434-5542; www.flogris.org
This stately late-Georgian mansion housed America's most celebrated art colony at the turn of the century. Paintings by Willard Metcalf, Childe Hassam and other artists are on display.
Krieble Gallery: Tuesday-Saturday 10 a.m.-5 p.m., Sunday 1-5 p.m.; Chadwick Studio: mid-May-October.

WHERE TO STAY
★★★BEE AND THISTLE INN
100 Lyme St., Old Lyme, 860-434-1667, 800-622-4946; www.beeandthistleinn.com
This 1756 inn is widely recognized by savvy travelers as one of the state's most romantic getaways. The antique-decorated rooms are cozy and clean, and the service is precise but never fawning.
11 rooms. Closed two weeks in January. No children under 12. Restaurant, bar. Spa. $151-250

★★★OLD LYME INN
85 Lyme St., Old Lyme, 860-434-2600, 800-434-5352; www.oldlymeinn.com
Located in the town's historic district, this classic bed and breakfast is close to Essex, Mystic Seaport, Mystic Aquarium and several local art galleries. Most guests, however, choose to stay put in their sumptuous rooms or watch the sunset from a deep Adirondack chair on the front lawn.
13 rooms. Complimentary breakfast. Restaurant, bar. $151-250

WHERE TO EAT
★★★BEE AND THISTLE INN
100 Lyme St., Old Lyme, 860-434-1667, 800-622-4046; www.beeandthistleinn.com
Romance is alive and well in the Bee and Thistle's white table-clothed main dining room. The formal, candlelit scene looks like something out of an Austen novel. But the food is all 21st-century, as chef Kristofer Rowe blends fresh produce with first-rate seafood and steak for hearty but arty meals.
American. Breakfast, lunch, dinner, Sunday brunch. Bar. Closed two weeks in January. $36-85

★★★OLD LYME INN
85 Lyme St, Old Lyme, 860-434-2600, 800-434-5352; www.oldlymeinn.com
The meat-heavy menu and clubhouse-like décor of the inn's grill room gives way to the dining room's more sophisticated appeal. The real draw is the mouth-watering homemade desserts like triple chocolate silk tower and "meltaway" chocolate cake.
American. Lunch, dinner. brunch. Bar. $36-85

OLD SAYBROOK
See also Essex, New London, Old Lyme
This shabby chic town at the mouth of the Connecticut River is full of magnificent second homes. Originally the site of Yale College, it's the third-oldest named community in the state.

WHAT TO SEE
FORT SAYBROOK MONUMENT PARK
Highway 154, Saybrook Point, Old Saybrook, 860-395-3152; www.oldsaybrookct.org
An 18-acre park with remains of Fort Saybrook, the state's first military fortification. Daily.

GENERAL WILLIAM HART HOUSE
350 Main St., Old Saybrook, 860-388-2622; oldsaybrookct.com
The 1767 Georgian-style residence of well-to-do New England merchant and politician William Hart features eight corner fireplaces, one of which is decorated with Sadler and Green transfer-print tiles illustrating *Aesop's Fables*.
June-August: Saturday-Sunday 1-4 p.m. or by appointment.

SPECIAL EVENTS
ARTS AND CRAFTS SHOW
Town Green, Main St., Old Saybrook, 860-388-3266; www.oldsaybrookct.com
More than 200 artists and crafts-persons are represented in this annual craft show.
Last full weekend in July.

CHRISTMAS TORCHLIGHT PARADE
Main Street, Old Saybrook, 860-388-3266; www.connecticutblues.com
Forty fife and drum corps march down Main Street during this parade.
Second Saturday in December.

WHERE TO STAY
★★★SAYBROOK POINT INN AND SPA
2 Bridge St., Old Saybrook, 860-395-2828, 800-243-0212; www.saybrook.com
Water views of Long Island Sound and the Connecticut River provide a postcard-perfect backdrop to this seaside getaway. Like many area inns, guest rooms here are replete with 18th-century period-style furnishings and accessories. A recent renovation brought a touch of luxury to the resort, from the Anichini linens on the beds and flat-screen TVs in the guest rooms to the full-service spa.
62 rooms. Restaurant, bar. Pool. Fitness center. Pets accepted. $151-250

★★★WATER'S EDGE RESORT AND CONFERENCE CENTER
1525 Boston Post Road, Westbrook, 860-399-5901, 800-222-5901;
www.watersedge-resort.com
Located on Long Island Sound, there's fun for the whole family at the Water's Edge Resort. Kids have their own activity center, but adults can also partake in a myriad of activities including softball, face painting, scavenger hunts, kite flying, football, horseshoes and volleyball. Rooms are decorated in Colonial style.
32 rooms. Restaurant, bar. Beach. Spa. $151-250

WHERE TO EAT
★★DOCK AND DINE
Saybrook Point, Old Saybrook, 860-388-4665; www.dockdinect.com

Fresh seafood is the focus at this casual waterfront restaurant. Choose from grilled fish served with a variety of sauces, lobster ravioli, creamy clam chowder and more.

Seafood, steak. Lunch, dinner. Closed Monday-Tuesday Mid-October-mid-April. Bar. Children's menu. $16-35

RIDGEFIELD
See also Stamford

It's not exactly Paris, but this southwestern Connecticut town does have a rare Champs Elysées-style boulevard. Ninety-nine feet wide, the street is lined with trees and stately houses. It was here that, in 1777, a pre-traitorous Benedict Arnold set up barricades and fought the Battle of Ridgefield.

WHAT TO SEE
ALDRICH CONTEMPORARY ART MUSEUM
258 Main St., Ridgefield, 203-438-4519; www.aldrichart.org

The museum has changing exhibits and a sculpture garden.

Tuesday-Sunday noon-5 p.m. Free admission on Tuesday.

KEELER TAVERN MUSEUM
132 Main St., Ridgefield, 203-438-5485; www.keelertavernmuseum.org

A restored 18th-century tavern, stagecoach stop and home that was once revolutionary patriot headquarters. A British cannonball is still embedded in the wall.

February-December: Wednesday, Saturday-Sunday 1-4 p.m. Closed January.

WHERE TO STAY
★★★THE ELMS INN
500 Main St., Ridgefield, 203-438-2541; www.elmsinn.com

Established in 1799, this is the oldest continuously run inn in the state. The property has been lovingly restored and now boasts historic appeal (antique furnishings, old-world charm) and modern conveniences (wireless Internet access, dry cleaning).

23 rooms. Complimentary breakfast. Restaurant, bar. $251-350

★★★STONEHENGE INN
35 Stonehenge Road, Ridgefield, 203-438-6511; www.stonehengeinn-ct.com

Set on a swan-filled lake, Stonehenge looks like an old white rambling farm-house. Rooms are elegant with English country style furnishings and service is attentive.

16 rooms. Complimentary breakfast. Restaurant, bar. $151-250

WHERE TO EAT
★★★THE ELMS
500 Main St., Ridgefield, 203-438-9206; www.elmsinn.com

A fireplace sets the tone at the Elms, where award-wining chef Brendan

Walsh creates standout Yankee cuisine. Dishes include pulled wild boar and lobster Shepherd's pie.

American. Lunch, dinner. Closed Monday-Tuesday. Reservations recommended. Outdoor seating. $16-35

STAMFORD

See also Greenwich, Ridgefield, Westport

Stamford is so close to New York, some label the growing city an out-of-state suburb. While it does have several resident commuters, not all its professionals travel to Manhattan. More than 20 Fortune 500 companies are headquartered here, making Stamford a booming business town in its own right with pretty marinas and beaches on Long Island Sound.

WHAT TO SEE
BARTLETT ARBORETUM AND GARDENS

151 Brookdale Road, Stamford, 203-322-6971; www.bartlettarboretum.org

Collections of dwarf conifers, rhododendrons, azaleas, wildflowers, perennials and witches brooms are open to the public, as are ecology trails and the natural woodlands surrounding the gardens.

Gardens daily 8:30 a.m.-sunset; visitors center Monday-Friday 8:30 a.m.-4:30 p.m.

WHERE TO STAY
★★HOLIDAY INN SELECT STAMFORD DOWNTOWN

700 E. Main St., Stamford, 203-358-8400, 888-465-4329; www.ichotelsgroup.com

After receiving a full renovation in 2008, this downtown hotel now features crisp, contemporary decor and updated amenities such as flat-screen TVs and wireless access. The restaurant, 700 Main, serves updated American dishes in a modern setting.

383 rooms. Restaurant, bar. Pool. Pets accepted. Complimentary breakfast. $61-150

★★★SHERATON STAMFORD HOTEL

2701 Summer St., Stamford, 203-359-1300, 800-325-3535;
www.sheraton.com/stamford

The Sheraton is 45 minutes from Manhattan, but most guests never make it into the city, preferring to explore Connecticut's fabled Gold Coast instead. Cream-colored walls, blue and white furnishings and lots of plants lend a coastal theme to the hotel. Pets are welcome here, thanks to the resort's "Love that Dog" program.

448 rooms. Restaurant, bar. Fitness center. Business center. $251-350

★★★STAMFORD MARRIOTT HOTEL & SPA

243 Tresser Blvd., Stamford, 203-357-9555, 800-732-9689; www.marriott.com

This hotel's biggest draw might be its prime location, right across the street from the Stamford Town Center Mall. If you can't find anything you like in those 130 stores, don't worry: The Marriott is also close to the Palace Theater, Playland Amusement Park, and the Whitney Museum.

506 rooms. Restaurant, bar. $251-350

WHERE TO EAT
★CRAB SHELL
46 Southfield Ave., Stamford, 203-967-7229; www.crabshell.com

A casual spot on Stamford Landing marina, this is a local favorite for fresh, affordable seafood. There are upscale options on the menu, such as filet of sole with lobster sauce, but the raw bar offerings and clam chowder are equally satisfying.

American, seafood. Lunch, dinner. Bar. Outdoor seating. $16-35

★★IL FALCO
59 Broad St., Stamford, 203-327-0002; www.ilfalco.com

Traditional Italian dishes are served in an elegant setting at this intimate bistro. Pastas, such as gnocchi with pesto, are made fresh and served alongside an extensive list of wines from around the world.

Italian. Lunch, dinner. Closed Sunday. Bar. $36-85

WASHINGTON
See also Litchfield

With its prime location in posh Litchfield County, Washington is a favorite destination for antiquing. Quaint churches and historic buildings dot the rolling landscape.

WHAT TO SEE
HISTORICAL MUSEUM OF GUNN MEMORIAL LIBRARY
5 Wykeham Road, Washington, 860-868-7756; www.gunnlibrary.org

This house, built in 1781, contains collections and exhibits on area history, paintings, furnishings, gowns, dolls, dollhouses and tools.

Hours for the library vary Monday, Tuesday, Thursday-Sunday. Closed Wednesday. Hours for the museum: Thursday-Saturday 10 a.m.-4p.m. and Sunday noon-4 p.m. Closed Monday-Wednesday.

INSTITUTE FOR AMERICAN INDIAN STUDIES
38 Curtis Road, Washington, 860-868-0518; www.birdstone.org

This museum features Northeastern Woodland Indian artifacts with a permanent exhibit hall. Exhibits include changing Native American art displays, a replicated indoor longhouse, an outdoor replicated Algonkian village and a simulated archaeological site.

Monday-Saturday 10 a.m.-5 p.m., Sunday noon-5 p.m.

WHERE TO STAY
★★★★★THE MAYFLOWER INN
118 Woodbury Road, Washington, 860-868-9466; www.mayflowerinn.com

This country inn, located less than two hours from New York City, evokes the feeling and quiet elegance of an English countryside hotel. Set on 28 acres of rolling hills, streams and lush gardens, guest rooms and suites are swathed in luxurious fabrics and feature four-poster, canopied beds, 18th and 19th-century art and modern touches like flat-screen TVs. The dining room's seasonal menu makes good use of fresh, local ingredients with dishes such as organic Atlantic salmon with fresh vegetables. The tap room has a more casual menu of Vermont cheddar-topped burgers and lemon-rosemary chicken. The sprawling spa is superlative.

24 rooms. No children under 12. Restaurant, bar. Spa. $351 and up

SPA
★★★★★THE MAYFLOWER SPA
118 Woodbury Road, Washington, 860-868-9466; www.mayflowerinn.com

The 20,000-square-foot Mayflower Spa, opened in 2006, features the same classic design, elegant furnishing and quiet luxury of its namesake inn. Those who come for the full spa experience receive a pre-arrival consultation to create a schedule of pampering services and fitness and nutrition classes. The spa has an indoor heated pool and mosaic-domed whirlpool. A wide variety of classes range from kickboxing to ballet. Private yoga classes and Pilates studios are also available. And guests are provided with goodies including yoga mats, MP3 players, loungewear and even rain boots should the need arise.

WESTPORT
See also Stamford

Much like neighboring Greenwich, Westport is home to successful corporate warriors. It's also full of thriving small businesses and notable actors and illustrators. The town is surrounded by wooded hills and Long Island Sound beaches, making it a pretty, if pricey, place to live.

SPECIAL EVENTS
LEVITT PAVILION FOR THE PERFORMING ARTS
Jesup Green, 260 Compo Road South, Westport, 203-226-7600;
www.levittpavilion.com

Nightly free outdoor performances of jazz, pop, rock, dance and children's music.

Late June-early August.

WHERE TO STAY
★★★INN AT NATIONAL HALL
2 Post Road W, Westport, 203-221-1351, 800-628-4255; www.innatnationalhall.com

This distinctive inn sits along the banks of the Saugatuck River and is within walking distance of shops, galleries and the beach. Slightly quirky with an Alice in Wonderland feel, the 1873 Italianate property has only 16 individually designed rooms and suites decorated in vibrant themes (the Watermelon Room, the Equestrian Suite). River views add an enchanting touch to the accommodations, and several chambers boast soaring two-story ceilings and crystal chandeliers.

16 rooms. Complimentary breakfast. Restaurant. Pool. Beach. Pets accepted. $251-350

WHERE TO EAT
★★★COBB'S MILL INN
12 Old Mill Road, Weston, 203-227-7221, 800-640-9365; www.cobbsmillinn.com

At the Cobb's Mill Inn, excellent service merges with an elegant, historic ambience. The cuisine is beautifully presented, and the setting is a rustic, cozy barn. Sample entrées such as olive oil poached halibut, or sake glazed sea bass. Seafood, steak. Lunch, dinner. Bar. Brunch. $36-85

★★THE RED BARN

292 Wilton Road, Westport, 203-222-9549; www.redbarnrestaurant.com

Housed in a namesake historic red barn, the restaurant serves an eclectic menu that features everything from filet mignon to eggplant parmesan. The barn's fireplaces make for a rustic setting.

American. Lunch, dinner, brunch. Children's menu. Outdoor seating. $36-85

WINDSOR LOCKS

See also Hartford

Located on the Connecticut River, this town is home to Bradley International Airport. The town takes its name from the locks located here on the Enfield Falls Canal.

WHAT TO SEE
NEW ENGLAND AIR MUSEUM

36 Perimeter Road, Windsor Locks, 860-623-3305; www.neam.org

One of the largest and most comprehensive collections of aircraft and aeronautical memorabilia in the world is located right next to Bradley International Airport. More than 80 aircraft, including bombers, fighters, helicopters and gliders, are on display; some date back to 1909. There's also a jet fighter cockpit simulator.

Daily 10 a.m.-5 p.m.

NODEN-REED HOUSE & BARN

58 West St., Windsor Locks, 860-627-9212

Situated in a 19th-century house and a barn are an antique sleigh bed, antique quilts, kitchen utensils and newspapers and periodicals from the 1800s.

May-October: Sunday 1-4 p.m.

OLD NEWGATE PRISON

115 Newgate Road, East Granby, 860-653-3563; www.eastgranby.com

Here, a 1707 copper mine was converted to a Revolutionary prison for Tories. It then became a state prison. Check out a self-guided tour of underground caverns where the prisoners once lived.

Mid-May-October: Wednesday-Sunday. 10 a.m.-4:30 p.m.

WHERE TO STAY
★HOMEWOOD SUITES

65 Ella Grasso Turnpike, Windsor Locks, 860-627-8463, 800-225-5466; www.homewoodsuites.com

This budget-friendly hotel underwent a recent renovation that introduced contemporary décor to the hotel's rooms and lobby. The hotel serves complimentary breakfast daily.

132 rooms. Fitness center. Pets accepted. Pool. Business center. $61-150

★★★SHERATON BRADLEY AIRPORT HOTEL

1 Bradley International Airport, Windsor Locks, 860-627-5311, 877-422-5311;
www.sheraton.com/bradleyairport

This hotel is well-situated near Bradley Airport, and a short drive south brings you to Hartford. Guest rooms are comfortable, with the Sheraton's signature Sweet Sleeper beds and soft, warm duvets. Room amenities include parking on the premises and a computer work station.

237 rooms. Restaurant, bar. Fitness center. Pool. Pets accepted. Business center. $61-150

MAINE

MAYBE IT'S THE FLAT YANKEE TWANG OR THE SALTY SEA AIR. WHATEVER IT IS, THERE IS something about Maine. With the highest tides in the country and a temperature that ranges from -46 F to 105 F, Maine is a popular state to visit year-round. There are 6,000 lakes and ponds and 3,500 miles of seacoast (though the water can be a bit chilly, with temperatures steady in summer in the 50s).

In 1604, St. Croix Island became Maine's first settlement, but it only lasted one winter. Another early settlement was established near Pemaquid Point, but it was the short-lived Popham Colony, at the mouth of the Kennebec River, that built America's first transatlantic trader in 1607, called the Virginia. Maine was a part of Massachusetts until 1820, when it was officially admitted to the Union.

Today, Maine is a vast playground of natural beauty, populated (in some places sparsely) by hearty Mainers who earn their stripes by surviving the long, dark winters. Most of Maine's 17.6 million acres of forest are open for public recreational use, including more than 580,000 acres owned by the state. Acadia National Park is one of the nation's wildest and most beautiful areas, now filled with a resurgent bald eagle population. Other wildlife can easily be seen in Maine, from the large numbers of seals and porpoises that swim in the waters off Penobscot Bay in summer to the pods of migratory whales that pass through each year.

In summer, the state swells with visitors who come to feast on lobster, sail the rugged, rocky coast, poke through antique shops in achingly quaint towns or even take a plunge in the perennially chilly coastal waters. Celebrities and the wealthy—including Martha Stewart, the Bush family, John Travolta and Stephen King—keep compounds here in places like Kennebunkport and Bar Harbor and occasionally add a dash of glamour to what is typically a humble, down-to-earth population.

Of course, fall rivals summer for the most popular time to visit New England's largest state and that's because of the resplendent display of autumn leaves the landscape produces each year. Tourists who come (in droves) during this time are called "leafpeepers." The state's inns, restaurants and roads are usually packed to capacity in September and October.

Local residents muddle through the summer and autumn crowds and dream of quiet, snowy winters, when they have the charms of this great state (mostly) to themselves again.

AUGUSTA

See also Bangor

Augusta, the capital of Maine, was settled in 1628 when settlers from Plymouth established a trading post on the site of Cushnoc, a Native American village. Soon after, in 1754, Fort Western was built to protect settlers against Native American raids, and from that, the settlement grew. Located 39 miles from the sea, Augusta is at the head of navigation on the Kennebec River.

WHAT TO SEE
BLAINE HOUSE

State and Capitol streets, Augusta, 207-287-2121; www.blainehouse.org

This is the 1833 house of James G. Blaine, Speaker of the U.S. House of Representatives and an 1884 presidential candidate. Since 1919, this 28-room house has been the official residence of Maine's governors. Originally built in the Federal style, it was remodeled several times and today appears semi-colonial.

Self-guided tours by appointment only. May 1-October 1: Tuesday-Thursday, 2-4 p.m.

MAINE STATE MUSEUM

83 State House Station, Augusta, 207-287-2301; www.state.me.us/museum

The museum houses exhibits of Maine's natural environment, prehistory, social history and manufacturing heritage.

Monday-Friday 9 a.m.-5 p.m., Saturday 10 a.m.-4 p.m., Sunday closed.

OLD FORT WESTERN

City Center Plaza, 16 Cony St., Augusta, 207-626-2385; www.oldfortwestern.org

This fort complex was built in 1754 by Boston merchants. The grounds feature a main house and reproduction blockhouse, watch boxes and palisade. The costumed staff interprets 18th-century life on the Kennebec River.

Memorial Day-Labor Day, daily 1-4 p.m.; after Labor Day-Columbus Day, weekends only 1-4 p.m.; November-March, limited Sundays.

STATE HOUSE

83 State House Station, Augusta, 207-287-2301

The original design for this impressive building was by Charles Bulfinch (architect of the Massachusetts State House), and dates back to the early 1800s. Remodeled and enlarged in 1910, it rises majestically above Capitol Park and the Kennebec River. On its 185-foot dome is a statue, designed by W. Clark Noble, of a classically robed woman bearing a pine bough torch.

Monday-Friday.

WHERE TO STAY
★★★BEST WESTERN SENATOR INN & SPA

284 Western Ave., Augusta, 207-622-5804, 877-772-2224; www.senatorinn.com

This hotel is the perfect jumping-off point for exploring Acadia or Maine's western mountains. Or stay put and enjoy the colonial charm of the rooms, the relaxing spa (complete with its own Jurlique store) or the American cuisine at the restaurant Cloud 9.

125 rooms. Pets accepted. Complimentary breakfast. Restaurant, bar. Fitness center. Spa. Pool. $151-250

★QUALITY INN & SUITES

65 Whitten Road, Augusta, 207-622-3776, 800-237-8466; www.augustaqualityinn.com

This budget-friendly hotel prides itself on offering clean, eco-friendly rooms featuring purified drinking water and updated amenities such as flat-screen TVs and new massage showers. The complimentary breakfast includes make

your own waffles and free newspapers.
58 rooms. Fitness center. Pool. $61-150

BAILEY ISLAND

Located at the end of Highway 24, along the northern shore of Casco Bay, Bailey Island is the most popular of the 365 Calendar Islands. Together with Orr's Island—to which it's connected by a cribstone bridge—Bailey is a resort and fishing center. Originally called "New Waggin" by an early trader from Kittery, Bailey Island was renamed after Deacon Timothy Bailey of Massachusetts, who banished early settlers and claimed the land for himself. Bailey Island and Orr's Island partially enclose an arm of Casco Bay called Harpswell Sound, the locale of John Whittier's poem "The Dead Ship of Harpswell" and of Harriet Beecher Stowe's "Pearl of Orr's Island."

WHAT TO SEE
GIANT STAIRCASE

Ocean Street, off Route 24
This is a natural rock formation dropping 200 feet in steps to ocean. Climbers can take in the view from the scenic overlook area.

WHERE TO EAT
★COOK'S LOBSTER HOUSE

Garrison Cove Road, Bailey Island, 207-833-2818; cookslobster.com
Try fresh-from-the-water lobster at this casual waterfront restaurant sandwiched on a peninsula on Casco Bay. The menu is simple and classic, with everything from boiled lobster to lobster rolls and clam chowder available. Seafood. Lunch, dinner. Bar. Children's menu. Outdoor seating. $36-85

BANGOR

See also Augusta

In 1604, Samuel de Champlain sailed up the Penobscot River to what is now Bangor and reported that the area was "most pleasant and agreeable," the hunting good and the oak trees impressive. Started as a harbor town, Bangor turned to lumber when the railroads picked up much of the shipping business. In 1842, it became the second-largest lumber port in the country.

Bangor received its name by mistake. An early settler, Reverend Seth Noble, was sent to register the new town under its chosen name of Sunbury. When officials asked Noble for the name, he thought they were asking him for the name of a tune he was humming and he replied "Bangor." Today, the city is the third largest in Maine and is a trading and distribution center.

WHAT TO SEE
BANGOR MUSEUM AND CENTER FOR HISTORY

159 Union St., Bangor, 207-942-1900; www.bangormuseum.com
The museum features exhibits of regional artifacts and the Quipus collection of historic clothing.
Tuesday-Saturday.

COLE LAND TRANSPORTATION MUSEUM

405 Perry Road, Bangor, 207-990-3600; www.colemuseum.org

The Cole Museum showcases the history of transportation in the American Northeast. The museum houses one of the largest collections of snow removal equipment found in one place anywhere in the country, as well as a cache of military vehicles. Historic photographs of Maine are also on display. May-mid-November, daily 9 a.m.-5 p.m.

MONUMENT TO PAUL BUNYAN

Bass Park, Main Street, Bangor

A 31-foot-tall statue commemorates the legendary lumberjack.

WHERE TO STAY
★FAIRFIELD INN

300 Odlin Road, Bangor, 207-990-0001, 800-228-2800; www.fairfieldinn.com

Located near Bangor's airport, this basic hotel has clean, updated rooms with luxury linens. The daily complimentary breakfast includes made-to-order waffles.

153 rooms. Fitness center. Pool, whirlpool. $61-150

BAR HARBOR

See also Blue Hill

Bar Harbor, the largest village on Mount Desert Island, has a summer population of more than 20,000 and is headquarters for the surrounding summer resort area. The island, which includes most of Acadia National Park, is mainly rugged granite, with many bays and inlets for sailing. In the mid-1800s, socially prominent figures, including publisher Joseph Pulitzer, had elaborate summer cottages built on the island. However, prosperity ended with the Great Depression, World War II and the Great Fire of 1947, which destroyed many of the estates and scorched more than 17,000 acres. As a result, instead of just evergreens, the forests in the area now have younger, more varied trees bearing red, yellow and orange leaves in fall.

WHAT TO SEE
ABBE MUSEUM

26 Mount Desert St., Bar Harbor, 207-288-3519; www.abbemuseum.org

This museum holds an extensive collection of Native American artifacts. The original location in Acadia National Park (open Memorial Day-mid-October) now houses exhibits on the archaeology of Maine and the history of the Abbe.

Daily 10 a.m.-6 p.m.; closed January.

BAR HARBOR HISTORICAL SOCIETY MUSEUM

33 Ledgelawn Ave., Bar Harbor, 207-288-0000; www.barharborhistorical.org

The museum features a collection of early photographs of hotels, summer cottages and Green Mountain cog railroad as well as hotel registers from the early to late 1800s, maps and a scrapbook of the 1947 fire.

June-October, Monday-Saturday 1-4 p.m.; winter, by appointment.

BAR HARBOR WHALE WATCH COMPANY

1 West St., Bar Harbor, 207-288-2386, 888-533-9253; www.whalesrus.com

The company offers a variety of cruises aboard catamarans *Friendship V* or *Helen H* to view whales, seal, puffin, osprey and more. Also offers nature cruises and lobster and seal-watching. Cruises vary in length and destination.

May-October daily. Depart from Bluenose Ferry Terminal.

FERRY SERVICE TO YARMOUTH, NOVA SCOTIA

121 Edens St., Bar Harbor, 207-288-3395; www.catferry.com

The passenger and car carrier Cat Ferry makes three-hour trips. See website for details on fares and scheduling.

THE JACKSON LABORATORY

600 Main St., Bar Harbor, 207-288-6000; www.jax.org

The center is an internationally known mammalian genetics laboratory conducting research relevant to cancer, diabetes, AIDS, heart disease, blood disorders, birth defects, aging, and normal growth and development. Audiovisual and lecture programs are often held here.

Early June-late August.

LOBSTER HATCHERY

1351 State Highway 3, Bar Harbor, 207-244-7330; www.theoceanarium.com

Young lobsters are hatched from eggs to ½ inch in length and then returned to the ocean to supplement the supply; guides narrate the process.

Daily, 9 a.m.-5 p.m. Mid-May-late-October, closed Sunday.

WHERE TO STAY

★★★BAR HARBOR HOTEL-BLUENOSE INN

90 Eden St., Bar Harbor, 207-288-3348, 800-445-4077; www.barharborhotel.com

From its hilltop location on Mount Desert Island, this hotel offers scenic views of Frenchman Bay. Explore nearby Acadia National Park or walk down to the dock and catch the *Cat Ferry* for a day trip to Yarmouth, Nova Scotia. The guest rooms feature traditional four-poster beds and balconies and include mini-refrigerators, CD and DVD players and bathrobes. Enjoy gourmet dining in the Rose Garden Restaurant.

98 rooms. Closed November-mid-April. Restaurant, bar. Fitness center. Pool. Business center. $151-250

★★BAR HARBOR INN

Newport Drive, Bar Harbor, 207-288-3351, 800-248-3351; www.barharborinn.com

Gorgeous views of the harbor and a classic gray shingled look make this inn a charming retreat. A new spa offers a full menu of facials, massages and body treatments.

153 rooms. Pets accepted. Complimentary breakfast. Restaurant, bar. Fitness center. Pool. Beach. $151-250

★★★THE BAYVIEW

111 Eden St., Bar Harbor, 207-288-5861, 800-356-3585;
www.thebayviewbarharbor.com

Located directly on the water, this 8-acre inn sits within five minutes of the town's center, but still offers a private setting. There are three buildings, including condos for guests on longer stays. Guest rooms are spacious and feature French doors that lead to wide, private decks overlooking the water. Luxurious furnishings, including four-poster beds, inlaid wood tables and armoires create a residential feel.

26 rooms. Complimentary breakfast. Fitness center. Tennis. Business center. Closed November-mid-May. $151-250

★★HARBORSIDE HOTEL & MARINA

55 West St., Bar Harbor, 207-288-5033, 800-328-5033; www.theharborsidehotel.com

A recent renovation updated this waterfront hotel in luxurious, English country style, from the new full-service spa to the formal dining room. Guest rooms feature luxury linens, gas fireplaces and flat-screen TVs.

187 rooms. Closed November-March. Complimentary breakfast. Restaurant, bar. Fitness center. Pool, whirlpool. $151-250

ALSO RECOMMENDED
CASTELMAINE

39 Holland Ave., Bar Harbor, 207-288-4563, 800-338-4563; www.castlemaineinn.com

Tucked away on a quiet side street, this inn is a Victorian-style house, circa 1886, located one mile from Acadia National Park and within walking distance of the ocean. It was once the summer residence of the Austro-Hungarian ambassador. Rooms showcase antiques and some are equipped with fireplaces.

★★★★★ MAINE

17 rooms. Closed November-April. Complimentary breakfast. $61-150

INN AT BAY LEDGE

150 Sand Point Road, Bar Harbor, 207-288-4204; www.innatbayledge.com

This inn, built in 1907, is located at the top of an 80-foot cliff on Mount Desert Island near Acadia National Park. Rooms are individually decorated with antiques.

10 rooms. No children under 16. Complimentary breakfast. Closed late October-April. Bar. $251-350

WHERE TO EAT
★★MAGGIE'S

6 Summer St., Bar Harbor, 207-288-9007; www.maggiesbarharbor.com

A sweet, local bistro housed in a charming blue house, this restaurant has a menu devoted to fresh, seasonal ingredients, with some produce organically grown by the owners. The lobster crepes are menu standouts, and the warm, dark chocolate pudding cake is the perfect end to a meal.

International. Dinner. Reservations recommended. Outdoor seating. Closed Sunday; late October-mid-June. Bar. $16-35

★★★READING ROOM
Newport Drive, Bar Harbor, 207-288-3351, 800-248-3351; www.barharborinn.com
Located on the oceanfront, this restaurant offers a panoramic view of the harbor and docks through large windows. Seafood is the star of the menu, with everything from lobster pie to local diver sea scallops available.
American. Breakfast, lunch, dinner, Sunday brunch. Bar. Children's menu. Reservations recommended. Closed December-March. $36-85

★ROUTE 66
21 Cottage St., Bar Harbor, 207-288-3708; www.bhroute66.com
An old-time diner loaded with Americana, Route 66 has an extensive menu of sandwiches, pizzas, salads and seafood. The classic shakes, smoothies and floats are worth the visit.
American. Lunch, dinner. Bar. Children's menu. Reservations recommended. Outdoor seating. Closed mid-October to mid-May. $16-35

BETHEL
See Augusta
Bethel, on both banks of the winding Androscoggin River, is built on Oxford Hills and is backed by the rough foothills of the White Mountains. In addition to being a year-round resort, it's an educational and wood products center. One of Maine's leading preparatory schools, Gould Academy (founded in 1836), is located here, as is Sunday River ski resort, one of New England's snowiest ski areas.

WHAT TO SEE
CARTER'S X-COUNTRY SKI CENTER
Intervale Road, Bethel, 207-824-3880; www.cartersxcski.com
Set on nearly one thousand acres with over 55 kilometers of groomed cross-country trails, the ski center provides rentals, lessons, a lounge, a shop and two lodges for guests.
December-March. Daily 10 a.m.-5 p.m.

DR. MOSES MASON HOUSE MUSEUM
14 Broad St., Bethel, 207-824-2908; www.bethelhistorical.org
The museum includes the restored 1813 home of the prominent congressman who served during Andrew Jackson's administration. The home features antique furnishings and early American murals.
July-Labor Day, Tuesday-Sunday 1-4 p.m.; rest of year, by appointment.

GRAFTON NOTCH STATE PARK
Highway 2, 207-824-2912; www.state.me.us
The Appalachian Trail passes through the notch. The park has interpretive displays, and scenic views. There is picnicking and fishing allowed on site. May 15-October 15; fee.

SUNDAY RIVER SKI RESORT
Sunday River Road, Bethel, 207-824-3000, 800-543-2754; www.sundayriver.com
Sunday River Resort features nine quad, four triple and two double chairlifts

(including four High-speed detachables and one surface lift). Ski patrol runs on site. There is a ski school along with rentals, ski shop and snowmaking. The resort has cafeterias restaurants and bars. Of the127 runs, the longest run is three miles. The longest vertical drop is 2,340 feet. There are 100 cross-country trails adjacent. Mountain biking is available in season.

Mid-November-mid-April, daily. May-Labor Day, daily. Labor Day-late October, weekends.

WHERE TO STAY
★★★BETHEL INN & COUNTRY CLUB
On the Common, Bethel, 207-824-2175, 800-654-0125; www.bethelinn.com

This hotel features rooms in three traditional colonial buildings as well as a series of luxury townhouses, perfect for families visiting the nearby slopes. In summer, there is a championship golf course designed by architect Geoffrey Cornish.

60 rooms. Pets accepted. Restaurant, bar. Fitness center. Pool. Golf. Tennis. $151-250

BLUE HILL
See also Bar Harbour

Named for a nearby hill that delivers a beautiful view of Mount Desert Island, Blue Hill evolved from a thriving seaport to a summer colony known for its crafts and antiques. Mary Ellen Chase, born here in 1887, wrote about Blue Hill in *A Goodly Heritage* and *Mary Peters*.

WHAT TO SEE
HOLT HOUSE
Water Street, Blue Hill, 207-326-8250; www.bluehillhistory.org

One of the oldest houses in Blue Hill; now home of the Blue Hill Historical Society, which features town memorabilia.

July-September, Tuesday, Friday, Saturday 11 a.m.-2 p.m.

RACKLIFFE POTTERY
132 Elsworth Road, Blue Hill, 207-374-2297; www.rackliffepottery.com

Family manufactures wheel-thrown dinnerware from native red-firing clay. There is an open workshop on site.

July-August, daily; rest of year, Monday-Saturday.

ROWANTREES POTTERY
84 Union St., Union, 207-374-5535

This company manufactures functional pottery and wheel-thrown handcrafted dinnerware.

June-September, Monday-Saturday; closed holidays.

WHERE TO STAY
★★★BLUE HILL INN
40 Union St., Blue Hill, 207-374-2844, 800-826-7415; www.bluehillinn.com

This federal-style house at the tip of the bay has operated as a bed and breakfast since 1840 and is on the National Register of Historic Places. For a more private retreat, choose one of the quaint guest rooms or the adjacent Cape House suite.

12 rooms. Restaurant. $151-250

BOOTHBAY HARBOR

See also Damariscotta, Monhegan Island

Native Americans were paid 20 beaver pelts for the area encompassing Boothbay Harbor. Today, it's a protected harbor, a haven for boatmen and the scene of well-attended regattas several times each summer. Boothbay Harbor, on the peninsula between the Sheepscot and Damariscotta rivers, shares the peninsula and adjacent islands with a dozen other communities, including Boothbay (settled 1630), of which it was once a part.

WHAT TO SEE
BOOTHBAY RAILWAY VILLAGE

586 Wiscasset Road, Highway 27, Boothbay, 207-633-4727; www.railwayvillage.org

The village includes historical Maine exhibits of rural life, railroads and antique autos and trucks. Rides are offered on a coal-fired, narrow-gauge steam train to an antique vehicle display. Also on exhibit are displays of early fire equipment, a general store, a one-room schoolhouse and two restored railroad stations.

Mid-June to September, daily.

BOOTHBAY REGION HISTORICAL SOCIETY MUSEUM

72 Oak St., Boothbay Harbor, 207-633-0820; www.boothbayhistorical.org

The museum displays artifacts of the Boothbay Region.

July-Labor Day, Wednesday-Saturday 10 a.m.-2 p.m.; rest of year, Friday-Saturday.

SPECIAL EVENTS
WINDJAMMER DAYS

192 Townsend Ave., Boothbay Harbor, 207-633-2353; www.boothbayharbor.com

Old schooners that previously sailed trade routes and now cruise the Maine coast sail en masse into the harbor. There is a waterfront food court, entertainment, street parade, as well as children's activities.

Late June.

WHERE TO STAY
★★BROWN'S WHARF MOTEL

121 Atlantic Ave., Boothbay Harbor, 207-633-5440, 800-334-8110;
www.brownswharfinn.com

Rooms at this waterfront inn are basic, but deliver great views of the harbor through large windows. Free wireless access is now available. The restaurant is a prime spot for sampling fresh steamed lobster.

70 rooms. Restaurant, bar. Closed November-April. $61-150

★★★SPRUCE POINT INN
88 Grandview Ave., Boothbay Harbor, 207-633-4152, 800-553-0289;
www.sprucepointinn.com
Located on a quiet peninsula on the east side of Boothbay Harbor, this retreat is an ideal getaway for families. Activities include swimming in salt and freshwater pools, kayaking, bicycling, fishing and hiking trails.
85 rooms. Closed mid-October-mid-May. Pets accepted. Restaurant, bar. Fitness center. Spa. Pool. Tennis. Business center. $151-250

WHERE TO EAT
★★★88 GRANDVIEW
88 Grandview, Boothbay Harbor, 207-633-4152, 800-553-0289;
www.sprucepointinn.com
At this restaurant, located inside the Spruce Point Inn, tables are covered with crisp white linens and are set with fine china. Seating is also provided on the enclosed sun-porch and outdoor deck with umbrella-topped tables overlooking the Atlantic Ocean. Dishes include candied duck breast and beef with Bordelaise sauce. A pianist performs nightly.
Continental. Dinner. Bar. Reservations recommended. Outdoor seating. Closed late October-mid-May. $36-85

★ANDREW'S HARBORSIDE RESTAURANT
12 Bridge St., Boothbay Harbor, 207-633-4074; www.andrewsharborside.com
This casual restaurant serves fresh seafood, from baked stuffed haddock to broiled scallops. The huge cinnamon buns served at breakfast are a local favorite.
American, seafood. Breakfast, lunch, dinner. Bar. Children's menu. Reservations recommended. Closed mid-October-Mother's Day. $16-35

★BLUE MOON CAFÉ
54 Commercial St., Boothbay Harbor, 207-633-2220;
www.bluemoonboothbayharbor.com
Breakfast standards are the draw at this cozy, casual restaurant. The menu includes breakfast burritos, fluffy pancakes, freshly made granola and more.
American. Breakfast, lunch. Outdoor seating. Closed November-March. $16-35

CAMDEN
See also Rockland
Used as the backdrop for the 1950s movie *Peyton Place*, Camden is the quintessential New England coastal town. Its unique setting makes it a popular four-season resort area. Activities include sailing, kayaking, swimming, camping, hiking, and in winter, skiing on a mountain with views of the ocean. The poet Edna St. Vincent Millay began her career in Camden.

WHAT TO SEE
CAMDEN HILLS STATE PARK
280 Belfast, Camden, 207-236-3109; www.state.me.us
Maine's third-largest state park surrounds 1,380-foot Mount Megunticook. The park's road leads to 800-foot Mount Battie.
Memorial Day-Columbus Day.

CAMDEN OPERA HOUSE

29 Elm St., Camden, 207-236-7963; www.camdenoperahouse.com

This Elm Street Theater offers musical and theatrical performances and concerts.

See website for ticket pricing and event details.

CAMDEN SNOW BOWL

Hosmer Pond Road, Camden, 207-236-3438; www.camdensnowbowl.com

The Snow Bowl offers a double chairlift and two T-bars. Ski patrol run regularly. Novices can rent equipment and attend ski school. There is also toboggan chute. Snowboarding is allowed. They make their own snow as necessary. There is a snack bar, as well as a lodge. The views of the ocean from the top of the mountain are breathtaking.

Late December-mid-March, daily.

CONWAY HOMESTEAD-CRAMER MUSEUM

Highway 1 and Conway Road, Camden, 207-236-2257; www.crmuseum.org/buildings

This authentically restored 18th-century farmhouse sits on a property that boasts a collection of carriages, sleighs and farm implements in an old barn. You will also find a blacksmith shop, a privy and an herb garden. Mary Meeker Cramer Museum contains paintings, ship models, quilts, costumes, documents and other memorabilia. The museum also features changing exhibits.

July and August, Tuesday-Friday.

MAINE STATE FERRY SERVICE

McKay St., and Highway 1, Lincolnville Beach, 207-789-5611; www.state.me.us

Twenty-minute trip to Islesboro (Dark Harbor) on the *Margaret Chase Smith*.

Mid-May-late October, weekdays, nine trips; Sunday, eight trips; rest of year, six trips daily.

WINDJAMMER SAILING

Camden Harbor, 800-807-9463; www.sailmainecoast.com

Old-time schooners leave from Camden and Rockport Harbors for half-day to six-day trips along the coast of Maine. For further information, rates, schedules or reservations, contact the Maine Windjammer Association.

May-October.

SPECIAL EVENTS
BAY CHAMBER CONCERTS

Rockport Opera House, Central St., Rockport, 207-236-2823;
www.baychamberconcerts.org

Classical music performances by Vermeer Quartet and guest artists.

July-August, Thursday-Friday evenings. Jazz musicians perform September-June (one show each month) Monday-Friday, 9 a.m.-5 p.m.

WINDJAMMER WEEKEND

Camden Harbor, 207-236-4404; www.windjammerweekend.com

This weekend is a celebration of Maine's windjammer fleet and features fireworks. Labor Day weekend.

WHERE TO STAY
★★★BLUE HARBOR HOUSE, A VILLAGE INN

67 Elm St., Camden, 207-236-3196, 800-248-3196; www.blueharborhouse.com
Built in 1768 as the home of the first Camden settler, James Richards, guest rooms are now filled with quilts and antiques. Enjoy a hearty breakfast before hiking Camden Hills State Park or taking a Penobscot Bay boat ride.
11 rooms. Complimentary breakfast. $151-250

★★★CAMDEN HARBOUR INN

83 Bayview St., Camden, 800-236-4266; www.camdenharbourinn.com
Influenced by its international owners, Camden Harbour Inn offers guests impeccable service, luxurious amenities and lovely views. Guests can expect to be spoiled with fine linens and towels, a king-size pillow-top mattress, luxe bathrobes, flat-screen TV and complimentary breakfast from the fine Natalie's restaurants.
18 rooms. Complimentary breakfast. $151-250

ALSO RECOMMENDED
CAMDEN WINDWARD HOUSE

6 High St., Camden, 207-236-9656, 877-492-9656; www.windwardhouse.com
This 1854 inn is located in the center of Camden's historic district, within walking distance to many restaurants, shops and Camden Harbor. Mount Battie and Camden Hills State Park are nearby. Rooms are individually decorated with antiques, and the inn has wireless access throughout.
8 rooms. No children under 12. Complimentary breakfast. Bar. $151-250

HAWTHORN INN

9 High St., Camden, 207-236-8842, 866-381-3647; www.camdenhawthorn.com
This 1894 Victorian inn is conveniently located near Camden's downtown area. The rooms all have private baths, and some display fireplaces, whirlpools and private decks with harbor views.
10 rooms. Closed January. No children under 12. Complimentary breakfast. $151-250

INN AT OCEAN'S EDGE

24 Stonecoast Rd., Lincolnville, 207-236-0945; www.innatoceansedge.com
This contemporary inn overlooks Penobscot Bay. Spacious rooms feature down duvet-topped beds, Jacuzzi tubs and ocean views. The outdoor infinity-edge pool overlooks the bay.
30 rooms. No children under 14. Complimentary breakfast. Fitness center. $151-250

INN AT SUNRISE POINT

Highway 1, Camden, 207-236-7716, 800-435-6278; www.sunrisepoint.com
This oceanfront hideaway is just minutes from Camden Harbor. Guests may choose to stay in a restored 1920s Maine-style cottage or in the main house. Breakfast is served in the conservatory and afternoon hors d'oeuvres are available in the library.
13 rooms. No children under 12. Complimentary breakfast. $251-350

MAINE STAY BED AND BREAKFAST

22 High St., Camden, 207-236-9636; www.mainestay.com

This bed and breakfast is situated inside a farmhouse built in 1802. The bright, cheerful rooms are decorated with antiques that include a 17th-century samurai chest.

8 rooms. No children under 12. Complimentary breakfast. $151-250

NORUMBEGA INN

63 High St., Camden, 207-236-4646; www.norumbegainn.com

This stone castle near the sea was designed and built by the inventor of duplex telegraphy and is located near Penobscot Bay. Offering panoramic views of the ocean, the property has been fully restored and is furnished with modern conveniences. Each room has a king bed and a private bath. Evening turndown service is provided.

13 rooms. No children under 7. Complimentary breakfast. $151-250

WHITEHALL INN

52 High St., Camden, 207-236-3391, 800-789-6565; www.whitehall-inn.com

This spacious resort inn was built in 1834 and was the location of a noted reading that poet Edna St. Vincent Millay gave a reading here in 1912. Rooms have been recently refreshed to include small flat-screen TVs and down duvets.

50 rooms. Closed mid-October-mid-May. Restaurant, bar. Tennis. Complimentary breakfast. $151-250

WHERE TO EAT

★★ATLANTICA

1 Bayview Landing, Camden, 207-236-6011; www.atlanticarestaurant.com

This casual bistro is decorated in a contemporary style that matches the straightforward, brightly flavored dishes on its menu. The lobster pot pie with matchstick fries and the grilled scallops with pumpkin risotto are rich and satisfying.

Seafood. Dinner. Bar. Reservations recommended. Outdoor seating. Closed Tuesday in winter; also month of January or March. $36-85

★★THE LOBSTER POUND

Highway 1, Lincolnville Beach, 207-789-5550; www.lobsterpoundmaine.com

Stop at this simple waterfront restaurant for fresh boiled lobster and lobster rolls. The menu also includes a selection of grilled steaks and dishes such as roast turkey.

American, seafood. Lunch, dinner. Children's menu. Reservations recommended. Closed November-April. Daily May-October. $16-35

★★★VINCENT'S

52 High St., Camden, 207-236-3391, 800-789-6565; www.whitehall-inn.com

Located in the quaint Whitehall Inn, this restaurant attracts visitors and local residents alike. The cuisine is New American with a healthy focus on seafood. Dine in the main dining room, the glass-enclosed dining porch, the seasonal side patio or order bar food in the adjacent lounge.

American. Breakfast, dinner. Bar. Reservations recommended. Outdoor seating. $16-35

★★WATERFRONT
40 Bayview St., Camden, 207-236-3747; www.waterfrontcamden.com
Originally a boat shed, this restaurant is located on Camden Harbor with docking and access for boaters and has specialized in presenting fresh regional seafood in both traditional and adventurous ways for more than 25 years. The décor includes open, beamed ceilings, hanging lanterns and a double fireplace; the outdoor deck is the place to be for an exceptional harbor view.
Seafood, steak. Lunch, dinner. Bar. Children's menu. Outdoor seating. $16-35

CHEBEAGUE ISLANDS
See also Portland
Little Chebeague and the Great Chebeague islands, off the coast of Portland in Casco Bay, were once a favorite camping spot of various tribes. The Native Americans had a penchant for clams, and the first European settlers found heaps of clamshells scattered across the land. Those shells were later used to pave many of the islands' roads, some of which still exist today.

Great Chebeague, six miles long and approximately three miles wide, is connected to Little Chebeague at low tide by a sandbar. There are various locations for swimming. Additionally, both islands are easy to explore on foot or bicycle. At one time, Great Chebeague was home to a prosperous fishing and shipbuilding community, and it was a quarrying center in the late 1700s. Today, it receives hundreds of visitors every summer.

WHAT TO SEE
CASCO BAY LINES
56 Commercial St., Portland, 207-774-7871; www.cascobaylines.com
Casco Bay Lines provides year-round ferry service from Portland, Commercial and Franklin streets. The trip is a one-hour crossing.
Daily.

CHEBEAGUE TRANSPORTATION
123 Roy Hill Road, Chebeague Island, 207-846-3700; www.chebeaguetrans.com
From Cousins Island, near Yarmouth, the trip is a 15-minute crossing. There is off-site parking available with shuttle service to ferry.
Daily.

CRANBERRY ISLES
See also Bar Harbor
The Cranberry Isles, named because of the rich, red cranberry bogs that once covered Great Cranberry Isle, lie off the southeast coast of Mount Desert Island. There are five islands in the group: Little and Great Cranberry, Sutton, Bear and Baker. Great Cranberry, the largest, covers about 900 acres. Baker Island is part of Acadia National Park, and Sutton is privately owned. In 1830, the islands petitioned the state to separate from Mount Desert Island.

WHAT TO SEE
ISLESFORD HISTORICAL MUSEUM
Main Street, and Sand Beach Road, Cranberry Isles, 207-244-9224;
www.mainemuseums.org
The museum holds exhibits on local island history from 1604.
Mid-June-September, daily.

DAMARISCOTTA
See also Boothbay Harbor, Monhegan Island
Damariscotta, whose name is an Abenaki word meaning "river of many
fishes," has a number of colonial, Greek Revival and pre-Civil War houses.
With the neighboring city of Newcastle across the Damariscotta River, this
is a trading center for a seaside resort region extending to Pemaquid Point
and Christmas Cove.

WHAT TO SEE
COLONIAL PEMAQUID STATE PARK
Colonial Pemaquid Road, New Harbor, 207-677-2423
Excavations have uncovered foundations of a jail, a tavern and private homes.
The park allows fishing and picnicking. A boat ramp and free parking are
available.
Memorial Day-Labor Day, daily.

FORT WILLIAM HENRY STATE MEMORIAL
New Harbor, 207-677-2423
In a reconstructed 1692 fort tower, the museum contains relics, portraits,
maps and copies of Native American deeds.
Memorial Day-September: daily.

PEMAQUID POINT LIGHTHOUSE PARK
Pemaquid Lighthouse, New Harbor, 207-677-2494; www.lighthouse.cc
The park includes an 1827 lighthouse that towers above the pounding surf
(not open to the public). The Fishermen's Museum is housed in an old light-
keeper's dwelling.
Memorial Day-Columbus Day, daily; rest of year, by appointment.

WHERE TO STAY
★★★THE BRADLEY INN
3063 Bristol Road, New Harbor, 207-677-2105, 800-942-5560; www.bradleyinn.com
This inn, built by a sea captain for his bride in 1880, is located at the tip
of Pemaquid Peninsula close to John's Bay and the Pemaquid Lighthouse.
Nearby activities include golfing, fishing, boating, walks on the beach, a winery, a nature area and fine restaurants. Rooms are individually decorated and
some feature fireplaces.
16 rooms. Closed January-March. Complimentary breakfast. Restaurant.
$251-350

★★★NEWCASTLE INN

60 River Road, Newcastle, 207-563-5685, 800-832-8669; www.newcastleinn.com

Overlooking gardens and the Damariscotta River, this Federal-style 1850 inn offers rooms and suites with four-poster or canopy beds, sitting areas or fireplaces. A four-course dinner preceded by complimentary hors d'oeuvres is served in one of the two dining rooms.

15 rooms. No children under 12. Restaurant, bar. Complimentary breakfast. $151-250

DEER ISLE

A bridge over Eggemoggin Reach connects these islands to the mainland. There are two major villages here, Deer Isle (the older) and Stonington. Lobster fishing and tourism are the backbone of the economy and sailing, tennis and golf are available in the area.

WHAT TO SEE
ISLE AU HAUT

Reached by ferry from Stonington, much of this island—with hills more than 500 feet tall, forested shores and cobblestone beaches—is in Acadia National Park.

ISLE AU HAUT BOAT SERVICES

Seabreeze Avenue, Stonington, 207-367-6516; www.isleauhaut.com

Service to the island and excursion trips are available. See their website for additional details on fares and scheduling.

WHERE TO STAY
★★★PILGRIMS INN

20 Main St., Deer Isle, 207-348-6615, 888-778-7505; www.pilgrimsinn.com

This restored historic wood-frame building was built in 1793 and houses eight-foot-wide fireplaces. Nearby are galleries and a famous art school. The chef prepares meals from local seafood, produce and fresh-grown ingredients from the garden.

16 rooms. Closed November-mid-May. Restaurant. Complimentary breakfast. Pets accepted.

FORT KENT

Fort Kent, at the northern end of famous Highway 1 (the other end is at Key West, Florida), is the chief community of Maine's "far north." A bridge across the St. John River leads to Clair, New Brunswick. The town is a lumbering, farming, hunting and fishing center. Canoeing, downhill and cross-country skiing, as well as snowmobiling are popular here. A campus for the University of Maine is located here.

WHAT TO SEE
FORT KENT BLOCKHOUSE

North edge of town, 207-941-4014

Built in 1839 during the Aroostook Bloodless War with Britain, the blockhouse was used as a guard post. The museum features antique hand tools and

interpretive displays. Picnicking is allowed on site.
Memorial Day-Labor Day, daily.

FORT KENT HISTORICAL SOCIETY MUSEUM AND GARDENS
54 W. Main St., Fort Kent, 207-834-5121
The former Bangor and Aroostook railroad station, built in early 1900s, now houses historical museum.
Usually last two weeks in June-August, Tuesday-Friday.

LONESOME PINE TRAILS
Forest Avenue, Fort Kent, 207-834-5202
On site there are thirteen trails, a 2,300-foot slope with 500-foot drop as well as a beginners slope and tow, a rope tow and T-bar. There is a ski school and rentals available. The ski patrol is on duty. There is also a lodge with concessions.
December-April.

SPECIAL EVENTS
CAN AM CROWN SLED DOG RACES
West Main Street, Fort Kent, 207-834-3312, 800-733-3563; http://can-am.sjv.net
Three races (30, 60 and 250-mile) begin on Main Street and finish at the Lonesome Pine Ski Lodge.
Late February-early March.

FREEPORT
See also Portland
Freeport is a historic seaside town that played a part in Maine's early history; papers were signed here, separating the state from Massachusetts in 1820. Today, the town is known as a destination for shopping. It is home to dozens of outlets and the renowned flagship L.L. Bean clothing and sporting goods store, which stays open 24 hours a day, selling everything from kayaks to bikes and thermal underwear to colorful fleece jackets.

WHAT TO SEE
ATLANTIC SEAL CRUISES
25 Main St., South Freeport. Depart from Town Wharf, 207-865-6112;
www.freeportusa.org
Cruises aboard a 40-foot, 28-passenger vessel on Casco Bay to Eagle Island and Robert E. Peary house museum; they also take seal and bird-watching trips, as well as fall foliage sightseeing cruises. Schedules vary and tickets can be purchased at Main Street office.
Daily 8 a.m.-7 p.m.

FACTORY OUTLET STORES
42-28 Main St., Freeport, 800-865-1994; www.freeportusa.com
Freeport is home to more than 170 outlet stores and centers that offer brand-name merchandise at discounted prices, including the famous L.L. Bean clothing and sporting goods flagship store, which stays open 24 hours a day.

MAST LANDING SANCTUARY

20 Gilsland Farm Road, Falmouth, 207-781-2330; www.maineaudubon.org

This 140-acre area is maintained by the Maine Audubon Society. Hiking and cross-country skiing available.

Daily.

WHERE TO STAY
★★★HARRASEEKET INN

162 Main St., Freeport, 207-865-9377, 800-342-6423; www.harraseeketinn.com

Three structures make up the inn: the Federalist House (1798), the Early Victorian House (1850) and a modern, colonial-style inn. Spacious guest rooms are decorated with antiques and cozy fireplaces. Tea is served in the paneled drawing room each afternoon, and there is a complimentary breakfast buffet each morning. This inn is located just two blocks from the L.L. Bean flagship store and the town's shopping outlets.

84 rooms. Pets accepted. Complimentary breakfast. Restaurant, bar. Pool. $151-250

ALSO RECOMMENDED
BREWSTER HOUSE BED & BREAKFAST

180 Main St., Freeport, 207-865-4121, 800-865-0822; www.brewsterhouse.com

Built in 1888, this waterfront inn's rooms are decorated with fresh floral prints and antique furniture. The inn includes a cozy parlor that is ideal for lounging, as you will find a warm, inviting fireplace.

7 rooms. No children under 8. Complimentary breakfast. $251-350

KENDALL TAVERN BED AND BREAKFAST

213 Main St., Freeport, 207-865-1338, 800-341-9572; www.kendalltavern.com

This bed and breakfast is located at the north end of Freeport. Built in 1832, the first floor was opened as a tavern, and a second story was added years later. Guest rooms feature antiques and handmade quilts. Each morning, a country-style breakfast is served in the dining room.

7 rooms. No children under 8. Complimentary breakfast. Pets accepted. $151-250

WHERE TO EAT
★GRITTY MCDUFF'S

187 Lower Main St., Freeport, 207-865-4321; www.grittys.com

Its location near the outlets makes Gritty McDuff's a popular spot to park for those who would rather sip a house-brewed beer than browse for bargains. The menu includes a wide selection of traditional pub dishes from fish and chips to sandwiches.

American, seafood. Lunch, dinner, late-night. Bar. Children's menu. Outdoor seating. $16-35

★★JAMESON TAVERN

115 Main St., Freeport, 207-865-4196; www.jamesontavern.com

Located in a house built in 1779, this traditional tavern serves a simple menu of pub fare and American classics. The lobster stew is a local favorite, as is the outdoor seating in summer.

Seafood, steak. Lunch, dinner. Bar. Children's menu. Reservations recommended. Outdoor seating. $16-35

★LOBSTER COOKER
39 Main St., Freeport, 207-865-4349; www.lobstercooker.net

A no-frills spot close to Freeport shopping, this restaurant offers a simple menu of lobster and other seafood, from lobster rolls to steamed clams. The clam and fish chowders win raves.

Seafood. Lunch, dinner. Children's menu. Outdoor seating. $16-35

★★★THE MAINE DINING ROOM
162 Main St., Freeport, 207-865-9377, 800-342-6423; www.harraseeketinn.com

This restaurant, located in the Harraseeket Inn, offers a cozy atmosphere, enhanced by two wood-burning fireplaces and windows overlooking the gardens. Organic and homegrown foods shine on the menu, and the wine selection is one of the largest in Maine.

American. Breakfast, dinner, brunch. Bar. Reservations recommended. $36-85

GREENVILLE

Greenville is a starting point for trips into the Moosehead Lake region. Until it was incorporated in 1836, it was known as Haskell in honor of its founder Nathaniel Haskell.

WHAT TO SEE

MOOSEHEAD MARINE MUSEUM
North Main Street, Greenville, 207-695-2716; www.katahdincruises.com/museum.html

This museum is located on the steamboat *Katahdin*, berthed in East Cove. There are exhibits of the steamboat era and the Kineo Hotel; cruises are also available.

July-Columbus Day.

ALSO RECOMMENDED

GREENVILLE INN
40 Norris St., Greenville, 207-695-2206, 888-695-6000; www.greenvilleinn.com

Spread out between a rambling Victorian and six individual cottages, this inn offers individually decorated rooms with private baths. The cottages are more rustic in décor, but include new pillow-top mattresses.

13 rooms. Complimentary breakfast. Restaurant, bar. $151-250

THE LODGE AT MOOSEHEAD LAKE
368 Lily Bay Road, Greenville, 207-695-4400, 800-825-6977;
www.lodgeatmooseheadlake.com

At this romantic retreat, lodge rooms and adjacent carriage house suites are adorned with charming rustic interiors including hand-carved poster beds. Most guest rooms feature sunset views over the water and Squaw Mountain. Explore nearby Lily Bay State Park or take part in the year-round recreations of the lake and surrounding wilderness.

5 rooms. No children under 14. Complimentary breakfast. Pets accepted. $251-350

KENNEBUNK

See also Kennebunkport, Portland

The inland sister to tony beach town Kennebunkport, this village is equally visually appealing and quaint. At one time, the original settlement that was to become Kennebunk used to be a part of Wells. When Maine separated from Massachusetts in 1820, Kennebunk separated from Wells. Once a shipbuilding community on the Mousam and Kennebunk Rivers, today, Kennebunk is the business center for the summer resort area that includes Kennebunkport and Kennebunk Beach.

WHAT TO SEE
BRICK STORE MUSEUM

117 Main St., Kennebunk, 207-985-4802; www.brickstoremuseum.org

This block of restored 19th-century buildings includes William Lord's Brick Store and exhibits of fine and decorative arts, historical and maritime collections.

Tuesday-Friday, 10 a.m.-4.30 p.m., Saturday 10 a.m.-1 p.m. Parking available.

WHERE TO STAY
THE BEACH HOUSE

211 Beach Ave., Kennebunk, 207-967-3850; www.beachhseinn.com

This circa-1890 inn is located on Kennebunk Beach, just two miles from Kennebunkport. Rooms are crisp and contemporary, with plush duvet-topped beds. Afternoon tea is served in the sitting room, which has a view of the ocean.

34 rooms. Complimentary breakfast. Reservations recommended. $351 and up

THE KENNEBUNK INN

45 Main St., Kennebunk, 207-985-3351; www.thekennebunkinn.com

Built in 1799, this cozy inn has been updated with streamlined, contemporary décor and modern touches such as wireless access. The inn's location in the center of Kennebunk makes it easy to walk to local shops and restaurants.

22 rooms. Pets accepted,. Complimentary breakfast. Restaurant. $61-150

WHERE TO EAT
★FEDERAL JACK'S RESTAURANT AND BREW PUB

8 Western Ave., Kennebunk, 207-967-4322; www.federaljacks.com

This casual restaurant features local beers made by the Kennebunkport Brewing Company alongside pub favorites. The clam chowder, steamed lobsters and haddock tacos are just a few menu highlights.

American, seafood. Lunch, dinner, late-night. Bar. Children's menu. Outdoor seating. $16-35

★★★GRISSINI
27 Western Ave., Kennebunk, 207-967-2211; www.restaurantgrissini.com
Grissini offers Tuscan cooking in an airy, loft-like setting. Features include a large stone fireplace, an open kitchen and an outdoor garden dining area. Pastas and pizzas are made fresh daily.
Italian. Dinner. Bar. Reservations recommended. Outdoor seating. $16-35

KENNEBUNKPORT
See also Kennebunk, Portland
At the mouth of the Kennebunk River, this quaint coastal town is a favorite summer destination of well-heeled New Englanders. The Bush family has its warm-weather compound here, and generations of bluebloods have checked into the historic Colony Hotel and walked along the beach to Walker's Point. In fall and winter, the town is equally appealing, with its many boutiques, restaurants and charming inns as diversions.

WHAT TO SEE
SCHOOL HOUSE

135 N. St., Kennebunkport, 207-967-2751; www.kporthistory.org
The 1899 schoolhouse is the headquarters of the Kennebunkport Historical Society. Houses collections of genealogy, photographs, maritime history and many artifacts and documents on Kennebunkport's history.
Tuesday-Friday.

WHERE TO STAY
★★THE BREAKWATER INN AND HOTEL

127-131 Ocean Ave., Kennebunkport, 207-967-5333; www.thebreakwaterinn.com
An inn has been in operation in this building for more than 150 years. The current version has cheerful accommodations, decorated in blue hues with a subtle nautical theme. The rooms are stocked with flat-screen TVs and DVD players and the onsite restaurant serves contemporary seafood dishes in an elegant setting with views of the river.
37 rooms. Complimentary breakfast. Restaurant. Spa. $251-350

★★★THE COLONY HOTEL

140 Ocean Ave., Kennebunkport, 207-967-3331, 800-552-2363;
www.thecolonyhotel.com/maine
Located on a rock promontory overlooking the Atlantic Ocean and the mouth of the Kennebec River, this hotel features a heated saltwater pool, beach and gardens. Other nearby activities include golfing, playing tennis, kayaking, bicycling, boating, shopping and touring art galleries. Maine lobster and local seafood are the focus at the hotel's restaurant.
125 rooms. Pets accepted. Restaurant, bar. Beach. Pool. Closed November-mid-May. $151-250

★★★KENNEBUNKPORT INN

One Dock Square, Kennebunkport, 207-967-2621, 800-248-2621;
www.kennebunkportinn.com
Built by a wealthy tea and coffee merchant in 1899, the Victorian mansion

was renovated to become an inn in 1926. Conveniently located in the heart of the historic seaport of Kennebunkport, this inn is an easy walk to the harbor and all the shops and galleries of Dock Square. Guest rooms feature period antiques and reproductions, high four-post beds, elegant fabrics and floral carpeting.

49 rooms. Complimentary breakfast. Restaurant, bar. Spa. Pool. $251-350

★★★NONANTUM RESORT

95 Ocean Ave., Kennebunkport, 207-967-4050, 800-552-5651;
www.nonantumresort.com

This is one of the oldest operating inns in the state. The beach is nearby, as is the Bush family compound for those hoping to glimpse the 41st or 43rd presidents. Maine seafood is the specialty at the onsite restaurant.

111 rooms. Restaurant, bar. Pool. Closed mid-November-April. $61-150

★★★★THE WHITE BARN INN

37 Beach Ave., Kennebunkport, 207-967-2321; www.whitebarninn.com

A cluster of cottages, restored barns and a circa-1860s house make up this quaint spot on the coast of Maine. The charming rooms and suites are decorated with antiques and feature wood-burning fireplaces, whirlpool tubs, and flat-screen TVs. Simple pleasures here include relaxing by the stone swimming pool, riding a bike along the coast, experiencing a spa treatment and having afternoon tea by the fire in the comfortable sitting room. The inn houses one of the region's most acclaimed restaurants, which serves New England cuisine in a rustic, candlelit setting.

25 rooms. Complimentary breakfast. Restaurant, bar. Spa. Pool. Business center. $351 and up

ALSO RECOMMENDED
BUFFLEHEAD COVE

Bufflehead Cove Lane, Kennebunkport, 207-967-3879; www.buffleheadcove.com

This secluded Victorian inn is spacious and old-fashioned. Located close to downtown Kennebunkport, guests may leisurely explore the local beaches or visit the numerous restaurants, art galleries, antique shops and old bookstores.

6 rooms. No children under 11. Complimentary breakfast. $251-350

CAPE ARUNDEL INN

208 Ocean Ave., Kennebunkport, 207-967-2125; www.capearundelinn.com

This recently renovated, Victorian-style 1890 inn, which overlooks the seacoast, also includes a 1950s-era annex and a carriage house. All of the rooms are individually decorated in English country style.

14 rooms. Complimentary breakfast. Restaurant. Closed mid-December-mid-April. $151-250

CAPTAIN FAIRFIELD INN

8 Pleasant St., Kennebunkport, 207-967-4454, 800-322-1928;
www.captainfairfield.com

This Federal-style 1813 historic bed and breakfast is at the heart of Kennebunkport. Guest rooms are fitted with antique and period furniture and each room has its own private bath and sitting area. The inn is surrounded by towering trees and gardens and overlooks the river and harbor. Captain Fairfield Inn is within walking distance to shops and art galleries, as well as the ocean and a variety of restaurants.

9 rooms. No children under 6. Complimentary breakfast. $151-250

THE CAPTAIN JEFFERDS INN

5 Pearl St., Kennebunkport, 207-967-2311, 800-839-6844; www.captainjefferdsinn.com

Built in 1804, this historic inn has been fully restored and is furnished with antiques and period reproductions. All rooms have private baths, fresh flowers, down-filled comforters and fireplaces. A complimentary three-course breakfast is included as are afternoon refreshments.

15 rooms. Pets accepted. No children under 8. Complimentary breakfast. Closed last two weeks in December. $251-350

THE CAPTAIN LORD MANSION

6 Pleasant St., Kennebunkport, 207-967-3141, 800-522-3141; www.captainlord.com

Set on an acre of gardens, this inn is decorated with a worldly mix of period furnishings and different themes. Repeat visitors are rewarded with an engraved stone in the Memory Garden after their tenth stay.

17 rooms. No children under 12. Complimentary breakfast. $61-150

ENGLISH MEADOWS INN

141 Port Road, Kennebunkport, 207-967-5766, 800-272-0698;
www.englishmeadowsinn.com

Housed in a Victorian farmhouse and an attached carriage house dating to the 1860s, this spacious inn is located amid sprawling grounds and gardens. Afternoon tea is served daily, and the rooms are individually decorated in English country style.

12 rooms. Pets accepted. Complimentary breakfast. Closed January. $61-150

OLD FORT INN

8 Old Fort Ave., Kennebunkport, 207-967-5353, 800-828-3678; www.oldfortinn.com

This inn contains guest rooms in a turn-of-the-century carriage house built of red brick and local stone. There is a tennis court and heated freshwater pool on site. Located just one block from the Atlantic Ocean, guests can explore nearby beaches, boutiques and art galleries.

16 rooms. Complimentary breakfast. Pool. Tennis. Closed mid-December-mid-April. $251-350

WHERE TO EAT
★BARTLEY'S DOCKSIDE

Western Avenue, Kennebunkport, 207-967-5050; www.bartleysdining.com

This simple waterfront restaurant serves fresh lobster, clams and more in a no-frills setting. Those with an appetite can opt for the jumbo, two-and-a-half pound steamed lobster, and finish it off with a slice of fresh-made blueberry pie.

Seafood. Lunch, dinner. Children's menu. Outdoor seating. $16-35

★NUNAN'S LOBSTER HUT

9 Mills Road, Kennebunkport, 207-967-4362

When all you want is a simple, steamed lobster, this is the place. Locals line up early at this no-reservation restaurant to dig into the huge, fresh lobsters, lobster rolls and blueberry pie.

Seafood. Dinner. Closed Columbus Day-May. $16-35

★★★STRIPERS

131-133 Ocean Ave., Kennebunkport, 207-967-5333; www.thebreakwaterinn.com

Its décor makes the restaurant feel like a modern seaside cottage, with a soft green banquette, steel-rimmed tabletops and a see-through aquarium wall that divides the entry from the main dining room. The menu includes options such as local Kennebunkport oysters, farm-raised striped bass, halibut and scallops. Located within the Breakwater Inn and Spa, Stripers is close to Dock Square's shops and galleries.

Seafood. Dinner, brunch. Bar. Reservations recommended. Outdoor seating. Closed late October-early April. $36-85

★★★★★THE WHITE BARN INN RESTAURANT

37 Beach Ave., Kennebunkport, 207-967-2321; www.whitebarninn.com

A New England classic, this charming candlelit space inside the White Barn Inn is bedecked with fresh flowers and white linen-topped tables. Executive chef Jonathan Cartwright creates delicious regional dishes accented with a European flair. The four-course prix fixe menu changes weekly, highlighting seafood from Maine's waters, as well as native game and poultry. The vast wine selection complements the cuisine, and a rolling cheese cart offers some of the best local artisans' products.

American. Bar. Jacket required. Reservations recommended. Closed three weeks in January. $86 and up

SPA

★★★★SPA AT WHITE BARN INN

37 Beach Ave., Kennebunkport, 207-967-2321; www.whitebarninn.com

Though located in a traditional (but luxurious) New England country inn, the Spa at White Barn Inn delivers minimalism without compromising luxury. Guests can request a light-of-the-moon plunge, which is a fizz of marine pebbles infused with mandarin orange and lemon essential oils, or an aroma sea bath. The nearby Kennebunk River provides the materials used in the spa's signature stone massage, while natural marine algae and Maine sea salts are incorporated into the body wraps.

KINGFIELD

See also Augusta

Located in the valley of the Carrabassett River, Kingfield once had several lumber mills. The town was named after William King, Maine's first governor, and was the birthplace of F.E. and F.O. Stanley, the twins who developed the Stanley Steamer. Canoeing, hiking and downhill skiing are available in nearby areas.

WHAT TO SEE
CARRABASSETT VALLEY SKI AREA
Sugarloaf Access Road, Kingfield, 207-237-2000; www.sugarloaf.com
There are approximately 50 miles of ski touring trails. The center offers school, rentals and a skating rink. There is also a trail information area and on site shop.
Early December-late April, daily.

SUGARLOAF/USA SKI AREA
Sugarloaf Access Road, Kingfield, 207-237-2000, 800-843-5623
This ski area features two quad, triple, eight double chairlifts and T-bar. There is a ski school, ski patrol, and rentals. Snowmaking is provided on site. Sugarloaf features a lodge, restaurants, coffee shop, cafeteria and bars. There is also a nursery, bank, health club and shops. There are also six Olympic runs, 45 miles of trails. The longest run is 3 ½ miles. There is a vertical drop of 2,820 feet and 65 miles of cross-country trails. Early November-May, daily.

WHERE TO STAY
★★★GRAND SUMMIT RESORT HOTEL
5091 Access Road, Kingfield, 207-237-2222, 800-843-5623; www.sugarloaf.com
Each room in this hotel has a view of the mountains and features oak furniture and brass fixtures. Guests can take advantage of skiing and golfing activities nearby. The hotel is located at the base of the slopes at Sugarloaf resort.
120 rooms. Restaurant, bar. Fitness center. Golf. Tennis. Ski-in/ski-out. $61-150

★★SUGARLOAF INN
Highway 27, Kingfield, 207-237-6814, 800-843-5623; www.sugarloaf.com
Basic, affordable rooms and ski-in/ski-out access make this Sugarloaf hotel a favorite with winter travelers. The inn features free wireless access and a cozy onsite pub.
42 rooms. Restaurant, bar. Pool. Golf. Tennis. $61-150

KITTERY
See also York
This old sea community has built ships since its early days. Kittery men built the Ranger, which sailed to France under John Paul Jones with the news of Burgoyne's surrender. Located across the Piscataqua River from Portsmouth, New Hampshire, Kittery is the home of the Portsmouth Naval Shipyard. The town also hosts several shopping outlets, featuring stores such as J. Crew and Calvin Klein.

WHAT TO SEE
FORT FOSTER PARK
Northeast via Highway 103 to Gerrish Island, 207-439-3800; www.kittery.org
This 92-acre park offers a pavilion, a beach, a baseball field and a fishing pier. Cross-country skiing is available in winter. Entrance fee per individual and per vehicle.

June-August, daily; May and September, Saturday-Sunday.

KITTERY HISTORICAL AND NAVAL MUSEUM
Highway 1 and Rogers Road, Kittery, 207-439-3080
Exhibits portray the history of the U.S. Navy and Kittery—Maine's oldest incorporated town—as well as southern Maine's maritime heritage.
June-October, Tuesday-Saturday 10 a.m.-4 p.m.

SARAH ORNE JEWETT HOUSE
5 Portland St., South Berwick, 207-384-2454; www.spnea.org/visit/homes/jewett
Novelist Sarah Orne Jewett spent most of her life in this 1774 Georgian residence. The interior was restored to re-create the appearance of the house during her time (1849-1909), and still contains some original 18th- and 19th-century wallpaper and fine paneling. Her bedroom-study has been left as she had arranged it.
June-mid-October, Friday-Sunday.

WHERE TO STAY
★COACHMAN INN
380 Highway 1, Kittery, 207-439-4434, 800-824-6183; www.coachmaninn.net
The simple rooms at this inn feature Colonial décor and free wireless access. The newly added guest lounge is fitted with high-definition TV, games and workstations.
43 rooms. Complimentary breakfast. Pool. $61-150

WHERE TO EAT
★CAP'N SIMEON'S GALLERY
90 Pepperell Road, Kittery Point, 207-439-3655; www.capnsimeons.com
Located in a 17th-century boathouse, this restaurant features nautical décor. There are views of the pier and lighthouses, and entertainment is offered on weekends.
Seafood. Lunch, dinner, Sunday brunch. Bar. Children's menu. $16-35

★★WARREN'S LOBSTER HOUSE
11 Water St., Kittery, 207-439-1630; www.lobsterhouse.com
This waterfront restaurant has an extensive menu of seafood dishes, including a lobster thermidor that is a tasty take on the classic recipe. The clam chowder is a menu standout, with a creamy base and rich, plump clams.
Seafood. Lunch, dinner. Sunday brunch. Bar. Children's menu. Outdoor seating. $16-35

LUBEC
Quoddy Head State Park, the easternmost point in the United States, is located in Lubec. There is a lighthouse here, as well as the Franklin D. Roosevelt Memorial Bridge, which stretches over Lubec Narrows to Campobello Island. Roosevelt summered here throughout much of his childhood and into his adult years.

WHAT TO SEE
ROOSEVELT CAMPOBELLO INTERNATIONAL PARK
459 Highway 774, New Brunswick, 506-752-2922; www.nps.gov/roca

This Canadian property is jointly maintained by Canada and the United States. At approximately 2,800 acres, it includes the 11-acre estate where Franklin D. Roosevelt had his summer home and was stricken with poliomyelitis. There are self-guided tours of the 34-room house, with interpretive guides available. Films shown in the visitor center; picnic sites in a natural area; observation platforms and interpretive panels at Friar's Head. There is no camping allowed.

Saturday before Memorial Day-October 31, daily.

WHERE TO STAY
HOME PORT INN
45 Main St., Lubec, 207-733-2077, 800-457-2077; www.homeportinn.com

Built in 1880, this inn features individually decorated rooms with views of the Bay of Fundy and Cobscook Bay. The daily breakfast includes house-made granola and fresh baked blueberry muffins.

7 rooms. Complimentary breakfast. Restaurant. Closed mid-October-late May. $61-150

WHERE TO EAT
★★HOME PORT INN
45 Main St., Lubec, 207-733-2077; www.homeportinn.com

Traditional tavern fare is served in a casual setting at this historic waterfront inn. Entrees include steak au poivre and steamed lobster. Desserts are made in house and feature berries and fruits in season.

American. Dinner. Reservations recommended. Closed November-April. $151-250

MONHEGAN ISLAND
See also Boothbay Harbor, Damariscotta, Rockland

The Monhegan Plantation, nine miles out to sea, approximately two miles long and one mile wide, is devoted to lobsters and summer visitors. Rockwell Kent and Milton Burns were among the first of many artists to summer here. Today, the warm-weather population is about 20 times the year-round number. There is more work in winter: by special law, lobsters may be trapped in Monhegan waters only from January to June. This gives them the other six months to grow. Thus, Monhegan lobsters command the highest prices.

Leif Ericson may have landed here in AD 1,000. In its early years, Monhegan Island was a landmark for sailors, and by 1611 it was well-known as a general headquarters for European fishermen, traders and explorers. For a time, the island was a pirate den. Small compared with other Maine islands, Monhegan is a land of contrasts. On one side of the island, sheer cliffs drop 150 feet to the ocean below, while on the other side Cathedral Woods offers visitors a quiet forest to explore.

WHAT TO SEE
MONHEGAN LIGHTHOUSE/MUSEUM

1 Lighthouse Hill, Monhegan Island, 207-596-7003; www.monheganmuseum.org

Historic lighthouse has been in operation since 1824; automated since 1959.

July 1-August 31: 11:30 a.m.-3:30 p.m.; select days in June and September: 1:30-3:30 p.m.

NORTHEAST HARBOR

See also Bar Harbor, Cranberry Isles

This coastal village is located on Mount Desert Island, a land of rocky coastlines, forests and lakes. The island is reached from the mainland by a short bridge.

WHAT TO SEE
FERRY SERVICE

33 Main St., Cranberry Isles, 207-244-3575

The ferry connects Northeast Harbor with the Cranberry Isles. The trip is a three-mile, 30-minute crossing.

Summer: daily; rest of year: schedule varies.

WOODLAWN MUSEUM (THE BLACK HOUSE)

172 Surrey Road, Northeast Harbor, 207-667-8671; www.woodlawnmuseum.com

Circa-1820 Federal house built by a local landowner is filled with period antiques. There is a garden as well as a carriage house with old carriages and sleighs.

May-October: Tuesday-Sunday; rest of year: by appointment.

WHERE TO STAY
★★★ASTICOU INN

15 Peabody Drive, Northeast Harbor, 207-276-3344, 800-258-3373; www.asticou.com

Rooms at this sprawling Victorian inn are decorated with oriental rugs and traditional furniture. The grounds include beautifully landscaped gardens, as well as clay tennis courts and an outdoor heated pool.

31 rooms. Off season, Monday-Friday. In season: daily. Restaurant, bar. Pool. Tennis. Spa. $251-350

WHERE TO EAT
★DOCKSIDER

14 Sea St., Northeast Harbor, 207-276-3965

This basic seafood restaurant serves lobster rolls alongside other summer favorites such as root beer floats and onion rings. The eatery also offers a selection of ice cream, and a side patio that's perfect for outdoor dining.

Seafood. Lunch, dinner. Children's menu. Outdoor seating. Closed Columbus Day-mid-May. $16-35

OGUNQUIT

See also Kennebunk, Kittery, York

Maine's "stern and rockbound coast" becomes a sunny strand here with a great white beach that stretches for three miles. The Ogunquit public beach is one of the finest on the Atlantic and offers marine views of Perkins Cove. The charming town has attracted a substantial art colony.

WHAT TO SEE
OGUNQUIT MUSEUM OF AMERICAN ART

543 Shore Road, Ogunquit, 207-646-4909; www.ogunquitmuseum.org
The museum, which overlooks the ocean and sculpture gardens, features 20th-century American sculpture and painting.
July-mid-October, daily.

SPECIAL EVENTS
OGUNQUIT PLAYHOUSE

10 Highway 1, Northeast Harbor, 207-646-2402; www.ogunquitplayhouse.org
Established in the early 1930s, the playhouse offers top plays and musicals with professional actors.
Late June-Labor Day weekend.

WHERE TO STAY
★★★ANCHORAGE BY THE SEA

125 Shore Road, Ogunquit, 207-646-9384; www.anchoragebythesea.com
This property has a prime location directly on the ocean. Rooms, spread out in several different buildings, are comfortable and have views of the sea. Some rooms feature fireplaces.
212 rooms. Complimentary breakfast. Restaurant. Pool. $61-150

★★MEADOWMERE

Highway 1, Ogunquit, 207-646-9661, 800-633-8718; www.meadowmere.com
Located in Ogunquit village, this hotel is loaded with amenities that appeal to families, from the pools to the onsite pub, game room and arcade. Rooms are basic, but wireless access and room service are available.
145 rooms. Complimentary breakfast. Restaurant. Fitness center. Pool. $151-250

★THE TERRACE BY THE SEA

23 Wharf Lane, Ogunquit, 207-646-3232; www.terracebythesea.com
This property manages to deliver a location that is close to both Ogunquit village and the town's white sandy beaches. The basic rooms include DVD players and free wireless.
36 rooms. Complimentary breakfast. Pool. Closed January-February. $

ALSO RECOMMENDED
HARTWELL HOUSE

312 Shore Road, Ogunquit, 207-646-7210, 800-235-8883; www.hartwellhouseinn.com
At this bed and breakfast, most rooms have French doors leading to terraces or balconies that overlook the gardens. A full gourmet breakfast and afternoon tea are served daily.
16 rooms. No children under 14. Complimentary breakfast. $151-250

WHERE TO EAT

★★★98 PROVENCE

262 Shore Road, Ogunquit, 207-646-9898; www.98provence.com

The cottage-like setting provides a warm, comfortable atmosphere. This welcoming country French restaurant tucked in a clapboard house offers an appealing menu with classics like fisherman soup or escargot.

French. Dinner. Bar. Closed Tuesday; mid-December-mid-April. $16-35

★★★ARROWS

Berwick Road, Ogunquit, 207-361-1100; www.arrowsrestaurant.com

This idyllic restaurant, housed in an 18th-century farmhouse, is a seasonal dining destination. Co-owners and co-chefs Clark Frasier and Mark Gaier bake their own breads, grow their own organic vegetables and offer a creative, elegant menu. The dining rooms are filled with fresh flowers from the onsite gardens, and the service is thoughtful and attentive.

American. Dinner. Bar. Reservations recommended. Closed Monday; also December-early April. $36-85

★BARNACLE BILLY'S

Perkins Cove, Ogunquit, 207-646-5575, 800-866-5575; www.barnbilly.com

Select your dinner from the onsite tank and then settle in for one of New England's best lobster bakes. The restaurant has its own boats, so the catch is fresh and served simply in a no-frills waterfront setting.

Seafood. Lunch, dinner. Outdoor seating. Reservations recommended. $16-35

★★BILLY'S ETC.

Oarweed Cove Road, Ogunquit, 207-646-4711; www.barnbilly.com

Serving a more extensive menu of New England fare than its sibling, Barnacle Billy's, this restaurant draws crowds for its fried clams, lobster stew and baked stuffed lobster. The waterfront patio is a prime spot for warm weather dining.

American, seafood. Lunch, dinner. Closed November-mid-April. Bar. Outdoor seating. Reservations recommended. $16-35

★★★CLAY HILL FARM

220 Clay Hill Road, Cape Neddick, 207-361-2272; www.clayhillfarm.com

This restaurant, housed in a historic 1780 farmhouse, is located on 30 acres of protected woodlands and certified by the National Wildlife Association as a wildlife habitat and bird sanctuary. The menu features fresh and seasonal dishes such as basil roasted haddock with tomato, cured olives and artichoke hearts.

Seafood. Dinner. Bar. Closed Monday-Wednesday, November-April. $36-85

★★GYPSY SWEETHEARTS

30 Shore Road, Ogunquit, 207-646-7021; www.gypsysweethearts.com

Housed in a converted Victorian, this restaurant serves eclectic dishes in a cozy setting and often features live jazz during dinner. Entrées include almond-crusted baked haddock and shelled lobster with tagliatelle.

International. Dinner. Bar. Reservations recommended. Outdoor seating.

Closed Monday. $16-35

★★★JONATHAN'S
92 Bourne Lane, Ogunquit, 207-646-4777; www.jonathansrestaurant.com
This restaurant is located in a house surrounded by gardens that was once the home of the owner's parents. It serves dishes created with fresh, seasonal ingredients (many of the fruits and vegetables come from the restaurant's own farm, as does the lamb).
American. Dinner. Bar. Closed Monday. $16-35

★★NO. FIVE-O
50 Shore Road, Ogunquit, 207-646-5001; www.five-oshoreroad.com
If you're craving seafood, but would rather skip the local lobster shacks in favor of something more sophisticated, try this contemporary restaurant. The menu includes everything from day boat haddock to baby back ribs. The lounge features a menu of design-your-own sandwiches.
American. Dinner. Bar. Reservations recommended. Outdoor seating. $16-35

★OARWEED COVE
Oarweed Road, Ogunquit, 207-646-4022; www.oarweed.com
This classic lobster shack serves fresh steamed lobsters along with sandwiches, salads and chowders. Desserts are made daily and take advantage of fresh fruits in season.
American, seafood. Lunch, dinner. Bar. Children's menu. Outdoor seating. Closed mid-October-early May. $16-35

★OGUNQUIT LOBSTER POUND
504 Main St., Ogunquit, 207-646-2516
There may be chowders and other seafood dishes on the menu at this basic restaurant, but the draw is the lobsters, priced by the pound and freshly boiled. In summer, individual covered picnic tables make for prime outdoor dining.
Seafood. Dinner. Closed mid-November-mid-February. Bar. Children's menu. Outdoor seating. $16-35

OLD ORCHARD BEACH
See also Kennebunk, Kennebunkport, Portland
This popular beach resort, located 12 miles south of Portland, is a longtime favorite on the Maine Coast. Its crescent beach is seven miles long and about 700 feet wide.

WHAT TO SEE
THE PIER
Old Orchard Beach
The pier extends 475 feet into the harbor and features shops, boutiques and a restaurant.
May-September, daily.

WHERE TO STAY
★THE EDGEWATER
57 W. Grand Ave., Old Orchard Beach, 207-934-2221, 800-203-2034; www.janelle.com
Though the building is a classic motel style, the rooms inside this waterfront hotel are updated with modern bathrooms and beach-inspired pastels. Some rooms feature full kitchenettes.
35 rooms. Closed mid-November-mid-March. Pool. $61-150

WHERE TO EAT
★★★JOSEPH'S BY THE SEA
55 W. Grand Ave., Old Orchard Beach, 207-934-5044; www.josephsbythesea.com
This upscale restaurant with waterfront views serves updated versions of American classics. Entrées include seared scallops with arugula and mustard vinaigrette, and baked stuffed lobster.
American, seafood. Breakfast, dinner. Bar. Reservations recommended. Outdoor seating. $16-35

★★OCEANSIDE GRILLE AT THE BRUNSWICK
39 W. Grand Ave., Old Orchard Beach, 207-934-4873; www.thebrunswick.com
Seafood is the specialty at this elegant dining room with views of the ocean. Besides steamed lobster, the menu includes fresh Maine shrimp, haddock, clams and more.
American, seafood. Lunch, dinner, late-night. Bar. Reservations recommended. Outdoor seating. $16-35

PORTLAND
See also Kennebunk, Kennebunkport, Old Orchard Beach
Maine's largest city is located on Casco Bay and dotted with islands that are popular with summer visitors. Because of its size, affordable housing and free-spirited feel, Portland is increasingly popular as an alternative to the nation's biggest cities (and absorbs plenty of Boston refugees). It's a city of fine elms, stately old homes, historic churches and charming streets. Portland was raided by Native Americans several times before the American Revolution. In 1775, it was bombarded by the British, who afterward burned the town. Another fire in 1866 wiped out large sections of the city. Henry Wadsworth Longfellow, the famed poet who lived in Portland, remarked that the ruins reminded him of Pompeii.

WHAT TO SEE
CHILDREN'S MUSEUM OF MAINE
142 Free St., Portland, 207-828-1234; www.childrensmuseumofme.org
This hands-on museum features interactive exhibits that allow children to become a Maine lobsterman, a storekeeper, a computer expert or an astronaut for the day.
Memorial Day-Labor Day, daily; rest of year, Tuesday-Saturday, 10 a.m.-5 p.m. Sunday, noon-5 p.m. Monday closed. Admission: $8 per person.

MAINE HISTORY GALLERY

489 Congress St., Portland, 207-774-1822; www.mainehistory.com

The gallery features the museum's collection of more than 2,000 paintings, prints and other original works of art, and approximately 8,000 artifacts. The collection includes costumes and textiles, decorative arts, Native American artifacts and archaeological material, political items and military artifacts. Changing programs and exhibits trace the history of life in Maine. Gallery talks and hands-on workshops are also offered.

Monday-Saturday 10 a.m.-5 p.m. Sunday noon-5 p.m.

PORTLAND HEAD LIGHTHOUSE MUSEUM

1000 Shore Road, Cape Elizabeth, 207-799-2661; www.portlandheadlight.com

The building is said to be first lighthouse authorized by the United States and the oldest lighthouse in continuous use. It was erected in 1791 on orders from George Washington.

June-October, daily. November-December and April-May, weekends 10 a.m.-4 p.m.

PORTLAND MUSEUM OF ART

7 Congress Square, Portland, 207-775-6148; www.portlandmuseum.org

The museum houses collections of American and European paintings, sculpture, prints and decorative art. On display is a State of Maine Collection with works by artists from and associated with Maine.

Free admission Friday evenings. May-October: daily; November-April: Tuesday-Sunday 10 a.m.-5 p.m., -Friday 10 a.m.-9 p.m., closed on New Year's Day, Thanksgiving, Christmas Day.

PORTLAND OBSERVATORY

138 Congress St., Portland, 207-774-5561; www.portlandlandmarks.org/observatory

This 1807 octagonal, shingled landmark is the last surviving 19th-century signal tower on the Atlantic. There are 102 steps to the top.

Memorial Day to Columbus Day, daily.

TATE HOUSE

1267 Westbrook St., Portland, 207-774-6177; www.tatehouse.org

The house is a 1755 Georgian structure built by George Tate, mast agent for the British Navy. Furnished and decorated in the period of Tate's residence, 1755-1800; 18th-century herb gardens.

Mid-June-mid-October: Tuesday-Sunday 10 a.m.-4 p.m.; weekends through October 31.

VICTORIA MANSION

109 Danforth St., Portland, 207-772-4841; www.victoriamansion.org

The building is one of the finest examples of 19th-century architecture surviving in the United States. The opulent 1858 Victorian interior includes frescoes, carved woodwork and stained and etched glass.

May-October, Monday-Saturday 10 a.m.-4 p.m.; closed Memorial Day.

WADSWORTH-LONGFELLOW HOUSE

489 Congress St., Portland, 207-772-1807;

www.mainehistory.org/house_overview.shtml

The boyhood home of Henry Wadsworth Longfellow was built in 1785 by the poet's grandfather, General Peleg Wadsworth, and is maintained by the Maine Historical Society. The house contains furnishings, portraits and personal possessions of the family.

June-mid-October, daily.

SPECIAL EVENTS
NEW YEAR'S EVE PORTLAND

582 Congress St., Portland, 207-772-5800

This spectacular New Year's party features more than 90 performances, mid-afternoon to midnight. It's a citywide, non-alcoholic celebration with parade and fireworks.

December 31.

OLD PORT FESTIVAL

549 Congress St., Portland, 207-772-6828;

www.portlandmaine.com

A celebration of Portland's restored waterfront district between Commercial Street and Congress Street. This one-day event features a parade, entertainment and food. Early June.

SIDEWALK ART SHOW

14 Ocean Great Way, Portland, 207-772-5800;

www.visitportland.com

Art and exhibits extend along Congress Street from Congress Square to Monument Square.

Third Saturday in August.

WHERE TO STAY
★★★BLACK POINT INN

510 Black Point Road, Scarborough, 207-883-2500, 800-258-0003;

www.blackpointinn.com

This seaside resort is located on a hill at the tip of Prout's Neck with the natural rugged beauty of the Maine coast on three sides. Each room is clad in period wallpaper and presents both porcelain and crystal lamps. Many of the rooms and cottages were former sea captains' homes.

65 rooms. Closed December-April. Pets accepted. Restaurant, bar. Fitness center. Beach. Pool. $251-350

★★EMBASSY SUITES

1050 Westbrook St., Portland, 207-775-2200, 800-753-8767;

www.embassysuitesportland.com

This hotel is located close to the Portland International Jetport and the Maine Mall (complimentary shuttle service is provided to both). The recently renovated guest rooms feature a separate sitting area and sleeping room, plush beds, two small desks and a wet bar with microwave. An evening manager's reception (with a three-piece band) is offered on Thursdays.

119 rooms. Pets accepted. Complimentary breakfast. Restaurant, bar. Fitness center. Pool. Business center. $151-250

★★★INN BY THE SEA
40 Bowery Beach Road, Cape Elizabeth, 207-799-3134, 800-888-4287;
www.innbythesea.com
This all-suite resort property features guest rooms with contemporary décor, porches and decks with a view of the ocean. A new spa offering a full menu of treatments was recently added to the list of onsite amenities, which also include tennis, shuffleboard, and volleyball. Rooms boast terrycloth robes and turndown service.
57 rooms. Pets accepted. Restaurant. Pool. Tennis. $151-250

★★★PORTLAND HARBOR HOTEL
468 Fore St., Portland, 207-775-9090, 888-798-9090; www.portlandharborhotel.com
This hotel is located in the Old Port district of downtown Portland, a fully restored area of Victorian buildings that houses restaurants, shops and galleries, just one block from the waterfront. An enclosed garden patio with a fountain is just off the lobby dining room. Guest rooms feature toile spreads, custom mattresses, luxury linens, feather pillows and duvets, and a two-level desk with leather chair.
97 rooms. Pets accepted. Restaurant, bar. Fitness center. Business center. $151-250

MAINE

70

★★★PORTLAND MARRIOTT AT SABLE OAKS
200 Sable Oaks Drive, South Portland, 207-871-8000, 800-752-8810;
www.marriott.com
Just a few miles from the Portland International Jetport and close to historic downtown Portland, this hotel is situated on a hill in a rural setting. A covered portico and a small pond with a fountain welcome guests at the hotel entry. Nearby activities include golf, tennis, a spa and the beach.
227 rooms. Pets accepted. Restaurant, bar. Fitness center. Pool. Golf. Business center. $151-250

★★★PORTLAND REGENCY HOTEL & SPA
20 Milk St., Portland, 207-774-4200, 800-727-3436; www.theregency.com
This small European-style hotel is located in Portland's Old Port waterfront district, surrounded by galleries, shops and restaurants. A circular brick driveway leads guests to the historic red brick building, built in 1895. The lobby and public rooms hold true to the hotel's heritage, with mahogany woodwork, Victorian furnishings and a "map room" with burgundy leather chairs. The period décor in the guest rooms includes two or four-poster beds and antique or reproduction dressers, tables and desks. The spa offers a complete selection of treatments.
95 rooms. Restaurant, bar. Fitness center. Spa. Business center. $151-250

ALSO RECOMMENDED
POMEGRANATE INN
49 Neal St., Portland, 207-772-1006, 800-356-0408; www.pomegranateinn.com

This inn, built in 1884, is small, yet sophisticated and located in the historic Western Promenade neighborhood. Antiques and art adorn the property. There is also an urban garden for guests to enjoy. The inn is located a short walk to the midtown arts district and there are museums, art galleries, boat rides, fine restaurants and recreational activities nearby.

8 rooms. No children under 16. Complimentary breakfast. $151-250

WHERE TO EAT
★★★BACK BAY GRILL
65 Portland St., Portland, 207-772-8833; www.backbaygrill.com
Located in downtown Portland in a restored 1888 pharmacy, this local favorite offers innovative cuisine and an intimate dining room. The pressed-tin ceiling adds to the ambience of the cozy rooms. The daily menu features fresh locally sourced foods (the restaurant is a member of the Maine Organic Farmers Growers Association) and emphasizes high-quality ingredients. Special dinners are offered with a prix fixe menu (wine tastings, wine dinners, lobster evenings).

American. Dinner. Closed Sunday. Bar. Reservations recommended. $36-85

★★FORE STREET
288 Fore St., Portland, 207-775-2717; www.forestreet.biz
James Beard award-winning chef Sam Hayward directs a kitchen devoted to fresh, seasonal, inspired cooking at this cozy restaurant in Portland's Old Port District. Ingredients, from day boat scallops to organic arugula, are sourced from local producers. Locals line up for the wood-oven roasted mussels and marinated hangar steak, and make sure to save room for the house-made ice creams, cakes and other desserts.

Seafood, steak. Dinner. Bar. Reservations recommended. $16-35

★★★PARK KITCHEN
422 N.W. Eighth Ave., Portland, 503-223-7275; www.parkkitchen.com
Located in a historic building along the North Park blocks, the food here is influenced by the seasons, with dishes such as lamb cassoulet making an appearance in winter, while salmon with cucumber and caraway is a summer specialty. Wines and microbrews are recommended for each entrée that chef Scott Dolich creates at this welcoming restaurant, which features an open kitchen.

American. Lunch, dinner. Brunch. Bar. Children's menu. Reservations recommended. Outdoor seating. Closed Monday. $16-35

★★RIBOLLITA
41 Middle St., Portland, 207-774-2972
This Italian bistro serves classic recipes in a casual setting. Pastas are house made and include gnocchi, fettuccini and more, often served with fresh seafood.

Italian. Dinner. Children's menu. Reservations recommended. Outdoor seating. Closed Sunday-Monday. $16-35

★★★THE ROMA CAFÉ
769 Congress St., Portland, 207-773-9873; www.theromacafe.com

Located in a circa-1887 Victorian mansion, this restaurant features small dining rooms with fireplaces, a beautiful carved wood staircase and beveled glass windows in a charming atmosphere. Menu offerings include seafood, lobster and Italian dishes.

Italian, seafood. Lunch, dinner. Bar. Reservations recommended. Closed Sunday-Monday. $16-35

★★★STREET & CO.
33 Wharf St., Portland, 207-775-0887

Located in the Old Port District on a cobblestone street, this 19th-century building was formerly a fish warehouse. The décor is upscale rustic, with exposed bricks, original plank hardwood flooring and beamed ceilings. Tables are heavy black stone slabs with rough-hewn wood legs. A fully open kitchen is opposite the center dining room, which offers large windows that open to the street. Only seafood is served, along with the freshest seasonal organic produce.

American, seafood. Dinner. Bar. Reservations recommended. $36-85

RANGELEY

There are 40 lakes and ponds within 10 miles of Rangeley. The six lakes that form the Rangeley chain—Rangeley, Cupsuptic, Mooselookmeguntic, Aziscoos, Upper Richardson and Lower Richardson—are spread over a wide area and give rise to the Androscoggin River. Some of Maine's highest mountains rise beside the lakes. The development of ski and snowmobiling areas has turned this summer vacation spot into a year-round resort.

WHAT TO SEE
RANGELEY LAKE STATE PARK
South Shore Drive, Rangeley, 207-864-3858; www.state.me.us/doc/parks

More than 690 acres roll through this park on Rangeley Lake. Swimming, fishing, boating (ramp, floating docks) and snowmobiling are all permitted. Picnicking and camping is allowed on site. Standard fees apply for camping or activities, see website for additional details.

May 15-October 1.

WILHELM REICH MUSEUM
19 Dodge Pond Road, Rangeley, 207-864-3443; www.wilhelmreichmuseum.org

Unusual stone building housing scientific equipment, paintings and other memorabilia of this physician-scientist. There is a slide presentation, nature trail and discovery room.

July-August, Wednesday-Sunday 1-5 p.m.; September, Sunday only 1-5 p.m.; rest of year, by appointment.

WHERE TO STAY
★★★RANGELEY INN
2443 Main St., Rangeley, 207-864-3341, 800-666-3687; www.rangeleyinn.com

The year-round resort offers skiing and snowmobiling in the winter and swimming and boating in the summer. This restored inn is located within the mountain lake wilderness of the Longfellow Mountains of western Maine. Moose and loons can be spotted nearby. Rooms have recently been updated with marble baths, English country decor and wireless access.

50 rooms. Pets accepted. Restaurant, bar. $61-150

WHERE TO EAT
★★★RANGELEY INN
2443 Main St., Rangeley, 207-864-3341; www.rangeleyinn.com

This romantic inn has been open for more than 90 years. Enjoy an elegant dinner in the main dining room, which showcases an ornate tin ceiling and chandeliers. Then retire to the pub that has a crackling fire in the fireplace and runs local microbrews on tap.

American, seafood. Breakfast, dinner. Bar. Children's menu. Outdoor seating. Closed Sunday-Thursday; also April-May. $16-35

ROCKLAND
See also Camden, Monhegan Island

This town on Penobscot Bay is the banking and commercial center of the region and the seat of Knox County. It is also the birthplace of poet Edna St. Vincent Millay. Its economy is geared to the resort trade, but there is commercial fishing and light industry.

WHAT TO SEE
FARNSWORTH ART MUSEUM AND WYETH CENTER
16 Museum St., Rockland, 207-596-6457; www.farnsworthmuseum.org

This museum is the cultural and educational center for the region. Collection of more than 10,000 works of 18th- to 20th-century American art. Center houses personal collection of Wyeth family (N.C., Andrew and Jamie) and archival material.

Memorial Day-Columbus Day, daily; January-March, Wednesday-Sunday 10 a.m.-5 p.m.; rest of year, Tuesday-Sunday 10 a.m.-5 p.m.; closed Thanksgiving, Christmas and New Year Day.

MAINE LIGHTHOUSE MUSEUM
1 Park Drive, Rockland, 207-594-3301; www.mainelighthousemuseum.com

There is a large collection of lighthouse lenses and artifacts in the museum. There is also a Civil War collection and an onsite museum shop.

Daily. Admission: adults $5, seniors $4, children under 12 free.

MAINE STATE FERRY SERVICE
517A Main St., Rockland, 207-596-2202; www.state.me.us/mdot/opt/ferry/215-info.php

Ferries make a 15-mile (1 hour, 15-minute) trip to Vinalhaven and a 12 ½-mile (1 hour, 10-minute) trip to North Haven. These trips run all year, with two to three trips daily. Also a 23-mile (2 hour, 15-minute) trip to Matinicus Island runs once a month.

WINDJAMMERS
Maine Windjammer Association, 800-807-9463; www.sailmainecoast.com
Twelve old-time schooners sail out for three to six days, following the same basic route through Penobscot Bay into Blue Hill and Frenchman's Bay, stopping at small villages and islands along the way. Each ship carries an average of 30 passengers. For further information, rates, schedules or reservations, contact the Maine Windjammer Association.
Memorial Day-Columbus Day.

SPECIAL EVENTS
MAINE LOBSTER FESTIVAL
Harbor Park, or at the public landing, Rockland, 207-596-0376, 800-562-2529;
www.mainelobsterfestival.com
A five-day event centered on Maine's chief marine creature, with a huge tent cafeteria serving lobster and other seafood. Parade, harbor cruises, maritime displays, bands, entertainment.
First weekend in August.

SCHOONER DAYS & NORTH ATLANTIC BLUES FESTIVAL
Rockland Harbor, 207-596-0376
Three-day festival celebrating Maine's maritime heritage, featuring a parade of the area's fleet of historic schooners, plus arts, entertainment, concessions, fireworks, blues bands and club crawl.
Weekend after July 4.

WHERE TO STAY
★★★SAMOSET RESORT
220 Warrenton St., Rockport, 207-594-2511, 800-341-1650; www.samoset.com
Named for the chief of the Pemaquid Indians who greeted the Pilgrims, this inn has welcomed guests since 1889. It is a year-round resort set on 230 ocean-side acres of the rugged coast of Maine. The resort has recently been refurbished and now features guest rooms with luxury linens and flat-screen TVs.
178 rooms. Restaurant, bar. Fitness center. Pool. Tennis. $151-250

WHERE TO EAT
★★★PRIMO
2 S. Main St., Rockland, 207-596-0770; www.primorestaurant.com
An ardent supporter of sustainable agriculture, chef Melissa Kelly uses mostly local, organic produce (much of it grown on the restaurant's farm) and incorporates vegetables, even in meat dishes. The menu, which changes weekly, draws from coastal Italy and France, and features everything from asparagus soup with goat cheese to olive oil-poached salmon with bitter greens and beets to wood-roasted oysters. Co-owner and pastry chef Price Kushner contributes equally savory desserts.
American menu. Dinner. Bar. Reservations recommended. Closed Tuesday. $36-85

SOUTHWEST HARBOR

See also Bar Harbor, Cranberry Isles

This is a prosperous, working seacoast village on Mount Desert Island. There are lobster wharves, where visitors can watch about 70 fishermen bring in their catch, and there are many shops where boats are constructed. Visitors can also rent sailboats and power boats in Southwest Harbor to explore the coves and islands; hiking trails and quiet harbors offer relaxation.

WHAT TO SEE
CRANBERRY COVE BOATING COMPANY
Southwest Harbor and Manset, 207-244-5882
On this cruise to the Cranberry Islands, you'll see native wildlife and learn island history. There are six departures daily, leaving from Upper Town Dock. Mid-June-mid-September, daily.

MAINE STATE FERRY SERVICE
Grandville Road, Bass Harbor, 207-244-3254; www.maine.gov
Ferry makes six-mile (40-minute) trip to Swans Island and 8 ¼-mile (50-minute) trip to Frenchboro (limited schedule). The ferries to Swans Island run all-year, one to six trips daily.

MOUNT DESERT OCEANARIUM
172 Clark Point Road, Southwest Harbor, 207-244-7330; www.theoceanarium.com
The oceanarium includes more than 20 tanks with Gulf of Maine marine creatures and exhibits on tides, seawater, plankton, fishing gear, weather. Inquire for information on special events.
Mid-May-mid-October: Monday-Saturday.

WENDELL GILLEY MUSEUM
4 Herrick Road, Southwest Harbor, 207-244-7555; www.wendellgilleymuseum.org
This art and natural history museum features a collection of bird carvings by local artist Wendell Gilley. There are changing exhibits of local and historical art and films.
June-October, Tuesday-Sunday 10 a.m.-4 p.m., May and November-December, Friday-Sunday 10 a.m.-4 p.m., closed Monday-Thursday. Admission: adults $5, children $2.

WHERE TO STAY
THE CLARK POINT INN
109 Clark Point Road, Southwest Harbor, 207-244-9828, 888-775-5953;
www.clarkpointinn.com
This inn is located in an 1857 Captain's house. Rooms are individually decorated in English country style and some include fireplaces.
5 rooms. Closed mid-October-April. No children under 8. Complimentary breakfast. Bar. $151-250

KINGSLEIGH INN
373 Main St., Southwest Harbor, 207-244-5302; www.kingsleighinn.com
Built in 1904, this inn features a wraparound porch. The English country

style rooms display down duvets, pillow-top mattresses and fresh flowers. 8 rooms. No children under 10. Complimentary breakfast. Bar. $61-150

WHERE TO EAT
★BEAL'S LOBSTER PIER
182 Clark Point Road, Southwest Harbor, 207-244-3202; www.bealslobster.com
This basic dockside restaurant serves lobsters and clams fresh from the boat. Chowders, sandwiches and ice cream are also available.
Seafood menu. Lunch, dinner. Outdoor seating. $16-35

YORK
See also Kittery, Ogunquit
Originally named Agamenticus by the Plymouth Company, the area was settled in 1624, chartered as a city—the first in America—in 1641 and renamed Gorgeanna. Following a reorganization in 1652, the "city" in the wilderness took the name York. The present-day York area includes York Village, York Harbor, York Beach and Cape Neddick.

WHAT TO SEE
EMERSON-WILCOX HOUSE
York and Lindsey Roads, York; www.oldyork.org
Built in 1742, with later additions, the Emerson-Wilcox House served (at various times) as a general store, a tavern and a post office, as well as the home of two of the town's prominent early families. It now contains a series of period rooms dating to 1750 and is furnished with antiques.

JOHN HANCOCK WAREHOUSE
York and Lindsey Roads, York, 207-363-4974; www.oldyork.org
Owned by John Hancock until 1794, this is one of the earliest surviving customs houses in Maine. The building is now used to interpret the maritime history of this coastal village.
Mid-June-mid-October: Tuesday-Saturday afternoons.

OLD GAOL
Lindsay Road, York
Built in 1719 with 18th-century additions, the jail is one of the oldest English public buildings in the United States and was used as a jail until 1860. On display are dungeons and cells for felons and debtors, as well as galleries of local historical artifacts and a late 1800s photography exhibit.

OLD YORK HISTORICAL SOCIETY
140 Lindsay Road, York, 207-363-4974; www.oldyork.org
Tour seven buildings dating to the early 1700s Mid-June-September. Visitor orientation and tickets are available at Jefferds Tavern. The Administration Office houses museum offices (Monday-Friday) and historical and research library.

SAYWARD-WHEELER HOUSE

9 Barrell Lane, York Harbor, 207-384-2454; www.spnea.org/visit/homes/sayward.htm

This is the home of 18th-century merchant and civic leader Tory Jonathan Sayward. Tours. June-October: first Saturday of the month.

WHERE TO STAY
★★★STAGE NECK INN

8 Stage Neck Road, York Harbor, 207-363-3850, 800-340-1130; www.stageneck.com

This inn is located on an ocean-bound peninsula in York Harbor. The resort offers a beach and is also close to the Kittery outlet malls, antiques shops, art galleries and historic attractions of York.

58 rooms. Restaurant, bar. Fitness room. Beach. Pool. Tennis. Spa. $151-250

ALSO RECOMMENDED
DOCKSIDE GUEST QUARTERS

22 Harris Island Road, York, 207-363-2868, 888-860-7428; www.docksidegq.com

This unique property is more like a compound than an inn, with rooms spread out over seven acres and located in a main house with several out buildings. Rooms are decorated with cheerful colors and contemporary furnishings, and have great views of the surrounding harbor.

25 rooms. Restaurant, bar. Closed weekdays late October-December, March-Memorial Day, December-February. $151-250

EDWARDS HARBORSIDE INN

Stage Neck Road, York Harbor, 207-363-3037; www.edwardsharborside.com

This turn-of-the-century house displays rooms with period furnishings and fireplaces. The inn features wireless access and complimentary breakfast.

9 rooms. Beach. $251-350

YORK HARBOR INN

Coastal Highway 1A, York Harbor, 207-363-5119, 800-343-3869;
www.yorkharborinn.com

Each room at this large inn is individually decorated with country prints, quilts and antiques. Some rooms feature fireplaces or Jacuzzi tubs. The on-site pub is a favorite local spot for casual dining, while the restaurant offers a more upscale environment.

54 rooms. Complimentary breakfast. Restaurant, bar. Beach. $151-250

WHERE TO EAT
★★DOCKSIDE

22 Harris Island Road, York, 207-363-2722, 888-860-7428; www.docksidegq.com

The staff at this restaurant sources seasonal, organic, local ingredients for its contemporary American menu. Sample entrées include pan-roasted native cod or grilled wild salmon with truffled potato purée.

Seafood, steak. Lunch, dinner. Bar. Reservations recommended. Outdoor seating. Closed Monday; day after Columbus Day-late May. $16-35

★★★YORK HARBOR INN
Highway 1A, York Harbor, 207-363-5119; www.yorkharborinn.com

Antique furnishings, floral wallpaper and lace curtains add to the ambience of this quaint, Colonial inn. The menu features local seafood, much of it caught close to the restaurant.

Seafood. Dinner, Sunday brunch. Children's menu. Reservations recommended. Closed Monday-Thursday (fall-spring). $16-35

MASSACHUSETTS

TO SOME, "NEW ENGLAND" MEANS ONE THING: MASSACHUSETTS. OVER FIVE CENTURIES, the Bay State has become the region's emblematic poster child, one rich in historical personality and modern diversions. Case in point: explorer John Cabot (his ancestors would become the ultimate Boston Brahmins) landed on these shores in 1497, just five years after Columbus' famed cross-Atlantic trip. The legendary Mayflower soon followed, establishing roots in what would become an area of American greats. Paul Revere, John Hancock, Sam Adams and, of course, the Kennedys all hailed from Massachusetts. So did literary giants like Ralph Waldo Emerson, Henry David Thoreau and Emily Dickinson. But for all its historical heft—it was local patriots who jump-started the American Revolution—the Bay State is not stuck in the past.

Boston, the biggest city in New England, is a lively metropolis, home to booming businesses and the fiercely followed Red Sox. Its residents live in a cross-section of neighborhoods along the Charles River. The North End, the city's Little Italy, bursts with gelaterias and red-sauce-heavy trattorias; the South End, by contrast, is awash in chic clothing boutiques and avant-garde eateries. To the west, north and south of the city stretch verdant, upscale suburbs and quiet, laid-back beach towns. Farther west, along the Massachusetts-New York border, is the Berkshires: a county so steeped in arts, culture and culinary experiences, it has become a go-to destination for people several states over.

And then there's Cape Cod and the Islands—Nantucket and Martha's Vineyard—a few of America's most sought-after summer spots. The area's hundreds of miles of coastline and soft, white-sand beaches are a vacationer's paradise. Locals live in gray-shingled homes in small beach hamlets and, for the most part, welcome visitors to their postcard-perfect Main Streets. The vibe is Puritan modern and slightly conservative, but fun loving.

It is often said that every town in Massachusetts plays a small part in the American story. A statewide trip takes travelers from Plymouth Rock, where it all began, to the battle of Bunker Hill, to the philosopher favorite Walden Pond, to the academic powerhouse Cambridge, and to the constantly innovating Boston. Indeed, the whole state is a melting pot of old traditions and modern ideas, lived out along a breathtaking coastline and a myriad of quiet hill villages.

AMHERST

See also South Hadley

This storied central Massachusetts town exudes academia. More than half its citizens are students (the other half might be professors), and its former natives include such scholarly types as Eugene Field, Emily Dickinson, Robert Frost and Noah Webster. The seat of Amherst College and the crown jewel of the University of Massachusetts system, this is a town filled with life, culture and ideas.

WHAT TO SEE
AMHERST COLLEGE

100 Boltwood Ave., Amherst, 413-542-2000; www.amherst.edu

One of the best liberal arts colleges in the country, Amherst enrolls some 1,550 students. On a tree-shaded green in the middle of town, its Robert Frost Library owns approximately half of Emily Dickinson's poems, as well as materials by Wordsworth, Eugene O'Neill and others.

EMILY DICKINSON MUSEUM: THE HOMESTEAD AND THE EVER-GREENS

280 Main St., Amherst, 413-542-8161; www.emilydickinsonmuseum.org

The Homestead was the birthplace and home of poet Emily Dickinson; the Evergreens housed her brother and his family. Select rooms are open for tours on a first-come, first-served basis.

March-May, September-October, Wednesday-Saturday 1-5 p.m.; June-August, Wednesday-Sunday 10 a.m.-5 p.m.; March-May and September-December, Wednesday-Sunday 11 a.m.-4 p.m.

ERIC CARLE MUSEUM OF PICTURE BOOK ART

125 W. Bay Road, Amherst, 413-658-1100; www.picturebookart.org

This 40,000-square-foot facility opened in 2002 as the first museum in the United States exclusively devoted to children's picture book art. Its founder, Eric Carle, has illustrated more than 70 picture books, including *The Very Hungry Caterpillar*, which has been published in more than 30 languages and has sold more than 18 million copies.

Tuesday-Friday 10 a.m.-4 p.m., Saturday 10 a.m.-5 p.m., Sunday noon-5 p.m.; open Mondays in July and August 10 a.m.-4 p.m.

UNIVERSITY OF MASSACHUSETTS

Massachusetts Avenue and North Pleasant Street, Amherst, 413-545-0111; www.umass.edu

Founded in 1863, and with 24,000 students, UMass-Amherst is the state's major facility of public higher education. It has more than 150 buildings on a 1,450-acre campus. Tours of campus are available.

Daily.

ANDOVER
See also Lowell

The seat of Boston's northern suburbs is a picturesque small city bursting with brick homes and quiet charm. Many of its residents commute to jobs in Boston. Many others are connected to the legendary Phillips Andover Academy—known simply as Andover—the posh prep school that is also the oldest incorporated school in the country.

WHAT TO SEE
PEABODY MUSEUM

175 Main St., Andover, 978-749-4490; www.andover.edu

This Native American archaeological museum has exhibits on the physical and cultural evolution of man and the prehistoric archaeology of New Eng-

land, the Southwest, Mexico and the Arctic.
Monday-Friday 8 a.m.-5 p.m., by appointment only.

PHILLIPS ANDOVER ACADEMY
180 Main St., Andover, 978-749-4000; www.andover.edu
Nearly 1,100 students make up this co-ed boarding school for grades 9-12.
Notable alumni include photographer Walker Evans, poet Oliver Wendell
Holmes, child-rearing expert Benjamin Spock and actor Humphrey Bogart.
The campus sits on 450 acres with 170 buildings. The Cochran Sanctuary, a
65-acre landscaped area, consists of walking trails, a brook and two ponds.

WHERE TO STAY
★★★ANDOVER INN
4 Chapel Ave., Andover, 978-475-5903, 800-242-5903; www.andoverinn.com
Located on the campus of Phillips Andover Academy, this neo-Georgian
country inn was built in 1930 to provide lodging for visiting parents and
alumni. The rooms are decorated in period furnishings.
23 rooms. Restaurant, bar. Complimentary breakfast. $61-150

★★ANDOVER WYNDHAM HOTEL
123 Old River Road, Andover, 978-975-3600; www.wyndham.com
Located just outside Andover's town center, this hotel offers updated rooms
with down duvets and flat-screen TVs. The hotel's restaurant and bar received a
renovation in 2009 and will feature an updated menu and contemporary décor.
293 rooms. Restaurant, bar. Pets accepted. $151-250

BOSTON
See also Braintree, Cambridge, Newton, Wellesley
With the culture of Chicago, the beauty of San Francisco and the diversity
of Paris, Boston is the social, financial, educational, historical, culinary and
sports center of New England. It should be no surprise that its nickname is
"The Hub," and most state happenings revolve around what's going on in
this port city of some 600,000 citizens. America's early settlers moved here
in the mid-1600s; their legacy is still very much alive in the old Colonials
of Charlestown and narrow, winding streets of the North End. Paul Revere's
fabled ride, and indeed the Revolution itself, started here, giving Boston
bragging rights over nearly every other American city.

Visitors can retrace Revere and other early patriots' steps along the Freedom Trail, a three-hour walking route that encapsulates much of the area's
history. Current citizens, though, leave the past to tourists and obsess instead over the Boston Red Sox and New England Patriots, two championship
teams known as much for their die-hard fans as for their athletic prowess.
Fenway Park, the oldest U.S. baseball stadium and home to the legendary
Green Monster, hosts the Red Sox (visitors would do well to take in a game
here while in town). Afterward, explore the city's neighborhoods, from the
upscale Beacon Hill to the bursting-with-life North End to the formerly Irish,
rapidly gentrifying South Boston (i.e. the "Southie" so well portrayed in local son Matt Damon's *Good Will Hunting.*)

Boston is perhaps best known for its top-tier universities—a whopping

100 in all—the most famous of which include Harvard, M.I.T., Boston University and the Berklee School of Music. During the academic year, students canvas Commonwealth Avenue and the Back Bay's Newbury Street shopping district, lending the whole city a youthful, energetic vibe (though older residents love to complain about the youngsters' rowdiness).

Students, locals and tourists alike love strolling through this walking city—possibly because of Boston drivers' rightful reputation as the worst in the world—especially along the landscaped Charles River Esplanade. The 18-mile-long waterside stretch has walking, running and biking trails, boathouses, tennis courts and plenty of shaded benches. On a summer day, the spot is packed with Bostonians getting exercise and checking out the evolving city skyline.

WHAT TO SEE
BOSTON AFRICAN AMERICAN NATIONAL HISTORIC SITE
14 Beacon St., Boston, 617-742-5415; www.nps.gov/boaf
Built by free black Bostonians in 1806, the building was an educational and religious center and site of the founding of the New England Anti-Slavery Society in 1832. The Meetinghouse is the starting point for the Black Heritage Trail, a walking tour conducted by the National Park Service that takes guests past black history-related sites.
May-September: daily; rest of year: Monday-Saturday.

BOSTON BALLET
19 Clarendon St., Boston, 617-695-6955; www.bostonballet.com
The Boston Ballet offers classic and contemporary performances by a company of some of the finest dancers in the world. If you're visiting in late November or December, don't miss *The Nutcracker*, performed annually before more than 140,000 people, which is the largest ballet audience in the world. Performances held October-May.

BOSTON BRUINS
TD Banknorth Garden, 100 Legends Way, Boston, 617-624-1000; www.bostonbruins.com
One of the great hockey traditions in the NHL, the Bruins were one of the league's "Original Six" teams.
September-May.

BOSTON CELTICS
226 Causeway St., Fourth Floor, Boston, 866-423-5849; www.nba.com/celtics
With 17 championships notched in its belt, Boston's pro basketball team has won more NBA titles than any other franchise.
October-June.

BOSTON COLLEGE
140 Commonwealth Ave., Chestnut Hill, 617-552-8000; www.bc.edu
This huge Catholic college of 14,500 students has a major presence in the city, thanks in part to its top-ranked basketball, hockey and football teams. The school's main campus in Chestnut Hill is full of old stone manors with stained-glass windows.

BOSTON COMMON

Beacon and Tremont Streets, Boston

The oldest public park in the United States, Boston Common is steeped in history. In the 1640s, farmers used the Common as a cattle pasture; later, the colonial militia used it to train soldiers. Colonists gathered here to listen to speeches, to witness public hangings and to watch spirited fencing duels. Today, the Common's 45 acres still act as a vibrant city center, an ideal place to stroll, in-line skate, play Frisbee, catch a free concert or enjoy a picnic. In the winter, the park's famous Frog Pond freezes over into a public ice skating rink.

Daily.

BOSTON HARBOR ISLANDS NATIONAL RECREATION AREA

408 Atlantic Ave., Suite 225, Boston, 617-223-8666; www.bostonharborislands.org

This national park is actually made up of several Boston Harbor islands, some open to the public, some private. Take the ferry to Georges Island; from there, a free water taxi sails you to Lovells, Peddocks, Gallops, Grape and Bumpkin islands. Each is unique, with features such as sand dunes, freshwater ponds and native wildlife. Camp on Lovells and Peddocks islands with a permit from the Metropolitan District Commission.

May-mid-October.

BOSTON PUBLIC GARDEN

Arlington, Boylston, Charles and Beacon Streets, Boston, 617-522-1966;
www.swanboats.com

Adjacent to Boston Common, this is the first botanical garden in the United States, with 24 acres featuring a splendid variety of flowers and ornamental shrubs. It's also home to the city's famous Swan Boats, which visitors can climb aboard for a 15-minute paddled ride around the garden's lagoon.

BOSTON PUBLIC LIBRARY

700 Boylston St., Boston, 617-536-5400; www.bpl.org

The stunning Italian Renaissance building by Charles McKim includes a central courtyard and fountain. Other highlights include mural decorations, bronze doors, sculptures and several reading rooms, including the Bates Room, where visitors can study and surf the Internet in silence.

Monday-Thursday 9 a.m.-9 p.m.; Friday-Saturday 9 a.m.-5 p.m.

BOSTON RED SOX

Fenway Park, 4 Yawkey Way, Boston, 617-267-9440; www.redsox.mlb.com

Going to Fenway isn't just about watching the Red Sox; it's about steeping yourself in tradition. Built in 1901, the park is home to the Green Monster, the infamous 37-foot, left-field wall. Cy Young pitched a perfect game at Fenway in 1904, and in 1914, a young Babe Ruth joined the home team. Today's 2004 and 2007 World Series Champs are no less impressive.

Regular tours. March-October.

BOSTON SYMPHONY ORCHESTRA/BOSTON POPS

301 Massachusetts Ave., Boston, 617-266-1492; www.bso.org

Symphony Hall is said to have perfect acoustics, a draw that packs the house despite lofty ticket prices. Both the old-school Boston Symphony Orchestra and the livelier Boston Pops perform here, when they're not giving free outdoor concerts on the Charles River Esplanade.

BSO performances October-April; Pops performances May-early July, mid-late-December.

BOSTON TEA PARTY SHIP AND MUSEUM

300 Congress St., Boston, 617-338-1773; www.bostonteapartyship.com

The museum ship is a replica of one of the three famous boats docked in the harbor the night of the Boston Tea Party. In 2001, the museum was badly damaged by a fire and closed for renovations. It's scheduled to reopen in the summer of 2010.

BOSTON UNIVERSITY

One Silber Way, Boston, 617-353-2300; www.bu.edu

A college of more than 28,000 students, B.U. encompasses an entire area of the city (not the least of which is the "B.U. Beach," a riverside strip of grassy lawn typically littered with sunbathing students). The Mugar Memorial Library houses the papers of Dr. Martin Luther King Jr., Robert Frost, Isaac Asimov and other writers and artists.

BUNKER HILL MONUMENT

43 Monument Square, Charlestown, 617-242-5641; www.nps.gov

Standing 221 feet high (that's 294 steps, with no elevator), the Bunker Hill Monument marks the site of the first major battle of the Revolutionary War. It was here that American Colonel William Prescott ordered his troops not to fire until "you see the whites of their eyes," so that bullets would not be wasted.

Daily.

CHARLES RIVER ESPLANADE

This flat, smooth asphalt path runs for 18 miles along the Charles River, from Boston to Cambridge to Watertown. During the summer months, active types stroll, jog, bike or blade the Esplanade; lazier locals picnic or sunbathe along both sides of the river. On a clear day, the river and skyline views are magnificent, some of the best in Boston. Rent a bike at Back Bay Bikes & Boards (336 Commonwealth Ave., 617-247-2336; www.backbaybicycles.com), Community Bicycle Supply (496 Tremont St., Boston, 617-542-8623; www.communitybicycle.com), Cambridge Bicycle (259 Massachusetts Ave., Cambridge, 617-876-6555) or Ata Cycle (1773 Massachusetts Ave., Cambridge, 617-354-0907; www.atabike.com). Rent rollerblades at Beacon Hill Skate Shop, (135 Charles St., 617-482-7400) or Blades Board & Skate (Boston and Cambridge, 617-437-6300; www.blades.com).

CHILDREN'S MUSEUM OF BOSTON

300 Congress St., Boston, 617-426-6500; www.bostonkids.org

With interactive exhibits on science, technology, art and culture, the Children's Museum lives up to its billing as "Boston's best place for kids 0-10." A kid-size construction site includes a mini artists' studio, real loom and weaving area, full-size wigwam and rock climbing area.

Saturday-Thursday 10 a.m.-5 p.m., Friday 10 a.m.-9 p.m.

COMMUNITY BOATING

21 David Mugar Way, Boston, 617-523-1038; www.community-boating.org

Community Boating runs the largest and oldest public sailing program in the country. Purchasing a two-day membership means unlimited use of boats, plus sailing, windsurfing or kayaking instruction.

April-November: daily; closed December-March.

COPLEY PLACE

100 Huntington Ave., Boston, 617-369-5000; www.shopcopleyplace.com

With more than 100 stores and a central glass atrium, Copley Place is devoted to upscale shopping and dining. Stores include Barneys, Neiman Marcus, Louis Vuitton, Christian Dior and Gucci.

Daily.

COPP'S HILL BURYING GROUND

Hull and Snow Hill Streets, Boston, 617-635-4505;
www.cityofboston.gov/freedomtrail/coppshill.asp

This is the second-oldest burying ground in Boston. Robert Newman, who hung the lanterns in the steeple of Old North Church, is buried here, as is the Puritan Mather family and African Americans from the nearby New Guinea Community, who lie in unmarked graves.

Daily.

DUCK TOURS

3 Copley Place, Suite 310, Boston, 617-267-3825; www.bostonducktours.com

This long-standing Boston tradition takes you from land to sea in a World War II half-boat, half-truck vehicle known as a Duck. Your "conDUCKtor" starts the 80-minute tour near the Boston Common and drives through the city before heading into the Charles River.

April-November: on the hour from 9 a.m. to one hour before sunset.

FANEUIL HALL MARKETPLACE

4 S. Market Building, Fifth floor Boston, 617-523-1300;
www.faneuilhallmarketplace.com

Faneuil Hall is more than just a shopping center: It has operated as a local marketplace since 1742, when wealthy merchant Peter Faneuil built and donated the area to the city. Today, it buzzes with tourists catching street performances or snacking on treats from indoor food mall Quincy Market.

Daily.

FRANKLIN PARK GOLF COURSE (WILLIAM J. DEVINE GOLF COURSE)

1 Circuit Drive, Dorchester, 617-265-4084; www.sterlinggolf.com

This 6,009-yard, par-70 golf course is the second-oldest public golf course in the country. Rates are reasonable, especially for kids under 18, and club rentals are just $10. The course is wide open but demanding, with some steep hills.

Daily dawn-dusk; closed for snow and inclement weather.

FRANKLIN PARK ZOO

1 Franklin Park Road, Dorchester, 617-541-5466; www.zoonewengland.org

The medium-sized zoo is home to "Bird's World," an indoor/outdoor aviary complex with natural habitats; an African tropical forest; a hilltop range with camels, antelopes and zebras; and a children's zoo. Daily.

FREEDOM TRAIL

99 Chauncy St., Suite 401 617-242-5642; www.thefreedomtrail.org

This two to three-hour walking tour takes visitors past some of Boston's most famous historical sites. It begins at the Boston Common and ends at the Bunker Hill Monument in Charlestown. Red bricks or red paint mark the trail, which you can follow on your own (free brochures are available) or with guided assistance.

GRANARY BURYING GROUND

Tremont and Bromfield Streets, Boston, 617-635-4505;
www.thefreedomtrail.org/visitor/granary.html

Revolutionary War heroes Paul Revere, John Hancock, Samuel Adams and Peter Faneuil (whose headstone is misspelled as "Peter Funal") lie here. The name comes from a grain storage building (a granary) that used to sit nearby. Daily 9 a.m.-7 p.m.

HAYMARKET

Blackstone Street, Boston

Rain or shine, winter or summer, Bostonians flock to Haymarket and its outdoor stalls for the freshest fruits, vegetables and seafood around.

INSTITUTE OF CONTEMPORARY ART

100 Northern Ave., Boston, 617-478-3100; www.icaboston.org

In late 2006, the ICA moved into its brand-new waterfront South Boston building. The four-floor museum now has a sizable theater with walls of glass, in addition to a large outdoor deck and several galleries showing permanent and temporary collections.

Tuesday, Wednesday, Saturday, Sunday 10 a.m-5 p.m., Thursday-Friday, 10 a.m.-9 p.m..

ISABELLA STEWART GARDNER MUSEUM

280 The Fenway, Boston, 617-566-1401; www.gardnermuseum.com

The museum is housed in the 19th-century home of Isabella Stewart Gardner. Collections include paintings and sculptures from around the world. On

weekends in fall, winter and spring, look for free afternoon concerts.
Tuesday-Sunday 11 a.m.-5 p.m.; concerts late September-May.

KING'S CHAPEL AND BURYING GROUND

58 Tremont St., Boston, 617-227-2155;
www.thefreedomtrail.org/visitor/kings-burying.html
King's Chapel, started by the Massachusetts Royal Governor, has held
church services at its location longer than any other church in the United
States. When the congregation outgrew the church in 1754, a new building
was erected around the old, which was then dismantled. The Burying Ground
next door is the oldest cemetery in Boston.
Daily; closed Sunday-Friday in winter.

L'ARTE DI CUCINARE

6 Charter St., Boston, 617-523-6032; www.cucinare.com
Michele Topor, a longtime resident of the North End and passionate gourmet
chef, leads 3½-hour tours of the North End Italian markets. Reservations are
required, and each tour is limited to 13 people.
Wednesday, Friday-Saturday.

LOUIS BOSTON

234 Berkeley St., Boston, 617-262-6100, 800-225-5135; www.louisboston.com
This men's and women's clothing emporium is considered among the finest
in the world. Housed in the historic former museum of science building, the
buyers here stock the shelves with hard-to-find labels from designers who
are ahead of their time.
Monday-Wednesday 11 a.m.-6 p.m., Thursday-Saturday 11 a.m.-7 p.m.

LOUISBURG SQUARE

Louisburg Square, Beacon Hill
This lovely little residential square is one of Boston's most coveted addresses.
Louisa May Alcott, William Dean Howells and other famous Bostonians—
including current Senator John Kerry—have had homes here.

MDC MEMORIAL HATCH SHELL

On the Charles River, between Storrow Drive and the water, 617-626-4970;
www.mass.gov
Packing as much as possible into the summer months, the Hatch Shell offers
free entertainment nearly every night of the week. Offerings range from dance
performances to rock concerts to the Boston Pops Fourth of July celebration.
Early June-early September.

MINUTEMAN COMMUTER BIKEWAY

www.minutemanbikeway.org
This suburban bike path begins near the Alewife 'T' station, goes through
Lexington and Arlington and ends at Bedford. The 11-mile path looks like a
miniature highway, complete with on and off-ramps, a center line and traffic
signs. The trail mimics portions of Paul Revere's famous ride.
Daily.

MOTHER CHURCH, THE FIRST CHURCH OF CHRIST, SCIENTIST CHRISTIAN SCIENCE CENTER

210 Massachusetts Ave., Boston, 617-450-2000; www.tfccs.com

This is the headquarters of the Christian Science Monitor, and the home of the Mapparium, a unique, acoustically perfect walk-through stained-glass globe.

Daily.

MUSEUM AT THE JOHN FITZGERALD KENNEDY LIBRARY

Columbia Point, Boston, 617-514-1600, 866-535-1960; www.jfklibrary.org

Designed by I.M. Pei, the library is a striking contemporary work of architecture. Inside are displays on Kennedy's life and presidency. The museum often hosts notable politicians and public figures for speeches and events.

Daily 9 a.m.-5 p.m.

MUSEUM OF AFRO AMERICAN HISTORY

46 Joy St., Boston, 617-720-2991 X.14; www.afroammuseum.org

The Museum of Afro American History preserves and exhibits the contributions of African-American Bostonians and New Englanders during colonial settlement and the Revolutionary War. The museum also features workshops for kids and adults, a public lecture series, storytelling for children, and poet and author visits.

Monday-Saturday 10 a.m.-4 p.m.

MUSEUM OF FINE ARTS

465 Huntington Ave., Boston, 617-267-9300; www.mfa.org

The MFA, Boston's answer to New York's Metropolitan Museum of Art, combines classic and contemporary art with ancient artifacts. The grand, white-stone building is practically an exhibit in itself.

Monday-Tuesday and Saturday-Sunday 10 a.m.-4:45 p.m., Wednesday-Friday 10 a.m.-9:45 p.m.

MUSEUM OF SCIENCE

1 Science Park, Charles River Dam and Storrow Drive, Boston, 617-723-2500; www.mos.org

The MOS's entertaining exhibitions include a T-rex model (complete with 58 teeth), presentations with live animals at the Wright Theater, a chick hatchery, and a lighthouse that explains light, optics and color. Also onsite is the Charles Hayden Planetarium.

Saturday-Thursday 9 a.m.-5 p.m., Friday 9 a.m.-9 p.m.

NEWBURY STREET

1-361 Newbury St., Boston, www.newbury-st.com

There's no better shopping street in New England than Newbury. Independent boutiques and well-known chain shops sell everything from baby gear to kitchen equipment to truffles to artwork. The street is also home to scores of spas and cafés, making it a one-stop shopping, eating and pampering destination.

NEW ENGLAND AQUARIUM

1 Central Wharf, Boston, 617-973-5200; www.neaq.org

The aquarium has a colorful array of dolphins, sea lions, penguins, turtles, sharks, eels, harbor seals and fish from around the world. Every 90 minutes, sea lions perform. There's also an IMAX theater.

Monday-Friday 9 a.m.-5 p.m., Saturday-Sunday, most holidays until 6 p.m.

NEW ENGLAND AQUARIUM WHALE WATCHES

Central Wharf, Boston, 617-973-5206; www.neaq.org

Stellwagen Bank, 25 miles from Boston, is a terrific area for whale-watching. From Boston, the New England Aquarium's tour takes you out to the feeding grounds of a variety of whales, many of which are endangered. Purchase tickets in advance. Boston Harbor Cruises (617-227-4321; www. bostonharborcruises.com) and Beantown Whale Watch (617-542-8000; ww.beantownwhalewatch.com) also operate whale cruises in Boston.

Mid-April-late October.

NICHOLS HOUSE MUSEUM

55 Mount Vernon St., Boston, 617-227-6993; www.nicholshousemuseum.org

The house features typical 1804 domestic architecture of Beacon Hill from its era, and is one of two homes on Beacon Hill open to the public. Attributed to Charles Bulfinch, the house has antique furnishings and art from America, Europe and the Orient from the 17th to early 19th centuries.

April-October: Tuesday-Saturday 11 a.m.-4 p.m.; November-March: Thursday-Saturday 11 a.m.-4 p.m.

OLD NORTH CHURCH

193 Salem St., Boston, 617-523-6676; www.oldnorth.com

Old North Church is the oldest church in Boston. On April 18, 1775, church sexton Robert Newman placed two lanterns in the steeple to signal that the British Army was heading up the Charles River. When Paul Revere saw the signal, he jumped on his horse and rode to Lexington to warn the militia. The next day, the shot heard round the world was fired on Lexington Green, officially beginning the Revolutionary War.

Daily, except January-February: closed Mondays.

OLD SOUTH CHURCH

645 Boylston St., Boston, 617-536-1970; www.oldsouth.org

A church community since 1669, Old South Church has a medieval architectural style that boasts impressive mosaics, stained glass and cherry woodwork. Worship is held on Sunday.

OLD SOUTH MEETING HOUSE

310 Washington St., Boston, 617-482-6439; www.oldsouthmeetinghouse.org

The most important date in Old South's history is December 16, 1773, when 5,000 colonists gathered at the church to protest the British tax on tea and decide on a course of action. From there, the men, dressed as Native Americans, snuck onto three ships laden with tea and dumped the cargo overboard.

Daily.

OLD STATE HOUSE/SITE OF BOSTON MASSACRE

206 Washington St., Boston, 617-720-1713; www.bostonhistory.org

The Old State House was originally built as the headquarters of the British government in Boston. It is now the city's oldest surviving public building. Inside, a museum exhibits the prominent role the building played in the American Revolution. In 1770, British troops shot into a crowd that had gathered here to hear a proclamation; the fallen are memorialized by a small circle of paving stones (it now sits under dense city traffic).

Daily 9 a.m.-5 p.m.

PARK STREET CHURCH

1 Park St., Boston, 617-523-3383; www.parkstreet.org

William Lloyd Garrison delivered his first antislavery address here in 1829. The church is often called "Brimstone Corner" because brimstone for gunpowder was stored here during the War of 1812.

Mid-June-August: limited hours; Sunday services all year.

PAUL REVERE HOUSE

19 N. Square, Boston, 617-523-2338; www.paulreverehouse.org

Built in 1680, the well-preserved Paul Revere House is Boston's oldest building. It still includes authentic furnishings and offers a rare glimpse of colonial life. Here, Paul Revere plied his silversmith trade and sold his wares, often in exchange for food or livestock. His successful ride to Lexington on April 18, 1775, was immortalized by Henry Wadsworth Longfellow in "The Midnight Ride of Paul Revere."

Mid-April-late October: daily 9:30 a.m.-5:15 p.m.; early November-mid-April: daily 9:30 a.m.-4:15 p.m.; closed Monday in January-March.

SAMUEL ADAMS BREWERY

30 Germania St., Boston, 617-522-9080; www.samueladams.com

Take a tour of the Boston Beer Museum and discover the critical details of the brewing process. While you're at it, sample a few Samuel Adams microbrews.

Tours, Thursday-Saturday.

THE SHOPS AT THE PRUDENTIAL CENTER

800 Boylston St., Boston, 800-746-7778; www.prudentialcenter.com

This indoor shopping mall includes Saks Fifth Avenue, Club Monaco, Barnes and Noble and more.

Daily.

STATE HOUSE

24 Beacon St., Boston, 617-727-3676; www.cityofboston.gov

The Massachusetts State House is an architectural marvel with a golden dome sheathed in 23-carat gold leaf (the original State House's was copper). Designed by Charles Bulfinch and built on land owned by John Hancock, the building's cornerstones were laid by many Bostonians, including Paul Revere, on July 4, 1795.

Monday-Friday 10 a.m.-3:30 p.m.

SUFFOLK DOWNS

111 Waldemar Ave., East Boston, 617-567-3900; www.suffolkdowns.com

Seabiscuit once won at Suffolk Downs, a local track that has been operating since 1935. The track offers pari-mutuel betting, which unlike casino gambling, doesn't involve betting against the house, only against other spectators. Daily.

TRINITY CHURCH

206 Clarendon St., Boston, 617-536-0944; www.trinitychurchboston.org

This Henry Hobson Richardson-built church was inspired by Phillips Brooks, the ninth rector of Trinity Church and author of the Christmas carol, "O Little Town of Bethlehem."
Daily.

USS CONSTITUTION

Charlestown Navy Yard, Boston National Historical Park, One Constitution Road,
Boston, 617-242-7511; www.cityofboston.gov

The oldest commissioned warship in the world got the nickname "Old Ironsides" during the War of 1812. Some 600 miles off the coast of Boston, it engaged the British *HMS Guerriere* in battle. While the *Guerriere* was badly damaged, cannonballs merely bounced off the *Constitution's* sides, as if they were made of iron (really, they are three layers of oak). In 1830, the ship was saved from the scrap heap because of public response to Oliver Wendell Holmes' poem "Old Ironsides." It was restored in 1925.
May-September, daily 9 a.m.-6 p.m., October-April, daily 10 a.m.-5 p.m.

CITI PERFORMING ARTS CENTER/THE SHUBERT THEATER

265 and 270 Tremont St., Boston, 617-482-9393; www.citicenter.org/theatres

Broadway shows, theater productions, dance and opera companies, and musical performers appear at the 3,600-seat Citi Performing Arts Center (formerly the Wang Theater), a world-class venue for the performing arts. The Shubert hosts an impressive array of quality local theater, dance and opera productions, many of which appeal to children.

SPECIAL EVENTS
BOSTON MARATHON

617-236-1652; www.bostonmarathon.org

The notoriously hilly and difficult Boston marathon is one of the most famous footraces in the world. To qualify, runners must have already posted an acceptable time in another marathon. (But that doesn't stop thousands of "scabs" from jumping into the race behind the pros.) Most of the city shuts down for the day, as fans line the route and cheer like crazy.
Third Monday in April.

FIRST NIGHT BOSTON

617-542-1399; www.firstnight.org

First Night is Boston's New Year's Eve celebration. The alcohol-free event begins with a Mardi Gras-style Grand Procession and features more than 250 performances in both indoor and outdoor venues. Those who can stay awake

are treated to a fireworks display at midnight.
December 31.

WHERE TO STAY

★★★BEACON HILL HOTEL
25 Charles St., Boston, 617-723-7575; www.beaconhillhotel.com

This petite boutique hotel is tucked between the shops and cafés of Charles Street, the neighborhood's main thoroughfare, in a historic townhouse building. The twelve guest rooms and one suite are delightful (if tiny!), with touches like plantation shutters and local photography, but it's the surroundings that make the hotel special. Spend a warm afternoon on the sunny roof deck, sipping wine and munching on modern French fare in the busy Beacon Hill Bistro downstairs. You might have to fight the well-heeled locals who come here for a table, but after tasting chef Jason Bond's seasonally inspired cuisine, you'll understand why they do. (Bonus for foodies: Breakfast in the Bistro is included in your stay.)

13 rooms. Restaurant. $251-350

★★★★★BOSTON HARBOR HOTEL
70 Rowes Wharf, Boston, 617-439-7000, 800-752-7077; www.bhh.com

Occupying an idyllic waterfront location, this quiet, luxurious hotel sits across from Boston's Financial District and along a stretch of land that was once dominated by an elevated highway. The staff at this full-service property is attentive. Rooms and suites are draped in rich colors (it is worth paying extra for a room with a view). In the summer, live music, dancing and an outdoor movie night take place on the hotel's outdoor patio. The hotel's Meritage restaurant is the domain of chef Daniel Bruce, whose dishes consist of the freshest local ingredients and are paired with wines by the glass or bottle from around the world. The Rowes Wharf water taxi whisks guests straight to the airport, avoiding Boston's notorious traffic.

230 rooms. Restaurant, bar. Fitness center. $351 and up

★★★BOSTON MARRIOTT COPLEY PLACE
110 Huntington Ave., Boston, 617-236-5800, 877-901-2079; www.copleymarriott.com

A fashionista's paradise, the 1,000-plus-room Back Bay Marriott lies adjacent to some of the city's best high-end shopping (including Barneys, Dior, Gucci and Jimmy Choo). Thanks to indoor walkways that connect the hotel with Copley Place, the Prudential Center and the Back Bay train station, guests can access some of Boston's sights without setting foot outside (a lifesaver when a Nor'Easter blows through town). Rooms aren't exceptional, but they do feature 300 thread-count sheets and 24-hour room service. Try to snag one on the concierge level, which has a private lounge, or one on a higher floor for views of Copley Square or the Charles River.

1,147 rooms. Restaurant, bar. $151-250

★★★BOSTON MARRIOTT LONG WHARF
296 State St., Boston, 617-227-0800, 800-228-9290; www.marriott.com

If you're traveling with children there may be no better place to stay than on Long Wharf. The historic waterfront location is surrounded by kid-friendly activities, from the street performers of nearby Quincy Market to the lively fish of the Aquarium. The Children's Museum is a short cab ride away. Add in the Marriott's indoor pool and the fact that the hotel sort of resembles a docked ship, and you've got a recipe for smiles. Of course, parents get some perks too, like 300-thread-count linens, flat-screen TVs and tons of local dining options.

412 rooms. Restaurant, bar. Fitness center. Pool. Business center. $151-250

★★★BOSTON PARK PLAZA HOTEL

50 Park Plaza, Boston, 617-426-2000; www.bostonparkplaza.com

From the bright red awnings to the always-busy restaurants (including celeb chef Todd English's Latin steakhouse Bonfire) to the hotel's dominating presence near the Public Garden (it takes up two giant blocks), there's nothing subtle about the Park Plaza. In fact, every U.S. President since the hotel's 1927 opening has stayed here. Multiple renovations mean some guest rooms are oddly proportioned (larger rooms were created by joining two minuscule ones), but all of them feature comfortable pillow-top mattresses. An update in 2008 added new carpeting, bedding and furniture; the property's common areas were upgraded in 2009.

941 rooms. Restaurant, bar. Fitness center. Business center. $251-350

★★★CHARLESMARK HOTEL

655 Boylston St., Boston, 617-247-1212; www.thecharlesmark.com

Walking down Boylston Street, it's easy to mistake the Charlesmark for just another swanky retail store or cocktail lounge. With a minimalist exterior and a busy ground-floor bar, it hardly looks like a place to stay. But the Back Bay townhouse, built as a private residence in 1892, contains a surprising number of cozy guest suites, and the service feels pleasantly personal compared to most Back Bay mega-hotels. Though small, all rooms are decked out in modern, minimalist style, giving it a fun, updated feel.

33 rooms. Bar. Business center. $151-250

★★★THE COLONNADE HOTEL

120 Huntington Ave., Boston, 617-424-7000, 800-962-3030; www.colonnadehotel.com

One of the last independent hotels in Boston, the Colonnade Hotel recently poured $20 million into a gut renovation of its rooms and public spaces, giving its once-tired interior a glossy new look. The lobby is done up with black woods, gleaming tile and detailed molding, while the guest rooms are dressed in soothing neutrals. Guests might not notice new little touches like extra outlets for charging up iPods and laptops, or the air-conditioning that senses when you've entered the room. But they are there, and they make a stay here very comfortable. For all the flashy upgrades, the hotel's greatest asset has remained untouched: On hot summer days, the glistening rooftop pool teems with sun worshippers.

285 rooms. Restaurant, bar. Fitness center. Pool. Business center. $251-350

★★★COPLEY SQUARE HOTEL

47 Huntington Ave., Boston, 617-536-9000; www.copleysquarehotel.com

One of Boston's most recognizable landmark hotels (the signature red sign can be seen from almost anywhere in Back Bay) received a major makeover in 2009. Upgrades restored its historic charm and lend a modern boutique-hotel feel to the 143-room hotel. New features include contemporary light fixtures, fabrics and glossy details in the lobby. Perks include complimentary coffee, tea and hot chocolate in the lobby 24 hours a day, wine from 5-6 p.m. and MP3 players that you can borrow during your stay. Xhale serves breakfast and dinner, and is a casual option with flat-screen TVs and plenty of room to spread out with your laptop. Nightlife options run the gamut from Saint, which features live DJ-music and dancing, to Minibar, a sophisticated martini bar.

143 rooms. Restaurant, bar. Pets accepted. $151-250

★★COURTYARD BOSTON COPLEY SQUARE

88 Exeter St., Boston, 617-437-9300; www.courtyardboston.com

If you're looking for a bed in Back Bay and prefer efficiency, the Courtyard in Copley is an easy and economical place to stay. Right in the center of Back Bay, between the Prudential Center and Copley Square, it's a quick walk to Newbury Street shopping, Boston Public Library and the Esplanade. (If you're in town for the Boston Marathon, you can't get any closer to the action; the finish line is just steps away from the entrance.)

81 rooms. Restaurant. Fitness center. $151-250

★★DOUBLETREE GUEST SUITES

400 Soldiers Field Road, Boston, 617-783-0090, 800-222-8733; www.doubletree.com

If you're coming to town to check out Boston's many colleges, this hotel's location in Allston (a neighborhood of Boston) makes a fine hub, as it's centrally located between B.U., Boston College, Harvard, MIT and Northeastern. Every room in the 15-story tower is a spacious suite, and extras like two TVs per suite and chocolate chip cookies at check-in will keep kids happy. Complimentary shuttles mean you can park your rental car at the hotel and not worry about navigating the city's notoriously confusing streets. Just be back in time to catch a show at Sculler's, one of the best jazz clubs in Boston.

308 rooms. Restaurant, bar. Fitness center. Pool. Business center. Pets accepted. $61-150

★★DOUBLETREE HOTEL BOSTON DOWNTOWN

821 Washington St., Boston, 617-956-7900; www.doubletree.com

Situated where downtown, the Theatre District and Chinatown meet, this Doubletree is prime real estate for nightlife-lovers. It's urban, for sure, but that's part of the draw. Inside, you can take refuge in the rooms' plush beds; the plain beige-and-white décor isn't much to speak of, but after experiencing the area's sensory overload, you won't feel like you're missing a thing. All guests enjoy access to the adjoining YMCA for workouts and swimming.

267 rooms. Restaurant, bar. Business center. $151-250

★★★THE ELIOT HOTEL

370 Commonwealth Ave., Boston, 617-267-1607, 800-443-5468; www.eliothotel.com

When you're staying at the plush Eliot Hotel, situated amid Commonwealth Avenue's multi-million dollar townhomes, private clubs and flowering tree-lined mall, feel free to take luxury for granted. All of the rooms are outfitted with marble bathrooms, down comforters and plush robes; with heavy toile drapes, dramatic valances and upholstered furniture, the style is classic through and through. Expect extras like 24-hour room service, clothes pressing and complimentary shoeshines. For guests with dogs, pet-sitting is available. Traveling foodies shouldn't miss chef Ken Oringer's James Beard Award-winning restaurant, Clio, for French-Asian cuisine; sushi bar Uni is ideal for a light bite.

95 rooms. Restaurant. Business center. $251-350

★★★THE FAIRMONT BATTERY WHARF BOSTON

Three Battery Wharf, Boston, 617-994-9000, 800-257-7544; www.fairmont.com

Located on the waterfront, this new hotel stands where shipyards and warehouses used to be. The location has its pros and cons. You are next to the North End (pro) where all the good restaurants are, but the area is still developing (con) so you might not get as much of a neighborhood feel. Still, you have water views and you can even take a water taxi here from the airport. Plus, the restaurant and outdoor patio are sure to be destinations come summer (especially since the complex includes residences). Rooms are modern and comfortable with large desks, marble baths, flatscreen TVs and iPod docking stations.

150 rooms. Restaurant, bar. Fitness center. Spa. Business center. $251-350

★★★THE FAIRMONT COPLEY PLAZA BOSTON

138 St., James Ave., Boston, 617-267-5300, 800-441-1414; www.fairmont.com

Don't let the imposing columned exterior (designed by Henry Janeway Hardenbergh, who also conceived New York's Plaza Hotel), glittering chandeliers and opulent trompe l'oeil ceilings fool you: this hotel is far from stuffy. Take it from black lab Catie, the Copley Plaza's "canine ambassador," who greets guests from the concierge desk. (Dog-loving guests can even sign up to take Catie on a walk.) Following $34 million in upgrades to the circa-1912 hotel, the guest rooms include minibars, marble bathrooms and windows that open. The traditional styling, however—striped wallpaper, flowery bedding, and mahogany furniture—has stayed put. Reserve a Fairmont Gold room, which comes with upgraded amenities and access to a private lounge with free refreshments.

383 rooms. Restaurant, bar. Fitness center. $251-350

★★★★★FOUR SEASONS HOTEL BOSTON

200 Boylston St., Boston, 617-338-4400, 800-330-3442; www.fourseasons.com

When it comes to superlative service, no one does it like the Four Seasons, and the Boston property is no exception. Guests at this parkside hotel, which lies directly across from the Public Garden and close to upscale retailers Escada, La Perla and Hermès, can expect to be spoiled. Room décor is not dramatic (the hotel calls the style "Beacon Hill residential"), but they're equipped for comfort, featuring plush slippers and robes, down pillows and DVD players for late-night movies. After check-in, head down for afternoon tea at the hotel's Bristol Lounge. With all the fixings of traditional English high tea service, like finger sandwiches and buttery scones, it's the definition of Old Boston refinement. A dip in the indoor pool, which overlooks the garden and State House, provides the perfect pre-dinner pick-me-up.

273 rooms. Restaurant, bar. Fitness center. Pool. Spa. Business center. $351 and up

★★HAMPTON INN & SUITES BOSTON CROSSTOWN CENTER

811 Massachusetts Ave., Boston, 617-445-6400; www.bostonhamptoninn.com

Picturesque surroundings are not this Hampton Inn's selling point; it overlooks not grassy gardens and historic landmarks, but rather a busy intersection by the highway (and a blighted area of town). But what it does offer—proximity to Boston University Medical Center and to one of Boston's hottest restaurant neighborhoods, the historic South End—makes it a viable and affordable option. Even better, there's a complimentary shuttle to destinations around Boston to save cab fare. Rooms are basic but well-maintained, and feature the chain's standard "Cloud Nine" bed. There's also an ample free breakfast that goes beyond basic bagels each morning.

175 rooms. Fitness center. Pool. Business center. $151-250

★HARBORSIDE INN

185 State St., Boston, 617-723-7500, 888-723-7565; www.harborsideinnboston.com

With no two rooms alike, this unpretentious hotel—sister property to Back Bay's Charlesmark Hotel—feels a bit like staying at a budget-friendly pensione in Europe. Rooms face either an indoor atrium or overlook the city streets (we'd pick the latter; the atrium-view rooms can feel fishbowl-like) and come pleasantly appointed; pale-colored linens and streamlined, light wood furniture lend even the cavernous interior rooms a little brightness.

98 rooms. $151-250

★★★HILTON BOSTON BACK BAY

40 Dalton St., Boston, 617-236-1100, 800-445-8667; www.hilton.com

This massive hotel fills with tourists and conventioneers year-round, and for good reason: a plethora of sights, including Fenway Park, Newbury Street and Copley Square are right down the street. That's not to say that you need to leave the property to sightsee; if you're lucky enough to have a room on one of the tower's upper floors, you may catch glimpses of sailboats on the Charles River or the lights of Fenway Park. Rooms are decked out in dark woods and modern neutrals, and bathrooms come stocked with Crabtree & Evelyn products.

385 rooms. Restaurant, bar. Fitness center. Pool. Business center. Pets accepted. $251-350

★★★HILTON BOSTON LOGAN AIRPORT

1 Hotel Drive, Boston, 617-568-6700, 800-445-8667; www.hilton.com

A round-the-clock shuttle to the terminals means you'll never miss a flight when you stay at this hotel; there's also a covered skybridge connecting the property to the airport in case you'd rather walk. Inside, guest rooms come equipped with Serta mattresses, Crabtree & Evelyn toiletries and flat-screen TVs; a giant 6,000-square-foot pool/spa/fitness complex makes your stay even cushier, so you can almost forget you're practically sleeping on the tarmac.

599 rooms. Restaurant, bar. Fitness center. Business center. Pool. Pets accepted. $251-350

★★HOLIDAY INN BOSTON AT BEACON HILL

5 Blossom St., Boston, 617-742-7630; www.ichotelsgroup.com

At the foot of Beacon Hill, an area packed with over-the-top, trend-conscious shops and restaurants, this Holiday Inn is a pleasantly utilitarian option. You won't find anything too fancy, but you will find friendly service, clean rooms, and—better yet—a prime location. Not only are the quaint shops of the Hill just around the corner, the hotel is also near Government Center, Quincy Market and the TD Banknorth Garden (great news for Bruins and Celtics fans). If you're in town to see a top doctor, its proximity to Massachusetts General Hospital also makes it a convenient choice.

303 rooms. Restaurant. Fitness center. Pool. Business center. $251-350

★★HOTEL 140

140 Clarendon St., Boston, 617-585-5600, 800-714-0140; www.hotel140.com

This hotel is a reliable, wallet-friendly choice that's close to the John Hancock and Prudential towers, as well as Back Bay station, where Amtrak's high-speed Acela departs for New York City and Providence. The historic building, which was the YWCA's first headquarters in the U.S., underwent a $30 million renovation in 2005, which brought both the hotel and its fellow tenants—like the Lyric Stage Company, located on the ground floor—up to date. Guest rooms are small and simply appointed with the basics; the rooms with one twin bed are almost hostel-like. If you're staying in Boston for a while, the hotel offers long-term rates and package deals.

54 rooms. Business center. Restaurant. Fitness room. Complimentary breakfast. $151-250

★★★HOTEL COMMONWEALTH

500 Commonwealth Ave., Boston, 617-933-5000, 866-784-4000;
www.hotelcommonwealth.com

It's hard to believe that the Hotel Commonwealth, which rises grandly over Kenmore Square and is just a baseball's throw from Fenway Park, hasn't been there forever. The stately hotel opened in 2003, and its architectural style is pure, traditional Boston. More than a place to lay your head, the complex includes the always-hopping brasserie Eastern Standard, and the cool Foundation Lounge. But it's the guest rooms that impress: Oversized, with 32-inch flat-screen TVs, luxe Italian linens and L'Occitane bath products, they offer an uncommon level of comfort.

150 rooms. Restaurant, bar. Fitness center. Business center. $251-350

★★★HYATT HARBORSIDE

101 Harborside Drive, Boston, 617-568-1234, 800-233-1234; www.hyatt.com

Airport hotels aren't known for being luxurious, but this Hyatt, located right next to the terminals, is well-appointed. Comfortable beds and soundproofed windows ensure you're well-rested for your morning flight, and a 24-hour business center lets you work at all hours (in case jet lag keeps you up). And there's hardly a better view of Boston than from the fitness center, so you can say one last goodbye to Boston before taking off.

270 rooms. Restaurant, bar. Business center. Pool. Fitness center. $151-250

★★★HYATT REGENCY BOSTON FINANCIAL DISTRICT

1 Ave., de Lafayette, Boston, 617-912-1234, 800-233-1234; www.hyatt.com

For business travelers coming to the Financial District, simple and reliable trumps buzz-worthy and overdone. When that's the case, this downtown Hyatt fits the bill. No cutting edge design features here; just 500 centrally located, well-equipped guest rooms at the ready. An indoor pool and eucalyptus steam room help you wind down after a day of meetings, while Sealy mattresses and Neutrogena products ensure you're comfortable.

500 rooms. Restaurant, bar. Fitness center. Business center. Pool. $251-350

★★★INTERCONTINENTAL BOSTON

510 Atlantic Ave., Boston, 617-747-1000, 800-972-3381;
www.intercontinentalboston.com

If most Boston hotels seem cramped, then the recently opened InterContinental Hotel is an oasis of space. As soon as you walk in the giant, marble-covered lobby, the soaring ceilings let you know you're not in old-school Boston anymore. Adding to the sense of openness is a giant outdoor patio, in addition to two acres of waterfront gardens, where you can dine outside. Rooms feature contemporary décor, flat-screen TVs and luxurious bathrooms with separate soaking tubs.

424 rooms. Restaurant, bar. Business center. Fitness center. Pool. Pets accepted. Spa. $251-350

★★★JURYS HOTEL

350 Stuart St., Boston, 617-266-7200; www.jurysdoyle.com

When friends ask how you passed the time in Boston, tell them you spent the night at the police station. If you'd stayed at Jury's, you'd be telling the truth. Formerly the Boston Police headquarters, the historic building now provides visitors with a surprisingly luxurious place to stay, with high-end amenities like down comforters, heated towel racks and multi-head showers in the bathrooms. Cuffs, the Irish bar on the ground floor, fills with revelers nightly (their volume increasing steadily as the hour approaches midnight), so it's not a spot to go for peace and quiet. If you love a scene, it's not a bad place to (not) sleep.

225 rooms. Restaurant, bar. Fitness center. Business center. $251-350

★★★THE LANGHAM BOSTON

250 Franklin St., Boston, 617-451-1900, 800-791-7781; www.langhamhotels.com

Near Faneuil Hall, the Freedom Trail and the North End, the Langham, housed in the former Federal Reserve building, is a great base for retracing the patriots' steps. Rooms have been freshened up with rich, jewel-toned fabrics and plasma TVs. The Asian-inspired Chuan spa is a great place for pampering, and the Julien Bar is a local favorite for power lunches. The long-standing weekend chocolate bar brunch is a favorite with locals for its overwhelming array of chocolate-based desserts and treats.

325 rooms. Restaurant, bar. $251-350

★★★LENOX HOTEL

61 Exeter St., Boston, 617-536-5300, 800-225-7676; www.lenoxhotel.com

You'd be hard-pressed to find a more action-packed home base in Boston than the Lenox Hotel. Located in the heart of Back Bay, an area that brims with activity, the Lenox sits on a corner that overlooks the Boston Marathon finish line, Copley Square and Boylston Street. While every other hotel seems to be redecorating in mid-century modern, the Lenox's elegantly traditional interior is refreshing. Wood detailing and brass chandeliers fill the lobby, while the rooms have satin damask bedding and floral upholstery. If you're in town during the winter months, request a room with a wood-burning fireplace. Aveda toiletries and access to the nearby Bella Sante spa up the frill factor. 212 rooms. Restaurant, bar. $251-350

★★★LIBERTY HOTEL

215 Charles St., Boston, 617-224-4000; www.libertyhotel.com

In 2007, Boston hipsters were blessed with the arrival of the Liberty Hotel, a jaw-dropping statement piece set in the previously vacant Charles Street Jail, first erected in 1851. Many of the one-time prison's historical details remain, including swinging iron cell doors, an impressive rotunda and exposed brick walls. Walking past barred windows en route to one of the lavishly appointed guest rooms—now stocked with Molton Brown bath products, sleek neutral linens, cozy knit blankets and flat-screen TVs—it's readily apparent that said rooms were once jail cells. The hotel's designers were not without a sense of humor: the lobby bar and restaurant Clink is a see-and-be-seen spectacle, night after night; celebrity mug shots grace the walls of downstairs bar Alibi. 298 rooms. Restaurant, bar. Fitness center. $351 and up.

★★★★MANDARIN ORIENTAL, BOSTON

800 Boylston St., Boston, 617-535-8888; www.mandarinoriental.com

Perhaps the most hotly anticipated real estate project to come to Boston in decades, the Mandarin Oriental (which include residences)—opened in October 2008—arrived to much fanfare. In addition to some of the city's chicest hotel accommodations, the property also includes a 16,000-square-foot spa, a vitality pool, a state-of-the-art Kinesis wall and three gourmet dining options, including the relocated upscale French restaurant, L'Espalier. Best of all, you're right on Boylton Street where all the great shopping is, and just minutes from the Charles River. 148 rooms. Restaurant, bar. Fitness center. Spa. Pool. Business center. $351 and up

★★★MILLENNIUM BOSTONIAN HOTEL

26 N. St., Boston, 617-523-3600, 800-343-0922; www.millenniumhotels.com

It's hard to get any closer to the action than the Millennium Bostonian, which sits at the edge of Quincy Market. A full renovation, completed in fall 2008, brings a much-needed touch of modern comfort to the formerly uninspiring interior spaces; guest rooms are decked out with Frette linens, pillow-top mattresses and flat-screen TVs. During the summer, book a room with a private balcony; in winter months, the rooms with fireplaces are cozy. Right across from touristy Faneuil Hall, the Millennium is ideal for visitors who don't want to walk far to see historic attractions. Guests also receive a discount at the adjacent Aveda Spa.

201 rooms. Restaurant, bar. Business center. Fitness center. $251-350

★★★NINE ZERO HOTEL

90 Tremont St., Boston, 617-772-5800, 866-646-3937; www.ninezero.com

Sometimes you just want a little glamour. When that's the case, there's Nine Zero. With its glossy interior of glass, stone, polished nickel, chrome and steel, the hotel feels modern and sophisticated. Chef Ken Oringer's onsite upscale steakhouse KO Prime draws an unfailingly stylish crowd. Don't be surprised if you run into a celebrity in the lobby; the hotel is a favorite of visiting stars who expect amenities like 24-hour room service. Upscale amenities include Frette linens, goose-down comforters and pillows, and local beauty guru Mario Russo's bath products.

190 rooms. Restaurant, bar. Pets accepted. $251-350

★★★OMNI PARKER HOUSE

60 School St., Boston, 617-227-8600, 800-843-6664; www.omnihotels.com

The storied Parker House hotel may have just undergone a $30 million renovation, but the circa-1855 hotel's main draw is its rich history—it was once the stomping ground of famed authors (Emerson, Thoreau) and presidents (Franklin D. Roosevelt, Ulysses S. Grant). Its restaurant, Parker's, was the birthplace of Boston cream pie (or so they claim…either way, it's tasty) and Parker House dinner rolls, as well as the spot where JFK held his bachelor party (in the press room). History buffs will also love its location on the Freedom Trail. The rooms, however, have everything that a 21st-century traveler needs, including work desks and flat-screen TVs.

551 rooms. Restaurant, bar. Fitness center. $251-350

★★★ONYX HOTEL

155 Portland St., Boston, 617-557-9955; www.onyxhotel.com

Positioned near the North End, this boutique hotel has a decidedly downtown feel, enhanced by a bold, contemporary décor. Rooms are done up in a palette of red, taupe and black, and feature down pillows, ultra-thick mattresses and suede furniture. The downstairs restaurant, The Ruby Room (which is—no surprise—all red) provides 24-hour room service. The hotel is particularly welcoming to pets, with treats, bowls and even welcome signs placed in the lobby.

112 rooms. Restaurant, bar. Fitness center. $251-350

★★★RENAISSANCE BOSTON WATERFRONT HOTEL

606 Congress St., Boston, 617-338-4111; www.marriott.com

One of the city's newest additions, the Renaissance Hotel, is bright, airy and right on the harbor. Many of the rooms have superb city and water views; they feel fresh and fun, with bold, splashy colors and patterns on the bed linens, furniture and throw pillows and huge HDTVs. Conveniently close to South Boston's new Convention & Exhibition Center, the Renaissance hosts a large number of business travelers in its straightforward but well-stocked rooms. While staying there, be sure to check out award-winning chef

Michael Schlow's newest venture, the seafood-heavy eatery 606 Congress, located on the first floor.

456 rooms. Restaurant. Fitness center. Pool. $251-350

★★★★THE RITZ-CARLTON, BOSTON COMMON

10 Avery St., Boston, 617-574-7100, 800-241-3333; www.ritzcarlton.com

This hotel's patrons receive perks like access to the enormous SportsClub/LA fitness center and spa, Bulgari toiletries, Bose radios and Bang & Olufsen stereos, all of which come standard with a stay here. Then there are the accommodations: even the most basic, pastel-toned guest rooms are nicely appointed with impossibly crisp bed linens, extra-fluffy pillows, three telephones (even in the bathroom) and large flat-screen TVs. Still not impressed? Have a bath butler come prepare an evening soak in your marble tub, then order room service at any hour you please. On weekdays, call for a complimentary limo ride to your morning meeting. Or reserve a room on the club level, which has its own lounge and concierge. Dogs are welcomed in style with the Pampered Pet Package, which includes bowls, biscuits and a personalized dog tag.

193 rooms. Restaurant, bar. Business center. Fitness center. Pets accepted. $351 and up

★★★SEAPORT HOTEL

1 Seaport Lane, Boston, 800-440-3318, 877-732-7678; www.seaportboston.com

Business travelers, welcome to your Eden. Catering largely to convention-goers and visitors to Boston's World Trade Center, the Seaport Hotel provides everything needed to set up an office-away-from-home, including two business centers, 24-hour business services, computer stations and private offices, and tons of meeting space. Rest up for your morning presentation on the guest rooms' 300-thread count, triple-sheeted beds and luxuriate in bathrooms stocked with oversized robes and towels. When the day is done, savor chef Rachel Klein's local, seasonal cuisine at Aura, or sip a martini at the new Tamo bar.

426 rooms. Restaurant bar. Pool. Fitness center. Business center. Pets accepted. $251-350

★★★SHERATON BOSTON HOTEL

39 Dalton St., Boston, 617-236-2000, 800-325-3535; www.sheraton.com

Size may not matter, but in the case of this Back Bay hotel, it can't be ignored. The largest hotel in the city, it contains a whopping 1,216 rooms and suites. That doesn't mean the hotel is cookie-cutter. While the standard rooms are small, the hotel's towering size means the views from most rooms' windows are stellar. And if you're here in summer, the 18-meter indoor/outdoor pool on the fifth floor is reason enough to book a room. It boasts a retractable roof and a deck, so on warm, clear days you can actually take in some sun (or, in the evening, the starry night sky).

1,216 rooms. Restaurant, bar. Pool. Fitness center. Business center. Pets accepted. $251-350

★★★★TAJ BOSTON
15 Arlington St., Boston, 617-536-5700, 877-482-5267; www.tajhotels.com

This venerable hotel, perched at the top of Newbury Street across from the Public Garden, hasn't changed much since it opened in the 1920s. Where else in town can you call for a bath butler (to fill your tub), a fireplace butler (to light your in-room hearth), or a technology butler (to ensure you don't miss a single email)? In true blueblood fashion, the décor is upscale, but not flashy, with richly-textured wall fabrics and tasseled drapes in a palette of beige, gold, rose and blue. Shoeshines, turndown service and high-end European toiletries are included, of course, as are the fantastic views of Newbury Street. The bar, with its original fireplace, dark wood paneling and cushy club chairs, is where Boston power deals are made.

273 rooms. Restaurant, bar. Fitness center. Business center. $351 and up

★★★WESTIN BOSTON WATERFRONT
425 Summer St., Boston, 617-532-4600; www.westin.com

Spacious and un-hotel like, the Westin Waterfront's lobby is the first sign you're not staying in a typical Boston hotel. The lobby bar, adorned with tall faux birch trees, is a Zen oasis; the giant wood-and-stone walls and ambient lighting feel spa-like. But once you've ascended to your hotel room, all the comforts you'd expect are there: the chain's trademark Heavenly Bed (swathed in crisp, high-quality white linens) and Heavenly Bath, slippers and robes, ergonomic desk chairs, turndown service and 24-hour room service. If you want to catch your flight without getting stuck in downtown traffic, catch the convenient water taxi, which will have you at Logan in plenty of time to hit the club lounge.

793 guest rooms. Restaurant, bar. Fitness center. Pool. Business center. $351 and up

★★★WESTIN COPLEY PLACE
10 Huntington Ave., Boston, 617-262-9600, 800-937-8461; www.westin.com

While a great location, flashy décor and fine dining are all well and good, Westin hasn't forgotten why you stay at a hotel: to sleep. Like the chain's other properties, every room in the Back Bay location has a Heavenly Bed with pillow-top mattress, plus a Heavenly Bath with dual showerheads. Even pets get the plush treatment with their own Heavenly dog beds. All this blissful snoozing is sure to leave you relaxed, well-rested and ready to take on all the nearby offerings: a steakhouse called The Palm and a local seafood spot Turner Fisheries; the indulgent Grettacole Spa; and, if you're in the mood for a little bit of flash after all that, a champagne bar.

803 rooms. Restaurant, bar. Pets accepted. Pool. Fitness center. Business center. $251-350

★★★★XV BEACON
15 Beacon St., Boston, 617-670-1500, 877-982-2226; www.xvbeacon.com

There's no such thing as a second-tier guest at XV Beacon; everyone is treated like a VIP. The service is suitably extravagant, with over-the-top amenities like complimentary Lexus sedan service to shuttle you around town as you please. Featuring an old-fashioned cage elevator and brass detailing, the hotel interior oozes Old Boston style. Every guest room has a poster bed, its own fireplace—a priceless amenity in the dead of winter—and Fresh toiletries; flowers greet you in your room. Come dinnertime, one of the city's top steakhouses, Mooo, is downstairs; its wine cellar is one of the most coveted private dining spaces in town. The hotel's stylishly dressed doormen are some of the city's friendliest and most knowledgeable, so be sure to get their tips for where to dine or shop.

61 rooms. Restaurant. Bar. Pets accepted. Fitness room. $351 and up

ALSO RECOMMENDED
CHARLES STREET INN
94 Charles St., Boston, 617-314-8900, 877-772-8900; www.charlesstreetinn.com
Step into the past without sacrificing modern conveniences at this charming city inn. The street-level reception and staircases are rather tight, but rooms are large and regal enough to qualify as decadent. Expect to find working fireplaces, massive antique armoires and heavily draped canopy beds in most. The hotel's location is ideal for exploring Beacon Hill, downtown or Back Bay on foot after a continental breakfast bounty is delivered to your door.

9 rooms. Complimentary breakfast. $251-350

GRYPHON HOUSE
9 Bay State Road, Boston, 617-375-9003, 877-375-9003;
www.gryphonhouseboston.com
More of a luxury bed and breakfast than a hotel, this circa-1895 brownstone stands at the juncture of Back Bay and Fenway. Each room is about the size of a studio apartment, has a working gas fireplace and wet bar, and is decorated in the Victorian style. The Kenmore subway stop, Boston University and Fenway Park are just moments away.

8 rooms. Complimentary breakfast. $151-250

NEWBURY GUEST HOUSE
261 Newbury St., Boston, 617-437-7666, 800-437-7668;
www.newburyguesthouse.com
A string of residences along upper Newbury Street was linked with indoor staircases and hallways to create this Back Bay bed and breakfast. Rooms tend to be on the small side, in part because private bathrooms were added when conversions were made. The décor is eclectic. A good value for its location; just ask for a rear-facing room to escape street noise.

32 rooms. Complimentary breakfast. $151-250

WHERE TO EAT
★★ABE & LOUIE'S
793 Boylston St., Boston, 617-536-6300; www.abeandlouies.com
With its prime Boylston Street location, this local, classic steak restaurant is consistently packed (a sprawling sidewalk patio for prime people watching doesn't hurt). Prime cuts of meat are served alongside steakhouse classics such as creamed spinach, hand-cut fries and New York cheesecake.
Steak. Lunch, dinner, brunch. Bar. Reservations recommended. Outdoor seating. $36-85

★★★AQUITAINE

569 Tremont St., Boston, 617-424-8577; www.aquitaineboston.com

Aquitaine feels a bit like a Parisian café parked in the middle of the South End. There's a chic clientele, the energizing hum of close-knit conversation, cozy banquettes and, of course, a menu of comfortable French classics. Regulars (mostly neighbors who live within walking distance) rave about the steak frites, but don't forgo the roast chicken, which can rival the comfort of a home-cooked meal minus the clean-up. Sunday brunch is a must; lines can be long but if the weather is nice, you won't mind waiting a few extra minutes for the classic omelette Basquaise, which oozes with ham and Gruyère goodness.

French. Dinner, brunch. Bar. Reservations recommended. $16-35

★★★AURA

1 Seaport Lane, Boston, 617-385-4300; www.seaporthotel.com

This casually elegant waterfront restaurant is based in the Seaport Hotel. So it's no surprise its menu focuses on fish: New England clam chowder, pan-roasted Maine diver scallops, Mediterranean-style swordfish and a seared loin of yellowfin tuna all make appearances. Desserts include maple ricotta cheesecake with Concord grape sorbet and a bittersweet chocolate tart with caramel ice cream.

Seafood. Breakfast, lunch, dinner, late-night, brunch. Bar. Children's menu. $36-85

★★B & G OYSTERS LTD

550 Tremont St., Boston, 617-423-0550; www.bandgoysters.com

A fresh-off-the-boat oyster house in New England's seafood capital? What a concept. Barbara Lynch couldn't agree more, especially after witnessing the immediate success of her intimate eatery (and we mean intimate, with limited table seating and a small bar surrounding the kitchen). Cool blue hues and sleek steel tables make the small room seem bigger than it is, and an open kitchen and oyster bar let you watch the shucking team in action. Boasting a dozen bivalve varieties daily, it's one of the best spots to sit and learn about oyster "terroir." The restaurant also has a chunky, meat-filled lobster roll (served with or without bacon), fried clams, charcuterie boards and entrées like Portuguese-style seafood stew. A patio opens up out back in the warmer months, and as with Lynch's other spots (The Butcher Shop and No. 9 Park), wine director Cat Silirie puts together a solid line-up of seafood-matching wines.

Seafood. Lunch, dinner. Outdoor seating. Closed holidays. $36-85

★★★BRAVO RESTAURANT

465 Huntington Ave., Boston, 617-369-3474; www.mfa.org

A favorite with ladies-who-lunch, this boldly colored restaurant is located on the second story of the Museum of Fine Arts. The restaurant's contemporary design reflects the museum's galleries of modern art (a few works are displayed on the eatery's walls). The chef incorporates fresh, local ingredients into an eclectic American menu. A wine tasting is offered on the last Wednesday of each month.

American. Lunch, dinner, brunch. Bar. Children's menu. Reservations recommended. $36-85

★★THE BUTCHER SHOP

552 Tremont St., Boston, 617-423-4800; www.thebutchershopboston.com

Inside Barbara Lynch's European-style butcher shop and wine bar, you can snack on the daily salami or simply shop for it. A selection of cured meats, cuts of beef and pâtés can be found inside the glass cases and on the menu, which has a number of substantial dishes available for lunch and dinner. If you're looking for a mid-afternoon snack, the hot dog with zucchini relish and house-made rosemary potato chips might be the best wiener you sample outside the ballpark. There is seating at the bar and along the windows (reservations are only accepted for parties of six or more), but some folks choose to stand beside the butcher block and graze on platters of cheese and charcuterie while drinking one of the robust wines listed on a chalkboard wall in the back.

American. Lunch, dinner, brunch. Children's menu. $36-85

★★★THE CAPITAL GRILLE

359 Newbury St., Boston, 617-262-8900; www.thecapitalgrille.com

Dark walls and an extensive single-malt Scotch list make this high-roller-frequented steakhouse a man's spot through and through. Its generous portions of well-marbled steak, creamed spinach and buttery mashed potatoes are hearty enough for the hungriest diner. The house specialty is the gargantuan dry-aged porterhouse. Weighing in at 24 juicy, bold ounces, it should come with its own defibrillator.

Steak. Dinner. Bar. Reservations recommended. $36-85

★★CARMEN

33 North Square, Boston, 617-742-6421; www.carmenboston.com

This jewel-boxed sized trattoria, located on picturesque, historic North Square, serves simple, seasonal Italian cuisine. The wine bar serves a selection of small plates, including marinated olives and roasted peppers, to complement the list of Italian wines. Pastas, such as linguine with clams, are made fresh daily. Because the North End is packed with charming cafés and pastry shops, Carmen does not serve dessert or coffee (take a short stroll instead to nearby Mike's Pastry for a superb cannoli).

Italian. Lunch, dinner. Closed Monday. Bar. $16-35

★★CASA ROMERO

30 Gloucester St., Boston, 617-536-4341; www.casaromero.com

If there weren't five feet of snow piling up outside half the year, you'd think you were in Mexico. Chef/owner Leo Romero has brought in dozens of imported Mexican artifacts to fill the cozy dining room, and his food drives the point home; he focuses on traditional Mexican dishes while incorporating local herbs and vegetables from his plot at the nearby community gardens. The results are flavor-packed and authentic. You can't go wrong with anything doused in his famous, richly layered mole sauce, and the beef tips simmered in a chile guajillo sauce carry a tasty kick. The secluded, plant-lined patio fills up on summer nights, so go early (and be prepared to wait) for one of the best alfresco meals this side of the border.

Mexican. Dinner, Sunday brunch. Bar. $36-85

★★★★CLIO
370 Commonwealth Ave., Boston, 617-536-7200; www.cliorestaurant.com

Chef and co-owner Ken Oringer's classical training (he was head of the class during his days at the Culinary Institute of America and snagged a James Beard Award) takes center stage at his original restaurant, Clio. With its leopard-print carpet and creamy walls, the room is as playful as the food. For example, he likes to show off different types of eel, when in season. Fresh fish plays a big role on the menu, and for those who prefer their seafood raw, Clio has a separate sashimi bar, Uni, where, for a hefty price, you can nibble on bite-sized spoons of sea urchin or fresh scallops. The place has a loyal following of both suited folks flexing their expense accounts and serious gourmands living for good food, but it also draws a fair number of local couples looking for a darkened corner in which to cuddle up.

French, Asian. Breakfast, dinner. Bar. Reservations recommended. Closed Monday. $36-85

★★★DAVIO'S
75 Arlington St., Boston, 617-357-4810; www.davios.com

This northern Italian steakhouse has been a Boston institution for more than 20 years. Its large dining room features dramatic high ceilings, a contemporary décor and imposing columns. An open kitchen lets diners watch chef Steve DiFillippo at work. Favored dishes include grilled porterhouse veal chops, hand-rolled potato gnocchi and a rich chocolate cake. Davio's To-Go Shop, serving delicious takeout such as pizza, sandwiches and dessert, is located next door.

Italian. Lunch, dinner, late-night. Bar. Children's menu. Reservations recommended. $36-85

★DURGIN PARK
340 Faneuil Hall Marketplace, Boston, 617-227-2038; www.durgin-park.com

This family-style stop sits inside the market building at Faneuil Hall and has done so since 1827. It draws visitors from every part of the world who settle into its checkered-cloth-covered picnic tables for down-and-dirty lobster bakes. Where else can you rub elbows (literally) with a family from Texas while digging into a plate of fried clams and a pot of baked beans? The menu carries everything from chicken fingers to New England corned beef and cabbage. Keep it simple and be sure to save room for the homemade Indian pudding. In the main dining room upstairs, mealtime can be loud and messy, while downstairs in the bar, there's always a game on one of the TVs and plenty of Sam Adams Lager on tap.

American. Lunch, dinner. Bar. Children's menu. Outdoor seating. $16-35

★★★EASTERN STANDARD
528 Commonwealth Ave., Boston, 617-532-9100; www.easternstandardboston.com

For a true smorgasbord of patrons, this Kenmore Square spot is it. You'll find every type, from students to financial power players. They're all sucking down classic cocktails and nibbling on hanger steak frites at the bar. The staff buzzes through all the commotion in the cavernous, red-accented dining room in vintage skirts or classic bartender vests, carrying a whirlwind of aromatic comfort food at every pass. From meatloaf and mashed potatoes to beef short-rib bourguignon, the menu hits all the classics. There's also a raw bar and a bar menu for lighter fare (including a superb Reuben made with Guinness-braised corned beef). The outdoor patio is a prime warm weather people-watching spot; but be wary on game days, as the place gets mobbed hours before the first pitch.

American. Breakfast, lunch, dinner. Outdoor seating. $16-35

★★FIGS

42 Charles St., Boston, 617-742-3447; 67 Main St., Charlestown, 617-242-2229; www.toddenglish.com

Todd English introduced gourmet pizza to Boston through Figs in the early 1990s, and locals have been coming here for the pies ever since. His inspired creations are all served on extra-crispy, super-thin crusts, which are weighted down with palate-tingling combinations like Gulf shrimp and caramelized leeks or crispy eggplant with dollops of whipped ricotta (you'll need a knife and fork for that one). If the pizzas aren't filling enough, there are dinner-sized salads, fried asparagus spears and rich, flavorful pastas to choose from. The 50-seat Charlestown location was actually home to the original Olives, which moved down the street before Figs opened up, and still boasts a boutique vibe and an amiable waitstaff, but no dessert.

Pizza. Lunch, dinner. $16-35

★FLOUR BAKERY

1595 Washington St., Boston, 617-267-4300;

12 Farnsworth St., Boston, 617-338-4333; www.flourbakery.com

This beloved South End sandwich shop and bakery seems to have a perpetual line snaking out of its glass door. The crowds have been following pastry chef Joanne Chang from her days at Rialto inside the Charles Hotel to what has blossomed into two locations of Flour (the other is in trendy Fort Point). Grab a seat at one of the communal tables and get to know your neighbors; the atmosphere is comfortable and cozy with stacks of alt-weekly newspapers for afternoon browsing and a chalkboard listing daily specials, a quote of the day and the weather. Chang makes addictive sticky buns and cookies, but the sandwiches are as tasty. Try the roast chicken sandwich with avocado and jicama or the curried tuna mixed with apples, carrots and golden raisins. The endless spread of sweets may appear overwhelming at first glance, but just pick one (or two or three); there isn't a bad choice among them.

Bakery. Breakfast, lunch. $15 and under

★★FRANKLIN CAFE

278 Shawmut Ave., Boston, 617-350-0010; www.franklincafe.com

Boston is an early-to-bed town, so finding a place to have a meal past midnight poses a challenge. Enter Franklin Café, a dimly lit neighborhood tavern that oozes cool and serves dinner long after other restaurants are dark. Dig into smoky, skillet-roasted mussels, duck quesadillas or classic steak frites while sipping a craft beer. Or order one of the specialty drinks: the blood orange martini is a stiff concoction made with vodka and Campari.

American. Dinner, late-night. Bar. $16-35

★★GINZA

16 Hudson St., Boston, 617-338-2261; www.ginzaboston.com

Those who believe Chinatown is best left to Chinese food haven't been to Ginza. Lauded as one of the top sushi restaurants in the city, Ginza puts out inventive rolls and pristine slivers of sashimi in frenetic order. Cooked dishes are popular, but not nearly as addictive. Don't mind the chintzy floral chair coverings and casual atmosphere; servers still manage to look hip in traditional kimonos while zipping between the wooden tables to the beat of Japanese pop lyrics. Fan favorites, like the gleaming sashimi appetizer and fashion maki (eel, avocado, cream cheese, cucumber and mountain burdock root), go down even quicker late at night—and we mean late, with a 4 a.m. last call on weekends—when the crowd gets younger and the music starts thumping. There's also a Brookline location, a favorite with B.U. students. Japanese. Lunch, dinner, late-night. Closed Thanksgiving. $16-35

★★★GRILL 23 & BAR

161 Berkeley St., Boston, 617-542-2255; www.grill23.com

Grill 23 fits all the major steakhouse stereotypes: massive cuts of prime, aged beef, a huge wine list plastered with inky reds and a well-suited corporate set swilling martinis at the bar. But there's more to this ornately outfitted, wood-paneled club than its Oriental rugs and polished marble floors. Executive chef Jay Murray is fanatical about where his beef comes from (in this case, all-natural Brandt beef) and how it's prepared. We'd be lying if we told you that people don't come just for the meat (they do). But Murray also supplies an impressive array of dayboat seafood and raw bar choices. There are a few inventive lamb and poultry dishes, too, and one of the restaurant's most famed sides: truffled tater tots.

Seafood, steak. Dinner. Bar. Reservations recommended. $36-85

★★★HAMERSLEY'S BISTRO

553 Tremont St., Boston, 617-423-2700; www.hamersleysbistro.com

Chef Gordon Hamersley came up with the right formula: Put simple ingredients into no-fuss dishes and serve them without a hint of pretension. It's worked for more than 20 years (diners pack the bright bistro-style dining room every night), and Hamersley still spends most of his time at the stove (sporting a Red Sox hat like the rest of his kitchen staff). The house specialty, chicken roasted with garlic, lemon and parsley, continues to draw faithful fans and the crispy polenta smothered in wild mushrooms is a nice blend of textured flavors. The seasonal bistro cuisine gets punched up with plenty of vegan options, and while her husband's in the kitchen, sommelier Fiona Hamersley is more than happy to guide you through the eclectic, though pricey, wine list.

French. Dinner. Bar. Reservations recommended. Outdoor seating. $36-85

★JASPER WHITE'S SUMMER SHACK

50 Dalton St., Boston, 617-867-9955; www.summershackrestaurant.com

An outpost of his larger Cambridge restaurant, Jasper White's Summer Shack is an amusing—and delicious—place to get shore-worthy seafood in the middle of town. The sound of cracking shells dominates the bustling dining room as hungry patrons dig into clambakes and crab legs; brown-paper tablecloths make for a handy backup napkin when you're in a pinch. On a cold Boston day, nothing beats a bowl of Bermuda fish and crab chowder, and if you're going for lobster, Jasper's pan-roasted preparation is a worthy splurge. Don't miss the oyster shooter: You'll get a whole oyster, cocktail sauce and vodka in one quick swallow. While a fierce debate rages in Boston as to who makes the best lobster roll, we think White's version is a worthy (and comparatively cheap) contender.

Seafood. Lunch, dinner. Bar. Children's menu. $16-35

★★★KO PRIME
Nine Zero Hotel, 90 Tremont St., Boston, 617-772-0202; www.koprimeboston.com

Chef Ken Oringer's foray into the world of steak has resulted in a stylish, upscale space that caters to the world-class travelers who frequent the hotel, as well as the city's food cognoscenti. Accented by leather and cowhides, the dining room is a trendy spot where diners dig into achingly tender braised Korubuta pork shoulder and Kobe iron steaks. Chef Jamie Bissonnette helms the kitchen, putting his charcuterie skills to good work and acquiring many ingredients from the hotel's rooftop garden and a host of local purveyors. There are a few seafood options if beef isn't your thing, and sides like short-rib mac and cheese and spaetzle with herbs and Parmesan balance out the plate. The cocktail list veers into the outrageous with a few liquid nitrogen-based creations.

Steak. Breakfast, lunch, dinner. $86 and up

★★★★L'ESPALIER
774 Boylston St., Boston, 617-262-3023; www.lespalier.com

This Back Bay institution moved from a 19th-century townhouse to a tony spot adjacent to the Mandarin Oriental in fall 2008, but managed to hold onto the bulk of its intimate charm. Dining here brings you back to another era (when men still wore coats and ties to dinner) and chef/proprietor Frank Mc-Clelland's over-the-top prix fixe menu only embellishes the experience. The dishes are a mix of French-influenced, traditional New England recipes like roasted Vermont rabbit with potato gnocchi and peas, and butter-poached Maine lobster with braised pork belly and sweet corn. His tasting menus can be amped up with caviar courses and an overflowing fromage cart, and the monster wine list puts plenty of stellar bottles alongside a few choices under $50. The cheese and wine nights are a riot – ask someone to sing the cheese song before the night ends.

French. Dinner, Saturday tea. $86 and up

★★LALA ROKH
97 Mount Vernon St., Boston, 617-720-5511; www.lalarokh.com

It's impossible to separate cuisine from culture at this romantic, Persian-themed dining spot. The interior is dotted with old maps and artifacts from Iran, making it seem somewhat out of place along the cobblestoned streets of Beacon Hill. Nevertheless, owners (and siblings) Babak Bina and Azita Bina-Seibel have created a homey spot to serve Azerbaijan-style cuisine from the northwest corner of Iran. Bina-Seibel loves to dish out slow-roasted meats, smoky spices and pickled accompaniments. Decadent cream sauces bring inventive flavors to heart-warming native dishes like Addas Pollo (fork-tender veal sitting atop Basmati rice sweetened by dates, currants and caramelized onion). Don't leave without sampling the bite-sized Baklavettes, which resulted in sticky fingers and a thoroughly sated sweet tooth.

Persian. Lunch, dinner. $16-35

★★LA VERDAD

Lansdowne St., Boston, 617-421-9595; www.laverdadtaqueria.com

If the Mexican wrestling masks that adorn the tiled dining room don't give it away, the enormous bar and wall of tequilas will show you that this place is built for fun and frivolity. Chef Ken Oringer proves that you don't have to live south of the border to replicate authentic Mexican street food, and his efforts have not gone unnoticed, as crowds pack this hopping Mexican taqueria whether there's a game at Fenway or not. Tortillas are handmade, tacos are served with traditional salsas and toppings, and ingredients are all fresh and local, including turkey, housemade sausage, fish and tongue. The bar whips up a killer margarita along with a range of other tequila-laced cocktails. If you're thinking of grabbing a postgame taco or two, you're not alone; lines can get surprisingly long at the takeout counter. You're better off waiting for a seat inside.

Mexican. Lunch, dinner. $16-35

★★LES ZYGOMATES

129 S St., Boston, 617-542-5108; www.winebar.com

The energy inside Les Zygomates (named for the facial muscles you use when smiling), will get you grinning despite your best efforts. This French-inspired wine bar boasts a split personality: One room offers a quiet retreat in which to grab a glass of wine and a light snack, while the other delivers lively jazz-fueled dinners night after night. The stage in the jazz room is on risers, so it sits higher than the tables, making every seat a good one for everyone to enjoy the nightly serenades. It's hard to imagine mediocre steak fries coming out of this classic French kitchen, and you won't have reason to with perfectly crispy fries and a reliably juicy cut of beef. The oysters on the half shell are another good bet. Prepare yourself for a big endeavor with the tome of a wine list, but the extensive by-the-glass section includes a reduced-price, three-ounce pour in case you want to try a few different varietals.

French. Lunch, dinner. Bar. Reservations recommended. Closed Sunday. $36-85

★★★LOCKE-OBER

3 Winter Place, Boston, 617-542-1340; www.lockeober.com

Chef Lydia Shire took over this aging, opulent city icon in 2001 and has managed to breathe a life back into the space without forgoing its Old World charm. Locke-Ober has long been a stomping ground for foodies, financiers and politicians (think stodgy old men who love mahogany) who fill the multi-roomed cavern; you can practically hear the echoes of Boston's 19th-century movers and shakers while perched at the front-room bar. The chef's updated take on traditional American fare has helped revive some Yankee classics such as clams casino and tiny pots of garlicky escargot. Shire also manages to give passé dishes like beef Stroganoff, made with hand-cut egg noodles or onion soup gratinée, a bit of an edge. You won't be hard-pressed to find a few octogenarians in the crowd, but if they are dining here after all those years, it must be worth it.

American. Lunch, dinner. Bar. Reservations recommended. Closed Sunday. $36-85

★★★MAMMA MARIA

3 N. Square, Boston, 617-523-0077; www.mammamaria.com

There may be a trattoria in every North End storefront, but picking one that actually goes beyond red sauce is a chore. Head straight to Mamma Maria, a romantic spot (at least when it's less crowded) that tries hard to veer away from cheesy pastas and generic meat sauces. The dining rooms are packed into a 19th-century brick townhouse (close to Paul Revere's house) that gives you an excuse to cozy up to someone you like. In the winter, the menu is filled with slowly braised sauces and meats to warm your bones; spring and summer find locally sourced asparagus, ramps and mushrooms tossed into a number of pastas and salads. If you're a sucker for classics, order the pasta Bolognese with homemade porcini pasta. Even your grandma can't make it this good.

Italian. Dinner. Bar. $36-85

★★★MASA

439 Tremont St., Boston, 617-338-8884; www.masarestaurant.com

Masa is a spicy little spot near the edge of the South End. In the bar area, which overlooks a chandelier-lit dining room, you can find killer margaritas and one of the city's most expansive tequila lists. They'll mix just about anything with the spirit, so be prepared for a good night out. The dining room is decorated with exposed brick walls, large mirrors, black-and-white checkered floors and flowing cream drapes. Settle into the oversized booths for a tapas combo platter of shredded chicken taquitos and a spicy ahi tuna ceviche. The brunch menu is also full of tapas-sized dishes, and late on Thursday nights the tables are pushed aside to make room for salsa dancing.

Southwestern. Dinner. Bar. Reservations recommended. Outdoor seating. $16-35

★★★★MERITAGE

70 Rowes Wharf, Boston, 617-439-3995, 800-752-7077; www.bhh.com

If the custom-made wine cases—and the 12,000 bottles they hold—flanking both ends of the contemporary rectangular room are any indication, they take their wine seriously. With more than 850 varietals, you'll be hard-pressed not to find a bottle that suits your mood and your menu selection. The carte du jour is even organized by styles, such as sparkling and full-bodied whites, to ensure that you get the most from your food and drink (and if you get confused, the affable and wine-versed staff is eager to assist). Chef Daniel Bruce incorporates local ingredients into his menu as often as possible, with dishes like maple-smoked salmon croustades with caramelized fennel and French bean salad (ideal with a crisp glass of prosecco), and wood-grilled filet mignon with soft whipped potatoes and horseradish onion cream (a perfect match for a rich cabernet). Every menu item can be ordered as a small or large plate, so feel free to share and taste more than a few.

International. Dinner, Sunday brunch. Bar. Reservations recommended. Closed Monday. $36-85

★★★METROPOLIS CAFÉ
584 Tremont St., Boston, 617-247-2931; www.metropolisboston.com

South Enders rely on Metropolis Café to feed them homey comfort fare with inspired touches. It's a tiny spot set in an old ice-cream parlor (the tin ceiling is still in place) and can feel cramped and comfortable all at once. Tables are nudged close together and servers can have a hard time maneuvering the crowded space, but that becomes a non-issue once you bite into something from the tightly edited menu. Specialties like horseradish-crusted salmon and rigatoni sprinkled with sausage are best at dinner, and you can't beat a bowl of the warm roasted-carrot soup with a touch of cilantro-jalapeño salsa on a cold afternoon. If you don't mind a wait (not a surprise with little more than a dozen tables), come for the acclaimed weekend brunch where the spicy huevos rancheros (fried eggs, tortillas and salsa) will start your day off with a bang.

American. Lunch, dinner, Saturday-Sunday brunch. $16-35

★★★THE METROPOLITAN CLUB
1210 Boylston St., Chestnut Hill, 617-731-0600; www.metclubandbar.com

Think all-American steakhouse next door meets modern urban night club and you've got The Met Club. Chef Todd Winer's specialties include a Myer rib eye for two, a bone-in veal parmigiana and a halibut for two with Italian pistachio butter. The sultry bar and lounge offers sexy cocktails and tempting snacks, including white garlic lobster pizza and Tokyo Kobe miniwiches.

Steak. Sunday brunch, lunch, dinner. Bar. Reservations recommended. $36-85

★★★MIEL
510 Atlantic Ave., Boston, 617-747-1000, 800-327-0200;
www.intercontinentalboston.com

This hotel brasserie is one of the few spots you can dine after 1 a.m. in this town, as it's actually open 24 hours a day, every day of the week. Named for the French word for honey, Miel shrugs off traditional hotel restaurant cues and instead acts as a fun, waterfront gathering spot for both guests and the building's residents. Inside, the spacious, country-yellow room is replete with wispy cream curtains and blond wood, and anchored by a huge wall of olive oil bottles. The menu is classically French with Pistou soup and bouillabaisse, and there's a daily raw bar. The chef does his best to insert local ingredients into the mix, but tends to lean on Gallic favorites—lavender, honey, olive oil—when making up the hearty dishes. Few things taste better after midnight than the Parisian crepe filled with ham and Swiss and topped with roquette, but if you can keep swinging until 5 a.m., the banana-nut French toast off the breakfast menu truly is the perfect nightcap.

French. Breakfast, lunch, dinner, late-night. Bar. Reservations recommended. Outdoor seating. $36-85

★MIKE'S CITY DINER
1714 Washington St., Boston, 617-267-9393; www.mikescitydiner.com

Bring your appetite to this no-frills diner. Locals line up early for a first-come, first-served table where you can dig into heaping portions of pancakes, scrambled eggs, hash and other classic dishes. The prices are rock-bottom, which makes this place a favorite of everyone from the mayor to the local cops who work the neighborhood.

American. Breakfast, lunch. $15 and under

★★★MISTRAL

223 Columbus Ave., Boston, 617-867-9300; www.mistralbistro.com

Mistral makes no apologies for its overdone décor and increasingly pricey food. It is, after all, still a favorite spot for Boston's beautiful set. The vaulted dining room is long and massive; towering arched windows flood the space with natural light and modernist accents. Chef/owner Jamie Mammano makes the food approachable but still throws in fussy details like a decadent foie gras and Dover sole. Mostly, guests come for his grilled thin-crust pizzas, spicy tuna tartare and the colorful cocktails. The bar is packed on weekends and there is an outstanding wine list to go along with Mammano's sophisticated cuisine. If noise is an issue, look elsewhere—weekends can get cacophonous.

French, Mediterranean. Dinner. Bar. Reservations recommended. $36-85

★★★MOOO RESTAURANT

XV Beacon Hotel, 15 Beacon St., Boston, 617-670-2515; www.mooorestaurant.com

Take your conventional idea of a steakhouse, turn it on its head, and you might get Mooo. (The name alone should be a hint). This restaurant is tucked inside XV Beacon Hotel and feels more like an urban French boîte than a place to dive into a plate of meat. The dishes are refined, but stick to steakhouse norms like massive portions and à la carte offerings. There are notable exceptions: alongside the standby filet and ribeye are soy-glazed short-ribs and skillet-roasted Cornish game hen. If you're on an expense account, live large with the $120 Kobe beef sirloin; if you're not, the Kobe dumpling for $19 will still satisfy. The notorious wine cellar made it mostly intact (you can still order ancient bottles that cost well into the thousands), but have added a few more affordable options to the list.

Steakhouse. Lunch, dinner. Reservations recommended. $36-85

★★MYERS + CHANG

1145 Washington St., South End, 617-542-5200; www.myersandchang.com

Bright, funky and colorful, this contemporary Chinese diner is the vision of chef Joanne Chang, who also owns Flour Bakery, and her husband Christopher Myers (of Radius and Via Matta). The concept is simple: easy, homestyle Chinese cuisine served all day long. Some menu items may appear to mimic what you'd find at a traditional takeout joint, but the similarities stop there. The scallion pancakes are grease-free and the pork stir-fry is served with crispy sweetbreads. Priced well below $20, most dishes are great for sharing, so you'll often find large groups passing around platters of food. At lunchtime it feels like a quiet café, but when the lights dim, the music goes up and it becomes something of a party scene.

Chinese. Lunch, dinner. Bar. $16-35

★★NEPTUNE OYSTER

63 Salem St, Boston, 617-742-3474; www.neptuneoyster.com

Dropping an oyster bar into the Italian-heavy North End might have been a gamble, but owners Jeff and Kelli Nace came out on top. The postage-stamp-size room has fewer than 30 seats (most of which are along the gleaming bar), but mirrors on the walls covered in the daily specials make it feel spacious. Behind the bar, servers put out frosty beers and chilled white wines while sharing space with the shucker, who rips through shells with amazing speed. Oyster varieties change daily and staples like the hot and buttery lobster roll or Cioppino, a tomato-based seafood stew, are year-round favorites. Self-proclaimed burger aficionados should try the Neptune Burger, a juicy beef patty topped with flash-fried oysters if only for its originality.

Seafood. Lunch, dinner. Bar. $16-35

★★★★NO. 9 PARK

9 Park St., Boston, 617-742-9991; www.no9park.com

The classic, dark-wood floors and cream-colored booths inside this historic Beacon Hill townhouse may not scream excitement. That reaction is reserved for the food, as award-winning chef Barbara Lynch (of B&G Oysters LTD and The Butcher Shop) uses local produce to churn out some of the city's most celebrated fare. She plays with both Italian and French techniques, giving herself the freedom to constantly re-create the contemporary menu, but a few winning dishes never stray far from the list: the prune-stuffed gnocchi topped with a healthy serving of seared foie gras and the crispy pork belly with braised Belgian endive and jalapeño aioli. The whole staff is trained under wine director Cat Silirie, so every server poses as a de facto sommelier ready with the story behind just about every bottle on the list. The bar staff, meanwhile, is helping lead a revival of the city's cocktail scene. The smooth vodka-lime Palmyra is a local favorite.

French, Mediterranean. Lunch, dinner. Bar. Reservations recommended. Closed Sunday. $36-85

★★★THE OAK ROOM

138 St., James Ave., Boston, 617-267-5300; www.theoakroom.com

The Oak Room is so richly elaborate and over the top that you might feel like you are walking into a staged murder mystery dinner theater. The baroque woodwork, intricately carved plaster ceiling and heavy burgundy drapes can be imposing. While it's hard not to be overshadowed by the décor, the food holds its own with winning dishes such as châteaubriand (this is a steakhouse, after all) with asparagus and a béarnaise sauce, and wild boar chops atop a cranberry-and-goat cheese tart. Hearty grilled fish, oysters Rockefeller and clams casino round out the (semi) lighter side. The bar and lounge are often flush with visitors checking out the constantly changing cocktail list. Order yourself a classic martini; it's served in a carafe that's chilled in a bucket of ice.

American. Breakfast, lunch, dinner, Sunday brunch. Bar. Children's menu. Reservations recommended. $36-85

★★★OLIVES

10 City Square, Charlestown, 617-242-1999; www.toddenglish.com

Chef Todd English's original restaurant still wows diners, despite the fact that he's not behind the stove nearly as much as he used to be. With 20 restaurants around the world and TV appearances galore, he's a bit busy these days. Instead, there's a team of devoted chefs pumping out his signature Mediterra-

nean cuisine from the open kitchen (you can reserve a table nearby to watch the action firsthand, as long as you don't mind shouting over the cacophony of kitchen rumbling). The high ceilings and pack-them-in mentality in the sleek dining room do not help the noise factor, but when food tastes this good, who cares? Dishes are spiked with regional ingredients like anchovies, feta cheese and, of course, olives, and the wood-grilled meats carry a pleasant, fire-roasted flavor. You'd be crazy not to try the signature classic-cut French fries, perfectly paired with any of the numerous (and slightly overpriced) wines by the glass.
Mediterranean. Dinner. $36-85

★★★O YA

9 East St., Boston, 617-654-9900; www.oyarestaurantboston.com
After opening O Ya, a tiny, modern den of Japanese treasures, chef/owner Tim Cushman quickly became the darling of local and national food writers. It's easy to see why: His fanciful take on Japanese cuisine, and sushi in particular, can be down-right mind-blowing. The dishes are bite-sized, for the most part, and involve complex ingredient pairings like foie gras with balsamic chocolate Kabayaki and Santa Barbara sea urchin with blood oranges and fresh wasabi. The presentation is as precise as the food is fresh, with dishes looking nearly too pretty to touch. Cushman's wife, Nancy, has crafted a sensational sake list to further rival the cuisine. Just be prepared: You'll reach deep into your pockets for such an extreme gustatory experience.
Japanese. Dinner. Bar. $86 and up

★★★PARKER'S

60 School St., Boston, 617-227-8600; www.omnihotels.com
Charles Dickens and Ralph Waldo Emerson ate here when they were in town, and John F. Kennedy's grandfather made Parker's the de facto headquarters of Massachusetts pols. The historical spot still attracts a cross-section of diners with a combination of classic and modern fare: steak au poivre with flaming tableside presentation is offered alongside pomegranate-glazed chicken, and salad selections include a "retro" chilled iceberg wedge and an arugula salad with pancetta, Parmesan and lemon-basil oil.
American. Breakfast, lunch, dinner. Bar. Children's menu. Reservations recommended. Closed Sunday. $36-85

★★PHO REPUBLIQUE

1415 Washington St., Boston, 617-262-0005; www.phorepublique.net
One of the first restaurants in the South End to try fusion cuisine, Pho Republique is still a neighborhood favorite. The atmosphere exemplifies Asian chic with walls dripping in flashy, graffiti-style characters, with low-lit lanterns dangling from above. The cocktails alone are worth the visit; many are mind-numbingly potent and made with fresh ingredients, like their mango martini. There's also a stellar sake selection that pairs well with the broad mix of noodles, spring rolls and curry dishes. Platters of dim sum go out to tables of diners seeking family-style portions and inexpensive (but tasty) snack food. It gets rowdy as the music volume increases toward the early morning hours, but the scene is a solid spot for group gatherings and people-watching.
Pan-Asian. Dinner, late-night. Bar. $16-35

★★★PIGALLE

75 Charles St. South, Boston, 617-423-4944; www.pigalleboston.com

By naming his restaurant after the red light district in Paris, chef/owner Marc Orfaly gives away his penchant for the exotic, but it comes out in his cooking, too. Though the menu reads like a traditional French bistro (duck liver terrine, halibut en croûte), a closer look shows a flair for Asian and sometimes Italian touches (wasabi oil and Chinese greens are served alongside that halibut). The atmosphere is intimate and personal (think tiny tables and low lighting), and the waitstaff is as attentive as they come in a French bistro. At the bar, snack-sized plates of Arancini are on offer beside santapan, a sampling of Malaysian street food. Reining things in is general manager Kerri Foley (Orfaly's wife), who maintains an immaculately crumb-free dining room.

French. Dinner. Closed Monday. $36-85

★★★RADIUS

8 High St., Boston, 617-426-1234; www.radiusrestaurant.com

Radius feels as moneyed and elitist as the power brokers and financial analysts who frequent it. The space is slick, modern, and appropriately, round, with a dining room flecked with silver and red hues, minimalist wall décor and an über-chill downstairs lounge. Unusually handsome servers in perfectly pristine suits take their jobs seriously, acting more like hosts than food-and-drink caddies. While co-owners Christopher Myers and Esti Parsons maintain the too-cool-for-school atmosphere, co-owner Michael Schlow stays busy keeping the restaurant on any Boston gourmand's short list. His inspired French cooking is spare (read: no heavy sauces, just bright, clean flavors and fresh, seasonal ingredients) and he flirts with techniques like foams and emulsions. Mostly, though, he sticks to what he knows best, like preparing simple fish dishes; he serves a trio of ceviches from time to time and does inspired work on a filet of cod. And Schlow's signature burger—it's only available at the bar—has gotten loads of press for its juicy, pure beef flavor. While you're there, order up a raspberry beret cocktail to go with your burger. It's a devilishly good and seriously addictive blend of Bombay gin, lime, raspberry purée and fresh ginger beer.

French. Lunch, dinner. Bar. Reservations recommended. Closed Sunday. $36-85

★★THE RED FEZ

1222 Washington St., Boston, 617-338-6060; www.theredfez.com

Housed inside a cavernous warehouse, this Moroccan-tiled gem was reborn in 2002 (it had been shuttered for many years after its heyday as a '70s hot spot). The space is surprisingly intimate with Persian rugs, exposed brick walls and arched windows. Laid-back diners fill up on a long list of Middle Eastern mezzes like spinach pie and falafel. There's a romantic outdoor patio off to the side that can get pretty festive on weekend nights. Jazz fans come in swarms for the Fez's Sunday brunch, where a mere sip of the strong Turkish coffee will have you amped all afternoon.

Middle Eastern. Dinner, late-night, Sunday brunch. Bar. Outdoor seating. $16-35

★★RISTORANTE TOSCANO

47 Charles St., Boston, 617-723-4090; www.toscanoboston.com

Thanks to a much-needed makeover, Ristorante Toscano, a Beacon Hill institution, has been revived into a sophisticated Italian café. Massive antique doors now decorate the space, and a glassed-encased wine cave—housing more than 1,000 bottles of Tuscan vino—sits at the heart of it all. At lunch, the floor-to-ceiling windows open out to the street, sending a breeze through the wood-floored room. The Caprese pie presents imported buffalo mozzarella and beefsteak tomatoes that look almost too pretty to eat. An all-Italian wine list leans heavily toward reds to match the flavorful food; you can sample many by quartino, which is about a third of a bottle.

Italian. Lunch, dinner. Bar. Reservations recommended. Closed Sunday. $16-35

★★★ROCCA KITCHEN & BAR

500 Harrison Ave., Boston, 617-451-5151; www.roccaboston.com

Inspired by her own Ligurian heritage, restaurateur Michela Larson built this space with wind-swept cliffs and the colors of a coastal town in mind. One of the few places that offers free parking in the South End, the two-story modern interior provides a low-key dinner venue for the growing neighborhood. The spacious outdoor patio with yellow shade umbrellas and chairs that are actually comfortable fills up with locals on warm afternoons, and the horseshoe-shaped bar is ideal for parties of one. The cuisine is based on Liguria as well; the warm ricotta is a terrific starter and the pesto is made by hand. There are a few housemade pastas (we particularly loved the hand rolled trofie), whole-roasted fish and soul-satisfying entrées like pork chop Milanese. Because most dishes top out around $25, there's plenty of room in your wallet for dessert, and you can't go wrong with the gelato—no surprise there.

Italian. Dinner. $36-85

★★★SAGE

1395 Washington St., Boston, 617-248-8814; www.sageboston.com

South End foodies were thrilled when Sage outgrew its North End digs and moved into a more spacious home on Washington Street. The move didn't diminish the charm. It's still a cozy place with a bustling bar and a simple, elegant dining room. Chef/owner Anthony Susi (who grew up in the North End, where his father ran a butcher shop) has more room (in the kitchen and elsewhere) to get his modern Italian fare into the hungry mouths of Italophiles. Dive into a plate of his hand-rolled gnocchi, which is doused in a seasonal sauce, or the creamy lobster fettuccine. If time is an issue, grab a spot at the bar and have your way with a few small plates (the bruschetta topped with Kobe beef and stuffed green peppers was our favorite). The wine list is mostly Italian and has some great bargains.

Italian. Dinner. Reservations recommended. Closed Sunday. $36-85

★★★SCAMPO

The Liberty Hotel, 215 Charles St., Boston, 617-224-4000; www.scampoboston.com

Chef Lydia Shire has made waves with her inventive ingredients and playful presentations, all while launching the culinary careers of dozens of Boston

chefs. Her most recent project, Scampo ("escape" in Italian) is set inside the Liberty Hotel, a former jailhouse turned über-cool destination. The atmosphere is anything goes, mixing casual hotel guests and leather-clad Euro-types with unassuming foodies. The fare is whimsical, yet rustic, and remains firmly rooted in Italy. Crispy brick-oven pizzas are layered with mounds of ingredients, and the spaghetti is tossed with everything from tomatoes to lobster. They also make their own mozzarella on site. Copper and brick outfit the room, which is an open configuration that makes it easy to see and be seen, even from the open kitchen. Escaping may prove to be more difficult.
Italian, American. Lunch, dinner. $36-85

★★SONSIE

327 Newbury St., Boston, 617-351-2500; www.sonsieboston.com
Despite its location at the scruffy lower end of Newbury Street, Sonsie lures high-brow Euro sophisticates on a regular basis. It also attracts stars like Matt Damon and Ben Affleck, who stop by when they're in town. The food is not bad, either, but make no mistake: people come for the scene. Shoppers crowd the window-front café tables, which look out over Newbury Street, to nosh on crispy, focaccia pizzas and spicy Cubano sandwiches; the ever-popular brunch is the perfect opportunity to people-watch at a leisurely pace. The dinner menu offers something for everyone. The wok-seared salmon with coconut green curry and purple sticky rice is tasty, and a side of deep-fried smoked onion rings are worth the calories every time. A swank little wine bar with a dozen tables has opened downstairs.
International. Breakfast, lunch, dinner, late-night, brunch. Bar. Reservations recommended. Outdoor seating. $16-35

★★★SORRELINA

1 Huntington Ave., Boston, 617-412-4600; www.sorellinaboston.com
It's hard to decide which lends more to the wow factor at this Back Bay restaurant: the sleek, contemporary design or the sophisticated Italian food. Cork floors, a white quartzite-terrazzo bar and low banquettes (all the better to see and be seen) make the room decidedly sexy. Though classics like spaghetti or veal Milanese make an appearance on the menu, chef/owner Jamie Mammano (also the talent behind Boston's Teatro, the Federalist and Mistral restaurants) dresses them up with gulf shrimp and chiles or saffron risotto. The exemplary wine list is punctuated by hard-to-find Italian bottles and balanced out with American and French selections.
Italian. Dinner. $36-85

★★STELLA

1525 Washington St., Boston, 617-247-7747; www.bostonstella.com
The South End had already reached critical mass of style when chef/owner Evan Deluty opened this hip Italian café. That didn't seem to matter, as locals still arrived in droves to slip into the cool all-white interior and sample dishes such as handmade linguine tossed with asparagus and a plain poached egg on top. Deluty's simply prepared pastas, pizzas and salads are brimming with local produce and heaps of flavor. The patio, accented by lemon-yellow umbrellas, carries a more casual vibe. The bar consistently buzzes from early evening until well past midnight (the kitchen stays open until 1:30 a.m.), and

the newly opened café next door provides sandwiches and take-away salads for daytime diners. Perhaps the best part of the meal is the bill, because few items cost more than $20. Go ahead, order that second glass of grappa.
Italian. Lunch, dinner. $16-35

★★TAPEO
266 Newbury St., Boston, 617-267-4799; www.tapeo.com
This tile-lined space captures the spirited atmosphere of a classic Madrid tapas bar, and the food is bona fide Spanish. Your first decision may be your easiest: order a pitcher of sangria. From there, the enormous list of hot and cold plates can be overwhelming, but you're unlikely to make a wrong move. Cold plates of jamón Serrano (sliced, cured ham) and anchovy fillets are tempting starters; larger hot plates like sizzling gambas al ajillo (garlic shrimp), patatas bravas (spicy potatoes) and platters of paella Valenciana are great for large groups to share. You'll often find celebratory crowds taking up large tables; for something quieter, request a corner table in the upstairs dining room. On a warm afternoon, the outdoor patio is aflutter with sangria-sipping people-watchers. If the wait is long, throw your name on the list and pass the time window-shopping.
Spanish, tapas. Dinner. Bar. Reservations recommended. Outdoor seating. $16-35

★★TARANTA
210 Hanover St., Boston, 617-720-0052; www.tarantarist.com
Peruvian and Italian cuisines collide, oddly enough, in Venezuela, which is where chef/owner Jose Duarte learned to prepare both. The menu at Taranta seamlessly fuses these two cultures into a cooking style that's utterly unique to the North End. Leaning heavily on Italian basics, Duarte plays with Peruvian ingredients in dishes like a cassava root gnocchi served with a slow-braised lamb ragout, and the espresso-crusted filet mignon over parsnip purée and sautéed escarole. Rare in the North End, this tri-level space feels expansive and open with exposed brick walls and windows overlooking Hanover Street (though the atmosphere does no favors for the noise level at times). Duarte has made strides to become one of the city's first green restaurants, and features a number of organic and biodynamic wines on his well-priced list.
Peruvian, Italian. Dinner. $36-85

★★TERRAMIA RISTORANTE
98 Salem St., Boston, 617-523-3112; www.terramiaristorante.com
Set on the corner of a tucked-away street in the North End, this perpetually crowded, 39-seat spot is as authentic as it gets with its white tablecloths, modern Italian fare and a long waiting list on busy nights. The menu's high notes involve updated classics enhanced with regional ingredients, such as creamy risotto peppered with chunks of Maine lobster or open-faced, seafood-filled ravioli. The cramped seating and gradually rising noise levels shouldn't thwart you; instead, prepare for jostling, lean in close and dive into three or four courses of well-prepared plates. Just don't plan on sticking around for dessert; they don't serve it.
Italian. Dinner. $36-85

★★★TOP OF THE HUB
800 Boylston St., Boston, 617-536-1775; www.topofthehub.net

If sweeping views are your thing, you'll want to add Top of the Hub to your short list of Boston must-visits. Located in Back Bay, this special-occasion spot specializes in elegant and romantic dining on the top floor of the Prudential building. The New American menu takes some chances, but for the most part stays true to the seasons, featuring a wide selection of fish, game, pork and beef. Main courses, such as the slow-roasted pork tenderloin (enough to feed a family of four), are ample; be prepared to share.

American. Lunch, dinner. Bar. Reservations recommended. $36-85

★★TORO
1704 Washington St., Boston, 617-536-4300; www.toro-restaurant.com

After running the kitchen at Clio for 10 years, chef Ken Oringer got antsy and decided to open a Spanish tapas bar as a side project. Inspired by his many travels to that country, he's crafted a menu filled with Spanish favorites like Iberian jamón and salt-crusted sea bass, as well as Kobe beef sliders and grilled corn smothered in aged Cotija cheese. The sangria is good, but the mojitos are better, and a nice selection of Spanish wines is listed on a chalkboard and served in standard juice glasses. Hipsters settle in beside suburbanites who have traveled far for the well-priced food in the brick-walled space, while everything from salsa music to Pearl Jam gets piped in through the sound system. Snagging a seat on the patio in summer is challenging, but worth the wait.

Spanish. Lunch, dinner, Sunday brunch. $36-85

★★TREMONT 647/SISTER SOREL
647 Tremont St., Boston, 617-266-4600; www.tremont647.com

Tremont 647 is a cozy neighborhood bistro known for its creative cocktail offerings and a menu of comfort food (lobster mac 'n' cheese is a standout). Next door is Sister Sorel, an equally welcoming bar with a few café tables and menu of small plates and sandwiches. Both spots offer the famous pajama brunch, a long-standing event during which locals line up in their, yes, pajamas to dine on gingerbread pancakes, mimosas and more.

American. Dinner, brunch. Bar. Outdoor seating. $16-35

★★★TROQUET
140 Boylston St., Boston, 617-695-9463; www.troquetboston.com

Troquet owners Chris and Diane Campbell take their wine and food-pairing skills seriously. So it's no surprise that this bistro wine bar boasts one of the most comprehensive lists in the city. The atmosphere is sophisticated yet understated, with impressive views of Boston Common and the State House. In contrast with the exhaustive wine list, chef Scott Hebert's food menu appears pleasantly limited, offering light dishes like East Coast halibut with lobster succotash and more substantial entrées such as pan-roasted rib steak with root vegetables and potato purée. A newly installed desserterie on the lower level is a relaxing spot to sample a smattering of creative sweet plates like the delicately crunchy milk chocolate mille feuille drizzled with a rum-and-honey reduction sauce.

French. Dinner. Bar. Reservations recommended. Closed Sunday-Monday. $36-85

★★★UNION BAR AND GRILLE

1357 Washington St., Boston, 617-423-0555; www.unionrestaurant.com

Union Bar and Grille's swank bar and black leather banquettes satisfy the South Enders who have a seemingly tireless appetite for just such an atmosphere (the funky, fruit juice-filled martinis may help; our vote goes to the apple blossom). The chef takes patrons' tastes seriously by putting out trendy dishes such as short-rib laced burgers and a rack of lamb drizzled with fig sauce; Union's 10K Tuna is a local favorite, appropriately named after the chef's spice rub won a contest for $10,000. Brunch here is as much a scene as dinner, with Bellinis and Pimosas (champagne with pomegranate purée) on just about every table alongside huge stacks of fluffy pancakes.

American. Dinner, Sunday brunch. Bar. $36-85

★★UNION OYSTER HOUSE

41 Union St., Boston, 617-227-2750; www.unionoysterhouse.com

As Boston's oldest restaurant, the Union Oyster House (which opened in 1826) can also be dubbed one of America's longest-running (it has the weathered wood floors to prove it). Still in its original building, the restaurant sits on the edge of Faneuil Hall and has been frequented by many notables including John F. Kennedy, whose favorite booth is labeled with a plaque. Today, Union Oyster sees more tourists than anything else, but for a creamy bowl of New England clam chowder or oysters on the half shell, it's a fine bet. The Lazy Man's Lobster is a popular dish for anyone who doesn't feel like donning a plastic bib, and the old-school raw bar is never short on oysters (or clams).

Seafood. Lunch, dinner, late-night. Bar. Children's menu. Reservations recommended. $16-35

★★★VIA MATTA

79 Park Plaza, Boston, 617-422-0008; www.viamattarestaurant.com

Via Matta may be the closest Boston will ever get to a celebrity hangout. Chef/owner Michael Schlow (who, with partners Christopher Myers and Esti Parsons, also owns Radius) attracts a line-up of big names like Billy Joel, Mick Jagger and Steven Tyler when they're in town. The place buzzes on celeb-less days, too (in fact, all of the hard surfaces make the dining room almost too loud). Schlow's take on simple Italian food includes big portions of chicken Milanese or tangy Sicilian tuna salad layered with white beans and caper berries. Afterward, indulge in the chocolate and hazelnut cheesecake with coconut gelato. There's a shaded outdoor patio hidden behind tall walls of climbing vines. The Enoteca/Caffe, a small candlelit bar at the front of the restaurant, dishes out late-night pizzas and other snacky small plates.

Italian. Lunch, dinner. Bar. Reservations recommended. Outdoor seating. Closed Sunday. $36-85

SPAS
★★★★★SPA AT MANDARIN ORIENTAL

Mandarin Oriental, 776 Boylston St., Back Bay, 617-535-8820;
www.mandarinoriental.com

Boston has always been a "hub" for luxury hotel experiences and the spa at the newly opened Mandarin Oriental is far from an exception. Sure, this

16,000-squarefoot space has all of the bells and whistles you'd expect: full-body massages, salt scrubs, anti-aging facials, spa pedicures. But, the Spa at Mandarin Oriental ups the ante with full-day location-specific programs like the Boston Breather that aims to counteract the stress of East Coast urban living with a welcoming foot ritual, Coffee and Frankincense Scrub, Aroma Stone Massage, facial of your choice and Luxury Mani-Pedi (plus lunch at the healthful Spa Café, since so many treatments are sure to leave you famished). If you need any more convincing that this is an above-and-beyond place, request a treatment in one of the spa suites, like the Mandarin Suite, which includes 700 square feet of ultimate privacy, a personal stone sauna, a soaking tub, two treatment tables (in case you want to invite a friend) and an enormous daybed for those who need yet another surface to recline on.

BRAINTREE

See also Boston

This city, just south of Boston, is the site of second President John Adams' estate. Though Adams was away for much of their marriage, first as a European ambassador during the Revolutionary War, and later in Philadelphia as president, his wife Abigail stayed behind and helped the farm and homestead flourish.

WHAT TO SEE
ABIGAIL ADAMS HOUSE

180 Norton St., Weymouth, 781-335-4205; www.abigailadamsbirthplace.org

This site is the birthplace of Abigail Smith Adams, daughter of a local clergyman, wife of President John Adams, mother of President John Quincy Adams.

July-Labor Day: Tuesday-Sunday.

ADAMS NATIONAL HISTORICAL PARK

135 Adams St., Quincy, 617-770-1175; www.nps.gov/adam

This park includes the birthplace of the second U.S. President John Adams, as well as Peacefield, his home following his retirement from Washington. The Stone Library was built in 1870 on the order of John Quincy Adams for the storage of the family's books and papers in a fireproof structure, and houses more than 14,000 volumes.

Daily, April-November, 9 a.m.-5 p.m.

GILBERT BEAN MUSEUM

786 Washington St., Braintree, 781-848-1640; www.braintreehistorical.org

This house contains 17th and 18th-century furnishings, military exhibits and local-historical displays.

Thursday-Saturday 10 a.m.-4 p.m. or by appointment.

WHERE TO STAY
★★★SHERATON BRAINTREE HOTEL

37 Forbes Road, Braintree, 781-848-0600, 800-325-3535; www.sheraton.com/braintree

Just 12 miles from Logan International Airport, near the JFK library and Bayside Exposition Center, the Sheraton Braintree is a good choice for those who want to visit Boston without paying the city's sky-high hotel rates. Relax in the indoor or outdoor pool, the sauna and the steam rooms or enjoy an invigorating workout at the extensive onsite health club that has racquetball, aerobics and Nautilus machines.

396 rooms. Restaurant, bar. $61-150

BREWSTER

See also Dennis

This quiet community on the inner arm of the Cape is dominated by miles of beautiful Cape Cod Bay beaches. Soft sand, gentle waves and plenty of shallow tide pools make Brewster an ideal family getaway.

WHAT TO SEE
CAPE COD MUSEUM OF NATURAL HISTORY

869 Main Street/Route 6A, Brewster, 508-896-3867; www.ccmnh.org

The museum displays exhibits on wildlife and ecology, and offers a library, lectures, field walks and trips to Monomoy Island.

February-March: Thursday-Sunday 11 a.m.-3 p.m.; April-May: Wednesday-Sunday 11 a.m.-3 p.m.; June-September: Daily 9:30 a.m.-4 p.m.; October-December: Wednesday-Sunday 11 a.m.-3 p.m.; Open only for special programs in January.

CAPE COD REPERTORY THEATER COMPANY

3299 Highway, 6A, Brewster, 508-896-1888; www.caperep.org

With both an indoor and outdoor theater, this troupe offers children's performances on Tuesday and Friday mornings in July and August. In addition, you'll find productions for the whole family in the outdoor theater in the woods near Nickerson State Park.

NEW ENGLAND FIRE & HISTORY MUSEUM

1439 Main St., Brewster, 508-896-5711

This six-building complex houses an extensive collection of firefighting equipment. Also on hand are a diorama of Chicago's 1871 fire, several antique engines, the world's only 1929 Mercedes-Benz fire engine, a life-size reproduction of Ben Franklin's firehouse, a 19th-century blacksmith shop, and the largest apothecary in the country (that's 664 gold-leaf bottles of medicine).

Memorial Day weekend-Labor Day, Monday-Saturday 10 a.m.-4 p.m., Sunday noon-4 p.m.; mid-September-Columbus Day, weekends.

NICKERSON STATE PARK

3488 Highway, 6A, Brewster, 508-896-3491; www.mass.gov

Nickerson State Park offers an unusual experience on Cape Cod: densely wooded areas that show no signs of the typical marshy Cape regions. The park has camping, challenging hiking trails, an eight-mile bike path, fishing, swimming, canoeing and bird-watching.

Daily.

OCEAN EDGE GOLF COURSE

2660 Highway, 6A, Brewster, 508-896-9000; www.oceanedge.com

This beautiful golf course, just a stone's throw from the ocean, offers 6,665 yards of manicured greens, plus five ponds for challenging play. Greens fees drop considerably in the off-season, and lessons from PGA pros are often available.

Daily; closed for snow and inclement weather.

WHERE TO STAY
★★★OCEAN EDGE RESORT

2907 Main St., Brewster, 508-896-9000, 800-343-6074; www.oceanedge.com

This sprawling 19th-century English country manor offers guests an oasis of comfort and privacy on Cape Cod Bay. Resort activities include golf, tennis, swimming, hiking and biking. Kids are welcome, but romantics shouldn't shy away; the estate is big enough for every type of family.

406 rooms. Restaurant, bar. $151-250

ALSO RECOMMENDED
BRAMBLE INN

2019 Main St., Brewster, 508-896-7644; www.brambleinn.com

This inn, located in a house built in the 1860s, feature rooms with four-poster beds and private baths. The cooked to order breakfast is a highlight.

8 rooms. No children under 8. Restaurant. Closed January-April. $61-150

OLD SEA PINES INN

2553 Main St., Brewster, 508-896-6114; www.oldseapinesinn.com

This grand inn is located in a building that was once a girls' boarding school. Rooms are decorated simply and filled with antiques.

24 rooms. No children under 8 (except in family suites). Complimentary breakfast. $61-150

WHERE TO EAT
★★★BRAMBLE INN

2019 Main St., Brewster, 508-896-7644; www.brambleinn.com

Chef/owner Ruth Manchester delivers creative cuisine and heartwarming hospitality at this cozy eatery in Brewster's historic district. The four quaint dining rooms, including an enclosed porch, are a comfortable setting for sampling the creative American cuisine (including espresso and spice rubbed filet mignon).

American menu. Dinner. Bar. Reservations recommended. Closed January-April. $36-85

★★BREWSTER FISH HOUSE

2208 Main St., Brewster, 508-896-7867;

This cozy restaurant specializes in local, fresh seafood. Entrées include grilled lobster with gnocchi, fava beans and corn, or grilled scallops. Because seating is first come, first served, arrive early to snag one of the 30 tables.

American, seafood. Lunch, dinner. Closed December-April. $36-85

★★★CHILLINGSWORTH

2449 Main St., Brewster, 508-896-3640, 800-430-3640; www.chillingsworth.com

The grand 300-year-old Chillingsworth Foster estate sprawls along the edge of the King's Highway. For the last 30 years, its restaurant has been synonymous with epicurean eating on Cape Cod. The formal dining rooms, furnished with antiques, are spread through the central house. The seven-course dinner is a contemporary interpretation of classic French cuisine: seared veal steak with truffle risotto, for example, or lobster with sautéed spinach and fennel. Plan to dress up and spend the whole evening tasting (quicker, lighter fare can be had in the more casual bistro on a glassed-in porch).

French. Lunch, dinner. Bar. Reservations recommended. Outdoor seating. Closed Monday; also December-mid-May. $36-85

BROOKLINE

See also Boston, Cambridge, Newton,

What started out as a commuter community has blossomed into a booming city in its own right. Directly to the east of Boston, Brookline began in the 1600s as a summer oasis for wealthy merchants and politicians. Centuries later, the town was still attracting notable Americans; Frederick Law Olmsted and John F. Kennedy both lived here (the latter's boyhood home is now open to the public). Today, Brookline's much-envied, Victorian-lined shady streets are home to moneyed families and one of the best school systems in the Boston area. The town's neighborhoods of Washington Square, Coolidge Corner and Brookline Village, with their shops, eateries and bars, attract younger residents and out-of-towners alike.

WHAT TO SEE
JOHN F. KENNEDY NATIONAL HISTORIC SITE

83 Beals St., Brookline, 617-566-7937; www.nps.gov/jofi

The birthplace and childhood home of the nation's 35th president has been restored to its 1917 state. Ranger-guided tours of the property are available. May-October, Wednesday-Sunday 10 a.m.-4:30 p.m.

WHERE TO STAY
★★HOLIDAY INN BOSTON-BROOKLINE

1200 Beacon St., Brookline, 617-277-1200; www.ichotelsgroup.com

An excellent alternative to staying in downtown Boston, this efficient hotel offers a quick commute into the city (the T's Green Line stop is right outside). If you're in town to see friends, visit the Longwood Medical area hospitals, or check out nearby Fenway Park, the area lets you skirt the maddening traffic that surrounds most Boston-area hotels. This hotel is nothing fancy, but it's basic and well-kept, with features like an indoor pool, a whirlpool, room service and shuttle service to select destinations in the city.

225 rooms. Fitness center. Pool. $151-250

WHERE TO EAT
★★★THE FIREPLACE

1634 Beacon St., Brookline, 617-975-1900; www.fireplacerest.com

Thanks to its yuppified neighborhood, the Fireplace can seem like a cross between *Friends* and *Cheers*, where everyone knows everyone else, and half the diners are just stopping to chat and sip a glass of Sancerre. Hungry patrons are devoted to the hearty fare—braised brisket, grilled halibut, gingerbread pudding—much of it made from scratch in the wood-fired oven or smoke box. The eponymous hearth provides welcome warmth and added coziness in winter months.

American. Lunch, dinner, brunch. Children's menu. $16-35

★★★FUGAKYU
1280 Beacon St., Brookline, 617-734-1268; www.fugakyu.net
Fugakyu stands out among all of Brookline's many sushi spots. Its Coolidge Corner location is huge and heavy on the blonde, wood-white screen décor. Larger parties can reserve private tatami rooms—complete with rice paper walls and sliding doors—and choose from a menu of soups, tempuras, stir-fries, noodles, pickle plates, sushi, sashimi, maki rolls and tableside braises. Diners rave about the tempura-fried green tea ice cream dessert topped with just a dab of red-bean paste.

Japanese, sushi. Lunch, dinner, late-night. Reservations recommended. Closed Sunday $16-35.

CAMBRIDGE
See also Boston

Across the Charles River from Boston, Cambridge seems a world away. Though connected to the state capital, and often lumped in with it geographically, the "People's Republic of Cambridge," as locals have christened it, has a decidedly different vibe. Famous for its universities (Harvard, M.I.T.), bustling squares and ethnically diverse residents (at least 80 different nations are represented by the city's public school kids), the area is a melting pot of people and ideas. The gritty, nightclub-filled streets of Central Square run into the vibrant back roads of Harvard Square and the mansion-lined Brattle Street, which in turn leads into family-friendly Huron Village. Farther to the east is Inman Square, a multicultural neighborhood overflowing with cafés, eateries and sweet little shops. Most of the city is easily accessible by public bus or train; those with more stamina should consider walking these historic, but very much alive, streets.

WHAT TO SEE
CAMBRIDGE ANTIQUE MALL
201 Monsignor O'Brien Highway, Cambridge, 617-868-9655; www.marketantique.com
Stroll through five floors of antique furniture, books, artwork, toys, clothing and more.

Tuesday-Sunday 11 a.m.-6 p.m.

CHRIST CHURCH
0 Garden St., Cambridge, 617-876-0200; www.cccambridge.org
Dating back to 1759, this Episcopal Church building is the oldest in Cambridge. The fine Georgian colonial designed by Peter Harrison was used as a barracks during the Revolution.

Daily.

FORMAGGIO KITCHEN

244 Huron Ave., Cambridge, 617-354-4750; www.formaggiokitchen.com

Whether you consider yourself a gourmet or a gourmand, you'll easily lose yourself in this culinary playground. With a selection of 200 artisan cheeses, fine pastas, international chocolates, exotic spices, mouthwatering snacks and Italian coffees, the famed Formaggio Kitchen is a food-lover's dream. Monday-Friday 9:00 a.m.-7:00 p.m., Saturday 9:00 a.m.-6:00 p.m., Sunday 10:00 a.m-4 p.m.

HARVARD MUSEUM OF NATURAL HISTORY

26 Oxford St., Cambridge, 617-495-3045; www.hmnh.harvard.edu

The Harvard Museum of Natural History is three museums in one: A botanical museum examines the study of plants, the museum of zoology explores the study of animals and a geological museum observes the study of rocks and minerals. All three explore the evolution of science and nature throughout time. Daily 9 a.m.-5 p.m.

HARVARD UNIVERSITY

24 Quincy St., Cambridge, www.harvard.edu;
Information center: 1350 Massachusetts Ave., Cambridge, 617-495-1573

America's oldest university was founded in 1636. Two years later, when a minister named John Harvard died and bequeathed half of his estate to the school, the college was named for him. The prototypical brick and quad-filled campus spans Harvard and Radcliffe colleges, as well as 10 graduate and professional schools.

HARVARD UNIVERSITY ART MUSEUMS

32 Quincy St., Cambridge, 617-495-9400; www.artmuseums.harvard.edu

Visit three museums in one: the Fogg Art Museum (includes wide-ranging collections of paintings and sculpture), the Busch-Reisinger Museum (features mostly German art) and the Arthur M. Sackler Museum (showcases ancient art, plus Asian and Islamic collections). Admission to one museum covers all three; allow a half-day for all. Free on Wednesdays and Saturdays until noon. Daily.

LIST VISUAL ARTS CENTER AT MIT

Wiesner Building, 20 Ames St., Cambridge, 617-253-4680; listart.mit.edu

The museum boasts changing exhibits of contemporary art. The MIT campus also has an outstanding permanent collection of outdoor sculpture, including works by Calder, Moore and Picasso, and significant architecture, with buildings by Aalto, Pei and Saarinen. October-June, daily.

LONGFELLOW NATIONAL HISTORIC SITE

105 Brattle St., Cambridge, 617-876-4491; www.nps.gov/long

This Georgian-style house, built in 1759, was Washington's headquarters during the 1775 siege of Boston, and later was Henry Wadsworth Longfel-

low's home from 1837 until his death in 1882.
Wednesday-Sunday, tours at 10:30-11:30 a.m. and 1-4 p.m.

MASSACHUSETTS INSTITUTE OF TECHNOLOGY
77 Massachusetts Ave., Cambridge, 617-253-1000; www.mit.edu
M.I.T. remains one of the greatest science and engineering schools in the world. On the Charles River, the campus' 135 acres house impressive neo-classic and modern buildings.
Monday-Friday.

MIT MUSEUM
265 Massachusetts Ave., Cambridge, 617-253-5927; web.mit.edu
Collections and exhibits interpret the Institute's social and educational history, developments in science and technology, and the interplay of technology and art.
Tuesday-Friday 10 a.m.-5p.m., Saturday-Sunday noon-5 p.m.; closed Monday.

PEABODY MUSEUM OF ARCHAEOLOGY AND ETHNOLOGY
11 Divinity Ave., Cambridge, 617-496-1027; www.peabody.harvard.edu
The Peabody Museum, one of the oldest anthropology museums in the world, traces human cultural history in the Western Hemisphere.
Daily.

RADCLIFFE COLLEGE'S SCHLESINGER LIBRARY CULINARY COLLECTION
10 Garden St., Cambridge, 617-495-8647; www.radcliffe.edu/schles
Through Radcliffe's culinary collection, you'll have access to more than 9,000 cookbooks. Although you can't borrow from the library, you can still tap into the books of some of the world's greatest chefs, including Samuel Narcisse Chamberlain, Julia Child and Sophie Coe.
Monday-Friday.

SPECIAL EVENTS
HEAD OF THE CHARLES REGATTA
2 Gerry's Landing Road, Cambridge, 617-868-6200; www.hocr.org
More than 300,000 spectators from all over the world descend on Boston for this three-mile rowing race that involves 7,000 athletes and 1,470 rowing shells. Olympic and World champions race each other on the Charles River, while countless fans tailgate and cheer along the shore.
Mid-October.

WHERE TO STAY
★★BOSTON MARRIOTT CAMBRIDGE
2 Cambridge Center, Cambridge, 617-494-6600, 800-228-9290; www.marriott.com
Busy Kendall Square provides the backdrop for this 26-story hotel. In fact, the Kendall/MIT subway stop is just downstairs, making jaunts to downtown Boston quick and easy. Try to lay claim to a room on one of the higher floors, for an impressive skyline view across the Charles River. All of the usual ac-

coutrements can be found in the comfortable guest rooms—down pillows, cable and high-speed Internet—but given the hotel's proximity to the best of both Cambridge and downtown, few guests spend their time holed up inside. 433 rooms. Restaurant, bar. $151-250

★★★CHARLES HOTEL

1 Bennett St., Cambridge, 617-864-1200, 800-882-1818; www.charleshotel.com

Celebrities, politicians and visiting dignitaries (not to mention the wealthy parents of Harvard students) all stay at the Charles, one of Boston's most beloved hotels. The guest rooms mix Shaker-inspired design with a multitude of modern amenities such as three two-line phones, Bose Wave radios, TVs in the bathrooms and more. Dine in either of its two restaurants, and be sure to tune into the sweet sounds of jazz at the Regattabar, where swinging national bands hit the stage. In winter, the hotel's courtyard becomes an ice-skating rink, while various community events, such as a farmer's market, take place here in the summer.

294 rooms. Restaurant, bar. Spa. Pets accepted. $251-350

★★★HOTEL MARLOWE

25 Edwin H. Land Blvd., Cambridge, 617-868-8000, 800-825-7140; www.hotelmarlowe.com

The Marlowe sets itself apart from other East Cambridge lodgings with its whimsical palette of crimson, deep blue and bright gold. Surrounded by luxury condos and a shopping mall, this modern hotel is less than a block from the Museum of Science. Amenities are top of the line (Frette linens, Aveda bath products), the in-room Sony PlayStations amuse youngsters, and the pet-friendly vibe is a big plus for animal lovers.

236 rooms. Restaurant, bar. Pets accepted. $251-350

★★★HYATT REGENCY CAMBRIDGE

575 Memorial Drive, Cambridge, 617-492-1234, 800-633-7313; www.hyatt.com

A riverside location makes the Cambridge Hyatt one of the chain's most distinctive Boston-area properties (though not as convenient to downtown); its unique ziggurat-shaped exterior rises grandly from the edge of the Charles. Inside it's mostly frills-free, but guests have the choice of rooms that face the interior atrium or ones with exterior views. Opt for the latter, especially if you can face the river and have a balcony; from upper floors there are excellent views of the Boston skyline. Amenities are fairly basic, but the rooms do have the chain's signature Hyatt Grand Bed, which almost guarantees a good night's rest.

469 rooms. Restaurant, bar. $151-250

★★★THE INN AT HARVARD

1201 Massachusetts Ave., Cambridge, 617-491-2222, 800-458-5886; www.theinnatharvard.com

Acclaimed postmodernist Cambridge architect Graham Gund showed great restraint in creating this neoclassical structure at the edge of Harvard Square. Guest rooms have a casual, homey feel, but a four-story atrium turns the reception area into a soaring library and lounge area. The university frequently

books many of the rooms for visiting scholars and dignitaries; just be sure to make reservations months ahead of a graduation or alumni weekend.
111 rooms. Restaurant, bar. $151-250

★★★KENDALL HOTEL

350 Main St., Cambridge, 617-577-1300; www.kendallhotel.com

Once a Victorian firehouse, the Kendall Hotel is on the National Register of Historic Places and, though thoroughly updated, maintains much of its timeworn charm. Each room is individually decorated and features elements like bright quilts and antique furniture; it's a bit like sleeping at your great-aunt's house (without the mothballs). A new seven-story tower added eight more guest rooms and four one-bedroom suites, all featuring more modern décor, but the feel is still cozy and casual. Don't miss the included breakfast buffet of homemade pastries and other sugary treats. Dinner in the Black Sheep restaurant is surprisingly upscale, with a changing menu of local and organic fare.

77 rooms. Restaurant, bar. Complimentary breakfast. $151-250

★★★LE MERIDIEN CAMBRIDGE MIT

20 Sidney St., Cambridge, 617-577-0200; www.starwoodhotels.com/lemeridien

This high-tech-themed hotel identifies closely with the similarly named school, as it even incorporates printed circuit-board designs into the bedroom furniture. Predictably, the hotel is wired every which way, with lightning-quick Internet access and Sony PlayStations in all guest rooms. The spot also functions as a conference and meeting center for cutting-edge companies in media, biotech, robotics and computing.

210 rooms. Business center. Restaurant, bar. $151-250

★★★ROYAL SONESTA HOTEL BOSTON

40 Edwin Land Blvd., Cambridge, 617-806-4200, 800-766-3782;
www.sonesta.com/boston

Set on perhaps the most picturesque stretch of the Charles River, the Royal Sonesta provides guests with spectacular views—think sailboats silhouetted by the city skyline—and waterfront living. It also contains one of the area's best Italian eateries, Restaurant Dante, which has earned many accolades since opening in 2006. Extras like high definition TVs, hypoallergenic down blankets and complimentary shuttle service (to account for its out-of-the-way spot) make staying here relaxing and worry-free; a visit to the Royal Treatments spa chills guests out even further.

400 rooms. Restaurant, bar. Business center. $251-350

★★★SHERATON COMMANDER HOTEL

16 Garden St., Cambridge, 617-547-4800; www.sheraton.com

If a visit to Harvard is what brings you to the Boston area, you won't find a better home base than the Commander, a landmark since 1927. It's smack in the middle of the sprawling campus, alongside the Cambridge Common park. The suites, of course, are lovely and spacious, with Colonial-style furniture and down duvets, but the best value may be the Club rooms: Located on "preferred" floors, these rooms include upgrades like free fitness center access and a private lounge serving complimentary breakfast, hors d'oeuvres and cocktails.

175 rooms. Restaurant, bar. Business center. $151-250

WHERE TO EAT
★★CHEZ HENRI
1 Shepard St., Cambridge, 617-354-8980; www.chezhenri.com

This cozy bistro delivers a reliable sampling of French and Cuban fare, including a sublime classic Cuban sandwich piled high with pork and spicy mustard. Entrées include sautéed rainbow trout with parsnip purée and paella made with fresh local seafood. The cocktail menu is one of the highlights of a visit, with classics such as caipirinhas and mojitos made from fresh muddled fruit.

Cuban, French. Dinner. Bar. $36-85

★★★CRAIGIE ON MAIN
853 Main St., Cambridge, 617-497-5511; www.craigieonmain.com

One of the many joys that go along with eating chef Tony Maws' food is knowing that he put his full attention into every dish that leaves the kitchen. Vegetables are pickled in house and consommés are strained and re-strained for just the right clarity and flavor profile. The chef often hits nearby farmers markets to create "market menus" on the day items become available. He's fanatical about crafting dishes from scratch and using organic ingredients whenever possible, which only enhance his intensely flavored bistro-style dishes. A decent-sized wine list is filled almost completely with organic and biodynamic producers and the plethora of house wines are unique…in that they're actually good.

French menu. Dinner. Reservations recommended. Closed Monday-Tuesday; also late June-early July. $16-35

★★★DANTE
Royal Sonesta Hotel, 40 Edwin H. Land Blvd., Cambridge, 617-497-4200; www.restaurantdante.com

Though this terraced restaurant is hidden away in the back of a Cambridge hotel, it boasts one of the best views of the city from across the Charles River. The patio is a prime spot in the summer months (Dante has a July Fourth bash every year) for taking in chef Dante de Magistris' precisely prepared Italian-inspired menu. In the dining room, cream-colored walls, warm lighting and lounge-like chairs keep diners relaxing tableside for hours. With its symphony of Mediterranean ingredients, the menu jumps from region to region, offering duck, oysters, sweetbreads and a number of cheeses. Try the chef's tasting menu for a multicourse sampling of it all—de Magistris tailors it to each table depending on the night (and his mood). The small bar fills up on weekends as revelers imbibe on flashy (though tasty) cocktails like sparkling sangria and delectable cosmos.

Italian. Lunch, dinner. $36-85

★★EAST COAST GRILL & RAW BAR
1271 Cambridge St., Cambridge, 617-491-6568; www.eastcoastgrill.net

Chef Chris Schlessinger's ode to barbecue and seafood has been serving hungry Cantabrigians for almost 25 years. The menu runs the gamut from oak smoked pit barbecue in the form of ribs, brisket and shredded beef or pork sandwiches, to grilled spiced mahi mahi and grilled white pepper crusted tuna. Locals line up for the Sunday brunch, which includes a make-your-own Bloody Mary bar.

Seafood. Dinner, Sunday brunch. Bar. $16-35

★★★HARVEST

44 Brattle St., Cambridge, 617-868-2255; www.harvestcambridge.com

Harvest's rustic ambiance—pewter tableware, dried flowers, dark wood—is at odds with the building's modern exterior. The restaurant is housed in an office building tucked just off Harvard Square, but boasts one of the area's best outdoor patios for warm weather dining. Inside, classic American dishes (don't miss the nightly risotto) are served from an open kitchen in the family-friendly dining room.

American. Lunch, dinner, Sunday brunch. Children's menu. $36-85

★★★OLEANA

134 Hampshire St., Cambridge, 617-661-0505; www.oleanarestaurant.com

Mediterranean menus are a dime a dozen in the Boston area, but few chefs coax out the cuisine's diverse influences as well as Oleana's chef/owner Ana Sortun. She matches Middle Eastern almonds with herbs from Provence in a chicken dish, and branches out with the likes of a Basque-influenced venison with caramelized turnip. Regulars enjoy the scallops with basmati-pistachio pilaf from the menu. The outdoor patio and fireplace-lit indoor rooms are inviting.

Mediterranean. Dinner. Bar. Reservations recommended. Outdoor seating. $36-85

★★★★RIALTO

1 Bennett St., Cambridge, 617-661-5050; www.rialto-restaurant.com

After nearly 12 years inside the Charles Hotel, Rialto recently received a makeover, reopening as a posh, more-polished version of itself with plantation shutters and crisp white table linens. As always, chef Jody Adams shines in the kitchen, letting her Italian cuisine take center stage. A few of her signature dishes (grilled Wolfe's Neck sirloin and slow-roasted Long Island duck breast, to name a few) can't be taken off the menu because they're so popular. Instead, she's added a handful of modern Italian specialties like gnocchi with rabbit Bolognese and spaghetti with lobster. The wine list is easy to dip in and out of with a few 4-ounce offerings (though the price may have you thinking you deserve a bottle), and the lounge is now a happening spot to grab drinks and appetizers from the bar.

Mediterranean. Dinner. Bar. Reservations recommended. $36-85

★★★SALTS

798 Main St., Cambridge, 617-876-8444; www.saltsrestaurant.com

With just 40 seats, the dining room at Salts feels almost like a private dinner party. Neighboring tables are often close enough for diners to overhear each other's conversations, making the room feel cozy and intimate (but less than ideal for a private affair). Warm, tableside candles and fresh bouquets complete the romantic ambience. Chef Gabriel Bremer puts finessed touches on his French-inspired dishes. The lavender-honey, whole-roasted boneless duck feeds two, which makes it the most popular romantic dish on hand. Bremer also has a light touch with seafood, allowing the dayboat halibut or sea trout flavors to shine. His wife, Analia Verolo, runs the dining room with precision and grace.

Contemporary American. Dinner. Reservations recommended. Closed Sunday-Monday. $36-85

★★★UPSTAIRS ON THE SQUARE

91 Winthrop St., Cambridge, 617-864-1933; www.upstairsonthesquare.com
As if plucked from a scene in *Alice In Wonderland*, this fluffy, pink-and-purple tinged dining room has whimsical touches splashed throughout (jewel tones and odd angles are used excessively in the second-floor dining room). It's a celebratory space and the food compliments the atmosphere. Dishes arrive in a flourish with seasonal ingredients like sweet peas, fava beans and pickled accompaniments sprinkled throughout. The bacon-wrapped beef tenderloin with ramp spaetzle, heirloom carrots and cilantro is a local favorite, as is the sweet watermelon gazpacho with poached shrimp. The Monday Club Bar and Zebra Room on the first floor are more casual (and affordable), with elegant salads and pizzas on the menu. When weather allows, the restaurant sets up pink umbrellas on its tiny outdoor patio. If you're looking for a spot to clink china and stretch your pinkies, afternoon tea is a Saturday dream with savory sandwiches and a slew of sweet treats such as butterscotch pudding and zebra cakes.

French, American. Lunch, dinner, Saturday tea. $36-85

CHATHAM

See also Orleans

Chatham is among the hubs of the Cape's social scene. Though tourists are hard to distinguish from blue-blooded locals, look closely. Year-rounders are most likely the ones sipping lemonade on the porches of their comfortable estates that look out over Pleasant Bay and Nantucket Sound. Monomoy Island, an unattached sand bar that stretches 10 miles into the sea, was once a haunt of "moon-cussers," beach pirates who lured vessels aground with false lights.

WHAT TO SEE
CHATHAM LIGHT

Bridge and Main Streets, Chatham, 508-430-0628;
This quintessential Cape lighthouse has been through many incarnations and restorations, but has always offered a superb view of the Atlantic and the seals on the beach below.
Daily.

MONOMOY NATIONAL WILDLIFE REFUGE

Monomoy Island, Chatham, 508-945-0594; www.monomoy.fws.gov
The refuge is 2,750 acres of a bird-lover's paradise. The spectacle is greatest in spring, when the inhabitants exhibit bright plumage while breeding.

WHERE TO STAY
★★★THE BRADFORD OF CHATHAM

26 Cross St., Chatham, 508-945-1030, 888-242-8426; www.bradfordinn.com
This traditional New England inn has rooms decorated in colonial style with fireplaces and four-poster beds. The guest rooms are arranged in a series of nine white-washed Cape Cod houses along a central yard, and each of them include wireless access.
38 rooms. No children under 12. Complimentary breakfast. $151-250

★★★CHATHAM BARS INN

297 Shore Road, Chatham, 508-945-0096, 800-527-4884; www.chathambarsinn.com
Built in 1814, this grand Cape Cod landmark has managed to maintain most of its historic charm. The guest rooms have 180-degree views of Pleasant Bay, with well-maintained gardens and a private beach (one of the few in the area) just outside. The resort recently added a large, state-of-the-art spa that offers plenty of pampering.
205 rooms. Restaurant, bar. Beach. $351 and up

★★★CHATHAM WAYSIDE INN

512 Main St., Chatham, 508-945-5550, 800-242-8426; www.waysideinn.com
This classic village inn dates back to the 1860s, as evidenced by the lobby's original knotty pine flooring. The informal and cozy property has 56 large, clean and comfortable rooms (a few have private balconies and jetted tubs). The grounds are within walking distance to the water and the town center.
56 rooms. Restaurant, bar. $251-350

★★★★WEQUASSETT RESORT AND GOLF CLUB

On Pleasant Bay, Chatham, 508-432-5400, 800-225-7125; www.wequassett.com
This country inn-resort hybrid appeals to antique lovers and activity junkies alike. Located on 22 acres, the full-service spot overlooks Pleasant Bay and the Atlantic Ocean. Suites take a cosmopolitan slant on country décor. Take advantage of the prestigious private Cape Cod National Golf Club.
104 rooms. Restaurant, bar. Beach. Closed December-March. $351 and up

ALSO RECOMMENDED
CAPTAIN'S HOUSE INN

369-377 Old Harbor Road, Chatham, 508-945-0127, 800-315-0728;
www.captainshouseinn.com
Once a sea captain's estate, this pretty inn was built in 1839 and features period wallpapers, Williamsburg antiques and elegantly refined Queen Anne chairs. Many of the guestrooms are named for the ships that once sailed the nearby seas.
16 rooms. No children under 12. Complimentary breakfast. Pool. Fitness center. $151-250

WHERE TO EAT
★★CHATHAM SQUIRE

487 Main St., Chatham, 508-945-0945; www.thesquire.com
This local tavern is a reliable choice for creamy clam chowder, lobster ravi-

oli, steamed mussels and other seafood dishes. Live bands play on weekends, when the atmosphere becomes boisterous and busy.

Seafood. Lunch, dinner. Bar. Children's menu. $16-35

★★IMPUDENT OYSTER
15 Chatham Bars Ave., Chatham, 508-945-3545

This classic bistro serves an eclectic menu with a spotlight on fresh, local seafood. Entrées include steamed mussels in garlic and white wine and duck breast in blackberry port sauce.

Seafood. Lunch, dinner. Bar. Children's menu. Reservations recommended. $36-85

★★★★TWENTY-EIGHT ATLANTIC
Pleasant Bay Road, Chatham, 508-432-5400, 800-225-7125; www.wequassett.com

Black truffle risotto, truffled salmon tartare and a petite clambake are among the enticing entrées offered at this waterfront restaurant located in the Wequassett Resort. The large, open dining room features featuring wide views of Pleasant Bay.

American. Breakfast, lunch, dinner. Bar. Children's menu. Reservations recommended. Outdoor seating. Closed December-March. $36-85

CONCORD
See also Lexington

About as old-school New England as it gets, Concord (along with neighboring Lexington) boasts the title "Birthplace of the Republic." A litany of American literary greats—Ralph Waldo Emerson, Henry David Thoreau, Nathanial Hawthorne, Louisa May Alcott—once called this country town home. The area got its name from the unusual "peace and concord" between its colonial settlers and the native population in the 17th century.

WHAT TO SEE
CODMAN HOUSE
Codman Road, Lincoln, 781-259-8843

Originally a two-story, L-shaped Georgian mansion, this 1740 house was more than doubled in size by Federal merchant John Codman to imitate an English-country residence.

June-mid-October, 1st Saturday of each month, tours: 11 a.m.-4 p.m.

CONCORD MUSEUM
200 Lexington Road, Concord, 978-369-9763; www.concordmuseum.org

On display are period rooms, galleries of domestic artifacts and decorative arts chronicling the history of Concord from Native American habitation to the present. Exhibits include Ralph Waldo Emerson's study, Henry David Thoreau's belongings used at Walden Pond and Paul Revere's signal lantern.

January 5-March 26: Monday-Saturday 11 a.m.-4 p.m., Sunday 1-4 p.m.; March 27-January 4: Monday-Saturday 9 a.m.-5 p.m., Sunday 12-5 p.m.; extended Sundays during June-August 9 a.m.-5 p.m.

DECORDOVA MUSEUM & SCULPTURE PARK

51 Sandy Pond Road, Lincoln, 781-259-8355; www.decordova.org

This museum has an eclectic collection of paintings, posters, photography, sculpture and media. The Sculpture Park displays large contemporary works throughout 35 wooded acres. In early June, rain or shine, the museum sponsors the Annual Art in the Park Festival and Art Sale.

Tuesday-Sunday 11 a.m.-5 p.m.

DRUMLIN FARM EDUCATION CENTER

208 S. Great Road, Lincoln, 781-259-2200; www.massaudubon.org

There is a demonstration farm with domestic and native creatures, gardens and hayrides.

Tuesday-Sunday. March 1-October 31: 9 a.m.-5 p.m.; November 1-February 28: 9 a.m.-4 p.m., Closed on Monday holidays, Thanksgiving, Christmas Eve, Christmas Day and New Year's Day.

FRUITLANDS MUSEUMS

102 Prospect Hill Road, Harvard, 978-456-3924; www.fruitlands.org

The Fruitlands Farmhouse contains the furniture, the books, and the memorabilia of the Alcott family and the Transcendentalists. The Shaker Museum has furniture and handicrafts, and the Picture Gallery houses American primitive portraits and paintings by Hudson River School artists. The American Indian Museum shows prehistoric artifacts and Native American art.

Mid-May-October, Monday-Friday 11 a.m.-4 p.m., Saturday-Sunday until 5 p.m.

GREAT MEADOWS NATIONAL WILDLIFE REFUGE

Lincoln Street, and 73 Weir Hill Road, Sudbury Center, 978-443-4661; www.fws.gov/northeast/greatmeadows

Great Meadows combines terrific dirt trails with a wildlife refuge that attracts more than 200 species of birds, including the magnificent great blue heron.

Daily dawn-dusk.

GROPIUS HOUSE

68 Baker Bridge Road, Lincoln, 781-259- 8098; www.spnea.org

This was the family home of Bauhaus architect Walter Gropius and the first building he designed after arriving in the United States in 1937.

June-October, first Saturday of the month. Tours: 11 a.m.-4 p.m.

MINUTE MAN NATIONAL HISTORICAL PARK

174 Liberty St., Concord, 978-369-6993; www.nps.gov/mima

The park consists of 900 acres along the Battle Road between Lexington and Concord. Walk the 5½-mile Battle Road Trail, stop at Hartwell Tavern to see reenactments of colonial life and continue to North Bridge, the site of the first battle of the Revolutionary War (a.k.a., the shot heard round the world). Spring, summer, fall: daily; winter: Saturday-Sunday.

OLD MANSE

269 Monument St., Concord, 978-369-3909; www.thetrustees.org

This was the parsonage of Concord's early ministers, including Reverend William Emerson, Ralph Waldo Emerson's grandfather. Nathaniel Hawthorne lived here for a time and made it the setting for Mosses from an Old Manse.

Mid-April-October, Monday-Saturday 10 a.m.-5 p.m.

ORCHARD HOUSE

399 Lexington Road, Concord, 978-369-4118; www.louisamayalcott.org

Louisa May Alcott wrote *Little Women* here.

Open year-round, hours vary seasonally.

RALPH WALDO EMERSON HOUSE

28 Cambridge Turnpike, Concord, 978-369-2236; www.rwe.org/emersonhouse

This was Ralph Waldo Emerson's home from 1835 to 1882.

Mid-April-late October, Thursday-Saturday 10 a.m.-4:30 p.m., Sunday from 1 p.m.

SLEEPY HOLLOW CEMETERY

Bedford Street, Concord; www.concordma.gov

The Alcotts, Ralph Waldo Emerson, Nathaniel Hawthorne, Margaret Sidney, Daniel Chester French and Henry David Thoreau are buried here.

WALDEN POND STATE RESERVATION

915 Walden St., Concord, 978-369-3254; www.mass.gov/dcr/parks/walden

Henry David Thoreau, the American writer and naturalist, made Walden Pond famous when he lived in a nearby rustic cabin for two years. The cabin still stands and is part of the park's collection. A 1 ½-mile trail circles the pond, perfect for hiking, running or swimming. Get here early—before 11 a.m.—the lot closes once it's full.

Daily.

WAYSIDE

455 Lexington Road, Concord; www.nps.gov/archive/mima/wayside/Planfrm1.htm

Well-known 19th-century authors Nathaniel Hawthorne, the Alcotts and Margaret Sidney, author of the *Five Little Peppers* books, lived here.

May-October.

SPECIAL EVENTS
PATRIOT'S DAY PARADE

Concord, 978-369-3120, 888-733-2678; www.concordnet.org

Patriot's Day commemorates the Battle of Lexington and Concord, which marked the beginning of the Revolutionary War on April 18, 1775. Schools and many businesses close, and the entire city celebrates. Watch parades and reenactments of the night of Paul Revere's famous ride, and at noon the famous Boston Marathon begins in Hopkinton.

Third Monday in April, one-day-only event.

WHERE TO STAY
★BEST WESTERN AT HISTORIC CONCORD
740 Elm St., Concord, 978-369-6100, 800-780-7234; www.bestwestern.com

This budget-friendly hotel recently underwent a renovation that updated the guest rooms with contemporary décor and wireless access. Breakfast is included with each stay.

106 rooms. Pets accepted. Pool. Fitness center. $61-150

★★★COLONIAL INN
48 Monument Square, Concord, 978-369-9200, 800-370-9200;
www.concordscolonialinn.com

Henry David Thoreau's family once owned the property, which has been an inn since 1889. Anchoring the western edge of Monument Square in historic Concord, the Colonial Inn is a short walk to the town's shops and cafés. Guest rooms are individually decorated and have been updated with four-poster beds. There are a variety of dining venues, including the main restaurant (for breakfast, lunch, dinner and Sunday brunch), the outdoor porch (formal High Tea) and a rustic, colonial tavern (beers, live jazz).

56 rooms. Restaurant, bar. $151-250

★★★HAWTHORNE INN
462 Lexington Road, Concord, 978-369-5610; www.concordmass.com

Built in 1870, the Hawthorne Inn is less than a mile east of the village center. The pink house is surrounded by gardens and its neighbors include Minuteman National Historic Park and the Wayside and Orchard houses. Nineteenth-century antiques, original artwork, Japanese woodcuts, pre-Columbian pottery, a kitschy collection of salt and pepper shakers, and books and old maps are displayed throughout the hotel.

7 rooms. Complimentary breakfast. $151-250

WHERE TO EAT
★★COLONIAL INN
48 Monument Square, Concord, 978-369-2373, 800-370-9200;
www.concordscolonialinn.com

The traditional dining room of Concord's Colonial Inn serves classic tavern fare to local diners. Entrées include brown sugar and apple cider brined salmon and chicken potpie.

American. Breakfast, lunch, dinner, Sunday brunch. Bar. Children's menu. Reservations recommended. Outdoor seating. $151-250

DEERFIELD

Twice destroyed by French and Native American attacks and almost forgotten by history, Deerfield was once the northwest frontier of New England. Today, it remains unspoiled by big business or big buildings, populated instead by historic homes, vast meadowlands and the nationally acclaimed prep school Deerfield Academy. The tiny village boasts one of the most beautiful lanes in America known simply as "The Street," a mile-long stretch of 80 houses dating from the 18th and early 19th centuries.

WHAT TO SEE
HISTORIC DEERFIELD

Highways 5 and 10, Deerfield, 413-774-5581; www.historic-deerfield.org

The town's main street maintains 14-historic houses furnished with collections of antique furniture, silver, ceramics and textiles. A 28,000-square-foot Collections Study Center features changing exhibits.

Daily walking tours and antique forums and workshops are available. Daily 9:30 a.m-4:30 p.m.

MEMORIAL HALL MUSEUM

10 Memorial St., Deerfield, 413-774-3768; www.deerfield-ma.org/museum.htm

Built in 1798, Deerfield Academy's first building contains colonial furnishings and Native American relics.

May-October, daily 11 a.m.-5 p.m.

WHERE TO STAY
★★★DEERFIELD INN

81 Old Main St., Deerfield, 413-774-5587, 800-926-3865; www.deerfieldinn.com

Early guests once pulled up to this historic inn by stagecoach; a few years later, visitors arrived on trolleys. Today, customers pull in behind the wheels of sleek German sports cars. The 1884 inn itself, however, hasn't changed much, as the sitting parlors still exhibit period wallpaper and antiques, and the 10 main rooms remain cozy with New England quaintness. Updates include sparkling bathrooms, four-poster beds and a 13-room barn annex. Though it's said an old-town ghost wanders its halls, the inn is perpetually packed; some Deerfield Academy parents book graduation rooms four years in advance.

23 rooms. Complimentary breakfast. Restaurant, bar. $151-250

WHERE TO EAT
★★★DEERFIELD INN

81 Old Main St., Deerfield, 413-774-5587, 800-926-3865; www.deerfieldinn.com

The aforementioned inn's dining room is among the finest—and only—dining options in the area. Reservations are a must, as Deerfield students typically pack the place on weeknights and weekends. The menu of classic New England cuisine changes seasonally.

American. Breakfast, dinner. Bar. Children's menu. Reservations recommended. $16-35

★★★SIENNA

6B Elm St., Deerfield, 413-665-0215; www.siennarestaurant.com

This contemporary 45-seat restaurant serves American cooking marked by French technique. Chef and owner Karl Braverman creates dishes influenced by seasonally available ingredients, such as duck with white potato, blood orange, bok choy and Spanish vinegar demi-glace.

American. Dinner. Closed Sunday and Tuesday. $16-35

DENNIS

See also Chatham, Orleans

Dennis is the seat of "the Dennises," a group of Cape Cod communities that includes Dennisport, East Dennis, South Dennis and West Dennis. It was here in 1816 that Henry Hall developed the commercial cultivation of cranberries. The town is well-known for its laid-back vibe and pristine beaches.

WHAT TO SEE
JOSIAH DENNIS MANSE

77 Nobscusset Road, Dennis, 508-385-3528; www.dennishistsoc.org

The restored home of the minister for whom the town was named has antiques, a Pilgrim chest, a children's room, a spinning and weaving exhibit and a maritime wing.

July-August, Tuesday and Thursday.

SPECIAL EVENTS
CAPE PLAYHOUSE

820 Main St., Dennis, 508-385-3911, 877-385-3911; www.capeplayhouse.com

The Cape Playhouse hosts both established Broadway stars and up-and-coming actors for two-week runs of musicals, comedies and dramatic plays. It's the oldest professional summer theater in the United States. On summer Friday mornings, it has special children's performances like puppetry, storytelling and musicals. The complex also houses the Cape Museum of Fine Arts, the Playhouse Bistro and the Cape Cinema.

Late June-Labor Day.

WHERE TO STAY
BY THE SEA GUESTS

57 Chase Ave., Dennisport, 508-398-8685, 800-447-9202; www.bytheseaguests.com

On a beachfront road facing Nantucket Sound, this inn has clean, bright rooms with chenille bedspreads and fine-art prints. The property's large veranda provides great scenery for alfresco morning meals.

12 rooms. Complimentary breakfast. Beach. $151-250

WHERE TO EAT
★★★RED PHEASANT INN

905 Main St., Dennis, 508-385-2133, 800-480-2133; www.redpheasantinn.com

Housed in a 200-year-old barn, this restaurant delivers quaint surroundings and fine food. The American menu consists of fish and meat specialties; lamb and game offerings change nightly. The 300-bottle wine list is extensive and features wines from around the world.

American. Dinner. Bar. Reservations recommended. $36-85

★★SCARGO CAFE

799 Main St., Dennis, 508-385-8200, 888-355-0112; www.scargocafe.com

A cozy fireplace sets the mood at this bistro, which serves a menu of seafood and steaks. The wine list is extensive and features several options available by the glass.

International. Lunch, dinner. Bar. Children's menu. Outdoor seating. $16-35

EASTHAM

See also Orleans

The Mayflower party met its first Native Americans in this quintessential Cape Cod town. Today, the Bayside spot is famous for Nauset Beach, a sprawling expanse of white sand that was once a ship graveyard.

WHAT TO SEE
EASTHAM HISTORICAL SOCIETY
190 Samoset Road, Eastham, 508-255-0558; www.easthamhistorical.org
This museum, housed in an 1869 schoolhouse, has Native American artifacts and farming and nautical implements.
July-August: Monday-Friday afternoons.

EASTHAM WINDMILL
Windmill Green, Eastham, 508-240-7211; www.easthamhistorical.org
This is the oldest windmill on the Cape. Built in 1680, it was restored in 1936.
Late June-Labor Day: daily.

WHERE TO STAY
★★FOUR POINTS BY SHERATON
3800 Highway 6, Eastham, 508-255-5000, 800-533-3986; www.fourpoints.com
This budget-friendly hotel features rooms with duvet-topped beds and flat-screen TVs. An interior atrium houses the hotel's heated pool.
107 rooms. Restaurant, bar. $61-150

★★THE INN AT THE OAKS
3085 County Road, Eastham, 508-255-1886, 877-255-1886; www.inattheoaks.com
Housed in a yellow Victorian, this inn features rooms individually decorated with antiques, and plenty of common areas in which to spread out (including a billiards room). The staff can arrange everything from spa services to kayak tours.
10 rooms. Complimentary breakfast. $151-250

ALSO RECOMMENDED
THE WHALEWALK INN
220 Bridge Road, Eastham, 508-255-0617, 800-440-1281; www.whalewalkinn.com
A stay at this stylish bed and breakfast is more like spending time at a friend's welcoming, elegant home. Rooms are individually decorated and include fireplaces and soaking tubs. The daily breakfast features freshly-baked breads and creative dishes such as frittata primavera and pecan waffles.
16 rooms. No children under 12. Complimentary breakfast. $251-350

FALL RIVER

See also New Bedford

In 1892, blue-collar Fall River was the site of one of the most famous murder trials in American history, after Lizzie Borden allegedly killed her father and stepmother with an axe (she was acquitted). Since then, the city has maintained a gritty, urban persona, thanks to its numerous industrial mills and factories.

WHAT TO SEE
BATTLESHIP COVE
5 Water St., Fall River, 508-678-1100
Onsite at the Cove are five World War II-era naval ships; the *Lionfish*, a World War II attack submarine, and the battleship *USS Massachusetts*. Commissioned in 1942, the latter was active in the war's European and Pacific theaters and now houses the state's official World War II and Gulf War Memorial. Also here are *PT Boat 796*, *PT Boat 617* and the destroyer *USS Joseph P. Kennedy Jr.*, which saw action in the Korean, Vietnam and Cuban conflicts. Daily 9 a.m.-6 p.m.

FALL RIVER HISTORICAL SOCIETY
451 Rock St., Fall River, 508-679-1071; www.lizzieborden.org
The 16-room Victorian mansion exhibits displays on the Fall River Steamship Line, dolls, fine art, glassware, costumes and Lizzie Borden trial artifacts.
May-October: Tuesday-Friday 9 a.m.-4 p.m.; additional weekend hours
June-September: Saturday-Sunday 9 a.m.-3 p.m.

LIZZIE BORDEN BED AND BREAKFAST
92 Second St., Fall River, 508-675-7333; www.lizzie-borden.com
In 1892, Lizzie Borden's father and stepmother were found murdered in their Fall River Greek Revival house. Borden was tried for the murder, but acquitted. Enterprising souls have turned the house into a bed and breakfast, where guests can learn about the murders over a breakfast similar to the one the Bordens ate before their deaths, and even spend a chilling night in the supposedly haunted house.

FALMOUTH
See also Martha's Vineyard
Falmouth, on the southwest corner of the Cape, boasts a whopping 68 miles of coastline and 12 public beaches. Its pride and joy is the Woods Hole Oceanographic Institution, the largest independent marine study facility in the world. Ferries run from Falmouth to Martha's Vineyard, but many vacationers make this upscale Cape town their final vacation destination.

WHAT TO SEE
ASHUMET HOLLY & WILDLIFE SANCTUARY
Ashumet and Currier Roads, Falmouth, 508-362-1426; www.massaudubon.org
This is a Massachusetts Audubon Society-run 45-acre wildlife preserve with a holly trail, herb garden and observation beehive.
Daily dawn-dusk.

BRADLEY HOUSE MUSEUM
573 Woods Hole Road, Woods Hole, 508-548-7270
Featured is a model of Woods Hole circa 1895, an audiovisual show of local history, and restored ships.
July-August, Tuesday-Saturday; June and September, Wednesday, Saturday; schedule may vary.

CAPE COD KAYAK

1270 Highway 28A, Cataumet, 508-563-9377; www.capecodkayak.com

This outfitter runs guided kayak tours on area lakes, rivers and harbors. Experienced kayakers can rent boats and head out on their own for up to a week. March-November; closed December-February.

SPECIAL EVENTS
FALMOUTH ROAD RACE

661 E. Main St., Falmouth, 508-540-7000; www.falmouthroadrace.com

Starting in Woods Hole and winding back into Falmouth Heights, this hilly and hot course meanders past breathtaking scenery. The 7.1-mile race allows entries by lottery; those who don't get in typically join the more than 70,000 spectators who line the course.

Third Sunday in August.

WHERE TO STAY
★★★COONAMESSETT INN

311 Gifford St., Falmouth, 508-548-2300; www.capecodrestaurants.org

North of town, in a shady, wooded area, lies the Coonamessett Inn. The property's five buildings are spread out over six landscaped acres that also host a barn, a carriage house and a caretaker's cottage. Sandy beaches, harbors and lots of antique shops are all nearby. The inn's rooms are spacious, with pine furniture, sitting areas, oversized closets, fresh flowers and refrigerators. Take advantage of the complimentary continental breakfast and/or try dinner at the inn's seasonal restaurant.

28 rooms. Complimentary breakfast. Restaurant, bar. $151-250

ALSO RECOMMENDED
CAPTAIN TOM LAWRENCE HOUSE

75 Locust St., Falmouth, 508-540-1445, 800-266-8139; www.captaintomlawrence.com

Vaulted ceilings, hardwood floors and a spiral staircase add to the romantic, old-world charm of this inn located within walking distance of the town's main street. Built in 1861, it is a former whaling captain's home.

7 rooms. Complimentary breakfast. Closed January. $151-250

INN ON THE SOUND

313 Grand Ave., Falmouth, 508-457-9666, 800-564-9668; www.innonthesound.com

The rooms at this waterfront inn are individually decorated in a fresh, modern style. A full gourmet breakfast is served daily and can be had in room, alfresco or in the inn's dining room.

10 rooms. No children under 18. $151-250

THE PALMER HOUSE INN

81 Palmer Ave., Falmouth, 508-548-1230, 800-472-2632; www.palmerhouseinn.com

This 1901 Queen Anne-style inn and guesthouse is open year-round. The Shining Sea Bikeway, ferries to the islands and beaches are all nearby. Rooms are individually decorated with antiques but feature luxury linens and mattresses.

16 rooms. No children under 10. Complimentary breakfast. $151-250

WHERE TO EAT
★THE FLYING BRIDGE
220 Scranton Ave., Falmouth, 508-548-2700; www.capecodrestaurants.org
Fresh seafood is the specialty at this waterfront restaurant. From lobster rolls to steamed lobster, crab cakes and wine poached scrod, the menu covers the gamut of classic New England recipes.
Seafood. Lunch, dinner. Bar. Children's menu. Outdoor seating. Closed late November-mid-March. $16-35

★★LANDFALL
2 Luscombe Ave., Woods Hole, 508-548-1758; www.woodshole.com/landfall
This restaurant is located on the waterfront in Woods Hole and features an extensive seafood menu. Entrées include lobster savannah, fresh grilled swordfish and seafood newburg.
Seafood. Lunch, dinner. Bar. Children's menu. Reservations recommended. Outdoor seating. Closed December-March. $16-35

FOXBOROUGH
See also Norfolk
This town, located between Providence and Boston, is home to Gillette Stadium, which hosts the New England Patriots football team and the New England Revolution soccer club.

WHAT TO SEE
NEW ENGLAND PATRIOTS
60 Washington St., Foxboro, 800-543-1776; www.patriots.com
Frequent NFL Super Bowl contenders, the Patriots call Foxborough's Gillette Stadium home. Game tickets can be ultra pricey, but the arena's top-notch amenities and die-hard fans make up for its steep costs.

NEW ENGLAND REVOLUTION
60 Washington St., Foxboro, 877-438-7387; www.revolutionsoccer.net
One of the top teams in major league soccer, the Revolution plays its home games at Gillette stadium. The Netside Terrace, a special seating area south of the pitch, costs $300 and includes parking, food and drinks for four. Closed October-March.

WHERE TO STAY
★★COURTYARD BOSTON FOXBOROUGH
35 Foxborough Blvd., Foxborough, 508-543-5222, 877-773-5738; www.marriott.com
This hotel, which received a recent makeover that introduced contemporary style to the property, is located close to Gillette Stadium. Rooms feature luxury bedding and flat-screen TVs.
161 rooms. Restaurant, bar. $61-150

GLOUCESTER
See also Ipswich
Thanks to George Clooney's tough-talking sea captain ("Are we men, or are we Gloucestermen?") in *The Perfect Storm*, this blue-collar seaside city has

experienced a renaissance. Tourists crowd the streets of this growing summer resort and embark on whale-watching cruises from its harbor. Fishing is still big business here; a rumored 10,000 local men have been lost at sea in the last three centuries.

WHAT TO SEE
BEAUPORT, THE SLEEPER-MCCANN HOUSE
75 Eastern Point Blvd., Gloucester, 978-283-0800; www.spnea.org
Henry Davis Sleeper, an early 20th-century interior designer, first built a 26-room house here in 1907. With the help of local architect Halfdan Hanson, he kept adding rooms until decades later, there were 40. Twenty-five are now on view and contain collections of antique furniture, rugs, wallpaper, ceramics and glass.
June-mid-October: Tuesday-Saturday, tours on the hour 10 a.m.-4 p.m.; open until 7 p.m. on Thursdays July-August.

CAPE ANN HISTORICAL MUSEUM
27 Pleasant St., Gloucester, 978-283-0455; www.capeannhistoricalmuseum.org
This museum has paintings by Fitz Hugh Lane, decorative arts and furnishings, and exhibitions on Cape Ann's history.
Tuesday-Saturday 10 a.m-5 p.m., Sunday 1-4 p.m.

HAMMOND CASTLE MUSEUM
80 Hesperus Ave., Gloucester, 978-283-2080; www.hammondcastle.org
Built by inventor Dr. John Hays Hammond, Jr. to resemble a medieval castle, this museum contains a rare collection of art objects, including an 8,200-pipe organ.
Memorial Day-Labor Day, daily; after Labor Day-Columbus Day, Thursday-Sunday; rest of year, Saturday-Sunday.

SARGENT HOUSE MUSEUM
49 Middle St., Gloucester, 978-281-2432; www.sargenthouse.org
This late 18th-century Georgian residence was built for Judith Sargent, an early feminist writer and sister of Governor Winthrop Sargent. Period furniture, china, glass, silver, needlework, Early American portraits and paintings by John Singer Sargent are on display.
Memorial Day-Columbus Day, Friday-Monday noon-4 p.m.

WHERE TO STAY
★BASS ROCKS OCEAN INN
107 Atlantic Road Gloucester 978-283-7600, 800-780-7234;
www.bassrocksoceaninn.com
This sprawling, historic inn features rooms with views of the ocean, spread out over three different buildings. Afternoon tea and cookies are served each day, and the inn offers activities ranging from croquet to darts and billiards. 51 rooms. Complimentary breakfast. Closed December-March. $151-250

GREAT BARRINGTON

See also Lenox

The once tiny, locals-only town of Great Barrington has slowly become the dining, shopping and cultural center of the Southern Berkshires. Tourists mob the streets and restaurants on summer weekends, leaving residents at once miffed at the crowds and grateful for the tourism dollars. The country spot has also become popular with the New York City set, which means things quiet down considerably in the winter. Hiking, biking, walking, skiing, snowshoeing and other outdoor activities abound here, as do music, theater and dance events.

WHAT TO SEE
CATAMOUNT SKI AREA
Highway 23, Great Barrington, 518-325-3200; www.catamountski.com
Night skiing is popular at this mountain, which has four double chairlifts, a ski school, equipment rentals, a cafeteria, a bar and a nursery. The longest run is two miles with a vertical drop of 1,000 feet.
December-March, daily. Monday-Friday 9 a.m.-4 p.m., Saturday and Sunday 10 a.m.-2 p.m.

COLONEL ASHLEY HOUSE
117 Cooper Hill Road, Sheffield, 413-229-8600; www.thetrustees.org
The elegance of this home reflects Colonel Ashley's prominent place in society. One political meeting he held here produced the Sheffield Declaration, the forerunner to the Declaration of Independence.
July-August, Wednesday-Sunday; Memorial Day-June and September-Columbus Day, weekends; open on Monday.

OTIS RIDGE
159 Monterey Road, Otis, 413-269-4444; www.otisridge.com
This ski resort has a double chairlift, a T-bar, a J-bar, three rope tows, ski patrol and school, rentals, plus a cafeteria. The longest run is one mile with a vertical drop of 400 feet.
December-March, daily.

RUBINERS CHEESEMONGERS & GROCERS AND RUBI'S CAFÉ
264 Main St., Great Barrington, 413-528-0488
This cheese shop, grocer and café carries charcuterie boards and beautiful, hard-to-find cheeses from around the world. Fresh, overstuffed sandwiches and tasty coffees are available at the café; the entrance is down the alley. Ask the staff at either to pack a picnic for your drive back.
Monday-Saturday 10 a.m.-6 p.m., Sunday 10 a.m.-4 p.m.; Rubi's, Monday-Saturday 7:30 a.m.-6 p.m., Sunday 7:30 a.m.-4 p.m.

SKI BUTTERNUT
380 State Road, Great Barrington, 413-528-2000, 800-438-7669;
www.butternutbasin.com
The family-friendly Butternut has a quad, triple and four double chairlifts, plus a pomalift and a rope tow. The cafeteria and wine room are better than

average and the slalom race course frequently attracts experts. The longest run is approximately 1½ miles; its vertical drop is 1,000 feet. There are also seven miles of cross-country trails.

December-March, daily.

SPECIAL EVENTS
BERKSHIRE CRAFT FAIR
Monument Mountain Regional High School, 600 Stockbridge Road, Great Barrington,
413-528-3346; www.berkshirecraftsfair.org

This annual juried fair typically attracts more than 100 artisans. Mid-August. Admission: adults $6, children 12 and under free.

WHERE TO STAY
THORNEWOOD INN & RESTAURANT
453 Stockbridge Road, Great Barrington, 413-528-3828, 800-854-1008;
www.thornewood.com

Each room at this country inn is furnished with antiques and wireless access. The landscaped, sprawling garden includes an outdoor pool.

13 rooms. No children under 12. Complimentary breakfast. Restaurant. $151-250

WINDFLOWER INN
684 S. Egremont Road, Great Barrington, 413-528-2720, 800-992-1993;
www.windflowerinn.com

On 10 acres of Berkshire hillside, this white clapboard country inn has a screened-in porch and antique-filled rooms. The estate dates back to the 1850s and is near the famous Tanglewood music center. Country chintzes, four-poster beds and wood burning fireplaces fill the rooms.

13 rooms. Complimentary breakfast. $151-250

WHERE TO EAT
★★★CASTLE STREET CAFÉ
10 Castle St., Great Barrington, 413-528-5244; www.castlestreetcafe.com

Chef/owner Michael Ballon's lively restaurant is divided into two parts: a fine-dining room and the more casual Celestial Bar. White tablecloths and candles decorate the former, while live music and multicolored pendant lamps set the tone in the (often very noisy) bar. The eatery's classic American food (think burgers and salads) is consistently fresh.

American. Dinner. Bar. Closed Tuesday. $16-35

★★★SPENCER'S
453 Stockbridge Road, Great Barrington, 413-528-3828, 800-854-1008;
www.thornewood.com

Located in the turn-of-the-century Thornewood Inn, Spencer's is a mellow, cozy restaurant favored by the area's many retirees. All produce is provided by the inn's own gardens, making dishes seasonal and flavorful.

American. Dinner Thursday-Saturday. Bar. Outdoor seating. $16-35

HARWICH

See also Chatham, Orleans

Like many Massachusetts towns, Harwich has been immortalized in some of the country's best-known books. The pretty Cape Cod spot stars in Joseph C. Lincoln's novels, Whittier's poems and James Fenimore Cooper's novel *The Spy*. Most of the area's seaside houses are owned by city dwellers who visit on weekends.

WHAT TO SEE
CAPE COD BASEBALL LEAGUE
11 North Road, Harwich, 508-432-3878; www.capecodbaseball.org
This is baseball as it should be: local, passionate, affordable and played only with wooden bats. The 10 teams are made up of college players from around the country who live with host families for the summer. Spectators sit on wooden benches, pack picnic lunches and cheer for their favorite players during each of the season's 44 games.
Mid-June-mid-August.

HARWICH HISTORICAL SOCIETY
80 Parallel St., Harwich, 508-432-8089; www.harwichhistoricalsociety.org
The society has Native American artifacts, a marine exhibit, cranberry industry articles and early newspapers and photographs. It's also the site of one of the first schools of navigation in the United States.
Usually mid-June-mid-October, Wednesday-Friday; schedule may vary.

SPECIAL EVENTS
CRANBERRY HARVEST FESTIVAL
Highway 58 N. and Rochester Road, Harwich, 508-430-2811;
www.harwichcranberryfestival.org
This festival is a family day with an antique car show, music, arts and crafts, fireworks, carnival and parade.
One weekend in mid-September.

WHERE TO STAY
★★THE COMMODORE INN
30 Earle Road, West Harwich, 508-432-1180, 800-368-1180; www.commodoreinn.com
This budget friendly inn is located close to the beaches of Nantucket Sound. Some rooms include Jacuzzi tubs and fireplaces.
27 rooms. Complimentary breakfast. Restaurant, bar. Pool. Closed November-April. $61-150

★THE SANDPIPER BEACH INN
16 Bank St., Harwich Port, 508-432-0485, 800-433-2234; www.sandpiperbeachinn.com
Simple rooms and a location close to the beach make this inn a good budget bet. Beach umbrellas, towels and chairs are provided, as is daily breakfast.
20 rooms. Beach. Complimentary breakfast. $61-150

WHERE TO EAT
★★BISHOP'S TERRACE
Route 28, West Harwich, 508-432-0253; www.bishopsterrace.com

This elegant restaurant, located in a former sea captain's house, serves classic American dishes and fresh seafood to Cape Cod's summer crowds. Entrées include pan seared local cod and crisp roast duck with port wine and pear sauce.

American. Dinner. Bar. Children's menu. Outdoor dining, June-October. Closed Monday; also Thanksgiving-Memorial Day. $16-35

★★L'ALOUETTE
787 Main St., Harwich Port, 508-430-0405; www.lalouettebistro.com

A charming French bistro located in central Harwich Port, L'Alouette makes good use of fresh local produce and seafood in its casual French menu. Dishes include steak frites with fresh asparagus and soy lacquered salmon.

French. Dinner. Reservations recommended. $36-85

HYANNIS AND BARNSTABLE
See also Martha's Vineyard, Nantucket Island, Yarmouth

The gateway to Cape Cod, Hyannis sees some six million visitors each year. Its seaside streets are well prepared, with multitudes of antique and specialty boutiques, fancy and casual eateries, libraries, museums and of course, the Kennedy Compound. In the surrounding area are tennis courts, golf courses, arts and crafts galleries and theaters. Tourists stream in and out by Amtrak rail, commuter flights, and ferries, giving this bustling city of 14,000 a very transient feel although those in the know stay put to decompress on the town's laid-back beaches.

WHAT TO SEE
CAPE COD PATHWAYS
3225 Highway 6A, Barnstable, 508-362-3828; www.capecodcommission.org/pathways

This network of walking and hiking trails is composed of a perfect mix of dirt, sand and gravel. It links to most Cape towns, thanks to the Cape Cod Commission, which oversees the trails and produces a detailed map. In early June, hearty souls hike from one end of the cape to the other on the Cape Walk; during the October Walking Weekend, guides lead groups on short and long hikes.

Daily.

CAPE COD POTATO CHIP COMPANY
100 Breed's Hill Road, Hyannis, 508-775-3358; www.capecodchips.com

Cape Cod chips, now sold all over the world, may be the area's most recognizable food product. Perhaps the best part about the onsite, self-guided tour is the free samples, though seeing the chips cook in huge kettles is a close second.

Admission:free. Monday-Friday 9 a.m.-5 p.m.

HYANNIS WHALE WATCHER CRUISES

Barnstable Harbor, 269 Mill Way, Barnstable, 508-362-6088, 888-942-5392;
www.whales.net

View whales aboard the *Whale Watcher*, a 297-passenger super-cruiser, custom designed and built specifically for whale-watching. An onboard naturalist narrates.

April-October, daily. Admission: adults $45, seniors 62 and over $40, children (4-12) $26, children 3 and under free.

JOHN F. KENNEDY HYANNIS MUSEUM

397 Main St., Hyannis, 508-790-3077; www.jfkhyannismuseum.org

Photographic exhibits and a seven-minute video narrated by Walter Cronkite focus on President Kennedy's relationship with Cape Cod.

Mid-April-October: Monday-Saturday 9 a.m.-5 p.m., Sunday and holidays noon-5 p.m.; rest of year: Thursday-Saturday 10 a.m.-4 p.m., Sunday and holidays noon-4 p.m. Closed in January. Admission: adults $5, children 10-17 $2.50, children under 10 free.

OSTERVILLE HISTORICAL SOCIETY MUSEUM

155 W. Bay Road, Osterville, 508-428-5861; www.osterville.org

The museum is housed in a sea captain's house with 18th- and 19th-century furnishings and a boat-building museum.

Mid-June-September, Thursday-Sunday 1:30-4:30 p.m.; and by appointment.

STEAMSHIP AUTHORITY

Ocean Street, Hyannis, 508-477-8600, 508-693-9130; www.steamshipauthority.com

Catch ferries to Woods Hole, Martha's Vineyard and Nantucket from the South Street dock. See website for schedule and ticket pricing.

WEST PARISH MEETINGHOUSE

2049 Meetinghouse Road, West Barnstable, 508-362-4445; www.westparish.org

This building is said to be the oldest Congregational church in the country. Regular Sunday services are held here all year.

Worship Sundays 10 a.m. Music programs.

SPECIAL EVENTS
CAPE COD OYSTER FESTIVAL

20 Independence Drive, Hyannis, 508-775-4746; www.capdecodclash.org

It's all you can eat at the Cape Cod Oyster fest and, thanks to local vineyards, all you can drink, too. Held at the Naked Oyster restaurant under a big tent, the event draws locals and tourists alike.

Late September.

FIGAWI SAILBOAT RACE AND CHARITY BALL

486 W. Hyannisport, 508-737-2987; www.figawi.com

The largest regatta on the East Coast, Figawi features 200 sailboats racing from Hyannis to Nantucket on Saturday, then back again in a Return Race on Monday. A black-tie charity ball precedes the event by one week. Held in

Hyannis (and also celebrated on Nantucket) and featuring live bands, dancing and a big feast; it's a major social event.
Memorial Day weekend.

POPS BY THE SEA

Town Green, Hyannis, 508-362-0066; www.artsfoundationcapecod.org
In early August, the Boston Pops makes its way to the Cape for a concert on the Hyannis Town Green. Each year brings a new celebrity guest conductor, from actors to poets to famous chefs. The performance serves as a fundraiser that supports the Arts Foundation of Cape Cod.

WILLOWBEND CHILDREN'S CHARITY PRO-AM

100 Willowbend Drive, Mashpee, 508-539-5030
The biggest names in professional golf pair up with celebrities for this annual charity golf event on Willowbend's course. The $20 fee is among the lowest you can pay to watch professional golf; the proceeds benefit a variety of children's charities.
Early July.

WHERE TO STAY
★ANCHOR-IN

One South St., Hyannis, 508-775-0357; www.anchorin.com
This hotel offers traditional (basic, no-frills) and deluxe (upgraded linens, amenities) rooms in a harborfront location. A new contemporary library, with a flat-screen TV and club chairs for lounging, and kitchen have been added.
43 rooms. Complimentary breakfast. Pool. $151-250.

★★COURTYARD CAPE COD HYANNIS

707 Highway, 132, Hyannis, 508-775-6600, 800-321-2211; www.marriott.com
A reliable choice in Hyannis, this budget-friendly hotel has rooms with updated linens, spacious work areas and ergonomic desk chairs. The hotel offers complimentary breakfast and includes an indoor pool.
119 rooms. Restaurant. Bar. $151-250

ALSO RECOMMENDED
ASHLEY MANOR

3660 Olde King's Highway, Barnstable, 508-362-8044, 888-535-2246;
www.ashleymanor.net
A garden and gazebo complete this beautiful inn, which features updated, elegantly decorated guest rooms filled with antiques. Unwind with a book in the library or with afternoon tea in front of the fire.
6 rooms. No children under 14. Complimentary breakfast. $61-150

WHERE TO EAT
★★DOLPHIN RESTAURANT

3250 Main St., Barnstable, 508-362-6610; www.thedolphinrestaurant.com
A casual family restaurant located in the center of quaint Barnstable, the Dolphin offers an eclectic array of dishes with a focus on fresh seafood. The

menu ranges from veal marsala to baked native cod.
American, seafood. Lunch, dinner. Bar. Children's menu. Reservations recommended. $16-35

★★FIVE BAYS BISTRO

825 Main St., Osterville, 508-420-5559; www.fivebaysbistro.com

Contemporary art and white linen draped tables set the scene at this modern bistro. The menu features dishes with a wide range of influences, from Asian (sesame encrusted tuna with wok-fried vegetables) to Italian (veal with linguine and spinach).
American menu. Dinner. Bar. $36-85

★★★NAKED OYSTER

20 Independence Drive, Hyannis, 508-778-6500; www.nakedoyster.com

What better place to try fresh-from-the-sea oysters and seafood than where they're sourced? This contemporary bistro provides a comfortable setting for doing so, and enhances the experience with dishes such as marinated Wagyu flank steak and parmesan risotto, as well as a lengthy wine list.
Seafood. Lunch, dinner. Bar. Closed Sunday. $16-35

★ORIGINAL GOURMET BRUNCH

517 Main St., Hyannis, 508-771-2558; www.theoriginalgourmetbrunch.com

Locals line up at this breakfast spot to order up custom-designed omelets, superlative eggs Benedict and thick French toast. A selection of sandwiches and burgers are available, as well.
American. Breakfast, lunch. $15 and under

★★★THE PADDOCK

20 Scudder Ave., Hyannis, 508-775-7677; www.paddockcapecod.com

Pressed linens and abundant flowers add sophistication to this family-friendly restaurant, while equestrian paintings and antiques lend a classic look and feel. The menu is full of fresh seafood (though poultry, steak and pasta also make appearances).
American. Lunch, dinner. Bar. Children's menu. Reservations recommended. Closed mid-November-March. $16-35

★★★THE REGATTA OF COTUIT

4631 Falmouth Road, Cotuit, 508-428-5715; www.regattaofcotuit.com

This 1790 stagecoach inn is run by chef Heather Allen, who cooks with French, American and Asian themes. The lacquered duck is a neatly Americanized version of Peking duck; and the Vietnamese-style fish and chips tempura is made from whatever the local fishermen catch that day. Owners Wendy and Brantz Bryan have accrued a nearly legendary wine list over the last three decades, making the Regatta a must-stop for wine lovers.
American. Dinner. Bar. Reservations recommended. Closed on Sunday, November-April. $16-35

IPSWICH

See also Gloucester

Ipswich is a summer resort town and home of Crane beach, one of the most beautiful stretches of sand in the state. The historic village has nearly 50 houses built before 1725, and many are from the 17th century.

WHAT TO SEE
CRANE BEACH

290 Argilla Road, Ipswich, 978-356-4354; www.ipswichma.com
Among the best beaches on the Atlantic coast, Crane has five miles of sand, lifeguards, bathhouses, a refreshment stand and walking trails.
Daily 8 a.m.-sunset.

JOHN HEARD HOUSE

54 S. Main St., Ipswich, 978-356-2811; www.ipswichmuseum.net
Bought as a memorial to Thomas F. Waters, this house has Chinese furnishings from the China sea trade.
May-mid-October, Wednesday-Saturday 10 a.m.-4 p.m., Sunday from 1 p.m.

THE JOHN WHIPPLE HOUSE

1 S. Village Green, Ipswich, 978-356-2811; www.ipswichmuseum.net
The 1640 house has 17th and 18th-century furniture and a lovely garden.
May-mid-October, Wednesday-Saturday 10 a.m.-4 p.m., Sunday from 1 p.m.

WHERE TO EAT
★★★1640 HART HOUSE

51 Linebrook Road, Ipswich, 978-356-1640; www.1640harthouse.com
Twenty years after the Pilgrims landed in the town of Ipswich, they built this now-restored house. This is upscale tavern dining at its best, with wood-beamed ceilings, rich, leather wingback chairs and a working fireplace. The menu features comfort food favorites, from hangar steak to corn chowder.
American. Lunch, dinner. Bar. Children's menu. Reservations recommended. $16-35

★CLAM BOX OF IPSWICH

246 High St., Ipswich, 978-356-9707; www.ipswichma.com/clambox
This quirky roadside clam shack (the building is in the shape of an open box) is renowned for its perfectly prepared, deliciously greasy fried clams. Besides the standard menu of fried seafood, there are sandwiches, including a terrific take on the classic lobster roll.
Seafood. Lunch, dinner. Credit cards not accepted.$15 and under

LEE

See also Great Barrington

Once an underappreciated Berkshire village, Lee has finally been discovered by summer and winter tourists. Its proximity to major cultural festivals and outdoor recreation makes it an ideal town in which to book a (often less expensive) room.

WHAT TO SEE
OCTOBER MOUNTAIN STATE FOREST
256 Woodland Road, Lee, 413-243-1778; www.mass.gov
The forest provides fine mountain scenery overlooking 16,000 acres of hiking, hunting and snowmobiling.

SANTARELLA
75 Main Road, Tyringham, 413-243-2819, 760-212-1577; www.santarella.us
The former studio of sculptor Sir Henry Kitson, creator of the Minuteman statue in Lexington, was built in the early 1920s. The roof was designed to look like the rolling hills of the Berkshires in autumn; the fronting rock pillars and grottoes are fashioned after similar edifices in Europe. This unique and charming setting is situated on a four-acre estate.

SPECIAL EVENTS
JACOB'S PILLOW DANCE FESTIVAL
358 George Carter Road, Becket, 413-243-0745; www.jacobspillow.org
America's oldest and most prestigious dance festival includes performances by international dance companies in the Ted Shawn Theatre and the Doris Duke Theatre.
Tuesday-Saturday, some Sundays. Late June-August.

WHERE TO STAY
APPLEGATE
279 W. Park St., Lee, 413-243-4451, 800-691-9012; www.applegateinn.com
This Georgian Colonial is a charming bed and breakfast built in the 1920s. Guests can stroll through six acres of rose gardens, perennial beds and apple trees.
11 rooms. No children under 12. Complimentary breakfast. Pool. $61-150

DEVONFIELD INN
85 Stockbridge Road, Lee, 413-243-3298, 800-664-0880; www.devonfield.com
Located in the heart of the Berkshires, this Federal-era manor house offers a comfortable stay. Rooms are individually decorated with antiques and some feature fireplaces.
10 rooms. No children under 10. Complimentary breakfast. $151-250

FEDERAL HOUSE INN
1560 Pleasant St., South Lee, 413-243-1824, 800-243-1824; www.federalhouseinn.com
This 1824 inn borders the Housatonic River and the Beartown State Forest. The rooms display a casual, country-style décor. Guests have access to golf and tennis at nearby Stockbridge Country Club.
10 rooms. No children under 12. Complimentary breakfast. Bar. $151-250

HISTORIC MERRELL INN
1565 Pleasant St., South Lee, 413-243-1794, 800-243-1794; www.merrell-inn.com
Listed on the National Register of Historic Places, this old stagecoach inn sits on two acres of picturesque Housatonic River-front property and is close to the Berkshire Mountains.
10 rooms. Complimentary breakfast. $61-150

WHERE TO EAT
★★CORK N' HEARTH
Route 20 Laurel Lake, Lee, 413-243-0535; www.corknhearth.com

This classic New England restaurant boasts views of Laurel Lake and a cozy wood-beamed interior. The menu includes grilled Atlantic salmon, roast duck and roasted pork prime rib.

Seafood, steak. Dinner. Bar. Children's menu. Closed Monday. $16-35

★★SULLIVAN STATION RESTAURANT
109 Railroad St., Lee, 413-243-2082; www.sullivanstationrestaurant.com

A former railroad depot is put to use at this casual restaurant. Burgers, sandwiches and salads are served alongside heartier entrées like prime rib au jus.

American. Lunch, dinner. Bar. Outdoor seating. Closed two weeks in late -February-early March. $16-35

LENOX
See also Stockbridge

Lenox is the Berkshires' most talked-about town. Its name has become synonymous with rambling summer homes, fine cuisine and intellectual pursuits. The Boston Symphony orchestra calls Tanglewood its summer base, and the literati find inspiration in Edith Wharton's former grand manse, the Mount. Many inns, bed and breakfasts and full-service resorts have opened in the surrounding hills.

WHAT TO SEE
EDITH WHARTON ESTATE (THE MOUNT)
Second Plunkett St., Lenox, 413-551-5104, 888-637-1902; www.edithwharton.org

Edith Wharton's summer estate was planned from a book she coauthored in 1897, *The Decoration of Houses*, and built in 1902. The enormous Classical Revival house is continuously being restored.

May-October: daily 9 a.m.-5 p.m.; November-mid-December: open on weekends 10 a.m.-4 p.m.

PLEASANT VALLEY WILDLIFE SANCTUARY
472 W. Mountain Road, Lenox, 413-637-0320; www.massaudubon.org

A sanctuary of the Massachusetts Audubon Society has 1,500 acres with seven miles of trails and a beaver colony.

Mid-June-Columbus Day. Admission: $4 for nonmember adults, $3 for nonmember children (3-12).

TANGLEWOOD
197 W. St., Lenox, 413-637-1600; www.bso.org

Nathaniel Hawthorne planned *Tanglewood Tales* here. Many of the 526 acres, developed into a gentleman's estate by William Aspinwall Tappan, take the form of formal gardens. Well-known today as the summer home of the Boston Symphony Orchestra, the outdoor music venue stages concerts—rock, country and classical—all season long.

Daily; free except during concerts.

SPECIAL EVENTS
SHAKESPEARE & COMPANY
70 Kemble St., Lenox, 413-637-1199; www.shakespeare.org

The professional theater company performs plays by Shakespeare and Edith Wharton on four stages (one is outdoors). The main season runs late June-early September.

Tuesday-Sunday. Free parking. Pets accepted.

WHERE TO STAY
★★★★★BLANTYRE
16 Blantyre Road, Lenox, 413-637-3556; www.blantyre.com

Gilded Age charm abounds at this Tudor-style mansion in the Berkshire Mountains. Blantyre's rooms maintain a decidedly British country style, with floral fabric, overstuffed furniture, and in some, fireplaces. Activities include croquet, tennis, swimming and the cultural festivals of Tanglewood and Jacob's Pillow. Dining at Blantyre is a special occasion. The chef even packs gourmet picnics for guests to take with them while exploring the region.

25 rooms. Children over 12 years only. Complimentary breakfast. Spa. Restaurant, bar. $351 and up

★★★CRANWELL RESORT SPA AND GOLF CLUB
55 Lee Road, Lenox, 413-637-1364, 800-272-6935; www.cranwell.com

This historic 100-year-old country hotel is set on a hill surrounded by 380 acres and a 60-mile view of the southern Berkshires. The 18-hole championship golf course is host to Beecher's golf school. Inside the sprawling mansion are an enormous new spa and fitness center, complete with yoga studios and a pool.

108 rooms. Restaurant, bar. Spa. Fitness center. $251-350

★★★GATEWAYS INN
51 Walker St., Lenox, 413-637-2532, 888-492-9466; www.gatewaysinn.com

A white-washed mansion is the setting for this country inn. The rooms are individually decorated with antiques, and some feature working fireplaces. The onsite restaurant is more than just a spot for breakfast; it's an elegant dining room where fresh pastas, grilled steaks and seafood are served each night.

11 rooms. Complimentary breakfast. Restaurant, bar. $151-250

★★★WHEATLEIGH
Hawthorne Road, Lenox, 413-637-0610; www.wheatleigh.com

Wheatleigh is a country house hotel of the finest order. The 19th-century Italianate palazzo is set on 22 acres of hills and Frederick Law Olmsted-designed gardens, and the estate shares in the grand Gilded Age heritage of the region. Guest rooms are comfortably elegant with English soaking tubs, exclusive bath amenities from Ermenegildo Zegna, raw silk coverlets and CD players. Details make the difference here, from the dazzling Tiffany windows to the ornate fireplace in the Great Hall. The restaurant, with its updated French dishes, draws gourmands.

19 rooms. No children under 9. Restaurant, bar. $351 and up

ALSO RECOMMENDED
BIRCHWOOD INN

7 Hubbard St., Lenox, 413-637-2600, 800-524-1646; www.birchwood-inn.com
This bed and breakfast is decorated with antiques and collectibles and features meticulously kept rooms and gardens. The house, a columned white Colonial, was built in 1767, and has served as an inn ever since.
11 rooms. Complimentary breakfast. Wireless access. Children 12 and over only. Pets accepted. $151-250

BROOK FARM INN

15 Hawthorne St., Lenox, 413-637-3013, 800-285-7638; www.brookfarm.com
An impressive library of poetry, fiction and history lends a literary feel to this property. The Victorian inn is close to Tanglewood and the area's many other cultural and outdoor activities.
15 rooms. No children under 15. Complimentary breakfast. $151-250

KEMBLE INN

2 Kemble St., Lenox, 413-637-4113, 800-353-4113; www.kembleinn.com
Located on three acres in the center of historic Lenox, this inn features magnificent views of the Berkshire Mountains. The guest rooms are named after American authors.
14 rooms. No children under 12. Complimentary breakfast. $151-250

ROOKWOOD INN

11 Old Stockbridge Road, Lenox, 413-637-9750, 800-223-9750;
www.rookwoodinn.com
This 1885 Victorian inn is furnished with English antiques and is located in the center of Lenox, close to the art, music and theater of Tanglewood. Some rooms feature fireplaces.
21 rooms. Complimentary breakfast. Pets accepted. $151-250

WHERE TO EAT
★★★BISTRO ZINC

56 Church St., Lenox, 413-637-8800; www.bistrozinc.com
This lively hotspot is a good choice for a preconcert meal. The contemporary décor features black-and-white herringbone tile, tin ceilings, pale yellow walls, burgundy banquettes and a large copper bar. French-American fusion standouts include ginger-encrusted salmon and entrecote aux oignons.
French. Lunch, dinner, late-night. Bar. Reservations recommended. $36-85

★★★BLANTYRE

16 Blantyre Road, Lenox, 413-637-3556; www.blantyre.com
Dining at the 1902 mansion is a rare culinary experience. Diners are treated to pre-dinner champagne and canapes on the terrace or in the Music Room before feasting on chef Christopher Brooks' rich, sophisticated fare. Antique glassware and place settings combine to create a romantic atmosphere, and the service is impeccable.
French. Breakfast, lunch, dinner. Jacket required. Reservations recommended. Bar. $36-85

★★CAFÉ LUCIA

80 Church St., Lenox, 413-637-2640; www.cafelucialenox.com

The menu at this charming Italian bistro focuses on seasonal, organic ingredients. Classic dishes on the menu include linguine with clams, osso bucco and roasted chicken with polenta.

Italian, seafood. Dinner. Bar. Outdoor seating. Tuesday-Saturday. Open Sundays on holiday weekends and in summer. $36-85

★★CHURCH STREET CAFÉ

65 Church St., Lenox, 413-637-2745; www.churchstreetcafe.biz

Located in the heart of historic Lenox, this casual café, decorated with the works of local artists, has served simple, approachable bistro cuisine in a cozy atmosphere for almost 30 years. The menu changes seasonally, but might include coq au vin, miso and orange glazed salmon, or grilled angus flat iron steak with mashed potatoes.

American. Lunch, dinner. Bar. Children's menu. Reservations recommended. Outdoor seating. Closed March-April; also Sunday-Monday in May-June and September-February. $36-85

★★★GATEWAYS INN

51 Walker St., Lenox, 413-637-2532, 888-492-9466; www.gatewaysinn.com

At the Gateways, the chefs use locally grown produce and dairy products in each dish on their seasonal menu. The best seat in the house is in the main dining room. Its French doors and terra cotta painted walls recall a Tuscan country inn.

American. Breakfast, lunch, dinner. Bar. Reservations recommended. Closed Monday in September-June. $36-85

★★★WHEATLEIGH

Hawthorne Road, Lenox, 413-637-0610; www.wheatleigh.com

Polished mahogany doors lead to the hotel's regal dining room, which was modeled in 1893 after a 16th-century Florentine palazzo. Dine on contemporary French cuisine in a sun-drenched room filled with oil paintings, hand-carved Chippendale chairs and a large wood-burning fireplace. Favorites on the menu include roasted Maine lobster and sweet corn soufflé with cassis ice cream.

French. Dinner, Sunday brunch. Bar. Reservations recommended. $86 and up

★★★THE WYNDHURST RESTAURANT

55 Lee Road, Lenox, 413-637-1364, 800-272-6935; www.cranwell.com

Cranwell Resort's main dining room is on the first floor of the 100-year-old Tudor mansion. Large windows offer vistas of the Berkshire Hills and the fireplace keeps the room warm on cold New England nights. The French and American cuisine highlights local produce, including game and cheeses.

American, French. Lunch, dinner. Reservations recommended. $251-350

LEXINGTON

See also Concord

Lexington is often referred to as the birthplace of American liberty. On its town green, on April 19, 1775, eight Minutemen were killed in what is sometimes considered the first organized fight of the War for Independence. As the British approached, American Captain John Parker told his men: "Stand your ground. Don't fire unless fired upon. But if they mean to have a war, let it begin here!" And so it did.

WHAT TO SEE
BATTLE GREEN

Center of town

The Old Monument, the *Minuteman* statue and the Boulder mark the line of the Minutemen, seven of whom are buried here.

BUCKMAN TAVERN

1 Bedford St., Lexington, 781-862-1703; www.lexingtonhistory.org

The minutemen assembled here before the battle.

Mid-April-May: weekends only; June-October: daily 10 a.m.-4 p.m.

HANCOCK-CLARKE HOUSE

36 Hancock St., Lexington, 781-862-1703; www.lexingtonhistory.org

Here, John Hancock and Samuel Adams were awakened by Paul Revere's alarm on April 18, 1775.

Mid-April-May: weekends only; June-October: daily; tours hourly 11 a.m.-2 p.m.

LEXINGTON HISTORICAL SOCIETY

1332 Massachusetts Ave., Lexington, 781-862-1703; www.lexingtonhistory.org

The society offers guided hours of revolutionary period houses.

Admission: for one house $6 adults, $4 children; for two houses $8 adults, $5 children.

MUNROE TAVERN

1332 Massachusetts Ave., Lexington, 781-862-1703; www.lexingtonhistory.org

This was the site of the British hospital after the battle. George Washington dined here in 1789.

Mid-April-October: tour at 3 p.m. daily.

NATIONAL HERITAGE MUSEUM

33 Marrett Road, Lexington, 781-861-6559, 781-457-4142; www.monh.org

The museum features exhibits on American history, including that of Lexington and the Revolutionary War.

Tuesday-Saturday 10 a.m.-4:30 p.m., Sunday from noon. Closed Mondays (except for selected holidays), Thanksgiving Day, Christmas Day and Easter Day.

SPECIAL EVENTS
REENACTMENT OF THE BATTLE OF LEXINGTON AND CONCORD
Lexington Green, Lexington, 781-862-1450; www.battleroad.org
The yearly reenactment of the opening battle of the Revolutionary War takes place at dawn on Patriots Day and includes a parade.
Monday nearest April 19.

LOWELL
See also Andover, Wilmington
In the 19th century, the powerful Merrimack River and its canals helped transform Lowell from a handicraft center to an industrial city. The Francis Floodgate, near Broadway and Clare Streets, was called "Francis's Folly" when it was built in 1848, but it saved the city from flood in 1936. A restoration of the historic canal system is underway, and the revitalized downtown district is sprouting urban chic stores and cafés.

WHAT TO SEE
AMERICAN TEXTILE HISTORY MUSEUM
491 Dutton St., Lowell, 978-441-0400; www.athm.org
The site's permanent exhibit, "Textiles in America," features 18th- to 20th-century textiles, artifacts and machinery that show the impact of the Industrial Revolution on labor.
Wednesday-Sunday 10 a.m.-5 p.m. Admission: $8 for adults, $6 for seniors. Free parking. Closed Monday-Tuesday.

LOWELL HERITAGE STATE PARK
160 Pawtucket Blvd, Lowell, 978-458-8750; www.mass.gov
Six miles of canals and two miles of park on the bank of the Merrimack River offer boating, a boathouse, a concert pavilion and interpretive programs. Schedule varies; call for details. Free parking is available to visitors.

LOWELL NATIONAL HISTORICAL PARK
246 Market St., Lowell, 978-970-5000; www.nps.gov/lowe
The nation's first large-scale center for the mechanized production of cotton cloth, Lowell became a model for 19th-century industrial development. This park was established to commemorate Lowell's unique legacy as the most important planned industrial city in America. It includes mill buildings and a five-and-a-half-mile canal system.
May-Columbus Day weekend.

NEW ENGLAND QUILT MUSEUM
18 Shattuck St., Lowell, 978-452-4207; www.nequiltmuseum.org
Changing exhibits feature antique, traditional and contemporary quilts.
Tuesday-Saturday 10 a.m.-4 p.m.; open Sundays from May-Decembeber noon-4 p.m. Closed on Mondays and major holidays. Admission: adults $5, seniors and students $4.

WHISTLER HOUSE MUSEUM OF ART

243 Worthen St., Lowell, 978-452-7641; www.whistlerhouse.org

The birthplace of the painter James Abbott McNeill Whistler. Exhibits include several of his etchings.

Wednesday-Saturday 11 a.m.-4 p.m. Admission: seniors $5, students $4.

WHERE TO STAY
★★★STONEHEDGE INN

160 Pawtucket Blvd., Tyngsboro, 978-649-4400, 888-649-2474;
www.stonehedgeinn.com

This contemporary inn is an American imitation of an English country manor. Large, comfortable rooms have spacious bathrooms with heated towel racks. Set on the grounds of a horse farm, the out-of-the-way spot is perfect for a romantic rendezvous or a corporate retreat.

30 rooms. Restaurant, bar. $151-250

WHERE TO EAT
★★COBBLESTONES

91 Dutton St., Lowell, 978-970-2282; www.cobblestonesoflowell.com

An elegant dining spot located in a historic building in downtown Lowell, this restaurant serves reliable, classic dishes in a candlelit room. Entrées include filet mignon with whipped potatoes and seared sea scallops with cheese tortellini.

American. Lunch, dinner, late-night. Bar. Children's menu. Closed Sunday; one week in August. Open Monday-Saturday. $16-35

★★★LA BONICHE

143 Merrimack St., Lowell, 978-458-9473; www.laboniche.com

Though the food is upscale, the dress is casual at this restaurant. The menu features an eclectic offering of dishes with a French accent, from grilled garlic chicken to duck with cranberry and orange.

International. Lunch, dinner. Closed Sunday-Monday first week of July. Bar. $16-35

★★★SILKS

160 Pawtucket Blvd., Tyngsboro, 978-649-4400, 888-649-2474;
www.stonehedgeinn.com

Said to have one of the world's most impressive wine caves, this out-of-the-way restaurant is an oenophile retreat. On 36 acres of horse country farm, the Stonehedge Inn's eatery proffers nearly 2,000 wines (its cellar allegedly houses more than 90,000 bottles). The food is equally impressive, and the service is anything but snooty.

French. Breakfast, lunch, dinner, Sunday brunch. Closed Monday. Outdoor seating. $36-85

MARBLEHEAD

See also Salem

Marblehead sits on a pretty peninsula 17 miles north of Boston. The town was settled in 1629 by hardy fishermen from England's West counties. It now boasts a beautiful harbor and a number of busy boatyards. Beaches, boating, fishing, art exhibits, and antique and curio shops abound—all combine to offer either quiet relaxation or active recreation.

WHAT TO SEE

ABBOT HALL

188 Washington St., Marblehead, 781-631-0000; www.abbothall.org

On display here are the "Spirit of '76" painting and the town's original deed.

Last weekend in May-last weekend in October: daily; rest of year: Monday-Friday.

JEREMIAH LEE MANSION

170 Washington St., Marblehead, 781-631-1768; www.marbleheadmuseum.org

Run by the Marblehead Historical Society, this mansion is where Generals Glover, Lafayette and Washington were entertained.

June-October, Tuesday-Saturday 10 a.m.-4 p.m.

KING HOOPER MANSION

8 Hooper St., Marblehead, 781-631-2608; www.marbleheadarts.org

This restored house features a garden and art exhibits. Mansion rooms include the parlor, dining room and wine cellar.

Tuesday-Saturday 10 a.m.-4 p.m., Sunday 1-5 p.m.

WHERE TO STAY

HARBOR LIGHT INN

58 Washington St., Marblehead, 781-631-2186; www.harborlightinn.com

Each room at this inn, housed in a building constructed in 1729, has a fireplace, canopy bed and Jacuzzi. Continental breakfast and fresh-baked cookies are served in the colonial dining room.

21 rooms. No children under 8. Complimentary breakfast. $61-150

WHERE TO EAT

★★MARBLEHEAD LANDING

81 Front St., Marblehead, 781-639-1266;

The lines are long at this waterfront seafood restaurant, and for good reason. Simple, steamed lobster and fresh seafood can be found in abundance on the menu at this casual spot.

Seafood. Lunch, dinner, Sunday brunch. Bar. Children's menu. Outdoor seating. $16-35

MARTHA'S VINEYARD

See also Hyannis and Barnstable, Nantucket

For an island less than 10 miles long and 20 miles wide, Martha's Vineyard has an outsized reputation. Along with neighboring Nantucket, the isle began as a whaling center and morphed into an offshore resort for the rich and fabulous. Its acres of soft, white-sand beaches, grassy dunes, craggy cliffs and cultivated farmland are almost too postcard-perfect. Not quite as ideal are the island's lofty prices: housing, shopping and dining here all come with hefty fees. Nevertheless, tourists continually pack the streets of Edgartown, Oak Bluffs and Vineyard Haven in the summer.

WHAT TO SEE
AQUINNAH CLIFFS
230 Jones Road, Falmouth Aquinnah, 508-540-0448, 508-444-0173;
www.aquinnahcliffs.com
These cliffs are national landmarks and the most photographed attraction on Martha's Vineyard. More than 150 feet tall and brilliantly colored, they were formed over millions of years by glaciers. Today, the cliffs are owned by the Wampanoag Indians, who hold them sacred. At their peak sits the Aquinnah Light lighthouse, commissioned by President John Adams in 1798. At the bottom of the cliffs is a beach where nude sunbathing is permitted.
April-November.

BLACK DOG BAKERY
3 Water St., Vineyard Haven, 508-693-4786; www.theblackdog.com
The Black Dog is more than just a bakery: it's a cultural phenomenon. Its logo—a black Labrador retriever—is omnipresent on T-shirts, hats, mugs and belts. The company's General Store has four Vineyard locations. All sell souvenirs and even dog treats. The bakery serves coffee, pastries, torts, truffles and other treats. Not to be outdone, the nearby Black Dog Tavern has tasty seafood and other island-appropriate dishes.
Daily 5:30 a.m.-5 p.m., till 9 p.m. in summer.

CHICAMA VINEYARDS
Stoney Hill Road, West Tisbury, www.chicamavineyards.com
The Vineyard was once a winemaking mecca; today Chicama is reviving the tradition. It produces a variety of wines, including merlot, chardonnay and cabernet. The onsite store also sells vinegars and salad dressings, mustards and chutneys, and jams and jellies. Tours and wine tastings are available. Hours vary; call ahead for details.

FEATHERSTONE MEETING HOUSE FOR THE ARTS
Barnes Road, Oak Bluffs, 508-693-1850; www.featherstonearts.org
This arts center offers tourists the hourly use of studios, as well as photography, woodworking, pottery, weaving and stained-glass classes. The Meeting House also includes a gallery of works from local artists and a camp for kids.
Daily; call for studio availability.

FELIX NECK SANCTUARY
Edgartown-Vineyard Haven Road, Vineyard Haven, 508-627-4850;
www.massaudubon.org
This 350-acre wildlife preserve is a haven for kids and bird-lovers alike. Six miles of trails (guided or self-guided) meander through meadows, woods, salt marshes and beaches. The visitor center has exhibits and a gift shop. In the summer, kids enroll in the site's Fern & Feather Day Camp.
Daily 8 a.m.-4 p.m.; closed Monday in September-May.

FLYING HORSE CAROUSEL

33 Oak Bluffs Ave., Oak Bluffs, 508-693-9481; www.mvpreservation.org/carousell

This carousel is the oldest in the country and a national historic landmark. Its flying horses are gorgeous, hand-carved and lifelike. Grasping the center brass ring earns you your next ride for free.

MENEMSHA FISHING VILLAGE

North Street, Menemsha

Menemsha is a picturesque fishing village, full of cedar-sided clam shacks, fishermen in waterproof gear and lobster traps strewn about. The movie *Jaws* was filmed here and the main street has a few shops.

MYTOI

Dike Road, Chappaquiddick, 508-693-7662; www.thetrustees.org

Although the Vineyard may not be a logical location for a Japanese garden, Mytoi has won praises for its mix of azaleas, irises, dogwood, daffodils, rhododendron and Japanese maple. The 50-year-old garden's centerpiece is a pond filled with goldfish and koi.

Daily.

OAK BLUFFS

www.ci.oak-bluffs.ma.us

In 1835, this Methodist community served as the site of annual summer camp meetings for church groups. The communal tents gave way to family tents, which in turn became wooden cottages designed to look like tents. Today, visitors to the community take in the town's resulting famous "gingerbread cottages."

OLD WHALING CHURCH

89 Main St., Edgartown, 508-627-4442; www.mvpreservation.org/whale

Built in 1843, this is a fine example of Greek Revival architecture. It's now a performing arts center with seating for 500.

VINCENT HOUSE

Pease's Point Way, Edgartown, 508-627-4440

Built in 1672, the oldest known house on the island has been carefully restored to allow visitors to see how buildings were constructed 300 years ago. June-early-October, daily 11 a.m.-3 p.m.; rest of year, by appointment.

VINEYARD HAVEN AND EDGARTOWN SHOPPING

508-693-0085; www.mvy.com

Vineyard Haven is where most of the island's year-round residents live, so its shops are a bit less upscale than those in ritzy Edgartown, where you could spend an afternoon or even an entire day opening your wallet. In both towns you'll find clothing boutiques (including Midnight Farm in Vineyard Haven, which is owned by Carly Simon), bookstores, jewelry shops, home accessories stores and gourmet boîtes.

VINEYARD MUSEUM

59 School St., Edgartown, 508-627-4441; www.marthasvineyardhistory.org

Four buildings, dating back to pre-Revolutionary War times, join together to form the Vineyard Museum. The Thomas Cooke House, a historic Colonial home, specializes in antiques and folk art; the Foster Gallery displays exhibits from the whaling industry; the Pease Galleries specialize in Native American exhibits; the Gale Huntington Library is a useful tool for genealogy.

THE YARD

Middle Road, Chilmark, 508-645-9662; www.dancetheyard.org

For 30 years, the Yard has hosted dance performances throughout the summer. The 100-seat theater makes its home in a renovated Chilmark barn and offers community dance classes and free performances for children and seniors. June-September. Admission: premium seating $50, general seating $25, seniors and under 30 $15.

SPECIAL EVENTS
STRIPED BASS & BLUEFISH DERBY

1A Dock St., Edgartown, 508-693-0085; www.mvderby.com

Just after midnight on the first day of the Derby, fishing enthusiasts seek out their favorite spots and cast off, hoping to land the big one. Whenever contestants haul in striped bass, bluefish, bonito or false albacore, the catch is weighed and measured at Edgartown Harbor. Prizes are awarded daily for big fish. A grand prize awaits the contestant who nets the largest catch caught during the tournament.
Mid-September-mid-October.

WHERE TO STAY
★★★BEACH PLUM INN

50 Beach Plum Lane, Menemsha, 508-645-9454, 877-645-7398;
www.beachpluminn.com

This Vineyard inn was built in 1890 from the salvage of a shipwreck. Set on a hilltop, it overlooks the ocean. A stone drive and garden-like path lead to the main house. Several other cottages dot the seven-acre property.
11 rooms. Complimentary breakfast. Restaurant. $151-250

★★★★CHARLOTTE INN

27 S. Summer St., Edgartown (Martha's Vineyard), 508-627-4751; www.charlotteinn.net

This inn is an oasis of tranquility even though it's located in the middle of the busiest town on Martha's Vineyard. Once you walk along the garden paths under the linden and chestnut trees, you just know this is a place coveted by those with a penchant for privacy and peace. Inside, the rooms are outfitted in elegant 19th-century art and original antiques. The guest rooms continue the luxe treatment with flat-screen TVs, down pillows and comforters, and Bulgari toiletries.
25 rooms. Restaurant. $351 and up

★★★HARBOR VIEW HOTEL

131 N. Water St., Edgartown, 508-627-7000, 800-225-6005; www.harbor-view.com

The renovated Harbor View combines the island's heritage with modern hotel amenities. Rooms are bright, airy and clean, and the service is top-notch. The hotel's lengthy veranda has many rocking chairs and overlooks Edgartown Harbor, making it the perfect perch from which to watch ships roll in.

124 rooms. Restaurant, bar. Pool. Golf. Spa. $61-150

★★★KELLEY HOUSE

23 Kelley St., Edgartown, 508-627-7900, 800-225-6005; www.kelley-house.com

Located in central Edgartown, this historic hotel offers rooms with beach-inspired décor spread out over several buildings. Extensive kids' programs are available for guests, and the property includes an outdoor pool. The Kelley House's pub, Newes From America, is a popular local spot for burgers, sandwiches and lobster rolls.

53 rooms. Complimentary breakfast. Restaurant. Pool. Golf. $151-250

★★MANSION HOUSE HOTEL & HEALTH CLUB

9 Main St., Vineyard Haven, 508-693-2200, 800-332-4112; www.mvmansionhouse.com

This hotel, housed in a vintage Victorian structure on Vineyard Haven's main drag, features renovated rooms with down duvets, flat-screen TVs and soaking tubs. The health club includes an indoor pool, and the spa offers a full range of services.

40 rooms. Restaurant, bar. Fitness center. Spa. $151-250

★THE NASHUA HOUSE HOTEL

30 Kennebec Ave., Oak Bluffs, 508-693-0043, 888-343-0043; www.nashuahouse.com

Basic but bright and clean rooms with shared baths make this historic Victorian Oak Bluffs hotel a popular budget choice. The staff keeps chocolate cookies on hand at the front desk and supplies rooms with bottled water and welcome baskets.

16 rooms. No children under 4. $61-150

★★★THE WINNETU INN & RESORT

31 Dunes Road, Edgartown, 508-627-4747; www.winnetu.com

This family-friendly resort has a prime location on the beautiful, uncrowded South Beach just outside Edgartown. The cheery rooms are decorated with beachy prints and feature kitchens that can be stocked with the inn's grocery service. Activities include weekly clambakes, movie nights and rides around the property on the restored fire engine.

52 rooms. Restaurant, bar. Pool. Tennis. $151-250

ALSO RECOMMENDED
ASHLEY INN

129 Main St., Edgartown, 508-627-9655; www.ashleyinn.net

Rooms at this bed and breakfast are individually decorated with country chintzes and antiques. Afternoon tea, cookies and lemonade are provided daily. The central Edgartown location makes the inn a good base for exploring the island's most refined town.

10 rooms. No children under 12. Complimentary breakfast. Restaurant. $61-150

THE HANOVER HOUSE

28 Edgartown Road, Vineyard Haven, 508-693-1066, 800-696-8633;
www.hanoverhouseinn.com

Set on a half-acre of land, this cozy bed and breakfast is walking distance to the ferry, shopping, restaurants and the library. Shuttles are available for travel to Edgartown and Oak Bluffs.

15 rooms. Complimentary breakfast. $151-250

HOB KNOB INN

128 Main St., Edgartown, 508-627-9510, 800-696-2723; www.hobknob.com

Attractive, individually designed rooms with luxury linens, flat-screen TVs and iPod docking stations are just one of the reasons this inn is consistently the most popular on the island. The innkeepers are devoted to sustainability, and as such offer organic gourmet breakfasts daily and Aveda natural bath products.

17 rooms. Complimentary breakfast. Spa. Fitness center. Business center. $151-250

OUTERMOST INN

171 Lighthouse Road, Chilmark, 508-645-3511; www.outermostinn.com

The inn's picture windows provide excellent views of Vineyard Sound and the Elizabeth Islands. The innkeeper, sibling to singer James Taylor, has created a bohemian home where meals are sourced from organic vegetables and herbs in the garden.

7 rooms. No children under 12. Complimentary breakfast. Restaurant, bar. $151-250

THORNCROFT INN

460 Main St., Vineyard Haven, 508-693-3333; www.thorncroft.com

Secluded on a tree-lined, three-acre peninsula, this charming, white-shuttered house has guest rooms with hot tubs and fireplaces. A full country breakfast can be eaten in the dining room or in-room.

14 rooms. Complimentary breakfast. $251-350

WHERE TO EAT

★★★ALCHEMY

71 Main St., Edgartown, 508-627-9999

A smart, casual crowd, including the occasional celebrity, frequents Edgartown's popular Alchemy. The American bistro offers upscale dining—don't miss the fried risotto balls—in a relaxing, two-story atmosphere. The happening bar and lounge are packed with local revelers after hours.

American. Lunch, dinner. Bar. Casual attire. Outdoor seating. Closed January. $36-85

★★THE AQUINNAH SHOP

State Road, Aquinnah, 508-645-3142

Perched atop the Aquinnah cliffs with a superb outdoor deck, this casual spot serves sandwiches, fresh baked pies, clam fritters and more. The eatery is also a popular spot for ice cream.

American. Breakfast, lunch, dinner. Children's menu. Outdoor seating.

Closed mid-October-Easter. $16-35

★★★BEACH PLUM INN RESTAURANT
50 Beach Plum Lane, Menemsha, 508-645-9454; www.beachpluminn.com
Every table at the renowned, out-of-the-way Beach Plum has an ocean view, making the eatery one of the most romantic places on the island. The seafood-heavy menu is makes use of local ingredients and includes dishes such as pan-seared hazelnut crusted halibut.
American. Dinner. Outdoor seating. Closed January-early May. $36-85

★COOP DE VILLE
Dockside Marketplace, Oak Bluffs, 508-693-3420; www.coopdevillemv.com
A casual Oak Bluffs spot with ample outdoor seating, this restaurant serves up reliable burgers and wings. The all-day raw bar includes clams, oysters and shrimp by the piece or by the dozen.
Seafood. Lunch, dinner. Bar. Outdoor seating. $16-35

★ESPRESSO LOVE CAFÉ
17 Church St., Edgartown, 508-627-9211; www.espressolove.com
Locals love the stiff cups of joe and fresh-made sandwiches at this charming eatery. The sprawling outdoor patio is a prime spot for lingering over house made brownies and desserts.
International. Breakfast, lunch, dinner. Children's menu. Reservations recommended. Outdoor seating. $16-35

★★★L'ETOILE
22 N. Water St., Edgartown, 508-627-5187; www.letoile.net
L'Etoile, once housed at the Charlotte Inn, is now at home in a relaxed location on North Water Street. The food is still served in a very formal atmosphere—and still costs a pretty penny—but the overall experience is now focused on the menu, not the staff's pomp. A brightly colored bar adjoins the restaurant; either room is a worthy place to dine in style.
French. Dinner. Bar. Jacket required. Reservations recommended. Closed Monday-Thursday off-season. $86 and up

★LATTANZI'S PIZZERIA
Old Post Office Square, Edgartown, 508-627-9084, 508-627-8854; www.lattanzis.com
Reliable pies, pastas and sandwiches make this pizza restaurant the island's go-to location for quick and tasty Italian. The pizzas are cooked in a wood-fired oven and come with a crispy thick crust.
Italian. Dinner. Children's menu. Reservations recommended. Outdoor seating. $15 and under

★LINDA JEAN'S
34 Circuit Ave., Oak Bluffs, 508-693-4093
This casual restaurant offers a full range of sandwiches, burgers and seafood for lunch and dinner, but is best known for its extensive breakfast.
American. Breakfast, lunch, dinner. Children's menu. Outdoor seating. $15 and under

★★LOLA'S SOUTHERN SEAFOOD

Beach Road, Oak Bluffs, 508-693-5007; www.lolassouthernseafood.com

Seafood is given a southern—and sometimes spicy—accent at this cozy bistro. Steamed lobster comes with maple garlic mashed potatoes, while north Atlantic salmon comes with a honey mango sauce. The restaurant hosts live bands playing everything from reggae to jazz on weeknights and some weekday evenings during summer.

American, seafood. Dinner, late-night, Sunday brunch. Outdoor bar. $16-35

★LOOKOUT TAVERN

8 Seaview Ave., Oak Bluffs, 508-696-9844; www.lookouttavern.com

With its outdoor patio overlooking Oak Bluffs' harbor, this seafood restaurant is a popular spot for lobsters, clams and fish tacos. The Boston cream pie cheesecake is a unique take on the classic dessert.

Seafood. Lunch, dinner. Bar. Outdoor seating. Closed November-April. $16-35

★★LURE GRILL

31 Dunes Road, Edgartown, 508-627-3663; www.winnetu.com

This casual, family friendly restaurant located within the Winnetu resort serves approachable seafood, burgers and steaks cooked over a wood-fired grill. The restaurant's activity area allows children to play in a dedicated spot while parents dine.

Seafood. Dinner. Labor Day-Columbus Day: closed Monday-Tuesday; Columbus Day-Thanksgiving: closed Monday-Thursday; closed Thanksgiving-May. $36-85

★THE NEWES FROM AMERICA

23 Kelly St., Edgartown, 508-627-4397; www.kelley-house.com/dining

This always-packed, family-friendly pub serves reliable sandwiches, burgers and seafood in a casual atmosphere. Local microbrews are available on tap.

American. Lunch, dinner. $15 and under

★★★OUTERMOST INN

81 Lighthouse Road, Aquinnah, 508-645-3511; www.outermostinn.com

Dining here is a serene experience, thanks to the refined inn's clifftop location and relaxed elegance. Fresh herbs and vegetables grown on the property influence the creative prix fixe menu. Wine lovers, take note: The restaurant is strictly BYOB.

American. Dinner. Reservations recommended. Closed Wednesday; also mid-October-mid-May. $36-85

★★SWEET LIFE CAFÉ

63 Circuit Ave., Oak Bluffs, 508-696-0200; www.sweetlifemv.com

Whether you're seated at a cozy table inside the grand Victorian in which this bistro is housed, or in its beautiful, flower-filled garden, you'll have a comfortable perch for sampling the flavorful, seasonal cuisine produced by chef Scott Ehrlich. Dig into sautéed halibut with sweet pea risotto, or grilled duck breast with potato purée. The wine list, selected by the restaurant's French owner, is extensive.

Seafood. Dinner. Reservations recommended. Outdoor seating. Closed January-March. $16-35

NANTUCKET

See also Hyannis and Barnstable, Martha's Vineyard

Generally regarded as even *more* exclusive than Martha's Vineyard, Nantucket is a small island full of sprawling cottages, endless soft-sand beaches, first-rate restaurants and breathtaking ocean vistas. The island was once a worldwide center for whaling, and many of the historic Nantucket Town houses were built as seaman's homes. In the peak summer season, the island's population skyrockets to nearly overcrowded proportions, as day-trippers and weekenders stream from the Steamship Authority ferries. Somehow, though, the island retains its charm and its flush residents take the tourists in stride. A plethora of outdoor activity can be explored here, from biking to swimming to sailing to tennis and golf. Siasconset (Sconset to natives) and Nantucket Town are the isle's shopping and dining hubs, though many small stores and eateries are sprinkled over the land's 49 square miles.

WHAT TO SEE

1800 HOUSE

8 Mill St., Nantucket, 508-228-1894; www.nha.org

This early 19th-century house has period furnishings, a large, round cellar and a kitchen garden.

ALTAR ROCK

Off Polpis Road, Nantucket

Altar Rock rises 90 feet above sea level and affords stunning views of Nantucket and the surrounding Cape. Go at dawn or dusk for the best views.

BARTLETT'S FARM

33 Bartlett Farm Road, Nantucket, 508-228-9403; www.bartlettsfarm.com

The Bartlett family has tilled the land of Nantucket's largest farm for nearly 200 years. Stop by for fresh vegetables, milk, eggs, cheese, freshly baked bread and cut flowers. A handful of prepared foods such as salads, pies, snacks, jams and chutneys are also available.

Daily 8 a.m.-6 p.m.

CISCO BREWERS

5 Bartlett Farm Road, Nantucket, 508-325-5929; www.ciscobrewers.com

Local beer-makers Cisco Brewers concoct dozens of micro-specialties such as Whale's Tale Pale Ale, Baileys Ale, Moor Porter, Capn' Swains Extra Stout, Summer of Lager and Baggywrinkle Barleywine. The Triple Eight Distillery and Nantucket Vineyards also have tasting rooms at the site, where you can sample everything from vodka to chardonnay. Onsite are guided tours of the brewery, vineyard and distillery.

Summer, Monday-Saturday 10 a.m.-6 p.m., Sunday until 5 p.m.; tours by appointment.

ENDEAVOR SAILING ADVENTURES

Straight Wharf, Nantucket, 508-228-5585; www.endeavorsailing.com

U.S. Coast Guard Captain James Genthner built his sloop, the *Endeavor*, and has been sailing it for more than 20 years. Take a 90-minute sail around Nantucket Sound and let Genthner and his wife, Sue, introduce you to Nantucket's sights, sounds and history.

May-October.

FIRST CONGREGATIONAL CHURCH

62 Centre St., Nantucket, 508-228-0950; www.nantucketfcc.org

Also called the Old North Church, this spot arguably offers Nantucket's best view of the island and surrounding ocean. To enjoy it, you'll have to climb the 120-foot-tall steeple's 94 steps.

Mid-June-mid-October, Monday-Saturday.

FOLGER-FRANKLIN MEMORIAL FOUNTAIN

Madaket Road, Nantucket, 508-228-1894

The fountain marks the birthplace of Abiah Folger, Benjamin Franklin's mother.

HADWEN HOUSE

96 Main St., Nantucket, 508-228-1894; www.nha.org

A Greek Revival mansion with furnishings from the whaling period.

Monday-Saturday 10 a.m.-5 p.m., Sunday from noon.

JETHRO COFFIN HOUSE (OLDEST HOUSE)

16 Sunset Hill Lane, Nantucket, 508-228-1894

Built in 1686, Oldest House is, true to its name, one of the oldest houses in the United States. The building was a wedding present given to the children of two feuding families (the Gardners and the Coffins) by their in-laws, who reconciled after the happy event.

Thursday-Monday, 11 a.m.-4 p.m. Closed December 1-4. Admission: adults $6, children 6-17 $3.

JETTIES BEACH

Bathing Beach Road, Nantucket, 508-228-2279; thejettiesnantucket.com

Kid-friendly Jetties is the best bet for beach-going families. There are restrooms, showers, changing rooms, a snack bar, lifeguards, rental chairs, a playground, volleyball and tennis courts, and a skateboarding park. You can also rent kayaks, sailboards and sailboats through Nantucket Community Sailing (508-228-5358).

Daily.

LOINES OBSERVATORY

59 Milk St., Nantucket, 508-228-9273; mmo.org

Named for the first professional female astronomer, the observatory lets guests peek through a telescope to view star-filled skies.

Monday, Wednesday, Friday evenings in summer, Saturday evenings year-round; closed Tuesday, Thursday, Sunday in summer, Sunday-Friday year-round.

MIACOMET GOLF COURSE
12 W. Miacomet Road, Nantucket, 508-228-9764, 508-325-0333;
www.miacometgolf.com
Nantucket's only public golf course offers nine holes (two are par-fives). Reserve a tee time at least a week in advance; the chances of playing in the summertime without a reservation are zero.
Daily.

MURRAY'S TOGGERY
62 Main St., Nantucket, 508-228-0437, 800-368-2134; www.nantucketreds.com
Murray's Toggery was the first store on the island to sell Nantucket Reds, the casual pink khaki pants that are a virtual beacon of preppiness in America.
Monday-Saturday 9 a.m.-7 p.m., Sunday 10 a.m.-6 p.m.; winter, Monday-Saturday 9 a.m.-5 p.m.

NANTUCKET HISTORICAL ASSOCIATION WHALING MUSEUM
15 Broad St., Nantucket, 508-228-1894; www.nha.org
This museum, redesigned and reopened in 2005, is the premier institution devoted to the history of the whaling industry. Inside are a 46-foot preserved sperm whale skeleton (the whale washed ashore in 1998) and many artifacts from the island's heyday as a center for whale oil production.
Mid-May-mid-October, daily 10 a.m.-5 p.m.; mid-October-mid-December, Thursday-Monday 11 a.m.-4 p.m.; closed mid-December-May.

NANTUCKET MARIA MITCHELL ASSOCIATION
4 Vestal St., Nantucket, 508-228-9198; www.mmo.org
The scientific library has historical documents, science journals and family memorabilia of the early astronomer. There's also a natural science museum with local wildlife, and an aquarium is nearby at 28 Washington Street.
Mid-June-August, Tuesday-Saturday; library also open rest of year, Wednesday-Saturday.

NANTUCKET TOWN
Nantucket, 508-228-1700; www.nantucketchamber.org/directory/merchants
Nantucket Town is a shopper's dream. A walk down its cobble stone main street involves passing by home, clothing, culinary, boat, jewelry, art and antique shops, most of which are tasteful and well-edited.

OLD MILL
50 Prospect St., Nantucket, 508-228-1894; www.nha.org/sites/oldmill
Believed to be the oldest windmill in the United States, this Dutch-style structure is impressive in its beauty and sheer vertical height of 50 feet. It was built in 1746 with salvaged oak that washed up on shore from shipwrecks. Inside are a research center and whaling museum.
June-August: daily; call for off-season hours.

RAFAEL OSONA AUCTIONS

21 Washington St., Nantucket, 508-228-3942; www.rafaelosonaauction.com

This spot hosts estate auctions on selected weekends (call for exact dates and times) that feature treasured pieces from both the United States and Europe. Late May-early December.

SIASCONSET VILLAGE

East end of Nantucket Island

Siasconset lies seven miles from Nantucket Town and can be reached by bicycle or shuttle bus (driving often takes twice as long due to traffic). This 18th-century fishing village features quaint cottages, grand mansions, restaurants, a few shops and a summer cinema.

SOMETHING NATURAL

50 Cliff Road, Nantucket, 508-228-0504; www.somethingnatural.com

Those looking for a casual breakfast or lunch should check out this bakery. This off-the-beaten-path shop makes healthy sandwiches, breads, bagels, salads and cookies. May-October.

THE STRAIGHT WHARF

Straight Wharf, Nantucket

Built in 1723, the wharf is Nantucket's launching area for sailboats, sloops and kayaks, but it's also a great shopping and eating area. Loaded with restaurants and quaint, one-room cottage shops, the wharf also features an art gallery, museum and outdoor concert pavilion.

STRONG WINGS SUMMER CAMP

9 Nobadeer Farm Rd., Nantucket, 508-228-1769; www.strongwings.org

Open for just two months every year, the Strong Wings Summer Camp enrolls kids ages 5-15 in three-day or five-day sessions, where they explore the area, mountain bike, hike, kayak, snorkel, rock climb and boogie board. Older kids learn search-and-rescue techniques. Late June-late August: daily.

THE SUNKEN SHIP

12 Broad St., Nantucket, 508-228-9226; www.sunkenship.com

The Sunken Ship is a full-service dive shop that offers lessons and rentals. The general store offers an eclectic array of maritime goods. Daily; call for closures.

THEATRE WORKSHOP OF NANTUCKET

2 Centre St., Nantucket, 508-228-4305; www.theatreworkshop.com

The theater has staged comedies, dramas, plays and dance concerts since 1985. Both professionals and amateurs make up the company, which offers up to 10 performances each summer.

WINDSWEPT CRANBERRY BOG

Polpis Road, Siasconset

To see how cranberries are grown and harvested, visit this 200-acre bog during the fall harvest (late September-October from dawn-dusk). At other times of the year, the bog is a peaceful place to walk and bike.

Daily dawn-dusk.

SPECIAL EVENTS
NANTUCKET ARTS FESTIVAL

508-325-8588; www.nantucketartscouncil.org

This weeklong festival celebrates a full range of arts on the island: films, poetry and fiction, acting, dance, paintings, photography and many other forms. Look for the wet-paint sale in which you can bid on works completed just that day.

Early October.

NANTUCKET FILM FESTIVAL

508-228-6648; www.nantucketfilmfestival.org

Like other film fests, this one screens new independent movies that may not otherwise garner attention. It's attended by screenwriters, actors, film connoisseurs and, occasionally, big-name celebrities. A daily event called Morning Coffee showcases a panel of the above participating in Q&As.

Mid-June.

NANTUCKET WINE FESTIVAL

508-228-1128; www.nantucketwinefestival.com

This weekend event includes tastings, seminars and several wine dinners. The Great Wine in Grand Houses event allows you to visit a private mansion, sip fine vintages drawn from nearly 100 wineries and dine on food prepared by some of the area's finest chefs. Reservations are required.

Mid-May.

WHERE TO STAY
★★CLIFFSIDE BEACH CLUB

46 Jefferson Ave., Nantucket, 508-228-0618; www.cliffsidebeach.com

Launched as a private beach club at the turn of the 20th century, this unique spot has a variety of sunny, simple rooms and suites, some housed in converted former bathhouses. Access to the beach and beach umbrellas, an on-site organic restaurant, and a new fitness facility and pool are included with each stay.

27 rooms. Closed November-April. Restaurant, bar. Beach. Spa. Pool. Complimentary breakfast. Fitness center. $151-250

★★★JARED COFFIN HOUSE

29 Broad St., Nantucket, 508-228-2400; www.jaredcoffinhouse.com

The location, right in the center of Nantucket Town, is the main draw at the Jared Coffin House, a historic property with rooms spread out over two buildings. Furnishings are colonial, and rooms have been updated with wireless access and luxury linens.

60 rooms. Restaurant, bar. $61-150

★★★WHITE ELEPHANT RESORT

50 Easton St., Nantucket, 508-228-2500, 800-445-6574; www.whiteelephanthotel.com

This harborfront hotel offers one of the most elegant places to stay on the island. Rooms are comfortable with plush beds and luxurious bath amenities. A handful of cottages with equally luxurious furnishings are available, as are the newly opened White Elephant Hotel Residences, an ultra-luxury selection of newly constructed rooms. The Brant Point Grill serves updated takes on classic New England cuisine. A full-service spa was recently added to the complex.

66 rooms. Restaurant, bar. Closed mid-December-March. Fitness center. $251-350

★★★★THE WAUWINET

120 Wauwinet Road, Nantucket, 508-228-0145, 800-426-8718; www.wauwinet.com

Staying at the Wauwinet is akin to being marooned on a remote island, but with impeccable service and amenities to make your stay more comfortable. Built in 1876 by ship captains, the Wauwinet is a grand resort secluded in the center of the island, featuring sophisticated, English, country-style rooms and suites, and private beaches fronting the harbor and Atlantic Ocean. The clay tennis courts are well maintained, and the restaurant, Toppers, has a 20,000-bottle wine cellar. A new spa offers a full menu of services.

36 rooms. Closed late October-early May. No children under 18. Complimentary breakfast. Restaurant. Tennis. Spa. $351 and up

ALSO RECOMMENDED
CARLISLE HOUSE INN

26 N. Water St., Nantucket, 508-228-0720; www.carlislehouse.com

The structure was built in 1765, and now houses an inn with rooms featuring fireplaces and four-poster beds.

17 rooms. Closed January-March. No children under 10. Complimentary breakfast. $61-150

CENTERBOARD GUEST HOUSE

8 Chester St., Nantucket, 508-228-9696; www.centerboardguesthouse.com

The updated, modern rooms at this bed and breakfast have flat-screen TVs, down duvets and full baths with Caswell and Massey bath products. The inn includes plenty of common space for spreading out, including a large parlor and an outdoor garden.

8 rooms. Closed January-February, Complimentary breakfast. $61-150

COBBLESTONE INN

5 Ash St., Nantucket, 508-228-1987; www.nantucket.net

The petite rooms at this cozy inn have fireplaces, colorful quilts and private baths. The innkeepers keep guests well supplied with snacks, sodas and a generous continental breakfast.

5 rooms. Closed January-March. Complimentary breakfast. $61-150

MARTIN HOUSE INN

61 Centre St., Nantucket, 508-228-0678; www.martinhouseinn.net

Located in a house built in 1803, this historic inn has rooms with four-poster or canopy beds and fireplaces. The inn provides afternoon snacks, wine and cheese and teas that can be enjoyed in the garden in warm weather.

13 rooms. Complimentary breakfast. Restaurant. $61-150

ROBERTS HOUSE INN

11 India St., Nantucket, 508-228-0600, 800-872-6830; www.robertshouseinn.com

Restored in 2003, this inn has rooms furnished with antiques and reproductions and private baths. Some rooms include Jacuzzi tubs.

45 rooms. Complimentary breakfast. $61-150

SEVEN SEA STREET INN

7 Sea St., Nantucket, 508-228-3577; www.sevenseastreetinn.com

Spread over three historic houses, this inn has rooms with canopy beds, high-definition TV and Jacuzzi tubs. Other amenities include iPod docking stations and rainshowers.

11 rooms. No children under 5. Complimentary breakfast. Closed January-mid April. Spa. $151-250

SHERBURNE INN

10 Gay St., Nantucket, 508-228-4425, 888-577-4425; www.sherburneinn.com

Built by whaling captain Obed Starbuck in 1831, this small inn has rooms decorated in cheerful colors. Breakfast and afternoon tea are served daily.

8 rooms. No children under 6. Complimentary breakfast. $61-150

VANESSA NOEL HOTEL

5 Chestnut St., Nantucket, 508-228-5300; www.vanessanoelhotel.com

This petite inn, opened by a New York-based designer, is housed above her eponymous shoe boutique. Rooms are simple but luxurious with plush beds, Frette linens and Bulgari bath products.

8 rooms. Complimentary breakfast. Bar. $351 and up

VERANDA HOUSE

3 Step Ln., Nantucket, 508-228-0695; www.theverandahouse.com

Renovations turned this classic inn into a chic, contemporary space with rooms kitted out with Frette linens, flat-screen TVs and luxury bath products. A full breakfast is served each day, and chocolate chip cookies are available each afternoon.

18 rooms. Complimentary breakfast. $351 and up

WHERE TO EAT

★★★21 FEDERAL

21 Federal St., Nantucket, 508-228-2121; www.21federal.com

Historic charm and contemporary panache come together at this stylishly clubby spot: a favorite of the islands who's who, both for its delectable New American cuisine and convivial bar. The well-rounded menu has a wide selection of meat, poultry and seafood, while the award-winning wine list delights oenophiles.

American. Dinner. Bar. Reservations recommended. Outdoor seating. Closed January-April. $36-85

★★★AMERICAN SEASONS

80 Center St., Nantucket, 508-228-7111; www.americanseasons.com

American Seasons' menu is refreshingly varied, and is divided to reflect regional cuisines: New England, Down South, the Wild West and the Pacific Coast. Thanks to meticulous attention to detail and fresh, local produce, the themed meals are a success. Regulars rave about the cooking and the folk-art-decorated, romantic dining room and patio.

American. Dinner. Bar. Reservations recommended. Outdoor seating. Closed January-March. $36-85

★ATLANTIC CAFÉ

15 S. Water St., Nantucket, 508-228-0570; www.atlanticcafe.com

This always bustling, family-friendly restaurant offers reliable burgers, sandwiches, salads and seafood in a setting close to the ferry piers. The large bar is a good perch for sampling local brews.

American. Lunch, dinner, late-night. Bar. Children's menu. Closed late December-early January. $15 and under

★★BLACK EYED SUSAN'S

10 India St., Nantucket, 508-325-0308; www.black-eyedsusans.com

Whether you come for the hearty, creative breakfasts or the romantic, candlelit dinners, you'll need to come early because this petite, popular restaurant does not take reservations. The classic diner-style counter provides a prime spot for watching the staff working in the open kitchen. The BYOB policy makes sampling a full meal of locally sourced seafood a budget-friendly option.

American. Breakfast, dinner. Credit cards not accepted. Closed Sunday; also November-March. $16-35

★★★BOARDING HOUSE

12 Federal St., Nantucket, 508-228-9622; www.boardinghouse-pearl.com

The restaurant's nouveau cuisine and sexy, youthful scene make the long waits worth it at this inspired eatery. Those in the know book a table outdoors to people-watch and stargaze as they eat. Others prefer the dimly lit downstairs dining room. Seafood and beef are the main ingredients behind the creative Asian-influenced menu; a comprehensive wine list ensures perfect pairings.

American. Lunch, dinner. Bar. Reservations recommended. Outdoor seating. $36-85

★★★CLUB CAR

1 Main St., Nantucket, 508-228-1101; www.theclubcar.com

The Club Car lounge is housed in a renovated train club car that once ran between Steamboat Wharf and Siasconset Village. Lunches and dinners offer sophisticated menus and a pianist performs nightly.

French. Lunch, dinner. Bar. Reservations recommended. Closed November-late May. $86 and up

★★★COMPANY OF THE CAULDRON
7 India St., Nantucket, 508-228-4016; www.companyofthecauldron.com
From its ivy-covered exterior to the soft glow of its candlelit dining room to its gentle harp soundtrack, this restaurant seems crafted straight from a romance novel. The menu features New American dishes and changes nightly. Seatings happen twice each night and feature a pre-determined menu of locally sourced ingredients.
International. Dinner. Reservations recommended. Closed Monday; also Mid-December-April. $36-85

★DOWNYFLAKE
18 Sparks Ave., Nantucket, 508-228-4533
Locals line up at this restaurant for satisfying, classic American breakfasts including fresh blueberry pancakes. The place is most popular, though, for its fresh-made doughnuts, baked each morning.
Breakfast, lunch. $15 and under

★FOG ISLAND CAFÉ
7 S. Water St., Nantucket, 508-228-1818; www.fogisland.com
This casual spot is known for its breakfasts, which include the popular fog-style chicken hash as well as cranberry pancakes and build-your-own omelets. The dinner menu includes dishes such as sesame crusted tuna and grilled salmon with lemon dill butter.
American. Breakfast, Lunch, dinner. Bar. Children's menu. Closed January-February. $15 and under

★★LE LANGUEDOC
24 Broad St., Nantucket, 508-228-2552; www.lelanguedoc.com
Classic French recipes fill the menu at this traditional restaurant, located in a historic house. Steak frites comes doused with bearnaise and alongside truffled greens, while pan-roasted lobster is served with creamy polenta.
French. Lunch, dinner. Bar. Reservations recommended. Outdoor seating. Closed February-March. $36-85

★★NANTUCKET LOBSTER TRAP
23 Washington St., Nantucket, 508-228-4200; www.nantucketlobstertrap.com
Lines are long at this traditional lobster restaurant, where things are kept simple with steamed lobsters served with fresh corn, boiled potatoes and bread and butter. The menu also includes clams, shrimp, steaks and chowder. Takeout dinners can be ordered ahead of time and are packed and ready to go for the beach or a picnic.
Seafood. Dinner. Bar. Children's menu. Outdoor seating. Closed October-April. $36-85

★★★ORAN MOR
2 S. Beach St., Nantucket, 508-228-8655; www.oranmorbistro.com
Climb the stairs to Oran Mor and discover a food lover's heaven. The eclectic menu echoes the restaurant's accessible elegance. Organic ingredients and

fresh seafood dominate the complex dishes. A friendly, knowledgeable staff caps off a fine-dining experience.

International. Dinner. Bar. Reservations recommended. Closed January-March. $36-85

★★★THE PEARL

12 Federal St., Nantucket, 508-228-9701; www.boardinghouse-pearl.com

This spot was among the first to bring city chic to Nantucket, appealing to a young, fashionable clientele that crowds the bar area on weekend nights. Asian flavors punctuate the Pearl's seafood dishes, while the drink menu is decidedly metropolitan, with various takes on martinis, cosmos and sake in addition to a complete wine and champagne list. There are only two seatings per evening, so reserve early.

International. Dinner, late-night. Bar. Reservations recommended. Closed October-April. $86 and up

★★★SUMMER HOUSE

17 Ocean Ave., Nantucket, 508-257-9976; www.thesummerhouse.com

The Summer House seduces with its oceanfront seating and superb cuisine. White wicker furnishings and ceiling fans set the scene for the refined New American cuisine. A more casual poolside lunch is also served.

American. Dinner. Bar. Outdoor seating. Closed mid-October-mid-May. $86 and up

★★★★TOPPER'S

120 Wauwinet Road, Nantucket, 508-228-0145, 800-426-8718; www.wauwinet.com

Chef David Daniels lends his extensive New England-honed skills to Toppers. Regulars know to order the seasonal prix fixe menu, which has locally inspired treats like lobster and chestnut soup, roasted sirloin of venison and housemade ice cream. His signature dishes, such as maple-glazed foie gras, potato-crusted Maine scallops and roasted New York duckling, are all outstanding. All meals can be paired with a selection from the award-winning 900-bottle wine list.

American. Lunch, dinner, Sunday brunch. Bar. Reservations recommended. Outdoor seating. Closed late October-early May. $86 and up

SPAS
★★★SPA BY THE SEA

120 Wauwinet Road, Nantucket, 508-228-0145, 800-426-8718; www.wauwinet.com

Indulge all your senses at this luxury spa located in the Nantucket seaside retreat The Wauwinet. Signature treatments, including the garden facial and Atlantic seaweed wrap, use local and sea-inspired ingredients. The spa herb garden, comfortable chaise lounges and sounds of rolling waves enhance the serene atmosphere.

NEW BEDFORD

See also Fall River

Herman Melville once said every house in New Bedford was harpooned, and then reeled in from the bottom of the sea. His metaphor held some truth; in his time, the city was the greatest whaling port in the world. But in 1857, when miners struck oil in Pennsylvania, this bustling sea-dependent spot became a veritable ghost town. It was eventually rebuilt around manufacturing but never quite recaptured the flourish of its earlier era. Today, the city is mostly urban and slightly gritty. Its past can be glimpsed in its monuments and museums, and in the sea captains' homes that still line its better streets.

WHAT TO SEE
BUTTONWOOD PARK & ZOO
425 Hawthorn St., New Bedford, 508-991-6178; www.bpzoo.org
The park has a greenhouse, ball fields, tennis courts, a playground, a picnic area and a fitness circuit. Zoo exhibits include elephants, lions, deer, bears, buffalo and a seal pool.
Daily 10 a.m.-5 p.m.

NEW BEDFORD WHALING MUSEUM
18 Johnny Cake Hill, New Bedford, 508-997-0046; www.whalingmuseum.org
The museum features an 89-foot half-scale model of the whale ship *Lagoda*. Galleries are devoted to scrimshaw, local artists, murals and a whale skeleton.
June-December: Daily 9 a.m.-5 p.m.; January-May: Monday-Saturday 9 a.m.-4 p.m., Sunday noon-4 p.m.; open until 9 p.m. every second Thursday of each month.

ROTCH-JONES-DUFF HOUSE AND GARDEN MUSEUM
396 County St., New Bedford, 508-997-1401; www.rjdmuseum.org
This Greek Revival mansion has been maintained to reflect the lives of three families that lived in the house.
Monday-Saturday 10 a.m.-4 p.m., Sunday noon-4 p.m.

SEAMEN'S BETHEL
15 Johnny Cake Hill, New Bedford, 508-992-3295;
Here is the circa 1832 "Whaleman's Chapel" referred to by Melville in *Moby Dick*. The prow-shaped pulpit was later built to represent Melville's description.
Daily.

SPECIAL EVENTS
FEAST OF THE BLESSED SACRAMENT
50 Madeira Ave., Hathaway St., and Tinkham Street, New Bedford, 508-992-6911;
www.portuguesefeast.com
This is the largest Portuguese feast in North America and features three days of entertainment, parades and amusement rides.
First weekend in August.

WHERE TO EAT
★★FREESTONE'S CITY GRILL
41 William St., New Bedford, 508-993-7477; www.freestones.com
Housed in a historic converted bank, this casual restaurant has an eclectic

menu that features everything from lobster rolls and filet mignon to pizzas. The cocktail list includes a lengthy selection of martinis and margaritas. Seafood. Lunch, dinner. Bar. Children's menu. $16-35

NEWBURYPORT

See also Ipswich

One of Massachusetts's best-kept secrets, Newburyport might be the ideal New England town. Smaller than a city but bigger than a village, this north shore spot is quaint without being saccharine and manageable without being boring. Its clean, safe streets exude history, especially those lined with stately Federalist ship captain's houses. Locals have an easy commute to Boston but rarely bother making the trip; everything they need, from sweet clothing boutiques to first-rate dining to the sandy shores of Plum Island, is right here.

WHAT TO SEE
COFFIN HOUSE

14 High Road, Newburyport, 978-462-2634; www.historicnewengland.org

This old home features 17th and 18th-century kitchens, in addition to a buttery and parlor with early 19th-century wallpaper.

June-mid-October, first Saturday of the month 11 a.m.-5 p.m.

CUSHING HOUSE MUSEUM

98 High St., Newburyport, 978-462-2681; www.newburyhist.com

This Federalist-style mansion was once the home of Caleb Cushing, the first U.S. envoy to China.

May-November, Tuesday-Friday 10 a.m.-4 p.m., Saturday from noon.

CUSTOM HOUSE MARITIME MUSEUM

25 Water St., Newburyport, 978-462-8681; www.customhousemaritimemuseum.org

Collections of marine artifacts, ship models and navigational instruments are on display here.

Mid-May-mid-December, Tuesday-Saturday 10 a.m.-4 p.m., Sunday and holiday Mondays noon-4 p.m.

PARKER RIVER NATIONAL WILDLIFE REFUGE

6 Plum Island Turnpike, Newburyport, 978-465-5753; www.fws.gov

This breathtaking, natural barrier beach is six-and-a-half miles long and the home of many species of birds, mammals, reptiles, amphibians and plants. Available are hiking, bicycling, waterfowl hunting and a nature trail. Daily.

WHERE TO STAY
★★GARRISON INN

11 Brown Square, Newburyport, 978-499-8500; www.garrisoninn.com

Rooms at this hotel, housed in a historic building, are basic, but it's the location in central Newburyport that's the draw. The rooms have been updated with flat-screen TVs and down featherbeds.

24 rooms. Restaurant, bar. Pool. Fitness center. Spa. $61-150

CLARK CURRIER INN

45 Green St., Newburyport, 978-465-8363; www.clarkcurrierinn.com

Rooms at this historic inn are individually decorated with antiques and repro-ductions. The Federal style building has been updated with wireless access and air-conditioning.

7 rooms. Complimentary breakfast. $61-150

WHERE TO EAT

★★★DAVID'S

11 Brown Square, Newburyport, 978-462-8077; www.davidstavern.com

A favorite of locals and visitors alike, this restaurant serves a wide variety of global fare. The downstairs pub delivers a casual atmosphere, while the upstairs dining room offers fine dining.

International. Dinner. Bar. Children's menu. $36-85

★THE GROG

13 Middle St., Newburyport, 978-465-8008; www.thegrog.com

This casual pub serves an eclectic menu of oysters, burgers, pasta and even Mexican dishes. Live musicians perform at the downstairs bar throughout the week.

International. Lunch, dinner. Bar. $16-35

★★MICHAEL'S HARBORSIDE

1 Tournament Wharf, Newburyport, 978-462-7785; www.michaelsharborside.com

With its waterfront location, this casual restaurant boasts a lively scene come summer. Seafood is the specialty of the house, with lobster rolls, fried cala-mari and classic baked haddock on the menu.

Seafood. Lunch, dinner. Bar. Outdoor seating. $16-35

★★TEN CENTER STREET

10 Center St., Newburyport, 978-462-6652; www.tencenterstreet.com

An 18th century bakery was the original occupant of this historic building, now in use as a chic, contemporary bistro. The upstairs dining room deliv-ers a more refined experience, while the downstairs pub has a bar and cozy booths. The dinner menu includes standouts such as truffled mac 'n' cheese and lobster chowder.

American. Lunch, dinner, Sunday brunch. Bar. Outdoor seating. Closed Monday. $16-35

NEWTON

See also Boston

Right outside Boston, the city of Newton is made up of 13 small subur-ban villages best known for their well-moneyed citizens and much-envied addresses. The various main streets have become shopping and dining des-tinations for families, while the city's five big schools—including Boston College—lend youthful energy to the area.

WHAT TO SEE
CHARLES RIVER CANOE & KAYAK CENTER
2401 Commonwealth Ave., Newton, 617-965-5110; www.paddleboston.com
Tourists who aren't afraid of getting a little wet love this Charles River entry point. Kayaks and canoes are available for rent.
April-October: daily.

JACKSON HOMESTEAD MUSEUM
527 Washington St., Newton, 617-552-7238; www.ci.newton.ma.us/jackson
Once a station on the Underground Railroad, the 1809 home of the Newton Historical Society has changing exhibits and a children's gallery.
Tuesday-Friday 11 a.m.-5 p.m., Sunday noon-5 p.m.

WHERE TO STAY
★★★BOSTON MARRIOTT NEWTON
2345 Commonwealth Ave., Newton, 617-969-1000, 800-228-9290; www.marriott.com
Ideal for business travelers, the Newton Marriot has a 24-hour, self-serve business center and more than 16,000 square feet of meeting space. Its prime location along the Charles River offers a great view.
430 rooms. Restaurant, bar. Fitness center. $61-150

★★★HOTEL INDIGO RIVERSIDE
399 Grove St., Newton, 617-969-5300; www.newtonboutiquehotel.com
Who'd have guessed you could find a little bit of Vegas-meets-South Beach in unassuming Newton, Massachusetts? But that's what the Hotel Indigo brought to town when it opened in summer 2008. Formerly a tired-looking Holiday Inn, the space has been transformed. Rooms are still on the small side, but they're now stocked with Aveda bath products, platform beds, all-marble bathrooms and flat-screen HDTVs. The best reason to stay here, though, is on the ground floor: Bokx109, a "concept" steakhouse with occasional celebrity guest chefs, and the Bokx Pool, an oddly appealing oasis replete with cabanas and cocktail service. Seasonal décor shifts mean the hotel gets a mini-facelift every couple of months.
193 rooms. Restaurant, bar. Fitness center. Pool. Business center. $151-250

★★★SHERATON NEWTON HOTEL
320 Washington St., Newton, 617-969-3010, 800-325-3535; www.sheraton.com
All rooms and suites at this recently renovated property have a contemporary décor with sleek white bedding, well-designed work areas and warm, mustard-colored walls. Those not wanting to shell out for Boston rates can stay here and hop the downtown express, which departs for Faneuil Hall every 20 minutes.
270 rooms. Restaurant, bar. Pool. Fitness center. $61-150

WHERE TO EAT
★★★LUMIERE
1293 Washington St., West Newton, 617-244-9199; www.lumiererestaurant.com
The words "warm" and "whimsical" best sum up the ambiance at this suburban French spot. The front door handle is a spoon, and Scrabble tiles line

the restroom doors. But the chef doesn't fool around with the contemporary French cuisine; it's fresh and straightforward, making this spot the best bistro for miles around.

French, menu. Dinner. $36-785

NORTH ADAMS

See also Williamstown

No town in the Berkshires has gone through a more dramatic transformation than North Adams (well, at least not recently). Thanks to Mass MoCA, the biggest modern art museum in the world, the former factory city suddenly finds itself a booming tourist center. Boutiques and eateries have followed suit, as has a crowd of young culture vultures eager to invest in the locale's emerging spirit.

WHAT TO SEE

KIDSPACE

87 Marshall St., North Adams, 413-664-4481; www.massmoca.org/kidspace

The museum's children's gallery presents contemporary art in a manner that is interesting and accessible, and has hands-on activity stations where kids can create their own art.

June-early September: daily noon-4 p.m.; rest of year: limited hours.

MASS MOCA

1040 Mass MoCA Way, North Adams, 413-664-4481; www.massmoca.org

The center for visual, performing and media arts features unconventional exhibits and performances by renowned artists and cultural institutions.

July-early September: daily 10 a.m.-6 p.m.; rest of year: Wednesday-Monday 11 a.m.-5 p.m.

MOHAWK TRAIL STATE FOREST

175 Mohawk Trail/Route 2, Charlemont, 413-339-5504;
www.mass.gov/dcr/parks/western/mhwk.htm

The forest has spectacular scenery and swimming, fishing, hiking, winter sports, picnicking, camping and log cabins.

MOUNT GREYLOCK STATE RESERVATION

Rockwell Road, North Adams, 413-499-4262; www.mass.gov/dcr/parks/mtGreylock

At 3,491 vertical feet, Mount Greylock is the highest point in the state. Fishing, hunting, cross-country skiing, picnicking and snowmobiles are allowed.

Mid-May-mid-October.

NATURAL BRIDGE STATE PARK

McCauley Road, off Route 8 North Adams, 413-663-6392;
www.mass.gov/dcr/parks/western/nbdg.htm

This park has a water-eroded marble bridge and 550-million-year-old rock formations popularized by Nathaniel Hawthorne. Picnicking is allowed in the park.

Mid-May-mid-October.

WESTERN GATEWAY HERITAGE STATE PARK

115 State St., North Adams, 413 663-6312;
www.mass.gov/dcr/parks/western/wghp.htm

A restored freight yard, with six buildings surround a cobbled courtyard and detailed historic exhibits on the construction of the Hoosac Railroad Tunnel. Daily.

SPECIAL EVENTS
FALL FOLIAGE FESTIVAL

6 West Main St, North Adams, 413-664-6180; www.fallfoliageparade.com

The festival featuers a parade, entertainment, dancing and children's activities. Late September-early October.

WHERE TO STAY
★★★THE PORCHES INN

231 River St., North Adams, 413-664-0400; www.porches.com

Directly across from Mass MoCA, this inn is housed in a row of vividly painted Victorian buildings, each of which has been restored and decorated with sleek, modern furnishings. There are porches and rocking chairs, but most guests ignore them in favor of the pool and luxe amenities.
52 rooms. Complimentary breakfast. Fitness center. $151-250

NORTHAMPTON

See also Springfield

Thanks to Jonathan Edwards, a Puritan who was once regarded as the greatest preacher in New England, Northampton was the scene of a frenzied religious revival movement in the early 18th century. However, the fervor had little lasting impact on the town, which is now full of first-class theaters and restaurants, antique shops and art galleries, and up-to-date hotels and inns. The area's thriving arts scene can be partly credited to its close proximity to five colleges: Mount Holyoke, Amherst, Hampshire, Smith and the University of Massachusetts.

WHAT TO SEE
ARCADIA NATURE CENTER AND WILDLIFE SANCTUARY, MASSACHUSETTS AUDUBON SOCIETY

127 Combs Road, Easthampton, 413-584-3009; www.massaudubon.org

On these 550 acres are an ancient oxbow of the Connecticut River, self-guided nature trails and an observation tower.
Tuesday-Sunday 9 a.m.-3 p.m.

CALVIN COOLIDGE MEMORIAL ROOM

20 West St., Northampton, 413-587-1011; www.forbeslibrary.org

On display are the late president's papers and correspondence.
Monday-Thursday, Saturday; schedule may vary.

HADLEY FARM MUSEUM

208 Middle St., Hadley, 413-584-1160;

A restored 1782 barn houses agricultural implements, tools and domestic

items dating back to the 1700s.
May-October, Wednesday-Saturday 11 a.m.-4 p.m., Sunday 1-4 p.m.

HISTORIC NORTHAMPTON MUSEUM HOUSES
46-66 Bridge St., Northampton, 413-584-6011; www.historic-northampton.org
These include the 1820 Damon House and the 1730 Parsons House.
Tuesday-Friday 10 a.m.-4 p.m., Saturday-Sunday from noon.

LOOK PARK
300 N. Main St., Florence, 413-584-5457; www.lookpark.org
In the park are a miniature train, the Christenson Zoo, boating, tennis, picnicking, playgrounds, ball fields and the Pines Theater.

MUSEUM OF ART
Elm Street, Northampton, 413-585-2760; www.smith.edu
This spot has a fine collection with an emphasis on American and European art of the 19th and 20th centuries.
September-May, Tuesday-Sunday; rest of year, Tuesday-Saturday.

SMITH COLLEGE
33 Elm St., Northampton, 413-584-2700; www.smith.edu
With 2,700 women, this is the largest private women's liberal arts college in the United States. On campus are Paradise Pond, the Helen Hills Chapel and the William Allan Neilson Library that has more than one million volumes.

SPECIAL EVENTS
THREE-COUNTY FAIR
Three-County Fairgrounds, Damon Road and Highway 9, Northampton, 413-584-2237; www.3countyfair.com
The nation's oldest agricultural fair has agricultural exhibits, horse racing and pari-mutuel betting.
Labor Day week.

WHERE TO STAY
★★★THE HOTEL NORTHAMPTON
36 King St., Northampton, 413-584-3100, 800-547-3529; www.hotelnorthampton.com
Built in 1927, this brick Colonial Revival building sits on a busy street opposite the restored Calvin Theater. A narrow glass greenhouse enwraps half the building and the hotel's public areas are adorned with Norman Rockwell prints and Japanese woodcuts. Colonial furnishings lend most guest rooms a stately vibe, while the hotel's two restaurants round out the experience.
106 rooms. Complimentary breakfast. Restaurant, bar. $151-250

WHERE TO EAT
★★EASTSIDE GRILL
19 Strong Ave., Northampton, 413-586-3347; www.eastsidegrill.com
With a lengthy menu offering a range of eclectic dishes, this casual bistro offers something for everyone. Entrées include baked Atlantic cod with lobster bisque, blackened ribeye and chicken etouffée.

American. Dinner. Bar. $16-35

ORLEANS

See also Chatham, Dennis

Orleans was supposedly named in honor of the French Duke of Orleans. Its history also includes the dubious distinction of being the only town in America to have been fired upon by the Germans during World War I. Today, tourists pass through this commercial hub along the way to Nauset Beach and the outer Cape.

WHAT TO SEE
ACADEMY OF PERFORMING ARTS

120 Main St., Orleans, 508-255-1963; www.apa1.org

The theater presents comedies, dramas, musicals, dance and workshops for all ages.

FRENCH CABLE STATION MUSEUM

41 S. Orleans Road, Orleans, 508-240-1735; www.frenchcablestationmuseum.org

Built in 1890 as the American end of the transatlantic cable from Brest, France, the museum has original submarine cable equipment.
July and August: Thursday-Sunday 1-4 p.m.; June and September: Friday-Sunday 1-4 p.m.

NAUSET BEACH

Beach Road, Orleans, 508-255-1386; www.capecod-orleans.com

One of the most spectacular ocean beaches on the Atlantic coast sits within the boundaries of Cape Cod National Seashore. Swimming, surfing, fishing are allowed at the beach. Lifeguards keep watch over beachgoers. There is a nominal parking fee.

ALSO RECOMMENDED
SHIP'S KNEES INN

186 Beach Road, East Orleans, 508-255-1312; www.shipskneesinn.com

This inn is a restored sea captain's house and is just steps from the ocean. The rooms are individually decorated in a nautical style and are furnished with antiques and four-poster beds.
16 rooms. No children under 12. Complimentary breakfast. $61-150

WHERE TO EAT
★★BARLEY NECK INN

5 Beach Road, East Orleans, 508-255-0212, 800-281-7505; www.barleyneck.com

Classic fine dining is the focus at the country house restaurant, set in a circa 1868 manor house. Choose from beef tenderloin, sole francaise, chicken pomodoro and more.
American. Dinner. Bar. Reservations recommended. $16-35

★THE BEACON ROOM

23 West Road, Orleans, 508-255-2211; www.beaconroom.com

This quaint bistro serves fresh seafood in a simple setting. Clam chowder and linguine in clam sauce are menu standouts.

American. Lunch, dinner. Bar. Outdoor seating. $16-35

★★★CAPTAIN LINNELL HOUSE

137 Skaket Beach Road, Orleans, 508-255-3400; www.linnell.com

Chef/owner Bill Conway delivers a delightful dining experience at this romantic restaurant. The grounds set the scene with a Victorian gazebo, lavender bushes and ocean breezes. Oil lamps and fresh flowers add to the main room's cozy, peaceful atmosphere. The skillfully prepared menu has highlights like veal with crab, bouillabaisse and pork tenderloin, and an extensive wine list is offered.

American. Dinner. Bar. Children's menu. Reservations recommended. Closed Monday; also mid-February-March. $36-85

★LOBSTER CLAW

Highway 6A, Orleans, 508-255-1800; www.lobsterclaw.com

For classic lobster bakes served in a kitschy setting (with plenty of fishing nets and nautical accents), the Lobster Claw can't be beat. The menu also includes a selection of grilled fish, sides and steaks.

American, seafood. Lunch, dinner. Bar. Children's menu. Closed mid-November-March. $16-35

★★MAHONEY'S ATLANTIC BAR AND GRILL

28 Main St., Orleans, 508-255-5505; www.mahoneysatlantic.com

This upscale bistro specializes in fresh, gourmet takes of classic seafood dishes, including pan roasted lobster with brandy flambé and blackened tuna sashimi. The bar offers an edited menu of smaller dishes and classic drinks.

American. Dinner. Bar. $16-35

★★NAUSET BEACH CLUB RESTAURANT

222 E. Main St., East Orleans, 508-255-8547; www.nausetbeachclub.com

Northern Italian cuisine is the focus at this upscale bistro. Pastas are made fresh each day, and the wine list includes a wide selection of Italian vintages.

Italian. Dinner. Bar. Reservations recommended. $36-85

★SIR CRICKET'S FISH AND CHIPS

38 Route 6A, Orleans, 508-255-4453

Prepare to dig in to crisp fried clams, superb lobster rolls and creamy chowder at this no-frills seafood shack. There are only a few tables and the place is usually crowded with locals, but takeout is available.

Seafood. Lunch, dinner. Credit cards not accepted. Children's menu. $15 and under

PITTSFIELD

See also Lenox, Stockbridge

Once widely regarded as the unwelcoming, gritty epicenter of the Berkshires, Pittsfield has recently started to return to its busy, beautiful small-town roots. The city's revitalized North Street once again boasts fine restaurants and shops, and its museums and theaters have also undergone facelifts. Instead of being a place that visitors drive through on their way elsewhere, Pittsfield is becoming a destination.

WHAT TO SEE
ARROWHEAD

780 Holmes Road, Pittsfield, 413-442-1793; www.mobydick.org

Herman Melville wrote Moby Dick while living here from 1850 to 1863. It's now the headquarters of the Berkshire County Historical Society.

Memorial Day weekend-October, daily 9:30 a.m.-4 p.m.

BERKSHIRE MUSEUM

39 South St., Pittsfield, 413-443-7171; www.berkshiremuseum.org

This is a museum of art, natural science and history, featuring American 19th- and 20th-century paintings; works by British and European masters; artifacts from ancient civilizations; exhibits on Berkshire County history; and children's programs.

Monday-Saturday 10 a.m.-5 p.m., Sunday noon-5 p.m.

BOUSQUET

101 Dan Fox Drive, Pittsfield, 413-442-8316; www.bousquets.com

The ski area has two double chairlifts, three rope tows, snowmaking, ski school, rentals, a cafeteria, bar and daycare. The longest run is one mile with a vertical drop of 750 feet. Night skiing is allowed.

December-March, daily.

HANCOCK SHAKER VILLAGE

Highways 20 and 41, Pittsfield, 413-443-0188; www.hancockshakervillage.org

A Shaker site from 1790 to 1960, this is now a living history museum of Shaker life, crafts and farming. A large collection of furniture and artifacts is housed in 20 restored buildings, including the Round Stone Barn.

JIMINY PEAK

37 Corey Road, Hancock, 413-738-5500; www.jiminypeak.com

This ski area has a six-passenger lift, three double chairlifts, a J-bar, two quads, three triple chairs, a ski school, rentals, a restaurant, two cafeterias, a bar and a lodge. The longest run is two miles with a vertical drop 1,140 feet. In the summer (Memorial Day through Labor Day), the mountain has trout fishing, 18-hole miniature golf course and an Alpine slide and tennis center.

Thanksgiving-early April, daily.

WHERE TO STAY
★★CROWNE PLAZA HOTEL

1 West St., Pittsfield, 413-499-2000, 800-227-6963; www.berkshirecrowne.com

Rooms at this business hotel feature updated linens and down duvets. The property includes an indoor pool and a fitness center.

179 rooms. Restaurant, bar. Pool. Business center. Spa. $61-150

PLYMOUTH

See also New Bedford

On December 21, 1620, 102 people stepped off the *Mayflower* to found the first permanent European settlement north of Virginia: Plymouth. Plagued by exposure, cold, hunger and disease during its first American winter, the colony was nearly wiped out. But the next year, the settlers were firmly established. Their landing site is memorialized by Plymouth Rock. Today, the town doubles as a summer resort oasis and fishing village, with tourists and locals going about their days together in ways those early citizens could hardly have imagined.

WHAT TO SEE
HARLOW OLD FORT HOUSE
119 Sandwich St., Plymouth, 508-746-0012; www.harlowfamily.com/hofh/index.htm
The site holds a circa 1677 Pilgrim house with crafts, candle-dipping demonstrations and an herb garden.
July-August, Tuesday-Friday.

HEDGE HOUSE
126 Water St., Plymouth, 508-746-0012; www.visit-plymouth.com
This 1809 house has period furnishings and special exhibits.
June-August: Wednesday-Sunday 2-6 p.m.

HOWLAND HOUSE
33 Sandwich St., Plymouth, 508-746-9590; www.pilgrimjohnhowlandsociety.org
This restored 1666 Pilgrim house has 17th and 18th-century furnishings.
Memorial Day-mid-October, Monday-Saturday.

MAYFLOWER SOCIETY HOUSE MUSEUM
4 Winslow St., Plymouth, 508 746-3188; www.themayflowersociety.com
This is the national headquarters of the General Society of Mayflower Descendants.
July-Labor Day: daily; Memorial Day weekend-June and early September-October: Friday-Sunday.

MYLES STANDISH STATE FOREST
194 Cranberry Road, South Carver, 508-866-2526;
www.mass.gov/dcr/parks/southeast/mssf.htm
The park consists of approximately 15,000 acres with swimming, fishing, boating, hiking, riding, hunting, picnicking and camping.

NATIONAL MONUMENT TO THE FOREFATHERS
Allerton Street, and Highway 44, Plymouth, 508-746-1790
This site was built between 1859 and 1889—at a cost of $155,000—to depict the virtues of the Pilgrims. At 81 feet high, it is the tallest solid granite monument in the United States.
May-October, daily.

PILGRIM HALL MUSEUM

75 Court St., Plymouth, 508-746-1620; www.pilgrimhall.org

Decorative arts and possessions of first Pilgrims and their descendants, plus the only known portrait of a *Mayflower* passenger, are on display here. Daily 9:30 a.m.-4:30 p.m.; closed January.

PLIMOTH PLANTATION/MAYFLOWER II

137 Warren Ave., Plymouth, 508-746-1622; www.plimoth.org

No, it's not a typo. The Plimoth Plantation, a re-creation of the 1627 Pilgrim village, uses the colony's old-fashioned spelling. Onsite actors pretend to have zero knowledge of the 21st—or even the 18th—century; they wear and use only the clothing, the equipment, the tools and the cookware the early settlers would have employed. The *Mayflower II* is a full-scale reproduction of the original built by J.W. & A. Upham with oak timbers, hand-forged nails, linen canvas sails and hemp rope.

March-November, daily.

PLYMOUTH COLONY WINERY

56 Pinewood Road, Plymouth, 508-747-3334; www.plymouthcolonywines.com

These working cranberry bogs are open to the public and give a good insight into cranberry harvest activities.

April-late December, daily; March, Friday-Sunday; also holidays.

PROVINCETOWN FERRY

10 Town Wharf, Plymouth, 508-746-2643, 800-242-2469; www.provincetownferry.com

A round-trip passenger ferry departs State Pier in the morning and returns in the evening.

Mid-June-Labor Day, daily; May-mid-June and after Labor Day-October, weekends.

RICHARD SPARROW HOUSE

42 Summer St., Plymouth, 508-747-1240; www.sparrowhouse.com

Dating to 1640, this is Plymouth's oldest restored home.

Open daily, except Wednesdays, 10 a.m.-5 p.m.

SPOONER HOUSE

27 North St., Plymouth, 508-746-0012; www.visit-plymouth.com

This 1747 home was occupied by the Spooner family for five generations and is furnished with its heirlooms.

June-October, Thursday-Saturday.

SPECIAL EVENTS
AUTUMNAL FEASTING

137 Warren Ave., Plymouth, 508-746-1622; www.plimoth.org

At Plimoth Plantation's 1627 Pilgrim Village, this is a harvest celebration with Dutch colonists from Fort Amsterdam re-creating a 17th-century event. There are on site activities, coupled with feasting and games.

WHERE TO STAY
★★RADISSON HOTEL PLYMOUTH HARBOR

180 Water St., Plymouth, 508-747-4900, 800-333-3333; www.radisson.com
Rooms at this central Plymouth hotel have recently been updated with down duvets and luxury linens. The property includes a large indoor pool and fitness center.
175 rooms. Restaurant, bar. $61-150

PROVINCETOWN
See also Chatham, Orleans, Truro and North Truro
Though its thunder has been stolen by Plymouth and that town's famous rock, Provincetown was actually the Mayflower's first docking site. Artists of all kinds converge in P'town, as those "in the know" call it, for the bustling—often too crowded—summer season. The town is known for its gay and lesbian scene, particularly during the July 4th holiday.

WHAT TO SEE
COMMERCIAL STREET

Commercial Street, Provincetown
Stretching more than three miles in length, this narrow street sports art galleries, shops, clubs, restaurants and hotels. When the street was constructed in 1835, all houses faced the harbor. Today, most homes have been turned 180 degrees to face the street (or have had a new front door crafted on the opposite side).

EXPEDITION WHYDAH'S SEA LAB & LEARNING CENTER

16 MacMillan Wharf, Provincetown, 508-487-8899; www.whydah.com
This is the archaeological site of the sunken pirate ship Whydah, which was struck by storms in 1717. Learn about the recovery of the ship's pirate treasure, in addition to the lives and deaths of pirates and the history of the ship and its passengers.
April-mid-October: daily; mid-October-December: weekends and school holidays.

PILGRIM MONUMENT & MUSEUM

1 High Pole Hill, Provincetown, 508-487-1310; www.pilgrim-monument.org
This is a 252-foot granite tower commemorating the Pilgrims' 1620 landing in the New World. Exhibits include whaling equipment, scrimshaw, ship models, artifacts from shipwrecks and a Pilgrim Room with a scale-model diorama of the *Mayflower*. Summer: daily.

PROVINCETOWN ART ASSOCIATION & MUSEUM

460 Commercial St., Provincetown, 508-487-1750; www.paam.org
Established in 1914, the collection is a virtual history of art on the Cape.
Late May-October: daily; rest of year: weekends.

WHALE WATCHING

306 Commercial St., Provincetown, 508-240-3636, 800-826-9300;
www.whalewatch.com

Visitors can take 3½ to 4-hour trips. Research scientists from the Provincetown Center for Coastal Studies are aboard each trip to lecture on the history of whales.

Mid-April-October, daily.

SPECIAL EVENTS
PROVINCETOWN PORTUGUESE FESTIVAL
MacMillian Wharf, Provincetown, 508-487-3424;

www.provincetownportuguesefestival.com

Provincetown's Portuguese community started this festival more than 50 years ago. Each year, in late June, the local bishop says mass at St. Peter's Church and then leads a procession to MacMillan Wharf, where he blesses a parade of fishing boats. The festival that follows features fireworks, concerts, dancing, and Portuguese art and food.

Last week in June.

WHERE TO STAY
★★★CROWNE POINTE HISTORIC INN
82 Bradford St., Provincetown, 508-487-6767, 877-276-9631; www.crownepointe.com

Five of the buildings at this downtown P'town inn date to the 1600s. Peaceful gardens, a fountain and a koi pond contribute to the mellow outdoor setting, while hardwood floors, antiques, crown molding and ceiling fans decorate the interiors. The guest rooms are large and offer extensive amenities; most rooms also have fireplaces and whirlpool tubs. Room stays include hearty breakfasts and evening cocktail receptions.

40 rooms. No children accepted. Complimentary breakfast. Restaurant, bar. Spa. $251-350

ALSO RECOMMENDED
FAIRBANKS INN
90 Bradford St., Provincetown, 508-487-0386, 800-324-7265; www.fairbanksinn.com

The rooms at this inn are spread out over three historic buildings, and feature colonial-style décor, period furnishings and flat-screen TVs. The courtyard garden is a charming spot for enjoying the ample daily breakfasts.

14 rooms. No children under 15. Complimentary breakfast. $61-150

SNUG COTTAGE
178 Bradford St., Provincetown, 508-487-1616, 800-432-2334; www.snugcottage.com

This charming inn is surrounded by lush gardens and features individually decorated rooms, many with fireplaces. The innkeeper provides snacks, drinks, afternoon wine and a full breakfast during stays.

8 rooms. Complimentary breakfast. $$

WHERE TO EAT
★★★BISTRO AT CROWNE POINTE INN
82 Bradford St., Provincetown, 508-487-6767; www.crownepointe.com

Paintings, fresh flowers and gleaming wood floors set the tone at this blufftop restaurant. The seasonal menu is skillfully served, and guests can substitute or order options made from scratch, without butter, cream or fatty oils.

American menu. Dinner. Bar. Reservations recommended. Closed Tuesday. $36-85

★FANIZZI'S BY THE SEA
539 Commercial St., Provincetown, 508-487-1964; www.fanizzisrestaurant.com
Waterfront views and a casual atmosphere make this Italian restaurant a favorite with locals. The menu includes dishes such as mustard nut crusted cod and freshly made tri-color tortellini.
American, Italian. Lunch, dinner. Bar. Children's menu. Reservations recommended. $36-85

★★FRONT STREET
230 Commercial St., Provincetown, 508-487-9715; www.frontstreetrestaurant.com
Chef owner Donna Aliperti creates, seasonally-focused food with an Italian accent at this sweet bistro in downtown P'Town. Choose from classics such as clams casino and eggplant parmesan, and wash them down with a selection from the wine list, with bottles from California and Italy.
Italian. Dinner. Bar. Reservations recommended. Closed January-April. $16-35

★★LOBSTER POT
321 Commercial St., Provincetown, 508-487-0842; www.ptownlobsterpot.com
An old-school favorite, located in the heart of Provincetown, this lobster shack is the place to go for clam chowder, lobster rolls and fresh boiled lobster. The Top of the Pot bar is a prime spot for views of the harbor and cocktails.
Seafood. Lunch, dinner. Bar. Children's menu. Closed December-March. $36-85

★★THE MEWS RESTAURANT & CAFÉ
429 Commercial St., Provincetown, 508-487-1500; www.mews.com
This two-level restaurant (fine dining on the first floor, café on the second) has waterfront views and an eclectic menu. Entrées include everything from curried chicken to filet mignon with bearnaise sauce.
International. Dinner, Sunday brunch. Bar. $16-35

★★NAPI'S
7 Freeman St., Provincetown, 508-487-1145, 800-571-6274;
www.napis-restaurant.com
The menu at this casual restaurant is extensive, but is best known for its vegetarian selection of raviolis, stir fries and burritos. Carnivores can dig into steak bearnaise, Thai chicken and shrimp and linguine with clams.
International. Dinner. Bar. Children's menu. Reservations recommended. $16-35

★★★RED INN RESTAURANT
15 Commercial St., Provincetown, 508-487-7334, 866-473-3466; www.theredinn.com
One of the best parts about this restaurant is its view of the harbor, the bay, the Long Point lighthouse and the shores of the Outer Cape. Diners get an eyeful of the panoramic display as they chomp on the house specialty: a tasty

porterhouse steak.

American. Dinner, brunch. Bar. Reservations recommended. $36-85

ROCKPORT

See also Gloucester, Ipswich

Rockport is a year-round artists' colony. A weather-beaten shanty on one of its many wharves has been the subject of so many paintings that it's now referred to as "Motif No. 1." Studios, galleries and summer cottages dot the shore of this quiet Cape Ann town, while tourists cruise its streets.

WHAT TO SEE
OLD CASTLE

Granite and Curtis Streets, Rockport, 978-546-9533;
www.sandybayhistorical.org/Castle.htm

This 1715 structure is a fine example of early 18th-century architecture and exhibits. July-August: Saturday; rest of year: by appointment.

THE PAPER HOUSE

52 Pigeon Hill St., Rockport, 978-546-2629; www.paperhouserockport.com

Newspapers were used in the construction of this house and its furniture. April-October: daily.

SANDY BAY HISTORICAL SOCIETY & MUSEUMS

40 King St., Rockport, 978-546-9533; www.sandybayhistorical.org

The museum has early American and 19th-century rooms and objects and exhibits on fishing, the granite industry and the Atlantic cable. Mid-June-mid-September: daily; rest of year: by appointment.

SPECIAL EVENTS
ROCKPORT CHAMBER MUSIC FESTIVAL

35 Main St., Rockport, 978-546-7391; www.rcmf.org

Soloists and chamber ensembles of international acclaim have performed at this art colony since 1982. A lecture series and family concert are also featured. Four weekends in June or July.

WHERE TO STAY
★★★EMERSON INN BY THE SEA

1 Cathedral Ave., Rockport, 978-546-6321, 800-964-5550;
www.emersoninnbythesea.com

This traditional country inn has hosted guests at its Pigeon Cove location since 1846. From March to the end of December, visitors can take in ocean views from the pool, porch, restaurant and most of the guest rooms. The rooms are decorated in country florals and feature wireless access. 36 rooms. Restaurant. Spa. $61-150

ALSO RECOMMENDED
ADDISON CHOATE INN

49 Broadway, Rockport, 978-546-7543, 800-245-7543; www.addisonchoateinn.com

This Cape Ann bed and breakfast is less than an hour's drive north of Boston.

The English country rooms are decorated with antiques and period pieces, and some have four-poster beds.
8 rooms. No children under 11. Complimentary breakfast. $61-150

THE INN ON COVE HILL
37 Mount Pleasant St., Rockport, 978-546-2701, 888-546-2701;
www.innoncovehill.com
This inn was built in 1791 from the proceeds of pirates' gold found nearby. Rooms are individually decorated with period furnishings.
8 rooms. Complimentary breakfast. Closed mid-October-mid-April. $61-150

SALEM
See also Marblehead
Despite its picturesque, idyllic streets, famous native son Nathaniel Hawthorne and its legacy as a major shipbuilding center, Salem will always be known for the brutal blip in its history. In 1692, at the peak of the town's infamous witch trials, 19 people were hanged on Gallows Hill, another was "pressed" to death and at least two others died in jail. A museum now memorializes the terrible events and much of the town's tourist trade revolves around the old trials.

WHAT TO SEE
CROWNINSHIELD-BENTLEY HOUSE
126 Essex St., Salem, 978-745-9500
Reverend William Bentley, minister and diarist, lived here from 1791 to 1819.
June-October, daily; rest of year, Saturday-Sunday, holidays.

DERBY HOUSE
174 Derby St., Salem, 978-740-1660; www.nps.gov/sama/historyculture/derby.htm
This was the home of maritime merchant Elias Hasket Derby, one of the country's first millionaires. The garden features roses, herbs and 19th-century flowers. Visits are by tour only; call to make an appointment.

GARDNER-PINGREE HOUSE
128 Essex St., Salem, 978-745-9500
Designed by Samuel McIntire, this 1804 house has been restored and handsomely furnished.
June-October: daily; rest of year: Saturday-Sunday, holidays.

HOUSE OF SEVEN GABLES
115 Derby St., Salem, 978-744-0991; www.7gables.org
Nathaniel Hawthorne's 1851 novel of the same name is said to have been inspired by this house.
Daily; weekends in October; closed first three weeks in January.

JOHN WARD HOUSE

161 Essex St., Salem, 978-745-9500
The house features 17th-century furnishings.
June-October, daily; rest of year, Saturday-Sunday, holidays.

PEABODY MUSEUM & ESSEX INSTITUTE

East India Square, Salem, 978-745-9500, 866-745-1876; www.pem.org/museum
The Peabody Museum, founded by sea captains in 1799, features five world-famous collections in 30 galleries.
Tuesday-Sunday and holiday Mondays: 10 a.m.-5 p.m.

PEIRCE-NICHOLS HOUSE

80 Federal St., Salem, 978-745-9500
One of the finest examples of McIntire's architectural genius, this 1782 home is authentically furnished.
By appointment only.

PIONEER VILLAGE: SALEM IN 1630

Forest River Park off W. St., Salem, 978-740-9636; www.essexheritage.org
A reproduction of an early Puritan settlement, the village has dugouts, wigwams and thatched cottages peopled by costumed interpreters.

ROPES MANSION AND GARDEN

318 Essex St., Salem, 978-745-9500; www.salemmass.com
This is a restored gambrel-roofed, Georgian and Colonial mansion furnished with period pieces. The garden, laid out in 1912, is known for its beauty and variety.
June-October: daily; limited hours Sunday.

SALEM MARITIME NATIONAL HISTORIC SITE

174 Derby St., Salem, 978-740-1660; www.nps.gov/sama
The site includes nine acres of historic waterfront. There are both self-guided and guided tours available.
Daily.

SALEM WITCH MUSEUM

19½ Washington Square, Salem, 978-744-1692; www.salemwitchmuseum.com
The Salem witch trials of 1692 are recreated here with a 30-minute narrated presentation that uses special lighting and life-size figures. (The exhibit may be frightening for young children.) Slightly less gruesome is the town's October Salem's Haunted Happenings, a Halloween festival that features street merchants, plays, witchy games and haunted houses.
Daily; extended hours in July and August.

WITCH DUNGEON MUSEUM

16 Lynde St., Salem, 978-741-3570; www.witchdungeon.com
Onsite is a reenactment of the witch trial of Sarah Good and a tour through a re-created dungeon where accused witches awaited trial.

April-November, daily.

WITCH HOUSE
310 Essex St., Salem, 978-744-8815; www.salemweb.com/witchhouse
This was the home of witchcraft trial judge Jonathan Corwin; some of the accused witches may have been examined here.
May-early November, daily 10 a.m.-5 p.m.; extended hours in October.

WHERE TO STAY
★★HAWTHORNE HOTEL
18 Washington Square West, Salem, 978-744-4080, 800-729-7829;
www.hawthornehotel.com
With its prime location in the heart of Salem, this historic hotel is hard to miss. The guest rooms feature colonial-style décor and free wireless access. The hotel's Tavern, with its wood burning fireplace, is a cozy spot for breakfast or lunch.
93 rooms. Restaurant. $61-150

WHERE TO EAT
★★THE GRAPEVINE
26 Congress St., Salem, 978-745-9335; www.grapevinesalem.com
This cozy bistro has a menu with an emphasis on hearty Italian cooking, from pappardelle bolognese to Tuscan seafood soup. The wine list includes reasonably priced bottles and half-bottles from around the world.
American, Italian. Dinner. Bar. Outdoor seating. $36-85

★★★LYCEUM
43 Church St., Salem, 978-745-7665; www.lyceumsalem.com
One of the area's top restaurants, this comfortable dining room is located in the building where Alexander Graham Bell made his first call in 1877. Seasonal, local ingredients shine in dishes such as pan-seared scallops with chorizo sausage and shitake risotto.
American. Lunch, dinner, Sunday brunch. Bar. $16-35

SANDWICH
See also Barnstable and Hyannis
Sandwich was the first established town on Cape Cod. Today, it's famous for its eponymous glass. The town, founded in 1639, is the oldest on Cape Cod.

WHAT TO SEE
HERITAGE MUSEUM AND GARDENS
67 Grove St., Sandwich, 508-888-3300; http://www.heritagemuseumsandgardens.org
Formerly the Heritage Plantation, Heritage Museum and Gardens has an eclectic mix of beautiful gardens, folk art, antique cars and military paraphernalia. Highlights include the 1800-era Old East Windmill and a restored 1912 carousel. Call ahead to find out about unique exhibits, displays and concerts.
May-October, daily; November-April, Wednesday-Sunday.

HOXIE HOUSE & DEXTER GRIST MILL

Water St., Sandwich, 508-888-1173

These are restored mid-17th-century buildings with an operating mill.
Mid-June-mid-October, daily.

SANDWICH GLASS MUSEUM

129 Main St., Sandwich, 508-888-0251; www.sandwichglassmuseum.org/glass_show

An internationally renowned collection of Sandwich Glass.
April-October, daily.

WHERE TO STAY
ISAIAH JONES HOMESTEAD

165 Main St., Sandwich, 508-888-9115, 800-526-1625; www.isaiahjones.com

An American flag and flower-lined porch adorn the exterior of this 1849
Victorian home. Decorated with antiques and country-patterned fabrics, the
guest rooms are spacious and include fireplaces.
7 rooms. No children under 16. Complimentary breakfast. $61-150

WHERE TO EAT
★★AQUA GRILLE

14 Gallo Road, Sandwich, 508-888-8889; www.aquagrille.com

This casual waterfront restaurant serves straightforward interpretations of
Cape favorites, including meaty, creamy lobster rolls and herb battered local
cod. The open-air deck is an ideal spot for sipping the special $5 martinis.
American, seafood. Lunch, dinner. Bar. Children's menu. Outdoor seating.
Closed November-mid-April. $16-35

★★BEE-HIVE TAVERN

406 Highway 6A, Sandwich, 508-833-1184; www.thebeehivetavern.com

A simple, family-friendly restaurant, the Bee-Hive serves seafood and classic bistro fare in a casual setting. Entrées include lobster pot pie and blackened salmon with barbecue sauce.
American, seafood. Lunch, dinner. Bar. Children's menu. $16-35

★★★THE DAN'L WEBSTER INN

149 Main St., Sandwich, 508-888-3623, 800-444-3566; www.danlwebsterinn.com

A former 1800s stagecoach inn once frequented by its namesake, this hotel
offers both a tavern and a white-tablecloth dining room. Chef and co-owner
Robert Catania buys some of his fish and hydroponic vegetables from a local
aquafarm, and he has built his wine list around his culinary aspirations.
American. Breakfast, lunch, dinner, Sunday brunch. Bar. Children's menu.
Reservations recommended. $16-35

SPRINGFIELD

See also Northampton

Springfield has a fine library, museums and a symphony orchestra, but it's
best known for being a major industrial city on the Connecticut River. The
game of basketball was first played here in 1891.

WHAT TO SEE
BASKETBALL HALL OF FAME
1150 W. Columbus Ave., Springfield, 413-781-6500; www.hoophall.com
This sports spot includes exhibits on the game, its teams and players. Inside the ball-shaped building are free movies, video highlights and life-size action blow-ups of Hall of Famers.
Daily.

INDIAN MOTORCYCLE MUSEUM
33 Hendee St., Springfield, 413-737-2624
This was part of the vast complex where Indian motorcycles were made until 1953. On display are historic bikes, an early snowmobile and a 1928 roadster.
Daily.

SPRINGFIELD ARMORY NATIONAL HISTORIC SITE
1 Armory Square, Springfield, 413-734-8551; www.nps.gov/spar
The old U.S. armory contains one of the largest collections of military small arms in the world. Exhibits include the "Organ of Guns," made famous by Longfellow's poem "The Arsenal at Springfield."
Daily 9 a.m.-5 p.m.

SPRINGFIELD MUSEUMS AT THE QUADRANGLE
220 State St., Springfield, 413-263-6800; www.springfieldmuseums.org
The site includes four museums and a library. *The George Walter Vincent Smith Art Museum* houses a collection of Asian armor, arms, jade, bronzes and rugs. T*he Connecticut River Valley Historical Museum* includes genealogy and a local history library. *The Museum of Fine Arts* has 20 galleries and an outstanding collection of American and European works. *The Science Museum* has an exploration center, early aviation exhibit, aquarium, planetarium, African hall and dinosaur hall.
All buildings Tuesday-Sunday.

STORROWTON VILLAGE
Eastern States Exposition, 1305 Memorial Ave., West Springfield, 413-205-5051;
www.thebige.com/village/storrowton_village.html
This group of restored Early American buildings includes a meeting house, schoolhouse and blacksmith shop.
June-August, Tuesday-Saturday; rest of year, by appointment.

SPECIAL EVENTS
EASTERN STATES EXPOSITION (THE BIG E)
1305 Memorial Ave., West Springfield, 413-737-2443; www.thebige.com
The largest fair in the Northeast has entertainment, exhibits, a historic Avenue of States, Storrowton Village, a horse show, agricultural events and a "Better Living Center" exhibit.
September.

WHERE TO STAY
★★★MARRIOTT SPRINGFIELD

1500 Main St., Springfield, 413-781-7111, 800-228-9290; www.marriott.com

At this business hotel, it's all about the beds. With extra-thick mattresses, duvets, bed skirts and plush pillows, the beds are reason enough to book a room here. Rooms also come with flat-screen TVs and polished granite bathrooms. The hotel is connected via enclosed walkway to a mall and complex with restaurants, art galleries, an African-American history museum and a billiards parlor.

265 rooms. Restaurant, bar. $151-250

★★★SHERATON SPRINGFIELD MONARCH PLACE HOTEL

1 Monarch Place, Springfield, 413-781-1010; www.sheraton-springfield.com

Guest rooms in this contemporary, urban spot surround a 12-story atrium, and the public areas feature local touches such as a folk art mural of Springfield's historical highlights. The hotel's Athletic Club is the largest hotel health club west of Boston, and spa services include everything from tanning to massages to manicures. Business travelers should ask for a smart room, which comes with a photocopier and fax machine.

325 rooms. Restaurant, bar. $151-250

WHERE TO EAT
★★STUDENT PRINCE & FORT

8 Fort St., Springfield, 413-788-6628; www.studentprince.com

This dark, wood-clad restaurant has been in operation for 75 years, and is known for its classic German menu. A large selection of imported German beers is available on tap to accompany the schnitzels, sauerbratens and goulash on the menu.

German. Lunch, dinner. Bar. $16-35

STOCKBRIDGE

See also Lenox, Pittsfield

Stockbridge's main drag was made forever famous by small-town life chronicler Norman Rockwell. The fact that the town still looks much as it appeared in his drawings continuously delights tourists, who crowd the area's shops and eateries in the summertime. West Stockbridge, by contrast, is a completely restored market village. Its own Main Street is lined with renovated, well-kept storefronts.

WHAT TO SEE
BERKSHIRE BOTANICAL GARDEN

Highways 102 and 183, Stockbridge, 413-298-3926; www.berkshirebotanical.org

This 15-acre botanical garden has perennials, shrubs, trees, antique roses, ponds, a wildflower exhibit, vegetable gardens and demonstration greenhouses. There is an on-site garden shop. They offer special events and lectures. Picnicking is allowed on the grounds.

May-October, daily.

CHESTERWOOD

284 Main St., Stockbridge, 413-298-3579; www.chesterwood.org

This was the grand early 20th-century summer residence and studio of Daniel Chester French, sculptor of the Minute Man statue in Concord and the Lincoln Memorial in Washington, D.C.

May-October, daily.

MISSION HOUSE

1 Sergeant St., Stockbridge, 413-298-3239; www.thetrustees.org

The house built in 1739 for the missionary Reverend John Sergeant and his wife, Abigail Williams, is now a museum of colonial life.

Memorial Day weekend-Columbus Day weekend, daily.

NAUMKEAG

1 Seargeant St., Stockbridge, 413-298-3239; www.thetrustees.org

Stanford White designed this Norman-style "Berkshire cottage" in 1886. The interior has antiques, Oriental rugs and a collection of Chinese export porcelain. The gardens include terraces of tree peonies, fountains and a birch walk.

Memorial Day weekend-Columbus weekend, daily.

NORMAN ROCKWELL MUSEUM

9 Glendale Road, Stockbridge, 413-298-4100; www.nrm.org

His eponymous museum maintains and exhibits the nation's largest collection of original art by Norman Rockwell.

Daily.

WHERE TO STAY
★★★THE RED LION INN

30 Main St., Stockbridge, 413-298-5545; www.redlioninn.com

Along with the street it sits on, the Red Lion Inn was immortalized by Norman Rockwell in his hearty, happy Stockbridge street scenes. Its guest rooms are well-appointed, though a bit snug. For roomier digs, book one of the inn's off-site suites, which are sprinkled among a handful of buildings throughout town, such as the former studio of artist Daniel Chester French and the former home of the Stockbridge Volunteer Fire Department.

100 rooms. Restaurant, bar. $151-250

★★★WILLIAMSVILLE INN

Highway 41, West Stockbridge, 413-274-6118; www.williamsvilleinn.com

Run by a German husband-and-wife team, the Williamsville Inn is a cross between Shaker austerity and comfort. Its blond-wood floors are spotless, as are its white bed linens and bath towels. Fresh flowers scent each room, and guests can walk through the property's extensive gardens.

16 rooms. Complimentary breakfast. Restaurant, bar. $61-150

ALSO RECOMMENDED
INN AT STOCKBRIDGE

Highway 7 N., Stockbridge, 413-298-3337; www.stockbridgeinn.com

An in-room decanter of port. Breakfast in a formal dining room. A large parlor with fireside chairs. A stroll through 12 secluded acres. Sound appealing? This 1906 Georgian-style inn has just eight guest rooms, allowing each visitor to savor the amenities. The Cottage House, added in 1997, has four junior suites. The Barn, built in 2001, provides four deluxe suites.

16 rooms. No children under 12. Complimentary breakfast. Fitness center. Spa. $251-350

THE TAGGART HOUSE

18 W. Main St., Stockbridge, 413-298-4303, 800-918-2680; www.taggarthouse.com
This lovingly restored 1800s country house fronts the Housatonic River. The rooms are luxurious and intimate, and replete with fine antiques.

4 rooms. Complimentary breakfast. $251-350

WHERE TO EAT
★★★THE RED LION

30 Main St., Stockbridge, 413-298-5545; www.redlioninn.com
It doesn't get any more classic than this fine dining restaurant. This inn's candlelit dining room is filled with antiques, colonial pewter and crystal. The contemporary New England menu emphasizes local, seasonal produce and offers several vegetarian options.

American. Lunch, dinner. Bar. Children's menu. Reservations recommended. Outdoor seating. $36-85

★★★WILLIAMSVILLE INN

Highway 41, West Stockbridge, 413-274-6118; www.williamsvilleinn.com
This cozy dining room has an open fireplace and plenty of candlelight. But what's really special about the German eatery is its open kitchen. Guests can watch chef/owner Erhard Wendt at work in his yellow-walled space (he often invites diners back for a closer look). The food is rich and savory—don't pass up any of the desserts.

French, German. Dinner, brunch. Bar. Reservations recommended. Outdoor seating. $36-85

TRURO & NORTH TRURO

See also Provincetown
Truro is perhaps the most sparsely settled part of Cape Cod, with great stretches of rolling moorland dotted only occasionally by small cottages. On the hill above the Pamet River marsh are two early 19th-century churches (one is the town hall). The surrounding countryside is popular with artists and writers.

WHAT TO SEE
HIGHLAND LIGHT/CAPE COD LIGHT

Highland Light Road, North Truro, 508-487-1121; www.lighthouse.cc/highland
This was the first lighthouse on Cape Cod. Built in 1798 and fueled with whale oil, it was rebuilt in 1853 and switched to an automated facility in 1986. It now shines for 30 miles, the longest visible range of any lighthouse on the Cape. The museum next door, housed in a historic building, is open from June-September and highlights the area's fishing and whaling heritage.

May-late October, daily.

TRURO HISTORICAL SOCIETY MUSEUM
6 Highland Road, North Truro, 508-487-3397; www.trurohistorical.org
The collection of artifacts from the town's past include shipwreck mementos, whaling gear, ship models, 17th-century firearms, a pirate chest and period rooms.
June-September, Monday-Saturday 10 a.m.-4:30 p.m., Sunday from 1 p.m.

WHERE TO STAY
★CROW'S NEST RESORT
496 Shore Road, North Truro, 508-487-9031, 800-499-9799; www.caperesort.com
The suites at this beach resort couldn't be closer to the water: all have water views, and are just steps to the beach. The décor is beach-inspired and streamlined, and the rooms feature free wireless and kitchens. Three fireplace-warmed cottages are also available.
33 rooms. Closed December-March. Beach. $61-150

WHERE TO EAT
★ADRIAN'S
535 Highway 6, North Truro, 508-487-4360; www.adriansrestaurant.com
The inside of this casual restaurant is warm and welcoming, but it's the sprawling outdoor deck that offers the best seating in summer. Breakfasts are hearty with dishes such as lobster Benedict; the dinner menu features Italian pastas, pizzas and entrées.
Italian. Breakfast, dinner. Bar. Children's menu. Outdoor seating. Closed mid-October-mid-May. $16-35

★★MONTANO'S
481 Highway 6, North Truro, 508-487-2026; www.montanos.com
Ample portions of reliable Italian dishes are served at this casual restaurant. The pizzas are made fresh with toppings such as housemade meatballs.
Italian, seafood. Dinner. Bar. Children's menu. $16-35

WELLFLEET
See also Provincetown, Truro and North Truro
Once a fishing town, Wellfleet dominated the New England oyster business in the latter part of the 19th century. It is now a summer resort and an art gallery town, and there's still plenty of oysters.

WHAT TO SEE
HISTORICAL SOCIETY MUSEUM
266 Main St., Wellfleet, 508-349-9157; www.wellfleethistoricalsociety.com
Marine items, whaling tools, Marconi memorabilia, needlecraft, a photograph collection, and marine and primitive paintings are on display here.
Late June-early September, Tuesday-Saturday; schedule may vary.

WELLFLEET BAY WILDLIFE SANCTUARY

291 Highway 6, South Wellfleet, 508-349-2615; www.wellfleetbay.org

Operated by the Massachusetts Audubon Society, the sanctuary has self-guiding nature trails and a natural history summer day camp for children.
Memorial Day-Columbus Day, daily; rest of year, Tuesday-Sunday.

WELLFLEET DRIVE-IN THEATER

Highway 6, Wellfleet, 508-349-7176; www.wellfleetdrivein.com

This is the only outdoor theater on the Cape. It projects a family-oriented double feature every evening under the stars.
Mid-October-mid-April.

WHERE TO EAT
★MOBY DICK'S

Highway 6, Wellfleet, 508-349-9795; www.mobydicksrestaurant.com

Fresh seafood served in a family-friendly atmosphere makes this restaurant a popular Cape spot. The chowder is creamy and filled with potatoes and clams, and the lobsters are steamed and served with corn on the cob.
Seafood. Lunch, dinner. Children's menu. Outdoor seating. Closed mid-October-April. $16-35

WILLIAMSTOWN

See also North Adams, Pittsfield

Most things in this Northern Berkshires town are centered around Williams College, one of the best-known liberal arts schools in the country. The very quiet, very remote hamlet is a perfect setting for a school campus, and a drive through the area reveals a myriad of playing fields and students shuffling to class.

WHAT TO SEE
STERLING AND FRANCINE CLARK ART INSTITUTE

225 South St., Williamstown, 413-458-2303; www.clarkart.edu

This museum houses more than 30 paintings by Renoir and other French Impressionists, as well as English and American silver and works by American artists like Homer, Sargent, Cassatt and Remington.
July-Labor Day, daily; rest of year, Tuesday-Sunday.

WILLIAMS COLLEGE

54 Sawyer Library Drive, Williamstown, 413-597-3131; www.williams.edu

This private liberal arts college has a student body of 1,950 and an idyllic campus. Its Chapin Library of rare books houses the four founding documents of the United States. The Hopkins Observatory has planetarium shows and the Adams Memorial Theater presents plays.

WILLIAMS COLLEGE MUSEUM OF ART

15 Lawrence Hall Drive, Williamstown, 413-597-2429; www.wcma.org

This spot is considered one of the finest college art museums in the country; it houses approximately 11,000 pieces.
Tuesday-Saturday 10 a.m.-5 p.m., Sunday from 1 p.m.

WHERE TO STAY
★★★1896 HOUSE
910 Cold Spring Road, Williamstown, 413-458-1896, 888-999-1896;
www.1896house.com
Among other options, guests can choose to stay in a brook or pondside room at this historic inn. The Brookside suite is hidden from the road by trees and features Cushman rock maple furniture, luxurious amenities and a beautiful gazebo. The pondside room has slightly fewer frills.
29 rooms. Complimentary breakfast. Restaurant. $61-150

★★★THE ORCHARDS
222 Adams Road, Williamstown, 413-458-9611, 800-225-1517;
www.orchardshotel.com
Grand gates of Vermont granite lead into this European chateau-style property just east of the village center. With bay windows and marble-floored baths, the rooms are decorated in English country style. Public spaces feature Oriental rugs and Austrian crystal chandeliers. The onsite restaurant serves a mix of continental and American cuisine; visitors can dine outdoors in the garden during summer months.
49 rooms. Restaurant, bar. $151-250

WHERE TO EAT
★★★GALA RESTAURANT & BAR
222 Adams Road, Williamstown, 413-458-9611, 800-225-1517;
www.galarestaurant.com
Gold and red brocade chairs and white tablecloths dress the room's interior at Gala, in the Orchards hotel. The chef incorporates high-quality local ingredients in the classic American dishes, which include apple and cheddar-stuffed pork chop, merlot-braised New Zealand lamb shank and seared Atlantic salmon. A wine cellar with a tasting room is used for chef's tables and private functions.
American menu. Breakfast, lunch, dinner, Sunday brunch. Bar. Reservations recommended. Outdoor seating. $16-35

★★WATER STREET GRILL
123 Water St., Williamstown, 413-458-2175
This casual bistro serves generous portions of salads, sandwiches and burgers. Desserts are made fresh and include bourbon pecan pie.
American. Lunch, dinner. Bar. Children's menu. $16-35

WORCESTER
See also Newton
One of the largest cities in New England, Worcester is an important industrial center. It's also another academic powerhouse: within the city limits are 12 colleges.

WHAT TO SEE
AMERICAN ANTIQUARIAN SOCIETY
185 Salisbury St., Worcester, 508-755-5221; www.americanantiquarian.org
This research library has the largest collection of source materials pertaining

to the first 250 years of American history.
Monday-Friday; Guided tours Wednesday afternoons.

ECOTARIUM
222 Harrington Way, Worcester, 508-929-2700; www.ecotarium.org
This museum has environmental science exhibits, a solar/lunar observatory, a multimedia planetarium theater and an African Hall.
Tuesday-Saturday 10 a.m.-5 p.m., Sunday from noon.

JOHN H. CHAFFY BLACKSTONE RIVER VALLEY NATIONAL HERITAGE CORRIDOR
414 Massasoit Road, Worcester, 508-755-8899; www.nps.gov/blac
This 250,000-acre region extends southward to Providence, Rhode Island and includes many points of historical and cultural interest.

SALISBURY MANSION
40 Highland St., Worcester, 508-753-8278; www.worcesterhistory.org/mansion.html
This was the house of leading businessman and philanthropist Stephen Salisbury.

WORCESTER ART MUSEUM
55 Salisbury St., Worcester, 508-799-4406; www.worcesterart.org
Fifty centuries of paintings, sculpture, decorative arts, prints, drawings and photography from America to ancient Egypt are on display here.
Wednesday-Sunday.

WHERE TO STAY
★★★BEECHWOOD HOTEL
363 Plantation St., Worcester, 508-754-5789, 800-344-2589;
www.beechwoodhotel.com
The hotel has a 24-hour fitness room and business center, which makes it ideal for business travelers. A polished foyer with marble floors, a small fireside seating area, and antique, stained-glass windows spice up the lobby.
73 rooms, Restaurant, bar. $151-250

★★★CROWNE PLAZA HOTEL
10 Lincoln Square, Worcester, 508-791-1600, 877-227-6963; www.cpworcester.com
The Crowne Plaza is located close to shopping malls and the booksellers' marketplace within 10 minutes of most area businesses. It also has a large indoor/outdoor pool and a courtyard landscaped with holly and flowering fruit trees. Ask for a room with a balcony, where you can enjoy morning coffee and a view of Lincoln Square.
243 rooms. Restaurant, bar. $61-150

WHERE TO EAT
★★★CASTLE
1230 Main St., Leicester, 508-892-9090; www.castlerestaurant.com
Owned and operated by the Nicas family since 1950, this "castle," complete with turrets, towers and a moat, always provides a unique dining experience.

Choose from one of the two distinctly different dining rooms, the Crusader or the Camelot; each has its own creative menu.

French. Lunch, dinner. Closed Monday. Bar. Children's menu. Outdoor seating. $36-85

YARMOUTH

See also Hyannis and Barnstable

Much of the Yarmouth area was developed on the strength of its 19th-century seafaring and fishing industries. Well-preserved houses line Main Street, where locals shop and stroll.

WHAT TO SEE

CAPE SYMPHONY ORCHESTRA

712A Main St., Yarmouth Port, 508-362-1111; www.capesymphony.org

This 90-member professional orchestra performs 15 indoor concerts throughout the year at Barnstable High School's 1,400-seat auditorium. Selections range from classical to pops to special children's events.

September-May; also two concerts in summer.

HISTORIC NEW ENGLAND

250 Highway 6A, South Yarmouth, 617-227-3957

This is a Georgian house adorned with 17th, 18th and 19th-century furnishings collected in the early 20th century.

June-October, first Saturday of the month.

WHERE TO STAY

★★★LIBERTY HILL INN

77 Main St., Yarmouth Port, 508-362-3976, 800-821-3977; www.libertyhillinn.com

The stately, whitewashed building that houses this charming inn was built in 1825. Rooms have antique furniture and oriental rugs and some bathrooms have original claw-foot tubs.

9 rooms. Complimentary breakfast. $61-150

ALSO RECOMMENDED

CAPTAIN FARRIS HOUSE BED AND BREAKFAST

308 Old Main St., South Yarmouth, 508-760-2818, 800-350-9477;

www.captainfarris.com

This bed and breakfast has beautifully landscaped lawns. Some rooms feature Jacuzzi tubs, and all are individually decorated with period furniture. Breakfast is served each day in a charming glass-enclosed courtyard.

10 rooms. No children under 10. Complimentary breakfast. Restaurant. $61-150

INN AT LEWIS BAY

57 Maine Ave., West Yarmouth, 508-771-3433, 800-962-6679; www.innatlewisbay.com

Located in a quiet seaside neighborhood one block from Lewis Bay, this Dutch colonial bed and breakfast serves full breakfasts each morning and refreshments each afternoon. Rooms feature colorful quilts and antiques.

6 rooms. No children under 12. Complimentary breakfast. $

WHERE TO EAT

★★INAHO

157 Route 6A Yarmouth Port, 508-362-5522

A huge menu of sushi and maki rolls is available at this streamlined Japanese restaurant. The special chef's choice menu is a multi-course tasting experience of the day's best fish, rolls and more.

Japanese, sushi. Dinner. $16-35

★★SKIPPER RESTAURANT

152 S. Shore Drive, South Yarmouth, 508-394-7406; www.skipper-restaurant.com

This classic seafood restaurant has been in business in its waterfront location since 1936. The décor is simple and nautical-themed, and the menu is loaded with classics like stuffed quahogs, clams casino and lobster ravioli.

Seafood. Lunch, dinner. Bar. Children's menu. Outdoor seating. Closed mid-October-mid-April. $16-35

NEW HAMPSHIRE

NEW HAMPSHIRE'S MOTTO, AS PROUDLY PROCLAIMED ON ITS LICENSE PLATES, IS "LIVE FREE or Die," a reference to the state's revolutionary spirit. Some from the surrounding states like to tease that the motto should be "Live Free and Die" because the granite state has markedly fewer laws restricting personal freedoms than any other state, from no helmet laws for motorcyclists over 18 to no seatbelts laws for car drivers and passengers over 18. But this atmosphere of free living is what is attracting more and more newcomers to New Hampshire, many who come for the low taxes and beautiful mountain scenery.

New Hampshire is famous for the important role it plays in national politics. The state traditionally holds the first presidential primary in the country, placing the laser focus of the media on its many small towns, their inhabitants and their voting habits.

The mountains in New Hampshire are known for their rugged "notches" (called "gaps" and "passes" elsewhere) and the old valley towns offer a serene beauty. Some of the best skiing in the East is available at several major resorts here. The state's many parks, antique shops, art and theater festivals and county fairs are also popular attractions, and more than half of New England's covered bridges are in New Hampshire.

In 1623, David Thomson and a small group of colonists settled on the New Hampshire coast near Portsmouth. These early settlements were part of Massachusetts. In 1679, they became a separate royal province under Charles the Second. In 1776, the Provincial Congress adopted a constitution making New Hampshire the first independent colony, seven months before the Declaration of Independence was signed. Although New Hampshire was the only one of the 13 original states not invaded by the British during the Revolution, its men fought long and hard on land and sea to bring about the victory. This strong, involved attitude continues in New Hampshire to this day.

BRETTON WOODS

See also Franconia

Bretton Woods is located in the White Mountains on a long glacial plain next to Mount Washington and the Presidential Range. Mount Washington was first sighted in 1497; however, settlement around it did not begin until 1771 when the Crawford Notch, which opened the way through the mountains, was discovered. In the 1770s, Governor Wentworth named the area Bretton Woods for his ancestral home in England. This historic name was set aside in 1832 when all the tiny settlements in the area were incorporated under the name of Carroll. For a time, a railroad through the notch brought as many as 57 trains a day and the area grew as a resort spot. A string of hotels sprang up, each more elegant and fashionable than the last. In 1903, the post office, the railroad station and the express office reverted to the traditional name: Bretton Woods. Today, Bretton Woods is a resort area at the base of the mountain.

WHAT TO SEE AND DO
BRETTON WOODS SKI AREA
Highway 302, Bretton Woods, 603-278-1000; www.brettonwoods.com

Bretton Woods has two high-speed quad, triple, two double chairlifts, and three surface lifts. They offer ski patrol, school, rentals and snowmaking. There is a restaurant, cafeteria, bar, child care and lodge on site. The longest run is two miles with a vertical drop of 1,500 feet. There are also 48 miles of cross-country trails.

Thanksgiving-April: daily. Night skiing early December--March: Friday-Saturday.

CRAWFORD NOTCH STATE PARK
Highway 302, Bretton Woods, 603-374-2272; www.nhstateparks.com

This notch is one of the state's most spectacular passes. Mounts Nancy and Willey rise to the west; Mounts Crawford, Webster and Jackson are to the east. Park headquarters is at the former site of the Samuel Willey house. The family of six and two hired men died in a landslide in 1826 when they rushed out of their house, which was left untouched. There are hiking and walking trails on the Appalachian system. Camping is allowed. There is an on-site interpretive center.

Late-May-mid-October.

WHERE TO STAY
★★★MOUNT WASHINGTON HOTEL
Highway 302, Bretton Woods, 603-278-1000, 800-258-0330;
www.mountwashingtonresort.com

This landmark hotel, opened in 1902 as a summer resort for wealthy Bostonians and New Yorkers, is a sprawling, well-preserved example of Spanish Renaissance architecture, tucked at the foot of the White Mountains. Rooms feature colonial-style furnishings and DVD players. A recently opened spa offers a range of treatments inspired by the hotel's mountain location. 200 rooms. Restaurant, bar. Fitness center. Pool. Golf,. Tennis. Business center. $251-350

WHERE TO EAT
★FABYAN'S STATION
Highway 302, Bretton Woods, 603-278-2222; www.mtwashington.com

Housed in a former railway station on the grounds of the Mount Washington Hotel, this family-friendly spot is popular for its pub-style fare. Burgers, ribs and wings are menu specialties.

American menu. Lunch, dinner. Bar. Children's menu. Casual attire. $16-35

CONCORD
See also Manchester

New Hampshire, one of the original 13 colonies, entered the Union in 1788, but its capital was in dispute for another 20 years. Concord finally won the honor in 1808. Building began for the state house immediately and finally finished in 1819. The legislature is the largest (more than 400 seats) of any state. Concord is the financial center of the state and offers a diverse range of industry.

WHAT TO SEE
CANTERBURY SHAKER VILLAGE

288 Shaker Road, Canterbury, 603-783-9511; www.shakers.org

Pay homage to New Hampshire's Shaker heritage with a visit to this National Historic Landmark museum, which offers guided and self-guided tours and a variety of exhibits.

Mid-May-late-October: daily 10 a.m.-5 p.m.; weekends in November; two days in December.

CHRISTA MCAULIFFE PLANETARIUM

2 Institute Drive, Concord, 603-271-7831; www.starhop.com

This living memorial to New Hampshire teacher Christa McAuliffe, who died aboard the U.S. space shuttle *Challenger* on January 28, 1986, offers a variety of shows designed for all ages in a 92-seat theater. Some shows are aimed at the very young while others boast 3-D computer graphic effects that are likely to impress all ages.

Saturday-Thursday 10 a.m.-5 p.m.; Friday until 9 p.m.

GRANITE STATE CANDY SHOPPE

9-17 Warren St., Concord, 603-225-2591, 888-225-2531; www.nhchocolates.com

Founded in 1927 by a Greek immigrant, Granite State Candy Shoppe is an old fashioned candy store. The candy shoppe is now owned by the founder's grandchildren, who still use many of his original copper kettles and dip each chocolate by hand.

MUSEUM OF NEW HAMPSHIRE HISTORY

6 Eagle Square, Concord, 603-228-6688; www.nhhistory.org

Founded in 1823, this historical museum houses permanent and changing exhibits, including examples of the famed Concord Coach; there is also a museum store.

Daily: Tuesday-Saturday 9:30 a.m.-5 p.m., Sunday noon-5 p.m.; Mondays 9:30 a.m.-5 p.m. from July 1-October 15 and December.

PIERCE MANSE

14 Penacook St., Concord, 603-225-4555

This was the home of President Franklin Pierce from 1842 to 1848. It was re-constructed and moved to the present site; the hosue contains many original furnishings and period pieces.

Mid-June-mid-October: Tuesday-Saturday 11 a.m.-3 p.m.; also by appointment.

STATE HOUSE

107 N. Main St., Concord, 603-271-2154

The interior of the State House has a Hall of Flags, as well as statues and portraits of state notables.

Monday-Friday.

WHERE TO EAT
★★ANGELINA'S RISTORANTE ITALIANO
11 Depot St., Concord, 603-228-3313; www.angelinasrestaurant.com

A casual Italian bistro with simple, white-washed walls and linen-covered tables, this restaurant is a reliable spot for sampling fresh-made pastas and favorites such as veal parmesan. The wine list features reasonably priced bottles with a focus on Italian wines.

Italian. Lunch, dinner. Reservations recommended. Lunch Monday-Friday, dinner Monday-Saturday; closed Sunday. $16-35

★ARNIE'S PLACE
164 Loudon Road, Concord, 603-228-3225; www.arniesplace.com

Place your order at the takeout window for pulled pork sandwiches, crispy onion rings or superlative ice cream, and then take a seat outside at this classic, summer-only restaurant. Locals swear by the fries, which are crispy, salty and purely addictive.

American. Lunch, dinner. Children's menu. Outdoor seating. No credit cards accepted. $15 and under

★MAKRIS LOBSTER AND STEAK HOUSE
354 Sheep Davis Road, Concord, 603-225-7665; www.eatalobster.com

Locals nearly overwhelm this simple seafood restaurant on weekends, and it's easy to understand why. An extensive menu features everything from lobster newburg to blackened swordfish served at budget-friendly prices. Fresh lobsters, clams and fish can be purchased to go at the onsite store.

Seafood, steak. Lunch, dinner, late-night. Bar. Children's menu. Outdoor seating. $16-35

DIXVILLE NOTCH

The small village of Dixville Notch shares its name with the most northern White Mountain passes. The Notch cuts through the mountain range between Kidderville and Errol. At its narrowest point, east of Lake Gloriette, is one of the most impressive views in the state. Every four years, Dixville Notch is invaded by the national news media, who report the nation's first presidential vote tally shortly after midnight on Election Day.

WHAT TO SEE
BALSAMS/WILDERNESS SKI AREA
1000 Cold Spring Road, Dixville Notch, 603-255-3400, 877-225-7267;
www.thebalsams.com

This ski area has a chairlift and two T-bars. There is ski patrol and school, as well as rentals and snowmaking should it be required. An onsite restaurant, cafeteria, bar, nursery and resort fulfills the immediate needs of guests. Their longest run is one mile, with a vertical drop of 1,000 feet.

December-March: daily. Cross-country trails.

WHERE TO STAY
★★★THE BALSAMS
1000 Cold Spring Road, Dixville Notch, 603-255-3400, 877-225-7267;
www.thebalsams.com
Built just after the Civil War, this 15,000-acre resort offers downhill ski-ing, cross-country skiing, snowboarding and ice skating; warmer months are spent playing golf or tennis and enjoying the great outdoors on nature walks. Operating on the all-inclusive American plan, the Balsams makes gourmet dining an integral part of the experience here.
212 rooms. Restaurant, bar. Fitness center. Pool. Golf. Tennis. Ski-in/ski-out. $151-250

EXETER
See also Portsmouth
A respected preparatory school and Colonial houses are a large part of Exeter's radical history. The town had its beginnings in religious nonconformity, led by Reverend John Wheelwright and Anne Hutchinson, both of whom were banished from Massachusetts for heresy. There was an anti-British scuffle in 1734, and by 1774, Exeter was burning Lord North in effigy and talking of liberty. It was made the capital of the state during the Revolution. Exeter is the birthplace of Daniel Chester French and John Irving.

WHAT TO SEE
AMERICAN INDEPENDENCE MUSEUM
1 Governors Lane, Exeter, 603-772-2622; www.independencemuseum.org
The site features a Revolutionary War-era state treasury building; the grounds house Folsom Tavern (1775). Free parking is available.
May-October, Wednesday-Saturday 10 a.m.-4 p.m.

PHILLIPS EXETER ACADEMY
20 Main St., Exeter, 603-772-4311; www.exeter.edu
The academy is a prestigious college preparatory school on 400 acres with more than 100 buildings. Founded in 1781 by John Phillips, who sought a school for "students from every quarter," Exeter is known for its student diversity. On campus there is a contemporary library (1971), designed by Louis I. Kahn; the Frederick R. Mayer Art Center and the Lamont Art Gallery.

FRANCONIA
See also Bretton Woods
Franconia is the gateway to the White Mountains. From here, explore the area's best hiking and skiing and in the fall, leaf peeping, as the annual pilgrimage to view the changing colors of the leaves is affectionately called.

WHAT TO SEE
FROST PLACE
Ridge Road, Franconia, 603-823-5510; www.frostplace.org
Two furnished rooms of Robert Frost's home are open to the public.
Admission: free to museum. July-Columbus Day, Wednesday-Monday afternoons; Memorial Day-June, Saturday-Sunday afternoons.

NEW ENGLAND SKI MUSEUM

Franconia Notch Parkway, Franconia, 603-823-7177, 800-639-4181; www.nesm.org

The museum details the history of skiing in the East; exhibits feature skis and bindings, clothing, art and photographs. There are vintage films as well. Admission: free. Memorial Day-Columbus Day and December-March, daily 10 a.m.-5 p.m.

WHERE TO STAY

★★★FRANCONIA INN

1300 Easton Road, Franconia, 603-823-5542, 800-473-5299; www.franconiainn.com

Located in the White Mountains but still close to the town center, this inn welcomes guests into an informal country-home atmosphere. The guest rooms are spacious and onsite activities include horseback riding, mountain biking, fishing and croquet.

34 rooms. Complimentary breakfast. Restaurant, bar. Pool. Tennis. Closed April-mid-May. $61-150

★★★LOVETTS INN

1474 Profile Road, Franconia, 603-823-7761, 800-356-3802; www.lovettsinn.com

Breathe in the fresh country air at this historic, romantic inn located in the White Mountains. Rooms feature floral chintzes and reproduction poster beds; some have fireplaces and Jacuzzi tubs.

18 rooms. Pets accepted; fee. Complimentary breakfast. Restaurant, bar. Pool. Closed April. $151-250

★★SUGAR HILL INN

Highway 117, Franconia, 603-823-5621, 800-548-4748; www.sugarhillinn.com

With bright, cheerful rooms decorated in fresh florals and checks, this inn delivers charm and style in a traditional white-washed building. The innkeeper is a culinary school grad, so the focus here is on food and hospitality. Breakfast and afternoon tea are included in the room rate; a spa room can be booked for hot stone and traditional massages.

15 rooms. Complimentary breakfast. Restaurant, bar. Spa. Closed one week in April. $151-250

ALSO RECOMMENDED

SUNSET HILL HOUSE–A GRAND INN

231 Sunset Hill Road, Sugar Hill, 603-823-5522, 800-786-4455;
www.sunsethillhouse.com

Built in 1882, the property features beautiful views of the mountains. The innkeepers offer an experience made up of thoughtful service, excellent food, and history-filled lodging.

28 rooms. Complimentary breakfast. Restaurant. Pool. Golf. $251-350

WHERE TO EAT

★★★THE FRANCONIA INN

1300 Easton Road, Franconia, 603-823-5542, 800-473-5299; www.franconiainn.com

This restaurant nestled among hills and mountains offers New American cuisine, drawing on regional specialties and influenced by the rich heritage of the area. Main courses include filet mignon with crab cakes and pepper-seared Atlantic salmon.

American. Breakfast, dinner. Closed April-mid-May. Bar. Children's menu. Reservations recommended. $16-35

★★POLLY'S PANCAKE PARLOR

672 Highway 117, Sugar Hill, 603-823-5575; www.pollyspancakeparlor.com

This sweet, no-frills restaurant specializes in pancakes and waffles made in a variety of batters and with toppings ranging from homemade maple syrup to fresh fruit. Simple sandwiches, quiches and salads round out the menu; a selection of freshly baked pies are offered daily.

American. Breakfast, lunch. Closed November-April. Children's menu. Reservations recommended. $16-35

FRANCONIA NOTCH STATE PARK

See also Franconia

This seven-mile pass and state park, a deep valley of 6,440 acres between the Franconia and Kinsman ranges of the White Mountains has been a top tourist attraction since the mid-19th century. Mounts Liberty (4,460 feet), Lincoln (5,108 feet) and Lafayette (5,249 feet) loom in the east, and Cannon Mountain (4,200 feet) presents a sheer granite face. The Pemigewasset River follows the length of the Notch. The park offers various recreational activities, including swimming at Sandy Beach.

WHAT TO SEE

CANNON MOUNTAIN SKI AREA

Franconia Notch State Parkway, Franconia, 603-823-8800; www.cannonmt.com

This ski area offers a tramway, two quad, three triple, two double chairlifts and a pony lift. There is ski patrol and ski school along with rentals and snowmaking, should either be required. The New England Ski Museum is on site. Their longest run is two miles with a vertical drop of 2,146 feet. Their tramway rises 2,022 feet vertically and makes the distance of one mile in six minutes.

Late November-mid-April, daily. Also operates Memorial Day-mid-October, daily; rest of year, weekends (weather permitting).

FLUME GORGE & PARK INFORMATION CENTER

Franconia Notch State Parkway, Franconia, 603-745-8391; www.flumegorge.com

This narrow, natural gorge and waterfall along the flank of Mount Liberty is accessible by stairs and walks. The information center offers a 15-minute movie every half-hour introducing the park.

Mid-May-late-October, daily 9 a.m.-5.30 p.m. Admission: adult $12, children 6-12 years $8, children under 5 free with adult.

OLD MAN OF THE MOUNTAIN HISTORIC SITE

Notch State Parkway

Discovered in 1805, the craggy likeness of a man's face was formed naturally of five layers of granite and was 40 feet high. It tumbled down on May 3, 2003. It was also known as the "Great Stone Face."

HAMPTON BEACH

See also Exeter, Portsmouth

This beachfront town has an old-fashioned boardwalk and plenty of sandy beaches. An annual seafood festival, held the week after Labor Day, is the town's biggest event.

WHAT TO SEE
FULLER GARDENS

10 Willow Ave., North Hampton, 603-964-5414; www.fullergardens.org

Former estate of the late Governor Alvan T. Fuller featuring extensive rose gardens, annuals, perennials, a Japanese garden and a conservatory. Mid-May-mid-October: daily 10 a.m.-5.30 p.m. Admission: adults $7, senior $6, student $5, children under 12 $3.

TUCK MEMORIAL MUSEUM

40 Park Ave., Hampton, 603-929-0781; www.hampton.lib.nh.us

This is home of the Hampton Historical Society. The museum house antiques, documents, photographs, early postcards, tools and toys. There is a trolley exhibit and other memorabilia of Hampton history. Onsite is also a restored one-room schoolhouse and fire station.
Mid-June-mid-September.

WHERE TO STAY
★★ASHWORTH BY THE SEA

295 Ocean Blvd., Hampton Beach, 603-926-6762, 800-345-6736;
www.ashworthhotel.com

Built in 1912 on oceanfront property in Hampton Beach, this inn has rooms decorated with contemporary décor. Some offer superb views of the ocean, and all have been updated with flat-screen TVs and upgraded bathrooms.
98 rooms. Restaurant, bar. Pool. Fitness room. Spa. $151-250

ALSO RECOMMENDED
D.W.'S OCEANSIDE INN

365 Ocean Blvd., Hampton Beach, 603-926-3542, 866-623-2674;
www.oceansideinn.com

This early-1900s beach house overlooking the Atlantic Ocean is an ideal getaway. The décor is colonial and some rooms have canopy beds.
Nine rooms. No children accepted. Complimentary breakfast. Beach.
Closed mid-October-mid-May. $151-250

HANOVER

See also Plymouth

Established four years after the first settlers came here, Ivy League institution Dartmouth College is an integral part of Hanover. Named for the Earl of Dartmouth, the school was founded by the Reverend Eleazar Wheelock "for the instruction of the youth of Indian tribes and others." Famous for its party scene, Dartmouth was the inspiration for the film *Animal House*.

WHAT TO SEE
DARTMOUTH COLLEGE
Main and Wheelock Streets, Hanover, 603-646-1110; www.dartmouth.edu
This Ivy League school of 5,400 students was founded in 1769 and is renowned for its business school and top-notch academics.

ENFIELD SHAKER MUSEUM
24 Caleb Dyer Lane, Enfield, 603-632-4346; www.shakermuseum.org
A museum devoted to Shaker culture sits on the site where the Shakers established their Chosen Vale in 1793. The museum includes exhibits, craft demonstrations, workshops, special programs and extensive gardens.
Monday-Saturday 10 a.m.-5 p.m. Sunday noon-5 p.m.

SAINT-GAUDENS NATIONAL HISTORIC SITE
139 Saint-Gaudens Road, Route 12A, Cornish, 603-675-2175; www.nps.gov/saga
This site is the former residence and studio of sculptor Augustus Saint-Gaudens (1848-1907). Saint-Gaudens' famous works *The Puritan*, *Adams Memorial* and *Shaw Memorial* are among the 100 works on display. Also includes formal gardens and works by other artists. There is often a sculptor-in-residence. The site has interpretive programs.
Memorial Day-October, daily 9 a.m.-4:30 p.m.

WEBSTER COTTAGE
32 N. Main St., Hanover, 603-643-6529
The circa 1780 residence of Daniel Webster during his last year as a Dartmouth College student is open for viewing.
Memorial Day-mid-October, Wednesday, Saturday-Sunday afternoons.

WHERE TO STAY
★★★HANOVER INN
Main and Wheelock Streets, Hanover, 603-643-4300, 800-443-7024;
www.hanoverinn.com
At this inn located just minutes from Dartmouth College, guest rooms are decorated with a colonial motif, and guests have access to athletic facilities at the university. The inn's restaurants server breakfast, lunch and dinner, and room service is available.
92 rooms. Pets accepted. Restaurant, bar. Fitness center. Airport transportation available. $251-350

WHERE TO EAT
★★JESSE'S
Lebanon Road, Hanover, 603-643-4111; www.blueskyrestaurants.com
With a log cabin feel, complete with a wood-burning fireplace and wood-clad walls, this steakhouse delivers reliable grilled meats. A new martini bar features offerings such as the Espressotini and Sour Apple martini.
Steak. Lunch, dinner. Bar. Children's menu. Outdoor seating. $16-35

★MOLLY'S

43 S. Main St., Hanover, 603-643-2570; www.mollysrestaurant.com

Popular for its fresh-baked pizzas, this casual pub has a full menu that ranges from burgers to pastas and salads. The outdoor patio makes securing a table easier in warm weather.

American. Lunch, dinner. Bar. Daily. $16-35

HOLDERNESS

See also Plymouth

Holderness is the shopping center and post office for Squam Lake, the second-largest lake in the state, and neighboring Little Squam. Fishing, boating, swimming, water sports and winter sports are popular in this area. The movie *On Golden Pond* was filmed here.

WHAT TO SEE
SQUAM LAKES NATURAL SCIENCE CENTER

23 Science Center Road, Holderness, 603-968-7194; www.nhnature.org

If this attraction looks familiar, perhaps you'll recognize it as the site where the 1981 movie *On Golden Pond*, with Henry Fonda and Katharine Hepburn, was filmed. Walking through the woods of this 200-acre wildlife sanctuary, you'll see black bears, deer, bobcats, otters, mountain lions, foxes and birds of prey in enclosed trail-side exhibits. You can also take the Explore Squam boat tour. Picnicking is allowed on site.

May-early November, daily 9:30 a.m.-4:30 p.m.

WHERE TO STAY
★★★MANOR ON GOLDEN POND

Manor Drive, Holderness, 603-968-3348, 800-545-2141;
www.manorongoldenpond.com

Modeled after an English country estate, this inn is located near Squam Lake. Rooms are decorated in chintzes and plaids, and some feature fireplaces or steam showers. Activities include tennis, badminton, croquet and access to a private beach.

25 rooms. No children under 12. Complimentary breakfast. Restaurant, bar. Pool. Tennis. $251-350

ALSO RECOMMENDED
GLYNN HOUSE INN

59 Highland St., Ashland, 603-968-3775, 800-637-9599; www.glynnhouse.com

This restored 1896 Queen Anne/Victorian is located near Squam Lake in the White Mountains. Rooms feature traditional furnishings and fabrics alongside updated touches such as flat-screen TVs and iPod players.

13 rooms. No children under 12. Complimentary breakfast. Pets accepted. $151-250

WHERE TO EAT
★★MANOR ON GOLDEN POND

Manor Drive, Holderness, 603-968-3348; www.manorongoldenpond.com

Dinner at this cozy inn on Squam Lake is a romantic experience. The location, high on a hill, provides spectacular views. The frequently changing à la carte menu includes New American dishes like duck hash Napoleon and sautéed mahi mahi.

American. Dinner, bar. $36-85

JACKSON

See also Plymouth

At the south end of Pinkham Notch, Jackson is a center for skiing and a year-round resort. The Wildcat River rushes over rock formations in the village; Wildcat Mountain is to the north. A circa-1870 covered bridge spans the Ellis River.

WHAT TO SEE
BLACK MOUNTAIN

Highway 16B, Jackson, 603-383-4490; www.blackmt.com

They have triple and double chairlifts, J-bar, ski patrol and school, rentals, cafeteria, and a nursery. Their longest run is one mile with a vertical drop of 1,100 feet.

JACKSON SKI TOURING FOUNDATION

153 Main St., and Highway 16A, Jackson, 603-383-9355; www.jacksonxc.org

They maintain 95 miles of cross-country trails, connecting inns and ski areas. Also provided is instruction, rentals, rescue service. December-mid-April, daily.

WHERE TO STAY
★★EAGLE MOUNTAIN HOUSE

Carter Notch Road, Jackson, 603-383-9111, 800-966-5779; www.eaglemt.com

An inn has operated in this location since 1879, but the white-washed historic structure that houses the Eagle Mountain House was built in 1916. Rooms feature cheerful floral fabrics, down duvets and wireless access. The on-site golf course has been in use since the 1920s.

96 rooms. Restaurant, bar. Fitness center. Pool. Golf. Tennis. Ski-in/ski-out. $151-250.

★★★INN AT ELLIS RIVER

17 Harriman Road, Jackson, 603-383-9339, 800-233-8309; www.innatellisriver.com

This luxurious inn offers rooms with period furnishings and a wide variety of amenities. Some rooms have whirlpool tubs or balconies, most have fireplaces. The surrounding area offers year-round activities such as cross-country skiing, golf, fishing, swimming and kayaking.

21 rooms. No children under 12. Complimentary breakfast. Restaurant, bar. Pool. Reservations recommended. $61-150

★★★INN AT THORN HILL

Thorn Hill Road, Jackson, 603-383-4242, 800-289-8990; www.innatthornhill.com

This historic inn puts a premium on luxury. Rooms have down duvet-topped beds, Jacuzzi tubs and TV/DVD players. A full gourmet breakfast is served each morning at the inn's restaurant.

25 rooms. No children under 8. Complimentary breakfast. Restaurant, bar. Fitness center. Spa. Pool. Ski-in/ski-out. $251-350

★★★WENTWORTH RESORT HOTEL
1 Carter Notch Road, Jackson, 603-383-9700, 800-637-0013; www.thewentworth.com
This elegant country inn, built in 1869, has been in continuous operation for more than a century. Located in the White Mountains, the year-round resort offers a fine-dining restaurant and recreational facilities.
51 rooms. Restaurant, bar. Pool. Golf. Tennis. Ski-in/ski-out. $151-250

WHERE TO EAT
★★CHRISTMAS FARM INN
Highway 16B, Jackson, 603-383-4313, 800-443-5837; www.christmasfarminn.com
Classic recipes receive a contemporary twist at this fine dining restaurant. Sample dishes such as honey soy glazed salmon or beef tenderloin with port wine reduction in a light-filled room filled with white-linen topped tables. American. Breakfast, dinner. Bar. Children's menu. Reservations recommended. $36-85

★★★INN AT THORN HILL
Thorn Hill Road, Jackson, 603-383-4242, 800-289-8990; www.innatthornhill.com
The dining room at this restaurant has a wood-burning fireplace and views of the countryside. The menu changes seasonally and serves dishes such as pan-seared tuna, grilled beef tenderloin and petite rack of veal. An extensive wine list is offered.
American. Breakfast, dinner. Bar. Reservations recommended. Outdoor seating. $36-85

★★WILDCAT INN & TAVERN
Highway 16A, Jackson, 603-383-4245, 800-228-4245; www.wildcattavern.com
Traditional fare such as rack of lamb and lobster mac and cheese are served in a casual setting at this rustic dining room. The tavern delivers a more casual menu of sandwiches and burgers along with live music on weekends. American. Lunch, dinner. Bar. Children's menu. Outdoor seating. Reservations recommended. $36-85

MANCHESTER
See also Concord, Nashua
Manchester is a city that has refused to bow to economic adversity. When the Amoskeag Manufacturing Company (cotton textiles), which had dominated Manchester's economy, failed in 1935, it left the city poverty-stricken. However, a group of citizens bought the plant for $5 million and revived the city. Now Manchester is northern New England's premier financial center.

WHAT TO SEE
CURRIER MUSEUM OF ART
150 Ash St., Manchester, 603-669-6144; www.currier.org
This is one of New England's leading small museums featuring 13th- to 20th-century European and American paintings and sculpture. They also house

New England decorative art, furniture, glass, silver and pewter. There are changing exhibitions, concerts, films and other programs. They offer tours of Zimmerman House, designed by Frank Lloyd Wright.

Sunday-Monday and Wednesday-Friday 11 a.m.-5 p.m.; Saturday 10 a.m.-5 p.m. (free admission 10 a.m.-12 p.m.); extended hours the first Thursday of every month; closed Tuesday.

MANCHESTER HISTORIC ASSOCIATION MILLYARD MUSEUM

129 Amherst St., Manchester, 603-622-7531; www.manchesterhistoric.org

This museum and library houses collections illustrating life in Manchester from pre-colonial times to present. There are permanent and changing exhibits as well as firefighting equipment, decorative arts, costumes and paintings.

Wednesday-Saturday 10 a.m.-4 p.m.

SCIENCE ENRICHMENT ENCOUNTERS MUSEUM

200 Bedford St., Manchester, 603-669-0400; www.see-sciencecenter.org

This museum houses more than 60 interactive, hands-on exhibits demonstrating basic science principles.

Monday-Friday 10 a.m.-4 p.m., Saturday-Sunday 10 a.m.-5 p.m.

WHERE TO STAY

★★★BEDFORD VILLAGE INN

2 Olde Bedford Way, Bedford, 603-472-2001, 800-852-1166;
www.bedfordvillageinn.com

This stately New England inn, housed in a converted 1800s barn, offers all-suite rooms, tastefully decorated with four-poster beds, Italian marble and whirlpool bathtubs. Guests and locals alike line up for breakfast and dinner in the on-site restaurant, where hearty takes on classic American recipes are served in a cozy space.

14 rooms. Restaurant, bar. $251-350

★★FOUR POINTS BY SHERATON MANCHESTER AIRPORT

55 John Devine Drive, Manchester, 603-668-6110, 800-368-7764;
www.fourpoints.com/manchester

A good bet for business travelers, this hotel is located near Manchester Airport and the Mall of New Hampshire and features simple rooms with updated contemporary décor. The on-site steakhouse features private micro-brews and a pub menu.

120 rooms. Pets accepted. Restaurant, bar. Fitness center. Pool. $61-150

★★RADISSON HOTEL MANCHESTER

700 Elm St., Manchester, 603-625-1000, 800-333-3333;
www.radisson.com/manchesternh

This downtown hotel features rooms with Sleep Number beds, fluffy down duvets and complimentary wireless access. The location near Manchester's Verizon Wireless Arena is ideal for catching local music and sports events.

251 rooms. Pets accepted. Restaurant, bar. Fitness center. Pool. $61-150

WHERE TO EAT
★★★BEDFORD VILLAGE INN
2 Village Inn Way, Bedford, 603-472-2001, 800-852-1166; www.bedfordvillageinn.com

Originally part of a working farm, this country inn is surrounded by gardens. Choose from eight separate dining rooms, each with its own distinct character (hand-painted murals, swag drapes, area rugs, or a roaring fireplace). The kitchen offers updated regional New England cuisine using only the freshest local ingredients.

American. Breakfast, lunch, dinner. Reservations recommended. Bar. $36-85

MEREDITH
See also Holderness, Plymouth

Between Lakes Winnipesaukee and Waukewan in the Lakes Region, Meredith is a year-round recreation area.

WHAT TO SEE
LEAGUE OF NEW HAMPSHIRE CRAFTSMEN—MEREDITH RETAIL GALLERY
279 Daniel Webster Highway, Meredith, 603-279-7920; www.nhcrafts.org

Works by some of New Hampshire's finest craftspeople are displayed and sold at this gallery.
Daily.

WINNIPESAUKEE SCENIC RAILROAD
Meredith, 603-279-5253; www.hoborr.com

Offers scenic train rides along the shore of Lake Winnipesaukee. Passengers board in Meredith or Weirs Beach. There are also fall foliage trains to Plymouth.
Memorial Day-October.

WHERE TO STAY
★★★THE INN AT BAY POINT
312 Daniel Webster Highway, Meredith, 603-279-7006, 800-622-6455;
www.millfalls.com

Located on the edge of Lake Winnipesaukee, this inn offers guests views of the lake from the large, comfortable rooms. Canoeing and other water sports are among the outdoor activities offered here, and there are plenty of shops and dining options in the surrounding area.

24 rooms. Complimentary breakfast. Restaurant, bar. Spa. Pool. Pets accepted. Closed midweek in winter. $151-250

THE INN AT MILL FALLS
312 Daniel Webster Highway, Meredith, 603-279-7006, 800-622-6455;
www.millfalls.com

This cozy inn, located in a historic mill complex in Meredith village, has rooms decorated in a simple, colonial style and a complimentary continental breakfast. Some rooms feature fireplaces and Jacuzzi tubs.

54 rooms. Restaurant, bar. Fitness room. Spa. Pool. $151-250

WHERE TO EAT
★★MAME'S
8 Plymouth St., Meredith, 603-279-4631; www.mamesrestaurant.com

Housed in a historic home, this American bistro serves an eclectic menu of dishes such as salmon Diane and chicken and broccoli pesto to a local crowd. The Sunday brunch features decadent dishes like french toast bananas foster.

American. Lunch, dinner, brunch. Bar. Children's menu. Reservations recommended. $16-35

MOUNT WASHINGTON
See also Bretton Woods

Mount Washington is the central peak of the White Mountains and the highest point in the northeastern United States (6,288 feet). At the summit, there is a 54-acre state park with an information center, a first-aid station, a restaurant and a gift shop. The mountain has the world's first cog railway, completed in 1869; a road to the top dates back to 1861. P.T. Barnum called the view from the summit "the second-greatest show on earth." The weather on Mount Washington is so violent that the timberline is at about 4,000 feet; in the Rockies it is nearly 10,000 feet. In the treeless zone are alpine plants and insects, some unique to the region. The weather station here recorded a wind speed of 231 miles per hour in April, 1934 (a world record). The lowest temperature recorded was −49 F; the year-round average is below freezing. The peak gets nearly 15 feet of snow each year.

WHAT TO SEE
COG RAILWAY
Highway 302, Bretton Woods, 603-278-5404, 800-922-8825; www.thecog.com

Allow yourself at least three hours for a round trip on the railway.
May-Memorial Day weekend: weekends; after Memorial Day weekend-November: daily.

GREAT GLEN TRAILS
Highway 16, Gorham, 603-466-2333; www.greatglentrails.com

Located at the base of Mount Washington, these all-season, non-motorized recreational trails feature biking programs (rentals), hiking programs (guided or self-guided), kayak and canoe tours, and workshops in summer. There is also cross-country skiing, snowshoeing and snow tubing in winter.
Daily; closed April.

MOUNT WASHINGTON AUTO ROAD
Highway 16, Gorham, 603-466-3988; www.mt-washington.com

The trip to the summit of Mount Washington takes approximately 30 minutes each way. Make sure your car is in good condition; check brakes before starting. Their guided tour service is available daily.
Mid-May-mid-October daily, weather permitting.

MOUNT WASHINGTON SUMMIT MUSEUM

Highway 302, Top of Mount Washington; 603-466-3388;
www.mountwashington.org/education/museum/

The museum features displays and exhibits on life in the extreme climate of the summit, rare flora and fauna, geology and history.
Memorial Day-Columbus Day: daily.

NASHUA

See also Manchester

Originally a fur trading post, Nashua's manufacturing began with the development of Merrimack River water power early in the 19th century. The city is the second largest in New Hampshire.

WHAT TO SEE
SILVER LAKE STATE PARK

Silver Lake Road, Hollis, 603-465-2342

The park includes a one-thousand-foot beach on a 34-acre lake. Swimming and picnicking are allowed on site. There is a bathhouse for guests.
Late June-Labor Day 9 a.m.-8 p.m.

WHERE TO STAY
★★★CROWNE PLAZA

2 Somerset Parkway, Nashua, 603-886-1200, 800-962-7482; www.cpnashua.com

Located 15 miles from Manchester Airport and 40 miles from Boston's Logan Airport, this full-service hotel is in the heart of New Hampshire's high-tech area. Rooms have been updated with luxury linens and flat-screen TVs.
230 rooms. Restaurant, bar. Fitness center. Pool. $151-250

★★★RADISSON NASHUA HOTEL

11 Tara Blvd., Nashua, 603-888-9970, 888-201-1718; www.radisson.com

This hotel with Tudor-style architecture offers a comfortable stay for both business and leisure travelers.
336 rooms. Pets accepted. Restaurant, bar. Pool. $151-250

NEW LONDON

See also Manchester

Located in the Lake Sunapee recreational area, this town has a charming main street and is close to many cross-country skiing and hiking trails.

WHERE TO STAY
★★★INN AT PLEASANT LAKE

853 Pleasant St., New London, 603-526-6271, 800-626-4907;
www.innatpleasantlake.com

Situated between the lake and Mount Kearsarge, this gabled country inn is decorated like a comfortable house and has access to a private beach. Fresh, local ingredients are put to good use in the new American recipes served in the elegant on-site dining room.
12 rooms. Complimentary breakfast. Restaurant. Beach. Closed one week in April and two weeks in November. $151-250

WHERE TO EAT
★★MILLSTONE
74 Newport Road, New London, 603-526-4201; www.millstonerestaurant.com
This casual bistro serves traditional recipes such as rack of lamb with mint sauce and fresh steamed Maine lobster. The extensive wine list features wines from around the world served by the glass and by the bottle.
American. Lunch, dinner, Sunday brunch. Bar. Children's menu. $16-35

★★ROCKWELL'S AT THE INN
353 Main St., New London, 603-526-2791, 800-526-2791; www.newlondoninn.net
Classic dishes are given a contemporary twist at Rockwell's at the Inn, the elegant dining room at the New London Inn. The tavern serves a more casual menu of sandwiches, salads and burgers.
American. Dinner, Sunday brunch. Bar. Children's menu. Reservations recommended. Outdoor seating. Closed Monday. $16-35

NORTH CONWAY
See also Jackson, Mount Washington
The heart of the famous Mount Washington Valley region of the White Mountains, this area also includes Bartlett, Glen, Jackson, Conway, Redstone, Kearsarge and Intervale. Mount Washington, seen from the middle of Main Street, is one of the great views in the East.

WHAT TO SEE
CONWAY SCENIC RAILROAD
38 Norcross Circle, North Conway, 603-356-5251; www.conwayscenic.com
Steam and diesel trains depart from a restored Victorian station (1874) for an 11-mile (55-minute) round trip. The Valley Train explores the Saco River valley. The Notch Train travels through Crawford Notch. There is also a railroad museum
Valley Train: Mid-May-October: daily; mid-April-mid-May, November-December: weekends. Notch Train: Mid-September-mid-October: daily; late June-mid-September: Tuesday-Thursday, Saturday.

ECHO LAKE STATE PARK
Highway 302, North Conway, 603-356-2672
This mountain lake lies in the shadow of White Horse Ledge. Travel a ccenic road to 700-foot Cathedral Ledge, a dramatic rock formation; there are panoramic views of the White Mountains and the Saco River Valley. Swimming and picnicking are permitted.
Late June-Labor Day.

MOUNT CRANMORE
Route 16 North Conway, 800-786-6754; www.cranmore.com
Mount Cranmore has express quad, triple, and double chairlifts to summit, as well as three double chairlifts to north, south and east slopes and four surface lifts. There is a ski patrol, school, rentals and snowmaking, They have a restaurant, bar and day care on site. The longest run 1¾ miles with a vertical drop of 1,200 feet.
November-April: daily.

WHERE TO STAY

★COMFORT INN

2001 White Mountain Highway, North Conway, 603-356-8811, 866-647-8483;
www.comfortinnnh.com

This budget-friendly hotel offers clean, basic rooms and amenities such as an indoor pool and free wireless access. Complimentary continental breakfast is included with each stay.

59 rooms. Fitness center. Pool. $61-150

★★NORTH CONWAY GRAND HOTEL

72 Common Court, North Conway, 603-356-9300, 800-648-4397;
www.northconwaygrand.com

Located near North Conway's shopping outlets, this sprawling resort attracts families with its guest room amenities, including Nintendo systems, DVD players and MP3 players. The resort also includes a movie room, tennis courts, children's programs and several restaurants.

200 rooms. Restaurant, bar. Fitness center. Pool. Tennis. $151-250

★★★WHITE MOUNTAIN HOTEL & RESORT

West Side Road, North Conway, 603-356-7100, 800-533-6301;
www.whitemountainhotel.com

Beneath the Whitehorse and Cathedral ledges and Echo State Park, this elegant English country inn offers outdoor activities including cross-country skiing, hiking and rock climbing. Rooms are decorated with colonial reproductions and feature flat-screen TVs.

80 rooms. Restaurant, bar. Fitness center. Pool. Golf. Tennis. Ski-in/ski-out. $151-250

WHERE TO EAT

★★★1785 INN

3582 White Mountain Highway, North Conway, 603-356-9025, 800-421-1785;
www.the1785inn.com

This restaurant offers an extensive continental menu that includes creative veal chops with mushroom and cabernet sauvignon reduction and seared sea scallops with leeks and artichokes. A wide selection of desserts is made daily, including the popular coffee buttercrunch pie.

American, continental. Dinner. Bar. $16-35

★BELLINI'S

1857 White Mountain Highway, North Conway, 603-356-7000; www.bellinis.com

This Italian bistro serves classic recipes such as fettuccini with bolognese sauce or fresh-made lasagna. The wine list includes selections from Italy's top winemaking regions.

American, Italian. Lunch, dinner. Bar. Children's menu. Outdoor seating. $16-35

★HORSEFEATHERS

2679 White Mountain Highway Main St., North Conway, 603-356-2687;
www.horsefeathers.com

This casual restaurant serves sandwiches, burgers and salads to a local crowd who come for specialties such as the pulled pork burrito or pastrami on rye. The menu also includes vegetarian selections like tofu pad thai and pasta prima vera.

American. Lunch, dinner, brunch. Bar. Children's menu. $16-35

PORTSMOUTH

See also Exeter

A tour of Portsmouth's historic houses reveals architecture from the Colonial and Federal periods into the 19th century. The one-time capital of New Hampshire, Portsmouth was also the home port of a dynasty of merchant seamen who grew rich and built accordingly. The U.S. Navy Yard located in Kittery, Maine on the Piscataqua River has long been Portsmouth's major industry. The peace treaty ending the Russo-Japanese War was signed at the Portsmouth Navy Yard in 1905.

WHAT TO SEE
FORT CONSTITUTION

New Castle, 603-436-1552; www.nhstateparks.com/fortconstitution.html

The first cannon was placed on this site in 1632; in 1694, it was known as Fort William and Mary. Information about a British order to stop gunpowder from coming into the colonies, brought by Paul Revere on December 13, 1774, caused the Sons of Liberty from Portsmouth, New Castle and Rye to attack and capture a fort that held five tons of gunpowder the next day. Much of this powder was used at Bunker Hill by the Patriots. This uprising against the King's authority was one of the first overt acts of the Revolution. Little remains of the original fort except the base of its walls. Fort Constitution had been built on the same site by 1808; granite walls were added during the Civil War. Mid-June-early September: daily; late May-mid-June, late September-mid-October: weekends, holidays only.

FORT STARK STATE HISTORIC SITE

Wild Rose Lane, New Castle, 603-436-1552; www.nhstateparks.com/fortstark.html

The site is a former portion of the coastal defense system dating to 1746, exhibiting many of the changes in military technology from the Revolutionary War through World War II. The fort is situated on Jerry's Point, overlooking the Piscataqua River, Little Harbor and Atlantic Ocean.

Late May-mid-October daily.

GOVERNOR JOHN LANGDON HOUSE

143 Pleasant St., Portsmouth, 603-436-3205; www.spnea.org

John Langdon served three terms as governor of New Hampshire and was the first president pro tempore of the U.S. Senate. The house's exterior proportions are monumental and the interior is embellished with excellent woodcarving and fine Portsmouth-area furniture. George Washington was entertained here in 1789. Surrounded by landscaped grounds with a gazebo, rose and grape arbor and restored perennial garden beds.

Tours: June-mid-October Friday-Sunday.

ISLES OF SHOALS

315 Market St., Portsmouth, 603-431-5500; www.islesofshoals.com

The *M/V Thomas Laighton* makes cruises to historic Isles of Shoals. They offer lobster clambake river cruises, fall foliage excursions and more. Mid-June-Labor Day daily.

JOHN PAUL JONES HOUSE

43 Middle St., Portsmouth, 603-436-8420; www.seacoastnh.com/touring/jpjhouse.html

The famous naval commander twice boarded at this circa 1758 house; now it's a museum containing period furniture, collections of costumes, china, glass, documents, weapons. Guided tours are offered. June-mid-October, daily.

MOFFATT-LADD HOUSE

154 Market St., Portsmouth, 603-436-8221; www.moffattladd.org

Built in 1763 by Captain John Moffatt, this house was later the home of General William Whipple, who was his son-in-law and a signer of the Declaration of Independence. Many original 18th- and 19th-century furnishings are on display. There are also formal gardens on site. Mid-June-mid-October, daily.

RUNDLET-MAY HOUSE

364 Middle St., Portsmouth, 603-436-3205; www.seacoastnh.com

The Federalist, three-story 1807 mansion sits on terraces and retains its original 1812 courtyard and garden layout. The house contains family furnishings and accessories, including many fine examples of Federalist craftsmanship and the latest technologies of its time. Guided tours are available. June-October first Saturday of the month.

STRAWBERY BANKE MUSEUM

454 Court St., Portsmouth, 603-433-1100; www.strawberybanke.org

The museum is a unique restoration of a 10-acre historic waterfront neighborhood on the site of the original Portsmouth settlement. Included are structures built between 1695 and 1950. Also offered on site are architectural exhibits, a pottery shop and demonstrations, family programs and activities, special events and tours.
May-October, daily 10 a.m.-5 p.m.; holiday hours in December.

WARNER HOUSE

150 Daniel St., Portsmouth, 603-436-5909; www.warnerhouse.org

This 1716 house is one of New England's finest Georgian houses, with scagliola in the dining room, restored mural paintings on the staircase walls, a lightning rod on the west wall said to have been installed by Benjamin Franklin in 1762 and five portraits by Joseph Blackburn. Guided tours. June-mid-October Monday-Saturday, Sunday afternoons.

WENTWORTH-GARDNER HOUSE

50 Mechanic St., Portsmouth, 603-436-4406; www.wentworthgardnerandlear.org

The 1760 house is an excellent example of Georgian architecture, and features elaborate woodwork. Mid-June-mid-October Thursday-Sunday noon-4 p.m.

WHERE TO STAY
★FAIRFIELD INN PORTSMOUTH SEACOAST
650 Borthwick Ave., Portsmouth, 603-436-6363, 800-228-2800; www.marriott.com
The rooms at this budget-friendly hotel are decorated with colorful, contemporary carpets and furnishings and feature free wireless access. A complimentary breakfast is included with each stay.
105 rooms. Pool. $61-150

★★HOLIDAY INN
300 Woodbury Ave., Portsmouth, 603-431-8000, 888-465-4329; www.holiday-inn.com
Business travelers flock to this Holiday Inn for its updated rooms, on-site fitness room and restaurant with room service. The fitness center was renovated in 2008 and includes new cardio machines and an indoor pool.
130 rooms. Restaurant, bar. Fitness center. $151-250

★THE PORT INN
505 Highway 1 Bypass South, Portsmouth, 603-436-4378, 800-282-7678; www.theportinn.com
This independent inn offers rooms decorated with cheerful chintzes and touches such as upscale bath amenities and mini kitchens. The pool area includes a barbecue grill and seating available for do-it-yourself outdoor dining.
57 rooms. Complimentary breakfast. Pool. $61-150

★★★SHERATON HARBORSIDE HOTEL PORTSMOUTH
250 Market St., Portsmouth, 603-431-2300, 800-325-3535; www.sheratonportsmouth.com
This large New England-style hotel features a brick and granite exterior with large-paneled windows. The interior is inviting and stylish, and the location is in the downtown historic district on the Piscataqua River.
220 rooms. Pets accepted. Restaurant, bar. Fitness center. Pool. Business center. $151-250

RHODE ISLAND

RHODE ISLAND'S MOTTO IS "HOPE," BUT A MORE APPROPRIATE MAXIM MIGHT BE "SIZE doesn't matter." The state is the smallest in the nation, more petite even than most neighboring state counties. But its pint size belies its influence as a historical, cultural and natural treasure trove, one that road trippers would be remiss to miss. For starters, the Ocean State has more than 400 miles of coastline, replete with sunning, swimming, sailing and fishing enclaves. Then there are the inland 1,000 or so square miles, studded with postcard-perfect working farms, quaint Colonial inns and protected nature reserves. Cities such as Providence and Newport supply the state with first-rate lodging and modern cuisine, while islands like Block Island give the harried a place to unwind.

All of this would no doubt have blown the feather cap off explorer Giovanni da Verrazano, who landed in Narragansett Bay in 1524, but it might not have surprised the state's founder, Roger Williams. Like thousands after him, Williams moved to Rhode Island to get away from it all. The "all" in his case was the puritanical tyranny of Massachusetts, but his tolerant 1636 settlement set the tone for times to come. The area quickly became known for its policy of religious and political freedom and, in 1663, King Charles II granted the colony a royal charter, creating the state of Rhode Island. Since then, the region has become a seat of firsts: Rhode Islanders were among the first colonists to attack the British; on May 4, 1776, the state was the first to proclaim independence (a full two months before the Declaration of Independence was signed); resident Samuel Slater built America's first water-powered cotton mill in 1790; and, in 1876, Newport held the country's first polo match. And it may not have been the first watering hole ever built, but Newport's 1673 White Horse Tavern is the oldest operating pub in the United States. It's small, but sturdy and still going strong.

BLOCK ISLAND
See also Providence, Newport

Twelve miles off the state mainland and a short ferry ride from Montauk, Block Island seems a world away. Blessedly absent from the 21-square-mile retreat are Long Island's weekenders and Newport's summer hordes. The scene here just feels milder and, technically, it is—once named Rhode Island's "air conditioned" resort, the atoll is up to 15 degrees cooler than the rest of the state. Named for Dutch explorer Adriaen Block, who landed here in 1614, the island was once a low-key fishing and farming community. Today, it's still low-key, and draws both city slickers and nature enthusiasts to its white-sanded shores. More than 40 rare and endangered species of plants and animals live here; most are protected by public land trusts like The Nature Conservancy, which designated Block Island "one of the twelve last great places in the Western Hemisphere."

WHAT TO SEE
MOHEGAN BLUFFS
West of the Southeast Light lighthouse off Mohegan Trail, these grand 200-

foot clay cliffs provide sightseers with an unparalleled ocean view.

NEW HARBOR
One mile west of the Mohegan Bluffs on Ocean Avenue, the mammoth New Harbor was formed when town planners cut through a sand bar to merge the sea with Great Salt Pond.

NORTH LIGHT
Built in 1867 at the tip of the island near Settler's Rock, this former light-house now houses a maritime museum. Its surrounding dunes host a seagull rookery and wildlife sanctuary.

WHERE TO STAY
★★SPRING HOUSE
52 Spring St., Block Island, 401-466-5844, 800-234-9263; www.springhousehotel.com
Housed in a whitewashed Victorian structure, perched on the ocean's edge, the Spring House Hotel offers rooms with basic, comfortable furnishings, pastel hues and floral fabrics. The on-site restaurant, Victoria's Parlor, serves classic New England fare and features an extensive martini menu.
50 rooms. Closed in winter. Complimentary breakfast. Restaurant, bar. $151-250

RHODE ISLAND'S EASTERN COASTLINE
Summer in Rhode Island's South County means beaches, boating and basking in the sun. It also means tourists galore. Navigating Newport traffic in August can induce road rage in the mildest-mannered of drivers; waiting in epic lines for ice cream can be a chore. Escape the crowds by taking a day trip along the state's quiet eastern coastline, through the (almost) untouched towns of Bristol, Tiverton and Little Compton. From downtown Providence, take Highway 195 east to exit 7, Highway 114 South. Drive through Barrington, Warren and Bristol. (Dozens of antique and second-hand shops line Warren's Main and Water streets.) Highway 114 becomes Hope Street in Bristol, where stately Federal-era houses (many of them now bed and breakfasts) hint at the town's pre-Civil War wealth. Continue over the Mount Hope Bridge into Portsmouth and turn left onto Highway 24. Cross the Sakonnet River Bridge into Tiverton, and turn right onto Highway 77 South. At the lone traffic light on 77, an intersection with Highway 179, is Tiverton Four Corners. Pause here for shopping and lunch at the town's boutiques and eateries, and don't miss a cone from 1920s sweet shop Gray's Ice Cream. Continue south on 77 toward Little Compton, past open fields with panoramic views of Narragansett Bay. Once a productive agricultural area, Little Compton is now a wealthy summer community; the restored-farmhouses-cum-stately-estates are a sight to be seen. You can double back on the same route or turn right onto Highway 24 North in Tiverton and drive into Fall River, Mass., then head west to Providence on Highway 195. Approximately 40 miles

---

.WHERE TO EAT
★FINN'S SEAFOOD
212 Water St., Block Island, 401-466-2473
With a menu that features the all-stars of summer seaside dining, from fresh-from-the-ocean steamers to buttery lobster salad rolls, Finn's delivers authentic New England recipes in a casual setting. The clam chowder, loaded with fresh clams and potatoes, and blue fish pate, are standouts.

Seafood. Lunch, dinner. Bar. Children's menu. $16-35

★★★HOTEL MANISSES DINING ROOM
1 Spring St., Block Island, 401-466-2836; www.blockislandresorts.com
Often praised for its seafood-heavy, contemporary American menu, romantics favor dining in the glass-enclosed garden room; sweet tooths adore rich homemade desserts like layered banana cream cake and Italian-style hot chocolate. A discreet, knowledgeable staff adds to the experience.
American. Dinner. Closed November-April. Bar. Reservations recommended. Outdoor seating. $36-85

★MOHEGAN CAFÉ
213 Water St., Block Island, 401-466-5911
This casual eatery, located steps from the Old Harbor ferry landing, has an eclectic menu featuring everything from burgers to burritos and pad thai, along with house-made beers.
American. Lunch, dinner. Bar. $16-35

BRISTOL
See also Portsmouth
Quaint little Bristol's history is surprisingly rife with strife. In the late 1600s, the Native American rebel leader King Philip headquartered his Wampanoag troops in the area, preparing them for the country's first major Colonist vs. Indian battle. The resulting yearlong King Philip's War began and ended on the Bristol peninsula, between Mount Hope and Narragansett bays. Civil War officer—and later, state governor and senator—General Ambrose Burnside also earned his military stripes in Bristol, which by the turn of the 18th-century had become the fourth-busiest port in the United States. Today, the town is well known for its quaint, seaside feel and the storied Herreshoff Boatyard where many an America's Cup champion was built.

WHAT TO SEE
BLITHEWOLD MANSION AND GARDENS
101 Ferry Road, Bristol, 401-253-2707; www.blithewold.org
This historic house's manicured trees, flowers and gardens combine with a sweeping sea view. Concerts are held on the grounds of this 45-room mansion in the summer.
Mansion, mid-April-Columbus Day, Wednesday-Sunday; grounds, daily 10 a.m.-5 p.m.

COGGESHALL FARM MUSEUM, COLT STATE PARK
Poppasquash Road, Bristol, 401-253-9062; www.coggeshallfarm.org
Set in the middle of Colt State Park, this working 18th-century farm has fresh vegetables and herbs as well as colonial craft demonstrations. Visitors with extra time can cruise the park's three-mile scenic drive around the former Colt family estate on Narrangansett Bay, or take advantage of area fishing, boating, hiking, picnicking and seasonal concerts in Stone Barn.
Farm museum: March-September: daily 10 a.m.-6 p.m.; October-February: daily 10 a.m.-dusk.

HERRESHOFF MARINE MUSEUM
1 Burnside St., Bristol, 401-253-5000; www.herreshoff.org

The Herreshoff Manufacturing Company produced some of the world's greatest yachts, including eight winners of the America's Cup. Permanent exhibits include big boats, steam engines, and photographs and memorabilia from the "golden age of yachting."

May-October: daily 10 a.m.-5 p.m., closed Monday Admission: adults 21 and older $8, seniors over 65 $7, student with student card $4, children under 12 no charge, members free.

WHERE TO EAT
★★LOBSTER POT
119 Hope St., Bristol, 401-253-9100; www.lobsterpotri.com

An oceanfront location and superb views provide the setting for this reliable seafood restaurant. Feast on an extensive raw bar menu featuring fresh oysters, clams and shrimp, or sample classics such as clam chowder and steamed lobsters.

American, seafood. Lunch, dinner. Closed Monday; also two weeks in March. Bar. Reservations recommended. Outdoor seating. $16-35

NARRAGANSETT
See also Newport

Before there was Monte Carlo, there was Narragansett. The southern Rhode Island city was once home to a lavish McKim, Mead and White-designed casino. Several summer "cottages" and hotels were built to house the well-heeled who flocked here to hobnob and gamble in the late 19th and early 20th centuries. The casino was devastated by fire in 1900, but its Tower still stands on Ocean Road. Today, Narragansett—named for its indigenous people—counts fishing and tourism as its leading industries. The city is also home to the University of Rhode Island's renowned Graduate School of Oceanography.

WHAT TO SEE
BLOCK ISLAND FERRY
Galilee State Pier, 304 Great Island Road, Point Judith, 401-783-4613;
www.blockislandferry.com

This automobile ferry provides service to Block Island from Point Judith and Newport. Daily.

POINT JUDITH
1460 Ocean Road, Narragansett, 401-789-0444

The lighthouse and station are closed to the public, but strolling Point Judith's historical grounds is free.

SOUTH COUNTY MUSEUM
Strathmore St., Narragansett, 401-783-5400; www.southcountymuseum.org

The museum exhibits 19th-century Rhode Island antique costumes, vehicles, toys and nautical equipment, as well as farm and blacksmithing displays. Also see a historic country kitchen, a general store, a cobbler's shop and a complete turn-of-the-century letterpress print shop.

May-June, September: Friday-Saturday 10 a.m.-4 p.m., Sunday noon-4 p.m.; July-August: Wednesday-Saturday 10 a.m.-4 p.m., Sunday noon-4 p.m.; special arrangements may be made for October visits by calling the museum.

THE TOWERS

35 Ocean Road, Narragansett, 401-782-2597; www.thetowersri.com

In 1900, McKim, Mead and White's grandiose casino—the landmark that solidified Narragansett as a summer destination for the rich and fashionable—was destroyed by fire. This Romanesque arch entryway, flanked by conical towers, is the only structural element that remains.

Various public events throughout summer.

SPECIAL EVENT
MID-WINTER NEW ENGLAND SURFING CHAMPIONSHIP

Narragansett Town Beach, 170 Clarke Road, Narragansett, 401-723-8795;
www.sne.surfesa.org

For information, contact the Northeastern Surfing Association, 126 Sayles Ave., Pawtucket.

Third Saturday in February.

WHERE TO EAT
★★COAST GUARD HOUSE

40 Ocean Road, Narragansett, 401-789-0700; www.thecoastguardhouse.com

Housed in an historic McKim, Mead and White building, this seafood restaurant serves steamed lobsters, grilled fish and more in an elegant setting. American, seafood. Lunch, dinner, Sunday brunch. Bar. Children's menu. Outdoor seating. Closed early January-mid-February. $$

NEWPORT

See also Narragansett, Portsmouth

If Jay Gatsby had a second summer home, it might have been in Newport. The laid-back resort town was once the epicenter of East Coast summer society, where the rich—August Belmont, Ward McAllister, William Astor, Stuyvesant Fish—built

megamansions that they called "cottages" along the city's now-public Cliff Walk. Their lavish and often outrageous soirées, some costing upwards of $300,000, were the talk of early 20th century Rhode Island. World War I dampened the revelry considerably, though many modern-day bluebloods still flock here for various seasonal affairs. Social registries aside, Newport is home to Rhode Island's first school and newspaper, as well as the country's earliest Quaker and Jewish communities. During the Revolutionary War, it was occupied by the British for two years before being recaptured by French allies. Throughout its history, the city has been famous for its boating and yachting culture, as shipbuilders and sailors still abound in town.

WHAT TO SEE
ASTOR'S BEECHWOOD

580 Bellevue Ave., Newport, 401-846-3772; www.astorsbeechwood.com
This mansion was the Italianate summer residence of socialite Caroline Astor (that's *the* Mrs. Astor). A theatrical tour of the house includes actors portraying Mrs. Astor's servants and society guests.
Mid-May-mid-December: daily; rest of year: weekends only.

BELCOURT CASTLE

657 Bellevue Ave., Newport, 401-846-0669; www.belcourtcastle.com
Designed by Richard Morris Hunt in French château style, this 1891-era 62-room house was the residence of Oliver Hazard Perry Belmont and his wife, Alva Vanderbilt Belmont. Belmont loved horses and his stables sit inside the main structure. The castle contains the largest collection of antiques and objects d'art in Newport. Special events scheduled throughout year.
Daily; closed January.

BREAKERS

44 Ochre Point Ave., Newport, 401-847-1000; www.newportmansions.org
With 70 rooms, the Northern Italian palazzo designed by Richard Morris Hunt is the largest of all Newport cottages. The children's playhouse cottage has a scale-size kitchen, fireplace and playroom. The mansion was built for Mr. and Mrs. Cornelius Vanderbilt in 1895.
Daily.

BRICK MARKET

121 Thames St., Newport, 401-846-0813; www.brickmarketnewport.com
Home of the Newport Historical Society, the Brick Market was built by Touro Synagogue architect Peter Harrison in 1762. The restored building, which once served as a market and granary, is now full of boutiques and restaurants.
Daily.

CHATEAU-SUR-MER

474 Bellevue Ave., Newport, 401-847-1000; www.newportmansions.org
This 1852 Victorian mansion was remodeled in 1872 by Richard Morris Hunt and has landscaped grounds with a Chinese moon gate. The house was built for William S. Wetmore, who made his fortune in the China trade.
Late June-early October, daily.

CLIFF WALK

Memorial Blvd., Newport, 401-847-1355; www.cliffwalk.com
This scenic walk overlooking the Atlantic Ocean adjoins many of Newport's famous cottages. It was designated a National Recreational Trail in 1975.

EDWARD KING HOUSE

Aquidneck Park, 35 King St., Newport, 401-846-7426, 866-878-6954
Richard Upjohn's 1895 mansion is considered one of the finest Italianate houses in the country.
Monday-Friday.

ELMS

367 Bellevue Ave., Newport, 401-847-1000; www.newportmansions.org

Modeled after the 18th-century Chateau d'Asnieres near Paris, this restored cottage from Newport's gilded age boasts elaborate interiors and formal, sunken gardens. The 1901 home was built for Edward J. Berwind, a Philadelphia coal magnate.

May-October: daily; November-March: Saturday-Sunday.

FRIENDS MEETING HOUSE

82 Touro St., Newport, 401-846-0813; www.newporthistorical.org

This was the site of the New England Yearly Meeting of the Society of Friends from 1699 to 1905. The expanded meetinghouse spans three centuries of architecture and construction. Guided tours are through the Newport Historical Society.

Mid-June-August: Thursday-Saturday. Tours hourly 10 a.m.-3 p.m.; also by appointment.

HISTORIC MANSIONS AND HOUSES

Combination tickets to the Elms, the Breakers, Rosecliff, Marble House, Hunter House, Château-sur-Mer, Kingscote and Green Animals topiary gardens are available at any of these houses.

HUNTER HOUSE

54 Washington St., Newport, 401-847-1000; www.newportmansions.org

An outstanding example of Colonial architecture, the 1748 Hunter House features a gambrel roof, 12-on-12 panel windows and a broken pediment doorway. It's furnished with pieces by famous 18th-century cabinetmakers Townsend and Goddard.

Late June-late September daily.

INTERNATIONAL TENNIS HALL OF FAME & MUSEUM

194 Bellevue Ave., Newport, 401-849-3990, 800-457-1144; www.tennisfame.com

The world's largest tennis museum features interactive and dynamic exhibits detailing the history of the sport. Tennis equipment, fashions, trophies and memorabilia are on display in the famous Newport Casino, built in 1880 and designed by McKim, Mead and White.

Daily. Grass courts available May-October.

KINGSCOTE

253 Bellevue Ave., Newport, 401-847-1000; www.newportmansions.org

A Gothic Revival cottage designed by Richard Upjohn. In 1881, McKim, Mead and White added the "aesthetic" dining room, which features a Tiffany-glass wall and Chinese paintings and porcelains. Built for George Noble Jones of Savannah, Georgia, Kingscote is considered the nation's first true summer "cottage."

June-October daily.

MARBLE HOUSE

596 Bellevue Ave., Newport, 401-847-1000; www.newportmansions.org

The front gates, entrance and central hall of this 1892 house are modeled after Versailles. It's named for the many kinds of marble used on its interior, which also features lavish use of gold. Original furnishings include dining room chairs made of gilded bronze. The house was built for Mrs. William K. Vanderbilt. On display are yachting memorabilia and a restored Chinese teahouse where Mrs. Vanderbilt held suffragette meetings.

April-October: daily; rest of year weekends.

NEWPORT ART MUSEUM AND ART ASSOCIATION

76 Bellevue Ave., Newport, 401-848-8200; www.newportartmuseum.com

Changing exhibitions of contemporary and historical art are housed in the 1864 mansion designed by Richard Morris Hunt in the "Stick-Style" and in the 1920 Beaux-Arts building. Available are lectures, performing arts events, evening musical picnics and tours.

Memorial Day-Labor Day: Tuesday-Saturday 10 a.m.-4 p.m., Sunday noon-4 p.m.; Labor Day-Memorial Day: Tuesday Friday 11 a.m.-3 p.m.; Saturday 10 a.m.-4 p.m.; Sunday noon-4 p.m.; Closed Monday.

OLD STONE MILL

Touro Park, Mill St., and Bellevue Ave., Newport, 401-846-1398;

The origin of this circular stone tower supported by arches is unknown. Although excavations (1948-1949) have disproved it, some people still believe it was built by Norsemen.

REDWOOD LIBRARY AND ATHENAEUM

50 Bellevue Ave., Newport, 401-847-0292; www.redwoodlibrary.org

Designed by master Colonial architect Peter Harrison, this is thought to be the oldest library building in continuous use in United States. It was used by English officers as a club during the Revolutionary War. Collections include original books and early portraits.

Monday, Friday-Saturday 9:30 a.m.-5:30 p.m.; Tuesday-Thursday until 8 p.m.; Sunday 1-5 p.m.

ROSECLIFF

548 Bellevue Ave., Newport, 401-847-6543; www.newportmansions.org

Modeled by Stanford White after the Grand Trianon at Versailles, Rosecliff has the largest private ballroom in Newport and a famous heart-shaped staircase. It was built for socialite Mrs. Hermann Oelrichs in 1902.

April-early November daily.

SAMUEL WHITEHORNE HOUSE

416 Thames St., Newport, 401-849-7300; www.newportrestoration.org

This 1811 house boasts exquisite furniture, silver and pewter made by 18th-century artisans, plus Chinese porcelain, Irish crystal, Pilgrim-era furniture and a garden.

May-October, Monday, Thursday-Friday 11 a.m.-4 p.m.; Saturday-Sunday 10 a.m.-4 p.m.; winter by appointment.

TOURO SYNAGOGUE NATIONAL HISTORIC SITE

85 Touro St., Newport, 401-847-4794; www.tourosynagogue.org

The first synagogue in America and a Georgian masterpiece by the country's first architect, Peter Harrison, the Touro contains the oldest Torah in North America, examples of 18th-century crafts and a letter from George Washington.

Admission: free.

TRINITY CHURCH

Queen Anne Square, Newport, 401-846-0660; www.trinitynewport.org

The first Anglican parish in the state (1698), the Trinity has been in continuous use since it was built. President George Washington and philosopher George Berkeley were communicants. The interior features Tiffany windows and an organ tested by Handel before being shipped from London. Tours are available.

WANTON-LYMAN-HAZARD HOUSE

17 Broadway, Newport, 401-846-0813; www.newporthistorical.org

This 1675 house is the oldest in Newport and one of the finest Jacobean homes in New England. It was the site of the 1765 Stamp Act riot. Its 18th-century garden has been restored. Guided tours are available.

Mid-June-late August: Thursday-Saturday; five tours daily; closed holidays.

WHITEHALL MUSEUM HOUSE

311 Berkeley Ave., Middletown, 401-846-3116; www.whitehallmuseumhouse.org

A restored, 1729 hip-roofed country house built by Bishop George Berkeley, the British philosopher and educator.

July-Labor day: Tuesday-Sunday 10 a.m.-4 p.m.; also by appointment.

SPECIAL EVENTS
NEWPORT MUSIC FESTIVAL

Newport, 401-849-0700; www.newportmusic.org

Chamber music held in Newport's fabled mansions.

Three concerts daily. Mid-July.

NEWPORT WINTER FESTIVAL

28 Pelham St., Newport, 401-847-7666, 800-326-6030;
www.newportevents.com/winterfest

The festival features ten days of food, festivities and music with more than 200 cultural and recreational events and activities.

Mid-February.

WHERE TO STAY
★★BEECH TREE INN & COTTAGE

34 Rhode Island Ave., Newport, 401-847-9794, 800-748-6565; www.beechtreeinn.com

This inn, located in a house built in the 1880s, has comfortable rooms, some with fireplaces or whirlpool tubs. The innkeepers prepare a full breakfast for guests daily.

8 rooms. $151-250

★★★CASTLE HILL INN & RESORT

590 Ocean Drive, Newport, 401-849-3800, 888-466-1355; www.castlehillinn.com

This colossal city landmark is located right off the famous Ocean Drive. The resort spans the main house, the adjacent Harbor House, a guest chalet and renovated private cottages, and it offers ocean views. Romantic and quiet (no kids allowed in the lobby), most rooms are filled with original antiques, gas fireplaces, marble baths and canopy beds. If you can tear yourself away from your suite, don't miss the lobby's evening fireside s'mores.

35 rooms. Complimentary breakfast. Restaurant, bar. Beach. $351 and up

★★★THE CHANLER AT CLIFF WALK

117 Memorial Blvd., Newport, 401-847-1300; www.thechanler.com

Offering one of the best opportunities in Newport to live out your own gilded age weekend, this lavishly restored mansion-turned-hotel is situated in a prime oceanfront spot along Cliff Walk. Each of Chanler's rooms is uniquely designed to represent a different historical period or theme. Its Ocean Villas have private water views, saunas and whirlpools. If you're feeling particularly indulgent, request a butler-drawn bath or in-room massage treatment.

20 Rooms. Restaurant, bar. $351 and up

★★★THE FRANCIS MALBONE HOUSE

392 Thames St., Newport, 401-846-0392, 800-846-0392; www.malbone.com

At the Malbone House, decorum still reigns with complimentary daily tea service and better yet, a full gourmet breakfast. The rooms are spacious, immaculate and tasteful, with Jacuzzis, fireplaces and fluffy comforters. The house dates back to 1760 and is within a convenient walking distance of Newport's shops and eateries.

20 rooms. Complimentary breakfast. $251-350

★★★HOTEL VIKING

1 Bellevue Ave., Newport, 401-847-3300, 800-556-7126; www.hotelviking.com

First built in 1926, the Hotel Viking, located in Newport's Historic Hill neighborhood, is listed on the National Register of Historic Places. The rooms feature four-poster beds and well-executed reproductions. The modern, full-service spa is a popular retreat for pampering. The Viking's vistas are sweeping, thanks to its off-the-beaten-path hilltop location far away from tourists, yet close enough to attractions like the Tennis Hall of Fame.

222 rooms. Restaurant, bar. $251-350

★★★HYATT REGENCY NEWPORT

1 Goat Island, Newport, 401-851-1234, 888-591-1234; www.newport.hyatt.com

On the tip of Goat Island, the Hyatt Regency overlooks Newport's harbor, Narragansett Bay and Jamestown Bridge. Pillow-top mattresses, plush duvets and Portico bath products lend each room a home-away-from-home feel, while a kid-friendly outdoor pool reminds guests they're on vacation (though business travelers can still sit in on conferences in the hotel's wired work center). No seaside trip is complete without a clambake and the Hyatt delivers this, too, with two do-it-yourself waterfront fire pits.

264 rooms. Restaurant, bar. Pool. Fitness center. Spa. $251-350

★★HYDRANGEA HOUSE INN

16 Bellevue Ave., Newport, 401-846-4435, 800-945-4667; www.hydrangeahouse.com

A sweet, small inn with individually decorated rooms, Hydrangea House sits in the heart of Newport's historic town center. Breakfast is served in a lavishly decorated formal dining room and features the inn's own house blend coffee and fresh-made breads and granola.

6 rooms. $251-350

★★IVY LODGE

12 Clay St., Newport, 401-849-6865, 800-834-6865; www.ivylodge.com

This Victorian mansion turned inn has rooms decorated with period furniture and a prime location close to Newport's historic mansions. Many of the rooms feature fireplaces and some have DVD players.

8 rooms. Complimentary breakfast. Business center. $251-350

★★★MARRIOTT NEWPORT

25 America's Cup Ave., Newport, 401-849-1000, 800-458-3066;
www.newportmarriott.com

The nautical-themed Marriott Newport seamlessly blends big-city service with small-town charm. Massive suspended sails hover over a lounge in the waterfront-facing, multilevel lobby; upstairs, sailboat-patterned quilts lay across white guestroom duvets.

319 rooms. Restaurant, bar. Fitness center. pool. $251-350

★★MILL STREET INN

75 Mill St., Newport, 401-849-9500, 800-392-1316; www.millstreetinn.com

If Newport's historic sights leave you fatigued with the past, retreat to this recently renovated, contemporary inn (housed in a historic building) where rooms are decorated with streamlined furnishings and neutral hues. New flat-screen TVs, Aveda bath products, Starbucks coffee and wireless Internet complete the up-to-date feel of this cheerful inn.

23 rooms. Complimentary breakfast. $251-350

★★★NEWPORT HARBOR HOTEL AND MARINA

49 America's Cup Ave., Newport, 401-847-9000, 800-955-2558;
www.newporthotel.com

Want to live like the Astors but lacking a seaside manse? Check in to the Newport Harbor Hotel. The Queen Ann Square spot overlooks its own 60-slip marina off Narragansett Bay. The surrounding acres include first-rate restaurants and shops, 19th-century mansions, a golf course, tennis courts and local wineries. Low-key blue and gray furniture decorates the hotel's lobby and guest rooms are stocked with televisions, DVDs and video games.

133 rooms. Restaurant, bar. $351 and up

WHERE TO EAT
★★★CANFIELD HOUSE

5 Memorial Blvd., Newport, 401-847-0416; www.canfieldhousenewport.com

This elegant restaurant once housed Newport's only gambling casino. Today, it is a place where both locals and tourists come for traditional American fare such as steaks, lamb and local seafood. High ceilings, dark wood paneling, crystal chandeliers, a prominent stained-glass window and other refined touches make any meal here a celebration. Alfresco dining is available on the covered porch during the warmer months, and more casual meals are available in the cellar pub.

American. Dinner. Bar. Children's menu. Reservations recommended. Outdoor seating. Closed Monday. $16-35

★★LA FORGE CASINO RESTAURANT

186 Bellevue Ave., Newport, 401-847-0418; www.laforgenewport.com

Situated on the grounds of the International Tennis Hall of Fame and offering views of the onsite grass courts, this restaurant serves classic American fare including baked stuffed lobster and clam chowder.

American. Lunch, dinner, Sunday brunch. Bar. Children's menu. Outdoor seating. $16-35

★★RHODE ISLAND QUAHOG COMPANY

250 Thames St., Newport, 401-848-2330; www.riquahogco.com

This casual seafood restaurant has a prime location in the heart of Newport's historic district, and as such is perpetually busy in summer months. Native quahogs, or clams, are served stuffed, in chowder and in clams casino, while pizzas, sandwiches and salads round out the rest of the menu.

Seafood. Lunch, dinner. Bar. Children's menu. Reservations recommended. Outdoor seating. Closed January-February. $16-35

★★★WHITE HORSE TAVERN

26 Marlborough St., Newport, 401-849-3600

If walls could talk, the White Horse Tavern's dark wooden planks would have much to say. Built in 1673, the downtown tavern is America's oldest watering hole. Its litany of owners have thankfully left the pub's brown clapboard exterior, stone fireplaces and exposed ceiling beams, all smack filled with centuries-old character. The only thing updated is the food, which highlights a menu of well-executed regional New England entrées.

American. Lunch, dinner, Sunday brunch. Bar. Reservations recommended. Outdoor seating. $36-85

PROVIDENCE

See also Bristol

Grateful that God's providence had led him to this spot, Roger Williams founded a town and named it accordingly. The early 1636 settlement, more farm town than urban center, soon morphed into an important port and industrial hub. Clipper ships left the harbor to explore China and the West Indies. Silver and jewelry artisans set up shop along the city's Colonial-lined streets. Today, Rhode Island's capital is the biggest metropolis in the state—which, with 160,000 residents isn't saying too much—and best-known for its outstanding universities: the liberal, Ivy League Brown, and the funky, alternative Rhode Island School of Design. Students are fixtures in the plethora of coffee shops and bars on bustling Thayer Street, while local Goodfellas frequent the trattorias of Federal Hill, Providence's Little Italy. The up-and-coming downtown area now has an upscale mall, a modern convention center and a booming nightlife scene. Still, perhaps in deference to the deferential Roger Williams himself, the city has maintained much of its old charm; contemporary hotels and office buildings share streets with historic houses, and the views of Narragansett Bay are as striking as ever.

WHAT TO SEE
ARCADE
65 Weybosset St., Providence, 401-273-9700
America's first indoor shopping mall, built in 1828, has national landmark status and more than 35 specialty shops and restaurants.

BROWN UNIVERSITY
45 Prospect St., Providence, 401-863-1000; www.brown.edu
Founded as Rhode Island College in 1764, the school was renamed for major benefactor Nicholas Brown in 1804. The 7,500-student Ivy is the seventh-oldest university in the country; its many libraries are free and open to the public.

CULINARY ARCHIVES & MUSEUM
315 Harborside Blvd., Providence, 491-598-2805; www.culinary.org
Dubbed the "Smithsonian of the food service industry," this museum contains more than 200,000 items related to the culinary arts.
Tuesday-Sunday 10 a.m.-5 p.m.

FIRST UNITARIAN CHURCH
1 Benevolent St., Providence, 401-421-7970; www.firstunitarianprov.org
At the top of this 1816 building is the largest bell ever cast by Paul Revere.

GOVERNOR STEPHEN HOPKINS HOUSE
15 Hopkins St., Providence, 401-421-0694; www.stephenhopkins.org
The 10-time governor of Rhode Island (he signed the Declaration of Independence) lived here.
April-December Wednesday, Saturday 1-4 p.m.; also by appointment.

JOHN BROWN HOUSE
52 Power St., Providence, 401-273-7507; www.rihs.org/Museums.html
George Washington was once a guest at this Georgian manse that now houses a museum of 18th-century china, glass and paintings, as well as John Brown's chariot, the oldest surviving American-made vehicle.
January-April, Friday-Saturday 10:30 a.m.-4:30 p.m.; May-December, Tuesday-Saturday 10:30 a.m.-4:30 p.m.

MUSEUM OF NATURAL HISTORY AND CORMACK PLANETARIUM
1000 Elmwood Ave., Providence, 401-785-9450; www.rogerwilliamsparkzoo.org
The museum features anthropology, geology, astronomy and biology displays; as well as educational and performing arts programs.
Daily 10 a.m.-5 p.m.; planetarium September-June Saturday-Sunday, July-August Tuesday.

OLD STATE HOUSE

150 Benefit St., Providence, 401-222-2678; www.preservation.ri.gov

The state General Assembly met here between 1762 and 1900. Independence was proclaimed in the State House two months before the Declaration was signed in Philadelphia.

Monday-Friday.

PROVIDENCE ATHENAEUM LIBRARY

251 Benefit St., Providence, 401-421-6970; www.providenceathenaeum.org

Housed in a Greek Revival building designed by William Strickland, this is one of the oldest subscription libraries in the United States. The rare book room includes original Audubon elephant folios and a small art collection.

September-May: Monday-Thursday 9 a.m.-7 p.m., Friday-Saturday until 5 p.m., Sunday 1-5 p.m.; June-Labor Day: Monday-Thursday 9 a.m.-7 p.m., Friday until 5 p.m., Saturday until 1 p.m.; closed Sundays and first two weeks of August.

PROVIDENCE CHILDREN'S MUSEUM

100 South St., 401-273-5437; www.childrenmuseum.org

Many hands-on exhibits, including a time-travel adventure through Rhode Island's multicultural history, a wet-and-wild exploration of water and a hands-on geometry lab, entertain kids at the museum.

September-March, Tuesday-Sunday 9 a.m.-6 p.m. and selected Monday holidays/Fridays until 8 p.m.; April-Labor Day, daily 9 a.m.-6 p.m.

RHODE ISLAND SCHOOL OF DESIGN

2 College St., Providence, 401-454-6100; www.risd.edu

Nearly 2,200 are enrolled here at one of the country's leading art and design schools.

RHODE ISLAND STATE HOUSE

82 Smith St., Providence, 401-222-2357; www.rilin.state.ri.us

Inside the 1901 capitol, designed by McKim, Mead and White, is an original Gilbert Stuart portrait of George Washington.

Monday-Friday 9-11 a.m.; closed second Monday in August.

ROGER WILLIAMS NATIONAL MEMORIAL

282 N. Main St., Providence, 401-521-7266; www.nps.gov

At the site of the old town spring, this 4 ½-acre park commemorates Roger Williams and the founding of Providence.

Daily.

ROGER WILLIAMS PARK

1000 Elmwood Ave., Providence, 401-785-9450; www.rogerwilliamsparkzoo.org

The park has 430 acres of woodlands, waterways and winding drives, plus greenhouses and a Japanese garden.

Daily.

ROGER WILLIAMS PARK ZOO

1000 Elmwood Ave., Providence, 401-785-3510; www.rogerwilliamsparkzoo.org
Ideal for kids, the zoo has a nature center, a tropical building, African plains and Marco Polo exhibits, and more than 600 animals.
Daily.

SPECIAL EVENTS
SPRING FESTIVAL OF HISTORIC HOUSES

21 Meeting St., Providence, 401-831-7440; www.ppsri.org
Sponsored by the Providence Preservation Society, the festival runs tours of grand old private houses and gardens.
Third weekend in June.

WATERFIRE

Waterplace Park, 101 Regent Ave., Providence, 401-272-3111; www.waterfire.org
Floating bonfires in the Providence River are accompanied by music.
Weekends, late May-late October.

WHERE TO STAY
★★CHRISTOPHER DODGE HOUSE

11 W. Park St., Providence, 401-351-6111; www.providence-hotel.com
A restored townhouse located near the state capitol building, this inn gets historic charm just right with bright, clean, streamlined rooms decorated with simple antique reproduction furnishings. A full breakfast is served daily and guests have access to a nearby fitness complex.
14 rooms. Complimentary breakfast. $61-150

★★COURTYARD PROVIDENCE DOWNTOWN

32 Exchange Terrace, Providence, 401-272-1191, 800-321-2211; www.courtyard.com
With refreshed guest rooms featuring contemporary décor, flat-screen TVs and free wireless access, this business-minded hotel is a good budget-friendly bet in downtown Providence. An onsite lounge, fitness center and indoor pool round out the amenities.
216 rooms. Restaurant, bar. $151-250

★★★MARRIOTT PROVIDENCE

1 Orms St., Providence, 401-272-2400, 800-937-7768; www.marriott.com
Located just off Interstate 95 (I-95), the Marriott can't be beat for convenience. Well-appointed rooms—think cushy armchairs, stately desks and a pillow menu—make it hard to beat for hospitality as well. Even kids get special treatment here in the form of poolside sand competitions and hotel-run scavenger hunts. Rows of classic Rhode Island Colonial homes, as well as plenty of shopping and eating options are nearby.
346 rooms. Restaurant, bar. $151-250

★★RADISSON HOTEL PROVIDENCE HARBOR

220 India St., Providence, 401-272-5577, 800-333-3333;
www.radisson.com/providenceri
This updated hotel features guest rooms with a contemporary décor and

views of Providence Harbor. The on-site restaurant serves breakfast, lunch and dinner, but room service offers an opportunity to linger in the special Sleep Number beds.

136 rooms. Restaurant, bar. $61-150

★★★THE WESTIN PROVIDENCE

1 W. Exchange St., Providence, 401-598-8000, 800-301-1111;
www.westin.com/providence

The downtown Westin is attached—via sky bridge—to Providence Place, the city's major mall. If browsing hundreds of boutiques isn't your thing, the modern two-tower hotel also provides plenty of other distractions, including a pool, fitness classes and extensive in-suite entertainment. Each room is outfitted with Starwood's signature "Heavenly Bed" and offers a flat-screen TV, a cordless phone, a dual-head shower and a better-than-average minibar. Canine guests are welcome, and they get their own bowls, treats and "Heavenly" dog beds, too.

364 rooms. Restaurant, bar. $251-350

WHERE TO EAT

★★★AL FORNO

577 S. Main St., Providence, 401-273-9760; www.alforno.com

Local favorite Al Forno has turned out primo pasta dishes for nearly three decades. Chef-owners (and cookbook authors) Johanne Killeen and George Germon preside over their rustic, two-story waterfront spot and infuse their Italian menu with Tuscan and Provençal flair. Housemade gnocchi with spicy sausage and the baked pasta with cream and four cheeses are among many mouthwatering must-eat dishes.

Italian. Dinner. Bar. Outdoor seating. Closed Sunday-Monday. $36-85

★★HEMENWAY'S SEAFOOD GRILL

121 South main St., Providence, 401-351-8570; www.hemenwaysrestaurant.com

An elegant downtown spot with floor-to-ceiling windows delivering outstanding views, this restaurant is a reliable choice for perfectly prepared seafood. Come for the steamers or clam chowder, but be sure to save room for the lobster ravioli and mile high key lime pie.

Seafood. Lunch, dinner. Bar. Outdoor seating. $16-35

★★★★MILL'S TAVERN

101 N. Main St., Providence, 401-272-3331; www.merchantcircle.com

From its smart design and young, energetic vibe to its appealing menu, this winning restaurant housed in a former mill turns tradition on its head. The menu echoes the classic-contemporary sentiment offering a wide variety of creatively prepared American seasonal dishes, many of which are cooked in the kitchen's wood-burning oven, wood grill and rotisserie. The warm, knowledgeable staff provides professional and thorough service without being stuffy or intrusive.

Contemporary American. Dinner. Bar. Reservations recommended. $36-85

★★★NEW RIVERS

7 Steeple St., Providence, 401-751-0350; www.newriversrestaurant.com

Fake fruit and wall-mounted plates have the potential to turn a good kitchen into kitsch. But while both Lucite pears and Majolica pottery are incorporated into New Rivers' décor, the overall ambiance is comfortable. The colorful downtown American bistro's seasonal menu is full of fresh, local ingredients; standout dishes include poached rabbit loin in sweet pea broth and roasted trout with cracked wheat and beets.

American. Dinner. Bar. Reservations recommended. Closed Sunday. $36-85

★★PANE E VINO

365 Atwells Ave., Providence, 401-223-2230; www.panevino.net

This Federal Hill Italian bistro delivers old school charm and perfect takes on tried and true recipes such as veal scaloppini or linguine with clams. The wine list offers a collection of unique bottles from Italy's best wine regions.

Italian. Dinner. Bar. Reservations recommended. $36-85

★★★POT AU FEU

44 Custom House St., Providence, 401-273-8953; www.potaufeuri.com

A formal, upstairs salon and a relaxed downstairs area make up Pot Au Feu, a traditional French bistro in the heart of Providence. The classic and regional French dishes—onion soup, salad niçoise, sweet and savory crepes—are authentic and delicious. The exposed brick walls and candlelit tables create a warm and cozy atmosphere.

French. Lunch, dinner. Bar. Reservations recommended. Closed Sunday. $16-35

WARWICK

See also Providence

Sometimes pretty, sometimes gritty, Warwick often (unfairly) gets a bad rap. The state's second-largest city is home to T.F. Green International airport and countless industrial warehouses, but it also has 39 miles of Narragansett Bay coastline and more than 15 picturesque marinas. Less populated than Providence, Warwick still has plenty of shopping and eating destinations, and its decentralized geography has given rise to a number of postcard-perfect villages such as Pawtuxet, Cowesett and Conanicut.

WHAT TO SEE
HISTORIC PONTIAC MILLS

334 Knight St., Warwick, 401-737-2700

A restored 1863 mill complex houses nearly 80 small businesses, artisans and shops, with an open-air market on weekends. Daily.

WALKING TOUR OF HISTORIC APPONAUG VILLAGE

3275 Post Road, Warwick, 401-738-2000, 800-492-7942

More than 30 historic and architecturally interesting buildings comprise this walking tour; brochure available through Warwick City.

SPECIAL EVENTS

GASPEE DAYS

Warwick, 401-781-1772, 800-492-7942; www.gaspee.com

A celebration of the capture and burning of the British schooner Gaspee by Rhode Island patriots includes arts and crafts, concerts, footraces, battle reenactments, parades and contests.

May-June.

WARWICK HERITAGE FESTIVAL

Warwick City Park, Warwick, 401-738-2000, 800-492-7942;

A weekend reenactment of the city's history.

November, Veterans Day weekend.

WHERE TO STAY

★★★CROWNE PLAZA

801 Greenwich Ave., Warwick, 401-732-6000, 800-227-6963; www.crowneplaza.com

Stranded travelers breathe a sigh of relief when checking into the Crowne Plaza, located three miles from the airport. At this tastefully decorated hotel, rooms come with marble baths, dark wooden desks, CD players, bathrobes and upscale toiletries, making overnights a pleasure. For the travel weary, there is a sleep amenity package that includes an eye mask, drape clip, earplugs, lavender spray and a night light.

266 rooms. Restaurant, bar. Pets accepted. $151-250

★★RADISSON HOTEL PROVIDENCE AIRPORT

2081 Post Road, Warwick, 401-739-3000, 800-333-3333; www.radisson.com/warwickri

A recent renovation left the rooms and public spaces at this airport hotel bright, cheerful and contemporary. Amenities are targeted to business travelers, with large work spaces and ergonomic desk chairs in each room. Round-the-clock airport transportation makes catching your flight a snap.

111 rooms. Complimentary breakfast. Restaurant, bar. $151-250

VERMONT

GREEN ROLLING HILLS, PICTURE-PERFECT VILLAGES, FIELDS DOTTED WITH BLACK-AND-WHITE cows. Vermont is every bit as bucolic as most imagine. But under that peaceful surface is an independent spirit that makes Vermont one of the most progressive, liberal states in the country. Vermonters are proudly individualist: one town threatened to secede from the U.S. over the Iraq war, and several towns have fought fiercely (but unsuccessfully) to stop Wal-Mart from opening in the state. And while modern Vermont is progressively leftist (it was one of the first states to sanction civil unions), that independent spirit is nothing new.

In 1724, Vermont became the last New England state to be settled. Ethan Allen and his Green Mountain Boys made Vermont famous when they took Fort Ticonderoga from the British in 1775. Claimed by both New York and New Hampshire, Vermont framed a constitution in 1777. It was the first state to prohibit slavery and the first state to provide universal male suffrage, regardless of property or income. For 14 years, Vermont was an independent republic, running its own postal service, coining its own money, naturalizing citizens of other states and countries and negotiating with other states and nations. In 1791, Vermont became the 14th state.

Tourism is a driving force in Vermont, with every town sprinkled with quaint bed and breakfasts, inns and restaurants. The state's many ski resorts often get top marks by national publications. A strong organic and environmentalist movement exists here, and chains are rare. It's not unusual to buy your gas from an independent gas station, or turn to a local bookshop for the latest bestseller.

That kind of grassroots populism is refreshing in an ever-homogenous America. Here you'll find tiny villages, outstanding fresh, organic food, topnotch skiing and the best maple syrup in the country. Burlington is a funky, artsy college town, while Montpelier is one of the country's prettiest state capitals. In between is a delightful landscape of adorable villages, each with a unique and proud character of its own.

ARLINGTON

See also Dorset, Bennington, Manchester and Manchester Center

The small town of Arlington, located in Southwestern Vermont, lies between the Green Mountains and the Taconic range. There are five mountain peaks located in the area. The American painter Norman Rockwell lived in the town during the 1940s.

WHAT TO SEE
NORMAN ROCKWELL EXHIBITION
3772 Highway 7A, Arlington, 802-375-6423;
www.vmga.org/bennington/normrockwell.html

Hundreds of magazine covers, illustrations, advertisements, calendars and other printed works are displayed in a historic 1875 church in the illustrator's former hometown. Hosts are Rockwell's former models.

Daily; May-October 9 a.m.-5 p.m.; November-April 10 a.m.-4 p.m.

WHERE TO STAY
★★★ARLINGTON'S WEST MOUNTAIN INN

144 W. Mountain Inn Road, and Highway 313, Arlington, 802-375-6516;
www.westmountaininn.com

This historic white, seven-gabled inn was built in 1849 and opened as an inn in 1978. Located on a mountainside overlooking the Battenkill River, the interior of the inn is furnished with a mix of antiques and country classics (pine paneling, fireplace, books, chess and checkers). Nearby activities include hiking, snowshoeing, canoeing, tubing, golfing and playing tennis.
20 rooms. Complimentary breakfast. Restaurant, bar. $151-250

ALSO RECOMMENDED
HILL FARM INN

458 Hill Farm Road, Arlington, 802-375-2269, 800-882-2545; www.hillfarminn.com

North of Arlington's town center, this charming inn lies on 50 acres fronting the Battenkill River. The land has sheep, goats and chickens wandering about outside to amuse kids and adults alike. There is also a historic guesthouse, a classic white farmhouse and several outlying cottages housing family suites and efficiencies. Inside, the guest rooms have simple country charm; there are no phones, but some rooms have televisions.
15 rooms. Complimentary breakfast. $61-150

WHERE TO EAT
★★★ARLINGTON INN

3904 Highway 7A, Arlington, 802-375-6532, 800-443-9442; www.arlingtoninn.com

This historic landmark inn was built in 1848 as a private home and has been in operation since 1888. The Victorian dining room serves classic dishes such as beef stroganoff and filet mignon. A fireplace keeps the room cozy in winter months.
American. Dinner. Bar. Children's menu. Reservations recommended.
Closed Monday; last week in April-first week in May; also Sunday in off-season. $36-85

BENNINGTON
See also Arlington, Manchester and Manchester Center

Bennington headquartered Ethan Allen's Green Mountain Boys—known to New Yorkers as the "Bennington Mob"—in Vermont's long struggle with New York. On August 16, 1777, this same "mob" won a decisive battle in the Revolutionary War. Bennington has three separate areas of historic significance: the Victorian and turn-of-the-century buildings downtown; the colonial houses, church and commons in Old Bennington (one mile west) and the three covered bridges in North Bennington.

WHAT TO SEE
BENNINGTON BATTLE MONUMENT

15 Monument Circle, Old Bennington,

A 306-foot monolith commemorates a Revolutionary War victory. There is an elevator to an observation platform
Mid-April-October, daily 9 a.m.-5 p.m.

BENNINGTON COLLEGE

Highway 67A and One College Drive, Bennington, 802-442-5401; www.bennington.edu
This small liberal arts college was founded in 1932 and became coeducational in 1969. The Visual and Performing Arts Center has special exhibits. The college hosts summer programs and performances.

BENNINGTON MUSEUM

75 Main St., Bennington, 802-447-1571; www.benningtonmuseum.org
This museum contains early Vermont and New England historical artifacts, including American glass, paintings, sculpture, silver and furniture. The Schoolhouse Museum contains Grandma Moses family memorabilia, a Bennington flag and other Revolutionary War collections.
Thursday-Tuesday 10 a.m.-5 p.m. Genealogical library by appointment.

OLD BURYING GROUND

1 Veterans Memorial Drive, Bennington, 802-447-3311; www.bennington.com
Poet Robert Frost and those who died in the Battle of Bennington are buried here.

OLD FIRST CHURCH

One Monument Circle, Old Bennington, Vt. Route 9 and Monument Avenue,
802-447-1223; www.oldfirstchurchbenn.org
Built in 1805, the church is an example of early colonial architecture. Guided tours. Memorial Day-June: weekends; July-mid-October: Monday-Saturday 10 a.m.-noon, 1-4 p.m., Sunday 1-4 p.m.

PARK-MCCULLOUGH HOUSE MUSEUM

One Park and West Street, North Bennington, 802-442-5441; www.parkmccullough.org
A 35-room 1865 Victorian mansion with period furnishings, stable with carriages. The rooms feature a costume collection, Victorian gardens and a child's playhouse. Special events are held throughout the year.
Mid-May-October: daily, tours 10 a.m.-4 p.m.; November-April: special events and group tours by appointment.

WOODFORD STATE PARK

142 State Park Road, Woodford, 802-447-7169; www.vtstateparks.com
At 2,400 feet, this 400-acre park has the highest elevation of any park in the state. Swimming, fishing, picnicking and boating (no motors; rentals) are allowed. There are a variety of nature and hiking trails. There are tent and trailer sites (as well as a dump station).
Memorial Day-Columbus Day.

WHERE TO STAY
★★★FOUR CHIMNEYS INN

21 W. Road, Bennington, 802-447-3500; www.fourchimneys.com
Guest rooms blend modern amenities with an Old-World feel at this elegant 1783 inn set on 11 acres of trees and rolling grass fields. The dining room serves updated American recipes at breakfast, lunch and dinner.
11 rooms. Complimentary breakfast. Restaurant, bar. $151-250

★HAMPTON INN
51 Hannaford Square, Bennington, 802-440-9862, 800-426-7866;
www.hamptoninn.com

With a location near Bennington's town center, this value-minded hotel is a good base for exploring Southern Vermont. The simple rooms at this Hampton Inn include updated linens and on-demand movies.

80 rooms. Complimentary breakfast. Fitness center. Pool. $61-150

BRANDON
See also Rutland

Brandon is a resort and residential town located at the western edge of the Green Mountains. The first U.S. electric motor was made in nearby Forestdale by Thomas Davenport.

WHAT TO SEE
MOUNT INDEPENDENCE
Highways 22A and 73 West, Orwell, 497 Mount Independence Road, Orwell,
802-759-2412; www.historicvermont.org/mountindependence

A wooded bluff on the shore of Lake Champlain, the site was part of the Revolutionary War defense complex. A fort built in 1776 across from Fort Ticonderoga was constructed to house 12,000 troops and protect the colonies from northern invasion. The area is the least disturbed major Revolutionary War site in the country; four marked trails show the ruins of the fort complex. Late May-mid-October, daily 9:30 a.m.-5 p.m.

STEPHEN A. DOUGLAS BIRTHPLACE
2 Grove St. (Highway 7), Brandon, 802-247-6401; www.brandon.org

Tour the cottage where the "Little Giant," once the Democratic nominee for president who lost to Abraham Lincoln, was born in 1813. Douglas attended Brandon Academy before moving to Illinois in 1833. Tours are by appointment.

WHERE TO STAY
★★★LILAC INN
53 Park St., Brandon, 802-247-5463, 800-221-0720; www.lilacinn.com

This Colonial home, built in 1909, is on the National Register of Historic Places. Decorated in Victorian style, rooms feature antiques, historical prints and artwork. Extensive gardens are found in back, along with a patio and gazebo. Enjoy a book in the library, practice on the putting green or take a drive to nearby historic Fort Ticonderoga.

9 rooms. Pets accepted. No children under 12. Complimentary breakfast. Restaurant, bar. $151-250

BURLINGTON
See also Shelburne

Located on Lake Champlain, Burlington is the largest city in Vermont. It's the site of the oldest university, the University of Vermont, and the oldest daily newspaper in the state. It's also the burial place of Revolutionary War hero Ethan Allen and the birthplace of philosopher John Dewey. It has a diverse range of industries and the lakefront area offers a park, dock and restaurants.

WHAT TO SEE
BOLTON VALLEY SKI/SUMMER RESORT
4302 Bolton Access Road, Bolton Valley, 877-926-5866; www.boltonvalleyvt.com
The resort has a quad, four double chairlifts, one surface lift, school, patrol, rentals, snowmaking, cafeteria, restaurants, bar and nursery. There are forty-three runs; the longest run is over three miles, and there is a vertical drop of 1,600 feet.
November-April: daily.

CHURCH STREET MARKETPLACE
2 Church St., Suite 2A, Burlington, 802-863-1648; www.churchstmarketplace.com
Four traffic-free blocks run from the Unitarian Church (designed in 1815 by Peter Banner) to City Hall at the corner of Main Street. The buildings are a mix of Art Deco and 19th-century architectural styles and house more than 100 shops, restaurants, galleries and cafés. The brick promenade offers vendors and street entertainers.

ETHAN ALLEN HOMESTEAD AND MUSEUM
1 Ethan Allen Homestead, Burlington, 802-865-4556; www.ethanallenhomestead.org
Ethan Allen had a colorful history as a frontiersman, a military leader, a land speculator, a suspected traitor and a prisoner of war. This preserved pioneer homestead was Allen's last home. Here you'll find a recreated hayfield and kitchen gardens, plus the 1787 farmhouse. One-hour guided tours are available.
Mid-May-mid-October: Thursday-Saturday 10 a.m.-4 p.m., Sunday 1-4 p.m.

ETHAN ALLEN PARK

1006 N. Ave Burlington and Ethan Allen Parkway, Burlington, 802-863-3489;
This was part of Ethan Allen's farm. Ethan Allen's Tower has views of Adirondacks and Lake Champlain to the west, Green Mountains to the east. Picnicking is allowed on site.
Memorial Day-Labor Day: Wednesday-Sunday afternoons and evenings.

LAKE CHAMPLAIN CHOCOLATES
750 Pine St., Burlington, 802-864-1808, 800-465-5909;
www.lakechamplainchocolates.com
Large glass windows give visitors a view of the chocolate-making process at this small-scale factory. The gift shop usually features in-store chocolate-making demonstrations on Saturdays, when the factory itself is closed.
Free factory tours: Monday-Thursday 9 a.m.-2 p.m. on the hour; free chocolate tastings: Friday 9 a.m.-2 p.m. on the hour; factory store: Monday-Saturday 9 a.m.-6 p.m., Sunday noon-5 p.m.

UNIVERSITY OF VERMONT

Waterman Building, 85 S. Prospect St., Burlington, 802-656-3480; www.uvm.edu

The university, founded in 1791, is the fifth-oldest university in New England and offers graduate and undergraduate programs. On campus is the Billings Center, the Bailey-Howe Library, the largest in the state, the Georgian-designed Ira Allen Chapel, named for the founder, and the Old Mill, a classroom building with cornerstone laid by General Lafayette in 1825.

SPECIAL EVENTS
DISCOVER JAZZ FESTIVAL

187 St. Paul St. Burlington, 802-863-7992; www.discoverjazz.com

A jazz extravaganza with more than 150 live performances takes place in city parks, clubs and restaurants.

Ten days in early June.

VERMONT MOZART FESTIVAL

3 Main St., Suite 217, Burlington, 802-862-7352; www.vtmozart.com

The festival features 26 chamber concerts in picturesque Vermont settings including the Trapp Family Meadow, Basin Harbor Club in Vergennes and Shelburne Farms on Lake Champlain.

Mid-July-early August.

WHERE TO STAY
★★BEST WESTERN WINDJAMMER INN & CONFERENCE CENTER

1076 Williston Road, South Burlington, 802-863-1125, 800-371-1125;
www.bestwestern.com

This budget-friendly option offers recently renovated rooms and complimentary breakfast as well as afternoon cookies and coffee. A complimentary airport shuttle is available.

159 rooms. Pets accepted. Restaurant. Fitness center. Pool. $61-150

★★DOUBLETREE HOTEL

1117 Williston Road, Burlington, 802-658-0250, 800-222-8733; www.doubletree.com

Located between downtown Burlington and Burlington airport, this hotel features rooms with contemporary décor and Doubletree's signature Sweet Dreams beds. The onsite restaurant serves traditional American fare in a casual environment.

130 rooms. Pets accepted, Restaurant, bar. Fitness room. Pool. $61-150

★★★THE ESSEX

70 Essex Way, Essex, 802-878-1100, 800-727-4295; www.innatessex.com

Each room at this inn is individually decorated with 18th-century, period-style furniture. The meals served at the restaurants are prepared by students at the New England Culinary Institute, and classes are offered that are open to the public. A new spa was added to the resort in 2009.

120 rooms. Pets accepted. Restaurant. $151-250

★★★SHERATON BURLINGTON HOTEL AND CONFERENCE CENTER

870 Williston Road, Burlington, 802-865-6600, 800-677-6576;
www.sheratonburlington.com

This full-service hotel is the only Sheraton located in Vermont. Rooms are comfortable with plush beds and wireless access. Club level guests have access to the club lounge, which serves complimentary breakfast and snacks daily.

309 rooms. Pets accepted. Restaurant, bar. Fitness center. Pool. Business center. $61-150

WHERE TO EAT
★DAILY PLANET

15 Center St., Burlington, 802-862-9647; www.dailyplanet15.com

A casual bistro set in downtown Burlington, this restaurant serves an eclectic menu that ranges from lobster crepes to southern pulled pork platters. The bar serves a selection of martinis and local micro-brews.

International. Dinner, late-night. Bar. Children's menu. Reservations recommended. Outdoor seating. $16-35

★★★PAULINE'S

1834 Shelburne Road, South Burlington, 802-862-1081; www.paulinescafe.com

This two-story restaurant serves fresh seasonal ingredients and a seafood-heavy menu. A $30 two-course dinner-for-two menu is offered at opening Sunday through Thursday.

American. Lunch, dinner, Sunday brunch. Bar. Children's menu. Outdoor seating. $16-35

DORSET

See also Arlington, Manchester and Manchester Center

This charming village is surrounded by hills that are 3,000 feet in altitude. In 1776, the Green Mountain Boys voted for Vermont's independence here, and in 1785, the first marble quarry in the country was opened on nearby Mount Aeolus.

SPECIAL EVENT
DORSET THEATRE FESTIVAL

Dorset Playhouse, 104 Cheney Road, Dorset, 802-867-2223; www.dorsettheatrefestival.com

A professional theater company presents six productions each season. Mid-June-Labor Day.

WHERE TO STAY
★★★DORSET INN

8 Church St. Dorset, 802-867-5500, 877-367-7389; www.dorsetinn.com

Established in 1796, this is the oldest, continuously operating inn in Vermont and it is rich with history; the Green Mountain Boys plotted their fight against the British here. Guest rooms feature private baths, antique furnishings and wall-to-wall carpet. There are no telephones in guest rooms, but some offer televisions. The onsite restaurant serves high-end comfort food, made from locally farmed products; dishes include smoked salmon and Asian spiked shrimp skewers.

29 rooms. Pets accepted. Complimentary breakfast. Restaurant, bar. Spa. $151-250

★★★INN AT WEST VIEW FARM

2928 Highway 30, Dorset, 802-867-5715, 800-769-4903; www.innatwestviewfarm.com

This restored farmhouse overlooks the Vermont countryside. Rooms are filled with antique reproductions and beds topped with down duvets, while the bathrooms have Caswell Masey bath products. A full breakfast of pancakes, eggs and other traditional dishes is served daily.

10 rooms. Restaurant, bar. $61-150

WHERE TO EAT

★★★BARROWS HOUSE INN

3156 Highway 30, Dorset, 802-867-4455, 800-639-1620; www.barrowshouse.com

Choose to sit in the clubby tavern, the bright greenhouse, on the small outdoor patio or in the more formal dining room while enjoying the regional cuisine served at this inn. The menus change seasonally and might feature black Angus filet mignon with port wine jus.

American. Breakfast, dinner. Bar. Children's menu. Reservations recommended. Outdoor seating. $16-35

★★INN AT WEST VIEW FARM

2928 Route 30, Dorset, 802-867-5715, 800-769-4903; www.innatwestviewfarm.com

Settle in to the simple dining room at this country inn and sample the traditional dishes on the seasonally influenced menu. Entrees include braised Niman Ranch short ribs with potato purée and pan-roasted free range chicken.

American. Dinner. Bar. Reservations recommended. Closed Tuesday-Wednesday. $36-85

GRAFTON

See also Manchester and Manchester Center

This New England village is a blend of houses, churches, galleries and antique shops, all circa 1800. Founded in pre-Revolutionary times under the patronage of George III, Grafton became a thriving mill town and modest industrial center after the damming of the nearby Saxton River. When water power gave way to steam, the town declined. Rescued, revived and restored by the Windham Foundation, its beauty remains intact. A creek runs through the picturesque town, and is a favorite among photographers.

WHAT TO SEE

GRAFTON PONDS CROSS-COUNTRY SKI CENTER

Townshend Road, Grafton, 800-843-1801, 802-843-2400; www.graftonponds.com

This center features more than 16 miles of groomed trails, a skiing school, rentals, concessions and a warming hut.

December-March: daily. In summer: walking and fitness trails (no fee).

THE OLD TAVERN AT GRAFTON

92 Main St., Grafton, 800-843-1801; www.old-tavern.com

Visited by many famous guests over the years, including several presidents and authors, this tavern was built in 1801. The interior is furnished with antiques and colonial décor. The former barn was converted to a lounge and an annex is restored from two houses. Dining is by reservation only.
May-March daily.

WHERE TO STAY
★★★OLD TAVERN AT GRAFTON

92 Main St., Grafton, 802-843-2231, 800-843-1801; www.old-tavern.com

This New England inn features guest rooms with antique Chippendale and Windsor furnishings and antique portraits and artwork. While rooms do not feature televisions, the inn is wired for wireless access. Guests will enjoy the afternoon tea, tennis courts and bicycles.
46 rooms. Closed April. No children under 7. Complimentary breakfast. Restaurant, bar. Tennis. $61-150

KILLINGTON

See also Plymouth

One of New England's most popular ski towns, Killington attracts scores every year thanks to its reliable and early-season snowmaking. The bars and lounges around Killington become a lively singles scene for skiing Bostonians come winter.

WHAT TO SEE
GIFFORD WOODS STATE PARK

34 Gifford Woods, Killington, 802-775-5354; www.vtstateparks.com

This 114-acre park has fishing and boating access to Kent Pond. Foot trails (Appalachian Trail passes through park). There is a forest with picnic facilities. Memorial Day-Columbus Day.

KILLINGTON RESORT

4763 Killington Road, Killington, 802-422-3261, 800-621-6867; www.killington.com

Killington Resort is comprised of 1,200 acres with seven mountains (the highest elevation is 4,241 feet). Two gondolas, six high-speed quad, six quad, six triple, four double chairlifts, eight surface lifts, patrol, school, rentals, snowmaking, mountaintop restaurant (with observation decks), six cafeterias, bars, children's center, nursery and lodging are all available on site. There are more than 200 runs, with the longest run 10 miles, with a vertical drop 3,150 feet. Snowboarding and snow tubing are also allowed.
October-June daily.

PICO ALPINE SLIDE AND SCENIC CHAIRLIFT

4763 Killington Road, Killington, 866-667-7426; www.killington.com

A chairlift brings you to the top of the mountain slope; you can control the speed of your own sled on the way down. There is a sports center and restaurant waiting below.
Late May-mid-October.

WHERE TO STAY
★★★INN OF THE SIX MOUNTAINS
2617 Killington Road, Killington, 802-422-4302, 800-228-4676; www.sixmountains.com
Located close to Killington ski resort, this inn offers an easy location from which to hit the slopes early in the morning. Cedars restaurant serves breakfast and the lounge is a great place for an après-ski drink.
100 rooms. Complimentary breakfast. Restaurant, bar. Fitness center. Pool. Tennis. Spa. $61-150

★★★RED CLOVER INN
7 Woodward Road, Mendon, 802-775-2290, 800-752-0571; www.redcloverinn.com
This 1840s country inn features views of the Green Mountains. Some rooms have fireplaces and four-poster beds. The inn's great room features a flat-screen TV, a film library and board games, while the complimentary daily afternoon tea service includes fresh-made scones, local jams and honeys and teas.
14 rooms. No children under 12. Complimentary breakfast. Restaurant, bar. $151-250

WHERE TO EAT
★★★HEMINGWAY'S
4988 Highway 4, Killington, 802-422-3886; www.hemingwaysrestaurant.com
Housed in a charming 19th-century house, Hemingway's offers a six-course menu, a four-course vegetable menu and a three-course prix fixe menu. Known for its American fare, the menu features dishes such as pan-roasted pork with braised Brussels sprouts, corn cake and bacon.
International menu. Dinner. October-mid-November. Bar. Casual attire. Closed Monday-Tuesday; also mid-April-mid-May. $86 and up

★★★RED CLOVER
7 Woodward Road, Mendon, 802-775-2290, 800-752-0571; www.redcloverinn.com
This 19th-century farmhouse inn offers sophisticated dining in four candlelit rooms. The menu changes frequently and includes entrées such as oven-roasted quail on a Tuscan bean salad or cider-marinated-salmon.
American menu. Breakfast, dinner. Bar. Business casual attire. Reservations recommended. Closed Monday-Wednesday. $36-85

LUDLOW
See also Plymouth
This southwestern Vermont town is close to Okemo Mountain and Ascutney Mountain ski resorts.

WHAT TO SEE
CROWLEY CHEESE FACTORY
14 Crowley Lane, Healdville, 802-259-2340, 800-683-2606;
www.crowleycheese-vermont.com
This company, opened in 1882, is the oldest cheese factory in the United States that still makes cheese by hand. There are display of tools used in early cheese factories and in home cheese making. You can both watch the process and sample the product. Monday-Friday.

GREEN MOUNTAIN SUGAR HOUSE

820 Highway 100 North, Ludlow, 800-643-9338; www.gmsh.com

This is a working maple sugar producer on shore of Lake Pauline.

WHERE TO STAY
★★★THE GOVERNOR'S INN

86 Main St., Ludlow, 802-228-8830, 800-468-3766; www.thegovernorsinn.com

The building dates back to 1890 and is a great example of Victorian architecture. Many rooms have period antiques and gas-lit stoves or fireplaces. Diners taken with the cuisine at the restaurant can participate in one of the Culinary Magic Cooking Seminars. The challenging slopes of Okemo Mountain are just a short distance from the Governor's Inn. A shuttle is available to the base of the mountain from the inn.

9 rooms. No children under 12. Complimentary breakfast. Restaurant. Closed late December; also two weeks in April and two weeks in November. $151-250

MANCHESTER

See also Arlington, Bennington, Dorset

Manchester and Manchester Center have been among Vermont's best-loved year-round resorts for 100 years. The surrounding mountains and ski resorts of Bromley Mountain and Stratton Mountain lure thousands each year. The addition of several upscale outlet shops (including Giorgio Armani, Escada and Reed and Barton) in and around the Manchester's town center make the area a busy year-round destination.

WHAT TO SEE
AMERICAN MUSEUM OF FLY FISHING

410 Main St., Manchester, 802-362-3300; www.amff.com

Founded in 1968 by fishermen who wanted to ensure that the history of their sport would not be lost, this museum is a hotspot for anglers of all ages. Collection of fly-fishing memorabilia and tackle of many famous persons, including Dwight D. Eisenhower, Ernest Hemingway, Andrew Carnegie, Winslow Homer, Bing Crosby and others.

Tuesday-Sunday 10 a.m.-4 p.m.

EQUINOX SKY LINE DRIVE

1A St. and Bruno Drive, Manchester and Manchester Center, 802-362-1114,

802-362-1115; www.equinoxmountain.com/skylinedrive

This spectacular five-mile paved road rises from 600 to 3,835 feet and delivers great views from the top of Mount Equinox. Fog or rain may make mountain road dangerous and travel inadvisable. No large camper vehicles are allowed on the property.

May-October: daily.

HISTORIC HILDENE

1005 Hildene Road, Manchester, 802-362-1788, 800-578-1788; www.hildene.org

The 412-acre estate of Robert Todd Lincoln (Abraham Lincoln's son) includes a 24-room Georgian manor house, held in the family until 1975.

The property has original furnishings, a carriage barn, formal gardens and nature trails.

Daily 9:30 a.m.-4:30 p.m.

MANCHESTER DESIGNER OUTLETS
Highways 11 and 30, Manchester Center, 802-362-3736;
www.manchesterdesigneroutlets.com

Many outlet stores can be found in this area, mainly along Highway 11/30 and at the intersection of Highway 11/30 and Highway 7A.

Monday-Saturday 10 a.m.-7 p.m., Sunday 10 a.m.-6 p.m.

WHERE TO STAY
★ASPEN MOTEL
5669 Main St., Manchester Center, 802-362-2450; www.theaspenatmanchester.com

This basic motor inn has clean, spare rooms at a budget-friendly price. The location is close to Manchester Center's shops and restaurants.

24 rooms. Pool. $61-150

★★★THE EQUINOX
3567 Main St., Manchester Village, 802-362-4700, 866-346-7625;
www.equinoxresort.com

Open since 1769, this resort has been visited by notables from the Lincolns to the Tafts and the Roosevelts, and it is listed on the National Register of Historic Places. Tucked at the base of Mount Equinox, the inn features loads of activities from golf at the Gleneagles golf course, to the onsite Orvis fly fishing and shooting schools, and its very own falconry center where you can learn about and practice flying raptors. A full-service spa is located on the property, as are three restaurants including the cozy and popular Marsh Tavern. The Equinox's owners also operate the nearby 1811 House Inn and Charles Orvis Inn.

180 rooms. Pets accepted. Restaurant, bar. Fitness center. Spa. Pool. Golf,. Tennis. Ski-in/ski-out. Business center. $251-350

★★★RELUCTANT PANTHER INN AND RESTAURANT
39 W. Road, Manchester, 802-362-2568, 800-822-2331; www.reluctantpanther.com

This inn was built in 1850 by a wealthy blacksmith. The owners have re-furbished the property, retaining two of the original fireplaces. Rooms are decorated with floral prints and plaids and feature flat-screen TVs.

21 rooms. No children under 14. Complimentary breakfast. Restaurant, bar. $151-250

ALSO RECOMMENDED
INN AT MANCHESTER
3967 Main St., Manchester, 802-362-1793, 800-273-1793; www.innatmanchester.com

This 19th-century Victorian structure has been beautifully restored to its original grandeur. Some rooms feature fireplaces and televisions. The inn's pub serves wines and local beers, and a full country breakfast is served each morning.

18 rooms. No children under 8. Pool. $151-250

THE INN AT ORMSBY HILL

1842 Main St., Manchester, 802-362-1163, 800-670-2841; www.ormsbyhill.com

Hospitality and relaxation abound at this tranquil location surrounded by views of the Green Mountains. The common areas feature a collection of china and unique fireplaces. Each room is individually decorated with a mix of antiques and country chintzes.

10 rooms. Complimentary breakfast. $151-250

SPA
★★★AVANYU SPA AT THE EQUINOX RESORT

3567 Main St., Manchester Village, 802-362-4700; www.equinoxresort.com

This 13,000-square-foot spa has a 75-foot heated indoor pool, a state-of-the-art fitness center, 10 treatment rooms, saunas and steam baths. Treatments include the Gentle Rain body treatment, where a sea salt, maple or citrus scrub is followed with a warm waterfall shower and an application of a rich body cream. Massage therapies like Flowing Water, Rolling Thunder and Dancing Wind simulate nature's energies through effleurage, deep tissue and gentle massage techniques.

MIDDLEBURY

See also Brandon

Benjamin Smalley built the first log house here just before the Revolution. In 1800, the town had a full-fledged college and, by 1803, there was a flourishing marble quarry and a women's academy run by Emma Hart Willard, a pioneer in education for women. Today, Middlebury is known for Middlebury College. A Ranger District office of the Green Mountain National Forest is also located here, and a map and guides for day hikes on Long Trail are available.

WHAT TO SEE
BREAD LOAF

121A S. Main St., Middlebury College, Freeman International Center, Middlebury, 802-443-5418; www.middlebury.edu

The site of the nationally-known Bread Loaf School of English in June and the annual Writers' Conference in August. The center is also the site of poet Robert Frost's cabin. In winter, it is the Carroll and Jane Rikert Ski Touring Center.

CONGREGATIONAL CHURCH

27 N. Pleasant St., Middlebury, 802-388-7634; www.midducc.org

The church was built after a plan in the *Country Builder's Assistant* and designed by architect Lavius Fillmore. Architecturally, the 1809 church is one of the finest in Vermont.

MIDDLEBURY COLLEGE

Middlebury College, Route 30, Middlebury, 802-443-5000; www.middlebury.edu

Middlebury College is famous for the teaching of arts and sciences and for its summer language schools as well as Bread Loaf School of English and Writers' Conference (see above).

MIDDLEBURY COLLEGE SNOW BOWL

Route 125, Middlebury, 802-388-4356; www.middlebury.edu

The ski area, owned by Middlebury College, has a triple and two double chairlifts, patrol, school, rentals, snowmaking, cafeteria. Fourteen runs. Early December-early April, daily.

VERMONT STATE CRAFT CENTER AT FROG HOLLOW

1 Mill St., Middlebury, 802-388-3177, 888-388-3177; www.froghollow.org

The center is housed in a restored mill overlooking Otter Creek Falls and has a sales gallery with works of more than 300 Vermont artists.
Special exhibitions, classes and workshops. Spring-fall, daily; rest of year, Monday-Saturday.

SPECIAL EVENTS
FESTIVAL ON THE GREEN

Middlebury Green, Main Street and Highway 7, Middlebury, 802-388-0216;
www.festivalonthegreen.com

Classical, modern and traditional dance; chamber and folk music; theater and comedy presentations.
Early July.

WINTER CARNIVAL

Middlebury College, Highway 30, Middlebury, 802-443-3100, 802-443-5483;
www.middlebury.edu

The oldest and largest student-run carnival in the country includes fireworks, an ice show and ski competitions; held on the campus of Middlebury College.
Late February.

WHERE TO STAY
★★★SWIFT HOUSE INN

25 Stewart Lane, Middlebury, 802-388-9925, 866-388-9925; www.swifthouseinn.com

This inn has three separate buildings, each with its own character and charm. Rooms are individually decorated and feature four-poster beds and handmade quilts. Some have fireplaces. The dining room serves fresh, seasonal dishes in an elegant setting.
20 rooms. Pets accepted. Complimentary breakfast. Restaurant. $151-250

ALSO RECOMMENDED
WAYBURY INN

457 E. Main, East Middlebury, 802-388-4015, 800-348-1810; www.wayburyinn.com

Constructed as a stagecoach stop, the building has been an inn since 1810. The rooms are decorated in country plaids and florals, and some feature claw foot tubs. The inn has an elegant dining room, as well as a casual pub.
14 rooms. Pets accepted. Complimentary breakfast. Restaurant, bar. $61-150

MONTPELIER

See also Waitsfield

Vermont's capital is one of the nation's most picturesque places, located on the banks of the Winooski River and made up of quaint brick buildings. A popular summer vacation area, Montpelier absorbs the overflow from the nearby ski areas in winter.

WHAT TO SEE
MORSE FARM

1168 County Road, Montpelier, 802-223-2740, 800-242-2740; www.morsefarm.com
Visit a maple sugar and vegetable farm set in a in rustic, wooded setting. You can tour the sugar house and view the sugar-making process in season. March-April. Daily.

STATE HOUSE

115 State St., Montpelier, 802-828-2228, 802-828-1411;
www.leg.state.vt.us/sthouse/sthouse.htm
Made in 1859 of Vermont granite, the dome of the capitol is covered with gold leaf.
Monday-Friday 8 a.m.-4 p.m.; guided tours, July-mid-October, Monday-Friday 10 a.m.-3:30 p.m., Saturday 11 a.m.-2:30 p.m.

THOMAS WATERMAN WOOD ART GALLERY

36 College St., Montpelier, 802-828-8743; www.twwoodgallery.org
The gallery features oils, watercolors and etchings by Wood and other 19th-century American artists. Also included are American artists of the 1920s and 1930s and changing monthly exhibits of works of contemporary local and regional artists.
Tuesday-Sunday noon-4 p.m.

VERMONT HISTORICAL SOCIETY MUSEUM

109 State St., Montpelier, 802-828-2291; www.vermonthistory.org
The museum features exhibits highlighting Vermont's history from 1600 to present day.
Tuesday-Saturday 10 a.m.-4 p.m., Sunday noon-4 p.m., May-October; closed holidays.

WHERE TO STAY
★COMFORT INN & SUITES AT MAPLEWOOD

213 Paine Turnpike North, Montpelier, 802-229-2222, 800-424-6423;
www.choicehotels.com
Rooms are basic and comfortable at this reliable Montpelier hotel. Free wireless access and complimentary breakfast are included with each stay.
89 rooms. Bar. $61-150

★★★INN AT MONTPELIER

147 Main St., Montpelier, 802-223-2727; www.innatmontpelier.com
Revisit the early 1800s at this historic inn, comprised of two stately buildings showcasing Greek and Colonial Revival woodwork, numerous fireplaces and

a spectacular front staircase. Rooms are decorated with antique furniture and rugs.

19 rooms. Complimentary breakfast. $61-150

★★★THE INN ON THE COMMON
1162 N. Craftsbury Road, Craftsbury Common, 802-586-9619, 800-521-2233; www.innonthecommon.com

This inn is made up of three restored Federal-style houses that feature colorful gardens and wooded hillsides. Rooms are individually decorated in a French country style. The dining room serves seasonal, local cuisine.

16 rooms. Pets accepted. Restaurant, bar. Pool. Tennis. $151-250

NEWFANE
See also Grafton

Originally settled high on Newfane Hill, this postcard-perfect Vermont town was a favorite vacation spot for American poet Eugene Field.

WHAT TO SEE
SCOTT COVERED BRIDGE
Route 30, Townshend, 802-257-0292

The longest single span bridge in the state (166 feet) was built with lattice-type trusses. The three span structure totals 276 feet. The other spans are of the king post-type trusses.

TOWNSHEND STATE FOREST
2755 State Forest Road, Townshend, 802-365-7500; www.vtstateparks.com

A 1,690-acre area with a foot trail to Bald Mountain (1,580 feet). Swimming is permitted at nearby Townshend Reservoir Recreation Area. There are hiking trails, picnic sites, tent and trailer sites; standard fees apply.

May-Columbus Day.

WHERE TO STAY
★★★WINDHAM HILL INN
311 Lawrence Drive, West Townshend, 802-874-4080, 800-944-4080; www.windhamhill.com

This charming, elegant 1825 country estate features rooms with fireplaces, plush beds and either spas or soaking tubs. The onsite restaurant serves full country breakfasts and simple, well-prepared dinners with entrées such as seared duck breast with blackberry demi-glace.

21 rooms. No children under 12. Restaurant. Pool. Tennis. $151-250

ALSO RECOMMENDED
FOUR COLUMNS INN
21 W. St., Newfane, 802-365-7713, 800-787-6633; www.fourcolumnsinn.com

Located in the center of Newfane and at the foot of a private mountain, this 16-room inn combines historic charm with modern flair. The décor is old-fashioned, with sleigh and iron four-poster beds. Many suites have two-sided fireplaces and most rooms have whirlpools or soaking tubs. While some

rooms are without TVs, all have wireless Internet access.
16 rooms. Pets accepted. Complimentary breakfast. Restaurant, bar. Pool.
$251-350

WHERE TO EAT
★★★FOUR COLUMNS
21 W. St., Newfane, 802-365-7713, 800-787-6633; www.fourcolumnsinn.com
Chef Greg Parks offers innovative and contemporary cuisine and an award-winning wine list at this welcoming inn. Dinner often features dishes such as grilled Angus tenderloin with green peppercorn vinaigrette or lobster wrapped in cabbage with buerre blanc.
American. Dinner. Bar. Reservations recommended. Outdoor seating.
Closed Tuesday. $36-85

★★★OLD NEWFANE INN
Highway 30, Newfane, 802-365-4427, 800-784-4427; www.oldnewfaneinn.com
Timbered ceilings and brick fireplaces add to the colonial charm of this historic 1787 landmark. Menu specialties include European classics such as chateaubriand and veal goulash.
Continental, French. Dinner, bar. Reservations recommended. Closed Monday; April-mid-May, November-mid-December. $16-35

NORTH HERO
This far northern Vermont town borders Lake Champlain and is close to both
New York State and Quebec, Canada.

WHAT TO SEE
NORTH HERO STATE PARK
3803 Lakeview Drive, North Hero, 802-372-8727; www.vtstateparks.com
A 399-acre park located in the north part of the Champlain Islands has extensive shoreline on Lake Champlain. Swimming, fishing, boating (ramps) and hiking (trails) are allowed; there is also a playground. There are tent and trailer sites (dump station). Standard fees apply.
Memorial Day-Labor Day.

SPECIAL EVENT
ROYAL LIPPIZAN STALLIONS OF AUSTRIA
Knight Point State Park, 44 Knight Point Road, North Hero, 802-372-8400,
800-262-5226; www.champlainislands.com
This is the summer residence of the stallions. There are performances Thursday and Friday evenings, Saturday and Sunday afternoons.
For ticket prices, contact Chamber of Commerce. July-August.

WHERE TO STAY
★★★NORTH HERO HOUSE INN
Highway 2, North Hero, 802-372-4732, 888-525-3644; www.northherohouse.com
This inn, built in 1800, is surrounded by views of the Green Mountains and Mount Mansfield. Rooms are decorated in a country style with antique furnishings. Breakfast is included with each stay.

26 rooms. Restaurant, bar. Tennis. $151-250

★★SHORE ACRES INN
237 Shore Acres Drive, North Hero, 802-372-8722; www.shoreacres.com
This resort, located on the shore of Lake Champlain, has simply decorated rooms with Shaker furnishings and colorful quilts that evoke summer camp décor. The inn offers scores of outdoor activities, including tennis, horseshoes and croquet.
23 rooms. Pets accepted. Restaurant, bar. Tennis. $61-150

WHERE TO EAT
★★NORTH HERO HOUSE
Highway 2, North Hero, 802-372-4732, 888-525-3644; www.northherohouse.com
With its colonial-style dining room and its eclectic menu of classic American dishes mixed with more contemporary fare, this restaurant inside the North Hero House is a popular local spot. Sample heartier entrées such as Yankee pot roast or stick to pub fare like fish and chips.
American menu. Dinner, Sunday brunch. Bar. Outdoor seating. $16-35

PLYMOUTH
See also Killington, Ludlow, Woodstock
This town hasn't changed much since July 4, 1872, when Calvin Coolidge was born in the back of the village store (which is still in business today). A country road leads to the cemetery where the former president and six generations of his family are buried. Nearby is the Coolidge Visitors Center and Museum, which displays historical and presidential memorabilia.

WHAT TO SEE
PRESIDENT CALVIN COOLIDGE HOMESTEAD
Coolidge Memorial Drive, Plymouth Notch, 802-672-3773; www.historicvermont.org/coolidge
In 1923, Calvin Coolidge was sworn in by his father in this house's sitting room, which has been restored to its early 20th-century appearance. The Plymouth Historic District also includes the General Store that was operated by the president's father, the house where the president was born, the village dance hall that served as the 1924 summer White House office, the Union Church with its Carpenter Gothic interior, the Wilder House (birthplace of Coolidge's mother), the Wilder Barn with 19th-century farming equipment, a restaurant and a visitor center with museum.
Late May-mid-October, daily 9:30 a.m.-5 p.m.

WHERE TO STAY
★★★HAWK INN AND MOUNTAIN RESORT
Route 100 South, Plymouth, 802-672-3811, 800-685-4295; www.hawkresort.com
From rooms at the inn to mountainside villas on the resort's nearly 1,200 acres, guests can try a variety of onsite activities including a spa and stables. The resort also includes a full-service spa plus an indoor pool and fitness room.
200 rooms. Restaurant, bar. Tennis. $251-350

RUTLAND

See also Brandon, Killington

This is Vermont's second-largest city. Its oldest newspaper, the *Rutland Herald*, has been published continuously since 1794. The world's deepest marble quarry is in West Rutland.

WHAT TO SEE
HUBBARDTON BATTLEFIELD AND MUSEUM

5696 Monument Hill Road, East Hubbardton, 802-759-2412;
www.historicvermont.org/hubbardton

On July 7, 1777, the Green Mountain Boys and colonial troops from Massachusetts and New Hampshire stopped British forces pursuing the American Army from Fort Ticonderoga. This was the only battle of the Revolution fought on Vermont soil and the first in a series of engagements that led to the capitulation of Burgoyne at Saratoga. Visitor Center with exhibits. There is a battle monument and trails. Picnicking is allowed on site.

Late May-mid-October: Thursday-Sunday 9:30 a.m.-5 p.m.

NEW ENGLAND MAPLE MUSEUM

Highway 7, Pittsford, 802-483-9414, 800-639-4280; www.maplemuseum.com

The museum holds one of the largest collections of antique maple sugaring artifacts in the world; there are two large dioramas featuring more than 100 hand-carved figures. There is a narrated slide show; as well as demonstrations and samples of Vermont foods. There is also a craft and maple-product gift shop.

Late May-October, daily 8:30 a.m.-5:30 p.m.; November-December, mid-March-late May, daily 10 a.m.-4 p.m.; closed January-February.

NORMAN ROCKWELL MUSEUM

654 Highway 4 E., Rutland, 802-773-6095; www.normanrockwellvt.com

More than 2,000 pictures and Rockwell memorabilia spanning 60 years of the artist's career. Includes the Four *Freedoms*, Boy Scout series, many magazine covers, including all 323 from the *Saturday Evening Post* and nearly every illustration and advertisement.

Daily.

WILSON CASTLE

West Proctor Road, Center Rutland, 802-773-3284; www.wilsoncastle.com

This 32-room, 19th-century mansion features 19 open proscenium arches, 84 stained-glass windows, 13 imported tile fireplaces, a towering turret and parapet. The home is filled with European and Asian furnishings as well as an art gallery featuring many sculptures. There are 15 other buildings on the property and a picnic area.

Guided tours. Late May-late October: daily 9 a.m.-6 p.m.; Christmas tours.

WHERE TO STAY
★BEST WESTERN INN & SUITES RUTLAND/KILLINGTON

One Route 4 East, Rutland, 802-773-3200, 800-720-7234; www.bestwestern.com

The condo-style suites at this hotel are a favorite with Killington skiers.

Rooms feature kitchens, pull-out sofas and updated linens.
56 rooms. Complimentary breakfast. Fitness center. Pool. Tennis. $151-250

★★HOLIDAY INN RUTLAND/KILLINGTON
2111 Highway 7 South, Rutland, 802-775-1911, 800-462-4810;
www.ichotelsgroup.com
Located close to downtown Rutland, this hotel has simple rooms decorated in
neutral tones and feature coffeemakers and refrigerators. The hotel includes
an indoor pool, a sauna and a fitness center.
151 rooms. Pets accepted. Restaurant, bar. Fitness center. Business center.
$151-250

★★★MOUNTAIN TOP INN
195 Mountain Top Road, Chittenden, 800-445-2100, 802-483-2311;
www.mountaintopinn.com
Located in the Green Mountains of Vermont, close to Killington ski resort,
the guest rooms at this inn are rustic and cozy, with down duvets and rich
chintzes. The resort is located 11 miles from Killington, and features an onsite equestrian center and Nordic ski and snowshoe center.
60 rooms. Closed April and first three weeks in November. Pets accepted.
Restaurant, bar. Pool. Golf. Tennis. $151-250

SHELBURNE

See also Burlington, Vergennes
With the Adirondack Mountains to the west and the Green Mountains on
the east, Shelburne is a small, friendly town that borders Lake Champlain.
The Shelburne Museum has one of the most comprehensive exhibits of early
American life.

WHAT TO SEE

SHELBURNE FARMS
1611 Harbor Road, Shelburne, 802-985-8686; www.shelburnefarms.org
Built at the turn of the 20th century, this is the former estate of Dr. Seward
Webb and his wife, Lila Vanderbilt. Located on the shores of Lake Champlain, the grounds, landscaped by Frederick Law Olmsted and forested
by Gifford Pinchot, once totaled 3,800 acres. Structures include the Webbs'
mansion, Shelburne House, which is a 110-room summer "cottage" built in
the late 1800s on a bluff overlooking the lake; a five-story farm barn; and
the coach barn, once the home of prize horses. Hayrides and walking trails
are also available. There is a cheese shop. Overnight stays at the property
are available.
Tours Memorial Day-mid-October, daily 9 a.m.-5:30 p.m.; off-season, daily
10 a.m.-5 p.m.

SHELBURNE MUSEUM
5555 Shelburne Road, Shelburne, 802-985-3346; www.shelburnemuseum.org
Founded by Electra Webb, daughter of Sugar King H.O. Havemeyer, this
collection of Americana art is located on 45 acres with 37 historic buildings
containing items such as historic circus posters, toys, weather vanes, trade

signs and an extensive collection of wildfowl decoys and dolls. American and European paintings and prints (including works by Monet and Grandma Moses) are on display, as well. Also here is the 220-foot side-wheel steamboat *Ticonderoga*, which carried passengers across Lake Champlain in the early part of the century and is now the last vertical beam passenger and freight side-wheel steamer intact in the United States. There is a working carousel and a 5,000-piece hand-carved miniature traveling circus, a fully intact lighthouse, a one-room schoolhouse, an authentic country store, the only two-lane covered bridge with footpath in Vermont, blacksmith shop, printing and weaving demonstrations, farm equipment and more than 200 horse-drawn vehicles on display.

May-October, daily 10 a.m.-5 p.m.

VERMONT TEDDY BEAR COMPANY

6655 Shelburne Road, Shelburne, 802-985-1319; www.vermontteddybear.com

The guided tour at this factory shows the process of handcrafting these famous stuffed animals. The onsite gift shop ensures that you won't go home empty handed; the Bear Shop opens at 9 a.m. daily.

VERMONT WILDFLOWER FARM

4750 Shelburne Ave., Shelburne, 802-425-3641; www.vermontwildflowerfarm.com

This farm holds acres of wildflower gardens, flower fields and woodlands, as well as a pond and brook.

April-October, daily 10 a.m.-5 p.m.

STOWE

See also Burlington

Boasting one of New England's most popular ski resorts, Stowe is a year-round destination thanks to its charming downtown and abundance of quaint inns and organic eateries. While the ski conditions on Mount Mansfield, Vermont's highest peak at 4,393 feet, generate the most buzz, more than half of Stowe's visitors coming during the summer. Warm-weather visitors can experience outdoor concerts, hiking, biking, golf, tennis and many events and attractions, including a factory tour at the nearby Ben & Jerry's headquarters.

WHAT TO SEE

ALPINE SLIDE

Stowe Mountain Resort, Spruce Peak, 5781 Mountain Road, Stowe, 802-253-3000, 800-253-4754; www.stowe.com

A chairlift takes riders to a 2,300-foot slide that runs through the woods and open field. Riders control their own speed on individual sleds.

Late June-Labor Day, daily 10 a.m.-5 p.m.; September-mid-October, weekends.

BEN & JERRY'S ICE CREAM FACTORY TOUR

Route 100, Waterbury, 866-258-6877; www.benjerry.com

This half-hour guided tour, offered every 30 minutes (and even more frequently in summer, spring and fall), takes visitors through the ice cream fac-

tory that cranks out such beloved flavors as Cherry Garcia and Chunky Monkey. The tour includes a seven-minute "moovie," views of the production line (except on weekends) and free samples in the FlavoRoom. There's also a gift shop, where you can pick up one of those famous tie-dyed cow T-shirts and a few pints to take home.
Daily.

MOUNT MANSFIELD GONDOLA

Stowe Mountain Resort, 5781 Mountain Road, Stowe, 802-253-3000, 800-253-4754
An eight-passenger enclosed gondola delivers riders to the summit of Vermont's highest peak. There is an on site restaurant and gift shop.
Mid-June-mid-October, daily 10 a.m.-5 p.m.

MOUNT MANSFIELD STATE FOREST

This 38,000-acre forest can be reached from Underhill Flats, off Highway 15, or from Stowe through Smugglers' Notch, north on Highway 108. The Long Trail leads to the summit of Mount Mansfield from the north and south. There are three state recreation areas in the forest.

STOWE MOUNTAIN RESORT

5781 Mountain Road, Stowe, 802-253-3000, 800-253-4754; www.stowe.com
Often named the best ski resort in the east, Stowe Mountain Resort features longer than average runs and ample snowmaking. The resort has a gondola, quad, triple and six double chairlifts, patrol, school, rentals, snowmaking, cafeterias, restaurants, bar, entertainment and nursery. They offer forty-seven runs, with the longest run more than 3½ miles and a vertical drop of 2,360 feet. Summer activities include an alpine slide (mid-June-early September, daily), mountain biking (rentals), gondola rides, in-line skate park, recreation trail, tennis, golf
Night skiing. Mid-November-mid-April, daily.

SPECIAL EVENT
STOWEFLAKE BALLOON FESTIVAL
Stoweflake Mountain Resort & Spa, 1746 Mountain Road, Stowe, 800-253-2232, 802-253-7355; www.stoweflake.com
More than 25 balloons are launched during this weekend-long festival.
Second weekend in July.

WHERE TO STAY
★★★GREEN MOUNTAIN INN
18 S. Main St., Stowe, 802-253-7301, 800-253-7302; www.greenmountaininn.com
This historic Colonial inn is surrounded by charming stores, galleries and restaurants. Rooms feature country-style quilts or chintzes, deep soaking tubs and some feature fireplaces.
104 rooms. Restaurant, bar. Fitness center. Pool. $151-250

★★★STOWEFLAKE MOUNTAIN RESORT & SPA
1746 Mountain Road, Stowe, 802-253-7355, 800-253-2232; www.stoweflake.com
This resort, the oldest in Stowe, recently underwent a major renovation and

added a 50,000-square-foot spa. Rooms are decorated in country quilts and feature pillow-top beds and down duvets. The restaurant serves innovative takes on American cuisine.

117 rooms. Restaurant, bar. Fitness center. Spa. Pool. Golf. $251-350

★★★TOPNOTCH RESORT AND SPA

4000 Mountain Road, Stowe, 888-460-5567, 800-451-8686; www.topnotchresort.com

This classic New England ski resort underwent a complete renovation in spring 2008. Rooms were updated with fresh, colorful country florals, pillow-topped beds and flat-screen TVs. A sprawling spa has been added to the resort and features 30 treatment rooms. The signature restaurant Norma's has a contemporary design and organic, seasonally-focused menu.

126 rooms. Restaurant, bar. Fitness center. Spa. Pool. Business center. Pets accepted. $251-350

★★TRAPP FAMILY LODGE

700 Trapp Hill Road, Stowe, 802-253-8511, 800-826-7000; www.trappfamily.com

Channel your inner Julie Andrews at this resort run by the Von Trapp family, the inspiration for the movie *The Sound of Music*. The rustic lodge overlooks a beautiful mountain range and is accented with hand-carved balustrades, pitched gables and a cedar shake roof. Activities include croquet, hiking, horse-drawn sleigh rides, pastry classes and cross-country skiing.

96 rooms. Restaurant, bar. Fitness center. Pool. Tennis. $151-250

ALSO RECOMMENDED
STONE HILL INN

89 Houston Farm Road, Stowe, 802-253-6282; www.stonehillinn.com

This inn is close to Stowe's antique shops, restaurants and activities. Rooms are individually decorated with flat-screen TVS and some feature fireplaces. Nine rooms. Closed April; also mid-November-mid-December. No children allowed. Complimentary breakfast. $251-350

VERGENNES

See also Middlebury, Shelburne

The oldest city in Vermont and the third oldest in New England, Vergennes is one of the smallest incorporated cities in the nation at one square mile.

WHAT TO SEE
BUTTON BAY STATE PARK

5 Button Bay State Park Road, Vergennes, 802-475-2377; www.vtstateparks.com

This 236-acre park on a bluff overlooking Lake Champlain was named for the button-like formations in the clay banks. Spectacular views of Adirondack Mountains. Swimming pool, fishing, boating (rentals), nature and hiking trails are some of the on site activities. There is also a naturalist museum. Memorial Day-Columbus Day.

JOHN STRONG MANSION

6656 Highway 17 West, West Addison, 802-759-2309;
www.vmga.org/addison/jstrong.html

A Federalist house built in 1795, the structure has been restored and furnished in the period.
Memorial Day-Labor Day, Saturday-Sunday 10 a.m.-5 p.m.

ROKEBY MUSEUM

4334 Highway 7, Ferrisburgh, 802-877-3406; www.rokeby.org

The ancestral home of abolitionist Rowland T. Robinson, built in 1785, was a station for the Underground Railroad. Artifacts and archives of four generations of the Robinson family are on display. Set on 85 acres, the farmstead includes an icehouse, a creamery and a stone smokehouse. Special events are offered year-round.
Tours. Mid-May-mid-October, house tours: Thursday-Sunday 11 a.m.,
12:30 p.m., 2 p.m.; grounds: year-round during daylight hours.

WHERE TO STAY
★★★BASIN HARBOR CLUB

4800 Basin Harbor Road, Vergennes, 802-475-2311; www.basinharbor.com

Located on Lake Champlain, this hotel offers accommodations in the lodge or in the cottages spread out over the property. Fresh local ingredients are used to prepare the breakfast and dinner served in the main dining room.
117 rooms. Pets accepted. Restaurant, bar. Fitness center. Beach. Pool.
Golf. Tennis. Closed November-mid-May. $151-250

WAITSFIELD

See also Warren

Located in the Mad River Valley, Waitsfield is a classic New England town close to local ski resorts. Rolling hills and bucolic farms dot the countryside.

WHAT TO SEE
MAD RIVER GLEN SKI AREA

Highway 17, Waitsfield, 802-496-3551; www.madriverglen.com

This ski resort has the country's oldest single chairlift, which was fully restored in 2006. Mad River Glen does not make snow, so conditions here depend on the weather. The area has three double and two single chairlifts, patrol, school, rentals, cafeterias, restaurant, bar and a nursery. There are forty-four runs, with the longest run three miles with a vertical drop of 2,000 feet.
December-April, daily.

WHERE TO STAY
★★TUCKER HILL INN

65 Marble Hill Road, Waitsfield, 802-496-3983, 800-543-7841; www.tuckerhill.com

A country inn with a variety of individually decorated rooms, the property has plenty of space to spread out including a pub, game room, living room and outdoor patio. A full breakfast is served daily in the skylit morning room.
18 rooms. Restaurant, bar. Pool. Tennis. $151-250

ALSO RECOMMENDED
1824 HOUSE INN BED AND BREAKFAST
2150 Main St., Waitsfield, 802-496-7555, 800-426-3986; www.1824house.com

This restored 1824 farmhouse features updated, colorful rooms with feather beds, Oriental rugs and down duvets. The inn has a comfortable common area with a TV, an outdoor Jacuzzi and a full breakfast is served daily.
8 rooms. $61-150

THE INN AT THE ROUND BARN
1661 E. Warren Road, Waitsfield, 802-496-2276; www.theroundbarn.com

Located on more than 200 acres of mountains, ponds and meadows, this inn has a round barn that is fully restored and is the setting for weddings, meetings and other functions. Rooms in the inn retain rustic details such as wood beamed ceilings or fireplaces.
12 rooms. Complimentary breakfast. Pool. $151-250

WARREN
See also Waitsfield

This northern Vermont town is close to ski areas Sugarbush and Mad River Glen. The town has several small bed and breakfasts and quaint restaurants that feed and house skiers at the end of a day on the mountain.

WHAT TO SEE
SUGARBUSH RESORT
1840 Sugarbush Access Road, Warren, 802-583-6300, 800-583-7669; www.sugarbush.com

The ski area has seven quad, three triple and six double chairlifts, four surface lifts, patrol, school, rentals, concession area, cafeteria, restaurant, bar and a nursery. There are more than 100 runs, with the longest run more than two miles, with a vertical drop of 2,650 feet.
Early November-late April, daily.

WHERE TO STAY
★★★THE PITCHER INN
275 Main St., Warren, 802-496-6350, 800-735-2478; www.pitcherinn.com

Rustic, yet rich guest rooms in the main house of this classic inn capture Vermont's colonial history, while two suites in the adjacent barn are perfect for families. Each room is decorated with a different theme, from fishing to skiing. The inn's restaurant serves breakfast and dinner and boasts a 6,500-bottle wine cellar. This inn also offers a locker room for ski storage and a boot and glove warmer.
11 rooms. Complimentary breakfast.. Restaurant, bar. $351 and up

★★★SUGARBUSH INN
1840 Sugarbush Access Road, Warren, 802-583-6114, 800-537-8427; www.sugarbush.com

Surrounded by slopes, hills and trails, this activity-oriented inn is between the towns of Waitsfield and Warren. Snowshoeing, snow tubing, ice skating and horse-drawn sleigh rides are available on the property.

143 rooms. Complimentary breakfast. Restaurant, bar. Fitness center. Pool. Golf. Tennis. Ski-in/ski-out. $151-250

WHERE TO EAT
★★★THE COMMON MAN
3209 German Flats Road, Warren, 802-583-2800; www.commonmanrestaurant.com

A restored 1880s barn is the setting for this traditional restaurant, where the menu runs the gamut from traditional American (New England fish stew) to more eclectic options such as homemade gnocchi with lobster. The center-piece of the restaurant is a huge stone fireplace. Dinner is often served to the tune of live jazz.

American. Dinner. Bar. Children's menu. Reservations recommended. Closed Sunday-Monday; two-four weeks in spring and November. $16-35

WEST DOVER
See also Bennington

A south central Vermont village, West Dover is located in the Green Mountains and near several ski resorts.

WHAT TO SEE
MOUNT SNOW SKI AREA
12 Pisgah Road, West Dover, 802-464-2151, 800-498-0479; www.mountsnow.com

The family-friendly ski area has two quads, six triples and nine double chair-lifts, and a ski patrol, school, rentals, snowmaking, cafeterias, restaurant, bars, entertainment and nursery. More than 100 trails are spread over five interconnected mountain areas. The longest run is 2 1/2 miles, with a vertical drop of 1,700 feet.

Half-day rates. November-early May: daily.

SPECIAL EVENTS
OKTOBERFEST & CRAFT SHOW
Mount Snow Resort, 12 Pisgah Road, West Dover, 802-464-2151, 800-498-0479;
www.mountsnow.com

New England artisans exhibit pottery, jewelry, glass, graphics, weaving and other crafts. The event features German-style entertainment.

Columbus Day weekend.

WHERE TO STAY
★★★THE INN AT SAWMILL FARM
Highway 100 and 7 Crosstown Road, West Dover, 802-464-8131, 800-493-1133;
www.theinnatsawmillfarm.com

This inn is housed in a converted barn, and the location is perfect for skiers looking to hit the slopes of nearby Mount Snow. Rustic, yet polished, weath-ered floors and hand-hewn posts and beams hint at the original construction. Rooms are decorated in country florals and with antiques and down duvet-topped beds.

21 rooms. Restaurant, bar. Fitness center. Pool. Tennis. Closed April-May. $351 and up

WHERE TO EAT
★★★THE INN AT SAWMILL FARM
Highway 100 and Crosstown Road, West Dover, 802-464-8131, 800-493-1133;
www.theinnatsawmillfarm.com

Exposed beams and chandeliers create a cozy setting for sampling the seasonal American menu of locally farmed game such as quail, pheasant, rabbit and venison. The wine list offers a selection of 1,285 wines from the 30,000-bottle cellar.

American. Breakfast, dinner. Bar. Reservations recommended. Closed April-May. $36-85

WINDSOR
See also Woodstock

Situated on the Connecticut River in the shadow of Mount Ascutney, Windsor was once the political center of the Connecticut Valley towns. The name "Vermont" was adopted, and its constitution was drawn up here. Many notable inventors (and inventions) were developed here in the 19th century, including the hydraulic pump, the sewing machine, the coffee percolator and various refinements in firearms.

WHAT TO SEE
CONSTITUTION HOUSE
16 N. Main St., Windsor, 802-672-3773; www.historicvermont.org

The house is an 18th-century tavern where the constitution of the Republic of Vermont was signed on July 8, 1777.

Museum: Late May-mid-October: Wednesday-Sunday 11 a.m.-5 p.m.

MOUNT ASCUTNEY STATE PARK
1826 Back Mountain Road Windsor, 802-674-2060; www.vtstateparks.com

This 1,984-acre park has a paved road to the summit of 3,144-foot high Mount Ascutney. Also available are hiking trails, picnicking, tent and trailer sites.

Memorial Day-Columbus Day.

VERMONT STATE CRAFT CENTER AT WINDSOR HOUSE
54 Main St., Windsor, 802-674-6729; www.vmga.org/windsor/vsscwindsor.html

This restored building features works of more than 250 Vermont craftspeople.
January-May: Thursday-Saturday 10 a.m.-6 p.m., Sunday 11 a.m.-5 p.m.;
June-December: Monday-Saturday 10 a.m.-6 p.m., Sunday 11 a.m.-5 p.m.

WHERE TO STAY
★★★JUNIPER HILL INN
153 Pembroke Road, Windsor, 802-674-5273, 800-359-2541; www.juniperhillinn.com

Housed in a 1902 Classical Revival mansion, perched atop 14 acres of hillside, the inn features individually decorated rooms. A 30-by-40-foot Great Hall includes a floor-to-ceiling fireplace, and the library in the west wing of the inn offers a great place to read or play board games. Past visitors include Teddy Roosevelt.

16 rooms. No children under 12. Complimentary breakfast. Restaurant.

Pool. Closed two weeks in November; three weeks in late March-early April. $151-250

WOODSTOCK
See also Killington, Plymouth
The historic charm of Woodstock has been preserved, at least in part, by determination. Properties held for generations by descendants of the original owners provided built-in zoning long before historic district status was achieved. When the iron bridge that crosses the Ottauquechee River at Union Street was condemned in 1968, it was replaced by a covered wooden bridge. The nearby town of Quechee is equally charming and is home to the famed Simon Pearce glass and pottery studio and restaurant.

WHAT TO SEE
KEDRON VALLEY STABLES
Highway 106 South, South Woodstock, 802-457-1480, 800-225-6301; www.kedron.com
The stables offer hayrides, sleigh rides, picnic trail rides, indoor ring rides and riding lessons by appointment.

MARSH-BILLINGS-ROCKEFELLER NATIONAL HISTORIC PARK
54 Elm St., Woodstock, 802-457-3368; www.nps.gov/mabi
The park includes the Marsh-Billings-Rockefeller mansion, which contains an extensive collection of American landscape paintings. The mansion is surrounded by the 550-acre Mount Tom forest. Interpretive tours are available. Reservations are recommended. The park also offers hiking, nature study and cross-country skiing.
Memorial Day-October, daily 10 a.m.-5 p.m.

SUICIDE SIX SKI AREA
South Pomfret Road, Woodstock, 802-457-1100; www.skivermont.com
This ski area has two double chairlifts, a J-Bar, patrol, PSIA school, rentals, snowmaking, cafeteria, wine and beer bar and a lodge. There are twenty-two runs; the longest run is one mile, with a vertical drop of 650 feet. The mountain is the site of the first ski tow in the United States (1934).
Early December-late March, daily.

VERMONT INSTITUTE OF NATURAL SCIENCE
Route 4, Quechee, 802-359-5000; www.vinsweb.org
The property includes a 47-acre mixed habitat site with trails. The VINS Nature Center includes the Raptor Museum, which has 26 species of hawks, owls and eagles
May-October, daily 9 a.m.-5:30 p.m.; November-April, daily 10 a.m.-4 p.m.

WOODSTOCK COUNTRY CLUB
14 The Green, Woodstock, 802-457-1100, 800-448-7900; www.woodstockinn.com
The country club includes an 18-hole championship golf course, 10 tennis courts, paddle tennis, a cross-country skiing center with more than 35 miles of trails, rentals, instruction and tours. The club has a restaurant and a lounge.

There is a fee for activities.
Daily; closed April and November.

WOODSTOCK HISTORICAL SOCIETY
26 Elm St., Woodstock; www.woodstockhistoricalsociety.org
The 1807 Dana House has 11 rooms spanning the period between 1750 and 1900 full of silver, glass, paintings, costumes, furniture and Woodstock-related artifacts and photographs.
Late May-late October: Monday-Saturday 10 a.m.-4 p.m., Sunday noon-4 p.m.

WHERE TO STAY
★★★KEDRON VALLEY INN
10671 S. Road, South Woodstock, 802-457-1473, 800-836-1193;
www.kedronvalleyinn.com
Located five miles outside Woodstock, this small historic inn is a great home base for guests focused on antique shopping or checking out the local shops. Most rooms have wood-burning stoves or fireplaces, and the décor is contemporary, country rustic.
26 rooms. Pets accepted. Restaurant, bar. Closed April. $151-250

★POND RIDGE MOTEL
506 Highway 4 West, Woodstock, 802-457-1667; www.pondridgemotel.com
A budget-friendly option with clean and basic rooms, this classic motel is located 1.5 miles from Woodstock's center. The motel overlooks a local river and pond.
20 rooms. $61-150

★★★QUECHEE INN AT MARSHLAND FARM
1119 Quechee Main St., Quechee, 802-295-3133, 800-235-3133;
www.quecheeinn.com
This inn was built in 1793 and has simply decorated rooms featuring colonial-style furniture, TVs and private baths. The inn's dining room is a popular local spot for traditional American fare.
24 rooms. Complimentary breakfast. Restaurant, bar. $151-250

★THE SHIRE RIVERVIEW
46 Pleasant St., Woodstock, 802-457-2211; www.shiremotel.com
Colonial-style furnishings and floral fabrics make up the basic rooms at this motel. Some rooms feature fireplaces, and most have views of the river.
42 rooms. $61-150

★★★★★TWIN FARMS
452 Royalton Turnpike, Barnard, 802-234-9999, 800-894-6327; www.twinfarms.com
This secluded, exclusive hideaway in central Vermont offers one of the most uniquely sybaritic lodging experiences to be had in America. With 10 private cottages and 10 sumptuous guest rooms, Twin Farms is designed to cater to the individual experience. Each room is decorated to reflect a different theme by renowned interior designer Jed Johnson; the Moroccan-influenced Meadow has Persian rugs and a mosaic-tiled fireplace, while the Scandina-

vian Barn has bleached pine floors, walls and rafters and crisp white and blue fabrics and upholstery. Meals are made to order and can be taken in the main dining room or the privacy of your cottage. The cost is all-inclusive.

16 rooms. Children not allowed. Complimentary breakfast. Restaurant, bar. Fitness center. Spa. Tennis. Ski-in/ski-out. $351 and up

★★★WOODSTOCK INN & RESORT

14 The Green, Woodstock, 802-457-1100, 800-448-7900; www.woodstockinn.com

The inn, the centerpiece of Woodstock, has been around since the 18th century. The rooms and suites capture traditional Vermont style, with handmade quilts, built-in alcoves and original prints. Downhill and cross-country skiing are two of the resort's most popular winter activities, while the Woodstock Country Club's prestigious course attracts golfers. Other popular activities include biking, canoeing, fishing, horseback riding and nature walks, and the town's shops are within walking distance. Three restaurants serve everything from gourmet cuisine to casual fare and traditional tavern-style food.

142 rooms. Restaurant, bar. Fitness center. Spa. Pool. Golf. Tennis. Ski-in/ski-out. Business center. $251-350

ALSO RECOMMENDED
APPLEBUTTER INN

Happy Valley Road, Woodstock, 802-457-4158; www.applebutterinn.com

Built in 1846, this inn used to be a stagecoach stop and a general store. Today, it features comfortable rooms decorated with oriental rugs, antiques and floral prints.

Six rooms. Complimentary breakfast. $61-150

THE LINCOLN INN AT THE COVERED BRIDGE

530 Woodstock Road, Woodstock, 802-457-3312; www.lincolninn.com

This renovated farmhouse's property (circa 1869) is bordered by the Ottauquechee River and a covered bridge. The inn's personality is quirky, with updated rooms with names like "yin yang" and "passion." The inn strives to offer the comforts of a traditional bed and breakfast without the stuffiness. As such, common areas are bright and spare, and creature comforts like fresh brewed Green Mountain coffee are on hand.

Six rooms. Complimentary breakfast. Restaurant. $61-150

MAPLE LEAF INN

Highway 12, Barnard, 802-234-5342, 800-516-2753; www.mapleleafinn.com

This property is located on 16 acres of maple and birch trees near the quaint town of Woodstock. The décor is classic country inn, with plenty of antiques, quilts and fireplaces to cozy up to.

Seven rooms. Complimentary breakfast. $151-250

PARKER HOUSE INN

1792 Quechee Main St., Quechee, 802-295-6077; www.theparkerhouseinn.com

A grand brick Victorian house built in 1857 and which served as a former senator's residence is the setting for this country inn. Rooms have been recently redecorated in French country style and feature spa showers and Jacuzzi tubs.

Seven rooms. Pets accepted. Complimentary breakfast. Restaurant. $61-150

WOODSTOCKER BED AND BREAKFAST

61 River St., Woodstock, 802-457-3896, 866-662-1439; www.woodstockervt.com

This quirky inn, which seems more like staying in a private home than a bed and breakfast, features rooms with contemporary décor, flat-screen TVs and new bathrooms. Guests love the 24-hour refreshment station stocked with serve-yourself goodies.

Nine rooms. Complimentary breakfast. $61-150

WHERE TO EAT

★★★BARNARD INN

5518 Highway 12, Barnard, 802-234-9961; www.barnardinnrestaurant.com

Built in 1796, this inn is quaint and simple in a charming New England way. The restaurant serves dishes prepared with French technique, such as steamed mussels with saffron and garlic.

French. Dinner. Bar. Children's menu. Closed Sunday-Monday. $151-250

★★★KEDRON VALLEY INN

Highway 106, South Woodstock, 802-457-1473, 800-836-1193;
www.kedronvalleyinn.com

This inn, located just outside Woodstock, is a local favorite for its cheerful rooms and reasonable prices. The menu at the inn's restaurant features Vermont-raised produce and meat.

American. Breakfast, dinner. Bar. Children's menu. Closed Tuesday-Wednesday, November-July, week of December 25. $16-35

★★★PRINCE AND THE PAUPER

24 Elm St., Woodstock, 802-457-1818; www.princeandpauper.com

Chef and owner Chris Balce offers a menu that changes seasonally. The house specialty is boneless rack of lamb in puff pastry with spinach and mushroom duxelles. For a lighter dinner, sample dishes from the bistro menu, including the freshly made pizzas.

American. Dinner. Bar. Reservations recommended. $36-85

★★★QUECHEE INN AT MARSHLAND FARM

1119 Quechee Main St., Quechee, 802-295-3133, 800-235-3133;
www.quecheeinn.com

The restaurant is in the main house of this inn, which dates back to 1793 and overlooks the Ottauquechee River. The cuisine is served in a casual but sophisticated setting, with a wine list to match.

American. Breakfast, dinner. Bar. Children's menu. Reservations recommended. Outdoor seating. $16-35

★★★SIMON PEARCE

1761 Main St., Quechee, 802-295-1470; www.simonpearce.com

Part of the glass-blowing and pottery complex that has become an emblem of Vermont, this spacious, contemporary restaurant has beautiful, forested views of the Ottauquechee River and a covered bridge. The cuisine is innovative American with Asian accents, and the breads and soups are homemade. American menu. Lunch, dinner. Bar. Reservations recommended. Outdoor seating. $36-85

★★★WOODSTOCK INN

14 The Green, Woodstock, 802-457-1100, 800-448-7900; www.woodstockinn.com
Nightly piano entertainment perfectly suits the romantic atmosphere at this quaint restaurant in the Woodstock Inn. The kitchen makes full use of local and seasonal produce with offerings like organic field greens with Vermont chevre, raspberries and maple mustard vinaigrette and chargrilled black Angus filet mignon with a Vermont gorgonzola crust and a cider reduction. American menu. Dinner, Sunday brunch. Bar. Children's menu. Reservations recommended. $36-85

INDEX

1640 Hart House (Ipswich), *153*
1785 Inn (North Conway), *227*
1800 House (Nantucket), *170*
1824 House Inn Bed and Breakfast (Waitsfield), *273*
1896 House (Williamstown), *206*
21 Federal (Nantucket), *176*
88 Grandview (Boothbay Harbor), *45*
98 Provence (Ogunquit), *65*

A

Abbe Museum (Bar Harbor), *39*
Abbot Hall (Marblehead), *162*
Abe & Louie's (Boston), *103*
Abigail Adams House (Braintree), *122*
Academy of Performing Arts (Orleans), *187*
Adams National Historical Park (Braintree), *122*
Addison Choate Inn (Rockport), *195*
Adrian's (Truro & North Truro), *204*
Al Forno (Providence), *246*
Alchemy (Martha's Vineyard), *167*
Aldrich Contemporary Art Museum (Ridgefield), *30*
Allis-Bushnell House And Museum (Madison), *19*
Alpine Slide (Stowe), *269*
Altar Rock (Nantucket), *170*
American Antiquarian Society (Worcester), *206*
American Independence Museum (Exeter), *214*
American Museum of Fly Fishing (Manchester), *259*
American Seasons (Nantucket), *177*
American Textile History Museum (Lowell), *160*
Amherst College (Amherst), *80*
Amistad Memorial (New Haven), *22*

Anchor-In (Hyannis and Barnstable), *151*
Anchorage by The Sea (Ogunquit), *64*
Andover Inn (Andover), *81*
Andover Wyndham Hotel (Andover), *81*
Andrew's Harborside Restaurant (Boothbay Harbor), *45*
Angelina's Ristorante Italiano (Concord), *213*
Applebutter Inn (Woodstock), *278*
Applegate (Lee), *154*
Apricot's (Farmington), *12*
Aqua Grille (Sandwich), *199*
Aquinnah Cliffs (Martha's Vineyard), *163*
The Aquinnah Shop (Martha's Vineyard), *167*
Aquitaine (Boston), *104*
Arcade (Providence), *243*
Arcadia Nature Center and Wildlife Sanctuary, Massachusetts Audubon Society (Northampton), *185*
Arlington Inn (Arlington), *250*
Arlington's West Mountain Inn (Arlington), *250*
Arnie's Place (Concord), *213*
Arrowhead (Pittsfield), *189*
Arrows (Ogunquit), *65*
Arts And Crafts Show (Old Saybrook), *29*
Ashley Inn (Martha's Vineyard), *166*
Ashley Manor (Hyannis and Barnstable), *151*
Ashumet Holly & Wildlife Sanctuary (Falmouth), *142*
Ashworth By The Sea (Hampton Beach), *217*
Aspen Motel (Manchester), *260*
Asticou Inn (Northeast Harbor), *63*
Astor's Beechwood (Newport), *236*
Atlantic Café (Nantucket), *177*
Atlantic Seal Cruises (Freeport), *52*

Atlantica (Camden), *48*

Audubon Center (Greenwich), *13*

Aura (Boston), *104*

Autumnal Feasting (Plymouth), *191*

Avanyu Spa at The Equinox Resort (Manchester), *261*

Avon Old Farms Hotel (Avon), *8*

Avon Old Farms Inn (Avon), *9*

B

B & G Oysters Ltd. (Boston), *104*

Back Bay Grill (Portland), *71*

Balsams/Wilderness Ski Area (Dixville Notch), *213*

The Balsams (Dixville Notch), *214*

Bangor Museum and Center For History (Bangor), *38*

Bar Harbor Historical Society Museum (Bar Harbor), *39*

Bar Harbor Hotel-Bluenose Inn (Bar Harbor), *40*

Bar Harbor Inn (Bar Harbor), *40*

Bar Harbor Whale Watch Company (Bar Harbor), *40*

Barley Neck Inn (Orleans), *187*

Barnacle Billy's (Ogunquit), *65*

Barnard Inn (Woodstock), *279*

Barrows House Inn (Dorset), *256*

Bartlett Arboretum and Gardens (Stamford), *31*

Bartlett's Farm (Nantucket), *170*

Bartley's Dockside (Kennebunkport), *58*

Basin Harbor Club (Vergennes), *272*

Basketball Hall Of Fame (Springfield), *200*

Bass Rocks Ocean Inn (Gloucester), *145*

Battle Green (Lexington), *159*

Battleship Cove (Fall River), *142*

Bay Chamber Concerts (Camden), *46*

The Bayview (Bar Harbor), *41*

The Beach House (Kennebunk), *55*

Beach Plum Inn Restaurant (Martha's Vineyard), *168*

Beach Plum Inn (Martha's Vineyard), *165*

Beacon Hill Hotel (Boston), *92*

The Beacon Room (Orleans), *187*

Beal's Lobster Pier (Southwest Harbor), *76*

Beauport, The Sleeper-Mccann House (Gloucester), *145*

Bedford Village Inn (Manchester), *222*

Bee And Thistle Inn (Old Lyme), *28*

Bee-Hive Tavern (Sandwich), *199*

Beech Tree Inn & Cottage (Newport), *239*

Beechwood Hotel (Worcester), *207*

Belcourt Castle (Newport), *236*

Bellini's (North Conway), *227*

Ben & Jerry's Ice Cream Factory Tour (Stowe), *269*

Bennington Battle Monument (Bennington), *250*

Bennington College (Bennington), *251*

Bennington Museum (Bennington), *251*

Berkshire Botanical Garden (Stockbridge), *201*

Berkshire Craft Fair (Great Barrington), *147*

Berkshire Museum (Pittsfield), *189*

Best Western at Historic Concord (Concord), *138*

Best Western Inn & Suites Rutland/ Killington (Rutland), *267*

Best Western Senator Inn & Spa (Augusta), *37*

Best Western Windjammer Inn & Conference Center (Burlington), *254*

Bethel Inn & Country Club (Bethel), *43*

Billy's Etc. (Ogunquit), *65*

Birchwood Inn (Lenox), *157*

Bishop's Terrace (Harwich), *149*

Bistro At Crowne Pointe Inn (Provincetown), *193*

Bistro Zinc (Lenox), *157*

Black Dog Bakery (Martha's Vineyard), *163*

Black Eyed Susan's (Nantucket), *177*

Black Mountain (Jackson), *220*

Black Point Inn (Portland), *69*

Blaine House (Augusta), *37*

Blantyre (Lenox), *156*, 157

Blithewold Mansion and Gardens (Bristol), *233*

Block Island Ferry (Narragansett), *234*

Blue Grass Festival (Norwich), *27*

Blue Harbor House, A Village Inn (Camden), *47*

Blue Hill Inn (Blue Hill), *43*

Blue Moon Café (Boothbay Harbor), *45*

Boarding House (Nantucket), *177*

Bolton Valley Ski/Summer Resort (Burlington), *253*

Boothbay Railway Village (Boothbay Harbor), *44*

Boothbay Region Historical Society Museum (Boothbay Harbor), *44*

Boston African American National Historic Site (Boston), *82*

Boston Ballet (Boston), *82*

Boston Bruins (Boston), *82*

Boston Celtics (Boston), *82*

Boston College (Boston), *82*

Boston Common (Boston), *83*

Boston Harbor Hotel (Boston), *92*

Boston Harbor Islands National Recreation Area (Boston), *83*

Boston Marathon (Boston), *91*

Boston Marriott Cambridge (Cambridge), *128*

Boston Marriott Copley Place (Boston), *92*

Boston Marriott Long Wharf (Boston), *92*

Boston Marriott Newton (Newton), *183*

Boston Park Plaza Hotel (Boston), *93*

Boston Public Garden (Boston), *83*

Boston Public Library (Boston), *83*

Boston Red Sox (Boston), *83*

Boston Symphony Orchestra/ Boston Pops (Boston), *84*

Boston Tea Party Ship and Museum (Boston), *84*

Boston University (Boston), *84*

Bousquet (Pittsfield), *189*

The Bradford of Chatham (Chatham), *134*

Bradley House Museum (Falmouth), *142*

The Bradley Inn (Damariscotta), *50*

Bramble Inn (Brewster), *124*

Bravo Bravo (Mystic), *21*

Bravo Restaurant (Boston), *104*

Bread Loaf (Middlebury), *261*

Breakers (Newport), *236*

The Breakwater Inn And Hotel (Kennebunkport), *56*

Bretton Woods Ski Area (Bretton Woods), *211*

Brewster Fish House (Brewster), *124*

Brewster House Bed & Breakfast (Freeport), *53*

Brick Market (Newport), *236*

Brick Store Museum (Kennebunk), *55*

Brook Farm Inn (Lenox), *157*

Brown University (Providence), *243*

Brown's Wharf Motel (Boothbay Harbor), *44*

Bruce Museum (Greenwich), *13*

Buckman Tavern (Lexington), *159*

Bufflehead Cove (Kennebunkport), *57*

Bunker Hill Monument (Boston), *84*

Bush-Holley House (Greenwich), *13*

The Butcher Shop (Boston), *105*

Butler-Mccook Homestead and Main Street History Center (Hartford), *15*

Button Bay State Park (Vergennes), *271*

Buttonwood Park & Zoo (New Bedford), *180*

By The Sea Guests (Dennis), *140*

C

Café Allegre (Madison), *19*

Café Lucia (Lenox), *158*

Calvin Coolidge Memorial Room (Northampton), *185*

Cambridge Antique Mall (Cambridge), *126*

Camden Harbour Inn (Camden), *47*

Camden Hills State Park (Camden), *45*

Camden Opera House (Camden), *46*

Camden Snow Bowl (Camden), *46*

Camden Windward House (Camden), *47*

Can Am Crown Sled Dog Races (Fort Kent), *52*

Candlewood Lake (Danbury), *9*

Canfield House (Newport), *241*

Cannon Mountain Ski Area (Franconia Notch State Park), *216*

Canterbury Shaker Village (Concord), *212*

Cape Ann Historical Museum (Gloucester), *145*

Cape Arundel Inn (Kennebunkport), *57*

Cape Cod Baseball League (Harwich), *148*

Cape Cod Kayak (Falmouth), *143*

Cape Cod Museum Of Natural History (Brewster), *123*

Cape Cod Oyster Festival (Hyannis and Barnstable), *150*

Cape Cod Pathways (Hyannis and Barnstable), *149*

Cape Cod Potato Chip Company (Hyannis and Barnstable), *149*

Cape Cod Repertory Theater Company (Brewster), *123*

Cape Playhouse (Dennis), *140*

Cape Symphony Orchestra (Yarmouth), *208*

The Capital Grille (Boston), *105*

Captain Fairfield Inn (Kennebunkport), *57*

Captain Farris House Bed and Breakfast (Yarmouth), *208*

The Captain Jefferds Inn (Kennebunkport), *58*

Captain Linnell House (Orleans), *188*

The Captain Lord Mansion (Kennebunkport), *58*

Captain Tom Lawrence House (Falmouth), *143*

Captain's House Inn (Chatham), *134*

Cap'n Simeon's Gallery (Kittery), *61*

Carbone's (Hartford), *17*

Carlisle House Inn (Nantucket), *175*

Carmen (Boston), *105*

Carrabassett Valley Ski Area (Kingfield), *60*

Carter's X-Country Ski Center (Bethel), *42*

Casa Romero (Boston), *105*

Casco Bay Lines (Chebeague Islands), *49*

Castelmaine (Bar Harbor), *41*

Castle Hill Inn & Resort (Newport), *240*

Castle Street Café (Great Barrington), *147*

Castle (Worcester), *207*

Catamount Ski Area (Great Barrington), *146*

Centerboard Guest House (Nantucket), *175*

The Chanler At Cliff Walk (Newport), *240*

Charles Hotel (Cambridge), *129*

Charles Ives Center For The Arts (Danbury), *9*

Charles River Canoe & Kayak Center (Newton), *183*

Charles River Esplanade (Boston), *84*

Charles Street Inn (Boston), *103*

Charlesmark Hotel (Boston), *93*

Charlotte Inn (Martha's Vineyard), *165*

Chateau-Sur-Mer (Newport), *236*

Chatham Bars Inn (Chatham), *134*

Chatham Light (Chatham), *133*

Chatham Squire (Chatham), *134*

Chatham Wayside Inn (Chatham), *134*

Chebeague Transportation (Chebeague Islands), *49*

Chesterwood (Stockbridge), *202*

Chez Henri (Cambridge), *131*

Chicama Vineyards (Martha's Vineyard), *163*

Children's Museum of Boston (Boston), *85*

Children's Museum of Maine (Portland), *67*

Chillingsworth (Brewster), *125*

Christ Church (Cambridge), *126*

Christa Mcauliffe Planetarium (Concord), *212*

Christmas Farm Inn (Jackson), *221*

Christmas Torchlight Parade (Old Saybrook), *29*

Christopher Dodge House (Providence), *245*

Church Street Café (Lenox), *158*

Church Street Marketplace (Burlington), *253*

Cisco Brewers (Nantucket), *170*

Citi Performing Arts Center/The Shubert Theater (Boston), *91*

Clam Box Of Ipswich (Ipswich), *153*

Clark Currier Inn (Newburyport), *182*

The Clark Point Inn (Southwest Harbor), *75*

Clay Hill Farm (Ogunquit), *65*

Cliff Walk (Newport), *236*

Cliffside Beach Club (Nantucket), *174*

Clio (Boston), *106*

Club Car (Nantucket), *177*

Coachman Inn (Kittery), *61*

Coast Guard House (Narragansett), *235*

Cobblestone Inn (Nantucket), *175*

Cobblestones (Lowell), *161*

Cobb's Mill Inn (Westport), *33*

Codman House (Concord), *135*

Coffin House (Newburyport), *181*

Cog Railway (Mount Washington), *224*

Coggeshall Farm Museum, Colt State Park (Bristol), *233*

Cole Land Transportation Museum (Bangor), *39*

Colonel Ashley House (Great Barrington), *146*

Colonial Inn (Concord), *138*

Colonial Pemaquid State Park (Damariscotta), *50*

The Colonnade Hotel (Boston), *93*

The Colony Hotel (Kennebunkport), *56*

Comfort Inn & Suites at Maplewood (Montpelier), *263*

Comfort Inn (North Conway), *227*

Commercial Street (Provincetown), *192*

The Commodore Inn (Harwich), *148*

The Common Man (Warren), *274*

Community Boating (Boston), *85*

Company of The Cauldron (Nantucket), *178*

Concord Museum (Concord), *135*

Congregational Church (Middlebury), *261*

Connecticut River Museum (Essex), *10*

Connecticut Storytelling Festival (New London), *26*

Constitution House (Windsor), *275*

Conway Homestead-Cramer Museum (Camden), *46*

Conway Scenic Railroad (North Conway), *226*

Cook's Lobster House (Bailey Island), *38*

Coonamessett Inn (Falmouth), *143*

Coop De Ville (Martha's Vineyard), *168*

Copley Place (Boston), *85*

Copley Square Hotel (Boston), *93*

Copper Beech Inn (Essex), *11*

Copp's Hill Burying Ground (Boston), *85*

Cork N' Hearth (Lee), *155*

Courtyard Boston Copley Square (Boston), *94*

Courtyard Boston Foxborough (Foxborough), *144*

Courtyard Cape Cod Hyannis (Hyannis and Barnstable), *151*

Courtyard New Haven at Yale (New Haven), *24*

Courtyard Providence Downtown (Providence), *245*

Crab Shell (Stamford), *32*

Craigie On Main (Cambridge), *131*

Cranberry Cove Boating Company (Southwest Harbor), 75

Cranberry Harvest Festival (Harwich), 148

Crane Beach (Ipswich), 153

Cranwell Resort Spa and Golf Club (Lenox), 156

Crawford Notch State Park (Bretton Woods), 211

Crowley Cheese Factory (Ludlow), 258

Crowne Plaza Hartford-Downtown (Hartford), 17

Crowne Plaza Hotel (Pittsfield), 189

Crowne Plaza Hotel (Worcester), 207

Crowne Plaza (Nashua), 225

Crowne Plaza (Warwick), 248

Crowne Pointe Historic Inn (Provincetown), 193

Crowninshield-Bentley House (Salem), 196

Crow's Nest Resort (Truro & North Truro), 204

Culinary Archives & Museum (Providence), 243

Currier Museum of Art (Manchester), 221

Cushing House Museum (Newburyport), 181

Custom House Maritime Museum (Newburyport), 181

D

D.W.'s Oceanside Inn (Hampton Beach), 217

Daily Planet (Burlington), 255

Dakota (Avon), 9

Danbury Plaza Hotel (Danbury), 10

Dante (Cambridge), 131

The Dan'l Webster Inn (Sandwich), 199

Dartmouth College (Hanover), 217-218

David's (Newburyport), 182

Davio's (Boston), 106

Decordova Museum & Sculpture Park (Concord), 136

Deep River Ancient Muster and Parade (Essex), 11

Deerfield Inn (Deerfield), 139

The Delamar (Greenwich), 13

Denison Homestead (Mystic), 20

Derby House (Salem), 196

Devonfield Inn (Lee), 154

Discover Jazz Festival (Burlington), 254

Dock And Dine (Old Saybrook), 30

Dockside Guest Quarters (York), 77

Docksider (Northeast Harbor), 63

Dockside (York), 77

Dolphin Restaurant (Hyannis and Barnstable), 151

Dorset Inn (Dorset), 255

Dorset Theatre Festival (Dorset), 255

Doubletree Guest Suites (Boston), 94

Doubletree Hotel Boston Downtown (Boston), 94

Doubletree Hotel (Burlington), 254

Downyflake (Nantucket), 178

Dr. Moses Mason House Museum (Bethel), 42

Drumlin Farm Education Center (Concord), 136

Duck Tours (Boston), 85

Durgin Park (Boston), 106

E

Eagle Mountain House (Jackson), 220

East Coast Grill & Raw Bar (Cambridge), 131

East Rock Park (New Haven), 23

Eastern Standard (Boston), 106

Eastern States Exposition (The Big E) (Springfield), 200

Eastham Historical Society (Eastham), 141

Eastham Windmill (Eastham), 141

Eastside Grill (Northampton), 186

Echo Lake State Park (North Conway), 226

Ecotarium (Worcester), 207

The Edgewater (Old Orchard Beach), 67

Edith Wharton Estate (the Mount) (Lenox), *155*

Edward King House (Newport), *236*

Edwards Harborside Inn (York), *77*

The Eliot Hotel (Boston), *94*

The Elms Inn (Ridgefield), *30*

Elms (Newport), *30, 237*

The Elms (Ridgefield), *30*

Embassy Suites (Portland), *69*

Emerson Inn By The Sea (Rockport), *195*

Emerson-Wilcox House (York), *76*

Emily Dickinson Museum: The Homestead and The Evergreens (Amherst), *80*

Endeavor Sailing Adventures (Nantucket), *171*

Enfield Shaker Museum (Hanover), *218*

English Meadows Inn (Kennebunkport), *58*

Equinox Sky Line Drive (Manchester), *259*

The Equinox (Manchester), *260*

Eric Carle Museum of Picture Book Art (Amherst), *80*

Espresso Love Café (Martha's Vineyard), *168*

The Essex (Burlington), *254*

Ethan Allen Homestead and Museum (Burlington), *253*

Ethan Allen Hotel (Danbury), *10*

Ethan Allen Park (Burlington), *253*

Eugene O'Neill Theater Center (New London), *24*

Expedition Whydah's Sea Lab & Learning Center (Provincetown), *192*

F

Fabyan's Station (Bretton Woods), *211*

Factory Outlet Stores (Freeport), *52*

Fairbanks Inn (Provincetown), *193*

Fairfield Inn Portsmouth Seacoast (Portsmouth), *230*

Fairfield Inn (Bangor), *39*

The Fairmont Battery Wharf Boston, *95*

The Fairmont Copley Plaza Boston (Boston), *95*

Fall Foliage Festival (North Adams), *185*

Fall River Historical Society (Fall River), *142*

Falmouth Road Race (Falmouth), *143*

Faneuil Hall Marketplace (Boston), *85*

Fanizzi's By The Sea (Provincetown), *194*

Farmington Antiques Weekend (Farmington), *12*

The Farmington Inn of Greater Hartford (Farmington), *12*

Farmington Valley Arts Center (Avon), *8*

Farnsworth Art Museum and Wyeth Center (Rockland), *73*

Feast of The Blessed Sacrament (New Bedford), *180*

Featherstone Meeting House for the Arts (Martha's Vineyard), *163*

Federal House Inn (Lee), *154*

Federal Jack's Restaurant and Brew Pub (Kennebunk), *55*

Felix Neck Sanctuary (Martha's Vineyard), *163*

Ferry Service to Yarmouth, Nova Scotia (Bar Harbor), *40*

Ferry Service (Northeast Harbor), *63*

Festival On The Green (Middlebury), *262*

Figawi Sailboat Race and Charity Ball (Hyannis and Barnstable), *150*

Figs (Boston), *107*

Finn's Seafood (Block Island), *232*

The Fireplace (Brookline), *125*

First Congregational Church (Nantucket), *171*

First Night Boston (Boston), *91*

First Unitarian Church (Providence), *243*

Five Bays Bistro (Hyannis and Barnstable), *152*

Flood Tide (Mystic), *22*

Florence Griswold Museum (Old Lyme), *28*

Flour Bakery (Boston), *107*

Flume Gorge & Park Information Center (Franconia Notch State Park), *216*

The Flying Bridge (Falmouth), *144*

Flying Horse Carousel (Martha's Vineyard), *164*

Fog Island Café (Nantucket), *178*

Folger-Franklin Memorial Fountain (Nantucket), *171*

Fore Street (Portland), *71*

Formaggio Kitchen (Cambridge), *127*

Fort Constitution (Portsmouth), *228*

Fort Foster Park (Kittery), *60*

Fort Kent Blockhouse (Fort Kent), *51*

Fort Kent Historical Society Museum and Gardens (Fort Kent), *52*

Fort Nathan Hale Park and Black Rock Fort (New Haven), *23*

Fort Saybrook Monument Park (Old Saybrook), *29*

Fort Stark State Historic Site (Portsmouth), *228*

Fort William Henry State Memorial (Damariscotta), *50*

Four Chimneys Inn (Bennington), *251*

Four Columns Inn (Newfane), *264*

Four Points by Sheraton Manchester Airport (Manchester), *222*

Four Points by Sheraton (Eastham), *141*

Four Seasons Hotel Boston (Boston), *95*

The Francis Malbone House (Newport), *240*

Franconia Inn (Franconia), *215*

The Franconia Inn (Franconia), *215*

Franklin Cafe (Boston), *107*

Franklin Park Golf Course (William J. Devine Golf Course) (Boston), *86*

Franklin Park Zoo (Boston), *86*

Freedom Trail (Boston), *86*

Freestone's City Grill (New Bedford), *180*

French Cable Station Museum (Orleans), *187*

Friends and Company (Madison), *19*

Friends Meeting House (Newport), *237*

Front Street (Provincetown), *194*

Frost Place (Franconia), *214*

Fruitlands Museums (Concord), *136*

Fugakyu (Brookline), *126*

Fuller Gardens (Hampton Beach), *217*

G

Gala Restaurant & Bar (Williamstown), *206*

Gardner-Pingree House (Salem), *196*

Garrison Inn (Newburyport), *181*

Gaspee Days (Warwick), *248*

Gateways Inn (Lenox), *158*

General William Hart House (Old Saybrook), *29*

Giant Staircase (Bailey Island), *38*

Gifford Woods State Park (Killington), *257*

Gilbert Bean Museum (Braintree), *122*

Ginza (Boston), *108*

Glynn House Inn (Holderness), *219*

Go Fish (Mystic), *22*

Governor John Langdon House (Portsmouth), *228*

Governor Stephen Hopkins House (Providence), *243*

The Governor's Inn (Ludlow), *259*

Grafton Notch State Park (Bethel), *42*

Grafton Ponds Cross-Country Ski Center (Grafton), *256*

Granary Burying Ground (Boston), *86*

Grand Summit Resort Hotel (Kingfield), *60*

Granite State Candy Shoppe (Concord), *212*

The Grapevine (Salem), *198*

Great Glen Trails (Mount Washington), *224*

Great Meadows National Wildlife Refuge (Concord), *136*

Green Mountain Inn (Stowe), *270*

Green Mountain Sugar House (Ludlow), *259*

Greenville Inn (Greenville), *54*

Grill 23 & Bar (Boston), *108*

Grissini (Kennebunk), *56*

Griswold Inn (Essex), *11*

Gritty Mcduff's (Freeport), *53*

The Grog (Newburyport), *182*

Gropius House (Concord), *136*

Grove Street Cemetery (New Haven), *23*

Gryphon House (Boston), *103*

Gypsy Sweethearts (Ogunquit), *65*

H

Hadley Farm Museum (Northampton), *185*

Hadwen House (Nantucket), *171*

Haight-Brown Vineyard and Winery (Litchfield), *18*

Hamersley's Bistro (Boston), *108*

Hammonasset Beach State Park (Madison), *19*

Hammond Castle Museum (Gloucester), *145*

Hampton Inn & Suites Boston Crosstown Center (Boston), *96*

Hampton Inn (Bennington), *252*

Hancock Shaker Village (Pittsfield), *189*

Hancock-Clarke House (Lexington), *159*

The Hanover House (Martha's Vineyard), *167*

Hanover Inn (Hanover), *218*

Harbor Light Inn (Marblehead), *162*

Harbor View Hotel (Martha's Vineyard), *166*

Harborside Hotel & Marina (Bar Harbor), *41*

Harborside Inn (Boston), *96*

Harlow Old Fort House (Plymouth), *190*

Harraseeket Inn (Freeport), *53*

Harriet Beecher Stowe Center (Hartford), *15*

Hartford Marriott Farmington (Farmington), *12*

Hartwell House (Ogunquit), *64*

Harvard Museum of Natural History (Cambridge), *127*

Harvard University Art Museums (Cambridge), *127*

Harvard University (Cambridge), *127*

Harvest (Cambridge), *132*

Harwich Historical Society (Harwich), *148*

Hawk Inn And Mountain Resort (Plymouth), *266*

Hawthorn Inn (Camden), *47*

Hawthorne Hotel (Salem), *198*

Hawthorne Inn (Concord), *138*

Haymarket (Boston), *86*

Head of the Charles Regatta (Cambridge), *128*

Hedge House (Plymouth), *190*

Hemenway's Seafood Grill (Providence), *246*

Hemingway's (Killington), *258*

Heritage Museum and Gardens (Sandwich), *198*

Herreshoff Marine Museum (Bristol), *234*

Highland Light/Cape Cod Light (Truro & North Truro), *203*

Hill Farm Inn (Arlington), *250*

Hill-Stead Museum (Farmington), *12*

Hilton Boston Back Bay (Boston), *96*

Hilton Boston Logan Airport (Boston), *96*

Hilton Mystic (Mystic), *21*

Historic Deerfield (Deerfield), *139*

Historic Hildene (Manchester), *259*

Historic Mansions And Houses (Newport), *237*

Historic Merrell Inn (Lee), *154*

Historic New England (Yarmouth), *208*

Historic Northampton Museum Houses (Northampton), *186*

Historic Pontiac Mills (Warwick), *247*

Historical Museum of Gunn Memorial Library (Washington), *32*

Historical Society Museum (Wellfleet), *204*

Hob Knob Inn (Martha's Vineyard), *167*

Holiday Inn Boston at Beacon Hill (Boston), *97*

Holiday Inn Boston-Brookline (Brookline), *125*

Holiday Inn Rutland/Killington (Rutland), *268*

Holiday Inn Select Stamford Downtown (Stamford), *31*

Holiday Inn (Portsmouth), *230*

Holt House (Blue Hill), *43*

Home Port Inn (Lubec), *62*

Homestead Inn (Greenwich), *14*

Homewood Suites (Windsor Locks), *34*

Horsefeathers (North Conway), *227*

Hotel 140 (Boston), *97*

Hotel Commonwealth (Boston), *97*

Hotel Indigo Riverside (Newton), *183*

Hotel Manisses Dining Room (Block Island), *233*

Hotel Marlowe (Cambridge), *129*

The Hotel Northampton (Northampton), *186*

Hotel Viking (Newport), *240*

House of Seven Gables (Salem), *196*

Howland House (Plymouth), *190*

Hoxie House & Dexter Grist Mill (Sandwich), *199*

Hubbardton Battlefield and Museum (Rutland), *267*

Hunter House (Newport), *237*

Hyannis Whale Watcher Cruises (Hyannis and Barnstable), *150*

Hyatt Harborside (Boston), *97*

Hyatt Regency Boston Financial District (Boston), *98*

Hyatt Regency Cambridge (Cambridge), *129*

Hyatt Regency Greenwich (Greenwich), *14*

Hyatt Regency Newport (Newport), *240*

Hydrangea House Inn (Newport), *241*

I

Il Falco (Stamford), *32*

Impudent Oyster (Chatham), *135*

Inaho (Yarmouth), *209*

Indian Leap (Norwich), *26*

Indian Motorcycle Museum (Springfield), *200*

Inn at Bay Ledge (Bar Harbor), *41*

The Inn at Bay Point (Meredith), *223*

Inn at Ellis River (Jackson), *220*

The Inn at Harvard (Cambridge), *129*

Inn at Lewis Bay (Yarmouth), *208*

Inn at Manchester (Manchester), *260*

The Inn at Mill Falls (Meredith), *223*

Inn at Montpelier (Montpelier), *263*

Inn at Mystic (Mystic), *21*

Inn at National Hall (Westport), *33*

Inn at Ocean's Edge (Camden), *47*

The Inn at Ormsby Hill (Manchester), *261*

Inn at Pleasant Lake (New London), *225*

The Inn at Sawmill Farm (West Dover), *274*

Inn at Stockbridge (Stockbridge), *202*

Inn at Sunrise Point (Camden), *47*

The Inn at The Oaks (Eastham), *141*

The Inn at The Round Barn (Waitsfield), *273*

Inn at Thorn Hill (Jackson), *220-221*

Inn at West View Farm (Dorset), *256*

Inn By The Sea (Portland), *70*

Inn of The Six Mountains (Killington), *258*

The Inn on Cove Hill (Rockport), *196*

The Inn on The Common (Montpelier), *264*

Inn on The Sound (Falmouth), *143*

Institute For American Indian Studies (Washington), *32*

Institute of Contemporary Art (Boston), *86*

Intercontinental Boston (Boston), *98*

International Tennis Hall of Fame & Museum (Newport), *237*

Isabella Stewart Gardner Museum (Boston), *86*

Isaiah Jones Homestead (Sandwich), *199*

Isle Au Haut Boat Services (Deer Isle), *51*

Isle Au Haut (Deer Isle), *51*

Isles Of Shoals (Portsmouth), *229*

Islesford Historical Museum (Cranberry Isles), *50*

Ivy Lodge (Newport), *241*

J

Jackson Homestead Museum (Newton), *183*

The Jackson Laboratory (Bar Harbor), *40*

Jackson Ski Touring Foundation (Jackson), *220*

Jacob's Pillow Dance Festival (Lee), *154*

Jameson Tavern (Freeport), *53*

Jared Coffin House (Nantucket), *174*

Jasper White's Summer Shack (Boston), *108*

Jean-Louis (Greenwich), *14*

Jeremiah Lee Mansion (Marblehead), *162*

Jesse's (Hanover), *218*

Jethro Coffin House (oldest House) (Nantucket), *171*

Jetties Beach (Nantucket), *171*

Jiminy Peak (Pittsfield), *189*

John Brown House (Providence), *243*

John F. Kennedy Hyannis Museum (Hyannis and Barnstable), *150*

John F. Kennedy National Historic Site (Brookline), *125*

John H. Chaffy Blackstone River Valley National Heritage Corridor (Worcester), *207*

John Hancock Warehouse (York), *76*

John Heard House (Ipswich), *153*

John Paul Jones House (Portsmouth), *229*

John Strong Mansion (Vergennes), *272*

John Ward House (Salem), *197*

The John Whipple House (Ipswich), *153*

Jonathan's (Ogunquit), *66*

Joseph's By The Sea (Old Orchard Beach), *67*

Joshua Hempstead House (New London), *25*

Josiah Dennis Manse (Dennis), *140*

Juniper Hill Inn (Windsor), *275*

Jurys Hotel (Boston), *98*

K

Kedron Valley Inn (Woodstock), *279*

Kedron Valley Stables (Woodstock), *276*

Keeler Tavern Museum (Ridgefield), *30*

Kelley House (Martha's Vineyard), *166*

Kemble Inn (Lenox), *157*

Kendall Hotel (Cambridge), *130*

Kendall Tavern Bed and Breakfast (Freeport), *53*

The Kennebunk Inn (Kennebunk), *55*

Kennebunkport Inn (Kennebunkport), *56*

Kensington (Norwich), *27*

Kidspace (North Adams), *184*

Killington Resort (Killington), *257*

King Hooper Mansion (Marblehead), *162*

Kingscote (Newport), *237*

Kingsleigh Inn (Southwest Harbor), *75*

King's Chapel And Burying Ground (Boston), *87*

Kittery Historical and Naval Museum (Kittery), *61*

Ko Prime (Boston), *109*

L

La Boniche (Lowell), *161*

La Forge Casino Restaurant (Newport), *242*

La Verdad (Boston), *110*

Lake Champlain Chocolates (Burlington), *253*

Lala Rokh (Boston), *109*

Landfall (Falmouth), *144*

The Langham Boston (Boston), *98*

Lattanzi's Pizzeria (Martha's Vineyard), *168*

Le Languedoc (Nantucket), *178*

Le Meridien Cambridge Mit (Cambridge), *130*

League of New Hampshire Craftsmen-meredith Retail Gallery (Meredith), *223*

Lenox Hotel (Boston), *99*

Les Zygomates (Boston), *110*

Levitt Pavilion for the Performing Arts (Westport), *33*

Lexington Historical Society (Lexington), *159*

Liberty Hill Inn (Yarmouth), *208*

Liberty Hotel (Boston), *99*

Lighthouse Point Park (New Haven), *23*

Lilac Inn (Brandon), *252*

The Lincoln Inn at the Covered Bridge (Woodstock), *278*

Linda Jean's (Martha's Vineyard), *168*

List Visual Arts Center at Mit (Cambridge), *127*

Litchfield History Museum (Litchfield), *18*

Litchfield Inn (Litchfield), *18*

Lizzie Borden Bed and Breakfast (Fall River), *142*

Lobster Claw (Orleans), *188*

Lobster Cooker (Freeport), *54*

Lobster Hatchery (Bar Harbor), *40*

Lobster Pot (Bristol), *194, 234*

Lobster Pot (Provincetown), *194*

The Lobster Pound (Camden), *48*

Locke-Ober (Boston), *110*

The Lodge at Moosehead Lake (Greenville), *54*

Loines Observatory (Nantucket), *171*

Lola's Southern Seafood (Martha's Vineyard), *169*

Lonesome Pine Trails (Fort Kent), *52*

Longfellow National Historic Site (Cambridge), *127*

Look Park (Northampton), *186*

Lookout Tavern (Martha's Vineyard), *169*

Louis Boston (Boston), *87*

Louisburg Square (Boston), *87*

Lovetts Inn (Franconia), *215*

Lowell Heritage State Park (Lowell), *160*

Lowell National Historical Park (Lowell), *160*

Lumiere (Newton), *183*

Lure Grill (Martha's Vineyard), *169*

Lyceum (Salem), *198*

Lyman Allyn Art Museum (New London), *25*

L'alouette (Harwich), *149*

L'arte Di Cucinare (Boston), *87*

L'escale (Greenwich), *14*

L'espalier (Boston), *109*

L'etoile (Martha's Vineyard), *168*

M

Mad River Glen Ski Area (Waitsfield), *272*

Madison Beach Hotel (Madison), *19*

Maggie's (Bar Harbor), *41*

Mahoney's Atlantic Bar And Grill (Orleans), *188*

The Maine Dining Room (Freeport), *54*

Maine History Gallery (Portland), *68*

Maine Lighthouse Museum (Rockland), *73*

Maine Lobster Festival (Rockland), *74*

Maine State Ferry Service (Camden), *46*

Maine State Ferry Service (Rockland), *73*

Maine State Ferry Service (Southwest Harbor), *75*

Maine State Museum (Augusta), *37*

Maine Stay Bed And Breakfast (Camden), *48*

Makris Lobster And Steak House (Concord), *213*

Mame's (Meredith), *224*

Mamma Maria (Boston), *111*

Manchester Designer Outlets (Manchester), *260*

Manchester Historic Association Millyard Museum (Manchester), *222*

Mandarin Oriental, Boston (Boston), *99*

Manor On Golden Pond (Holderness), *219*

Mansion House Hotel & Health Club (Martha's Vineyard), *166*

Maple Leaf Inn (Woodstock), *278*

Marble House (Newport), *238*

Marblehead Landing (Marblehead), *162*

Mark Twain House (Hartford), *16*

Marriott Newport (Newport), *241*

Marriott Providence (Providence), *245*

Marriott Springfield (Springfield), *201*

Marsh-Billings-Rockefeller National Historic Park (Woodstock), *276*

Martin House Inn (Nantucket), *176*

Masa (Boston), *111*

Mass Moca (North Adams), *184*

Massachusetts Institute of Technology (Cambridge), *128*

Mast Landing Sanctuary (Freeport), *53*

Max Downtown (Hartford), *17*

The Mayflower Inn (Washington), *32*

Mayflower Society House Museum (Plymouth), *190*

The Mayflower Spa (Washington), *33*

MDC Memorial Hatch Shell (Boston), *87*

Meadowmere (Ogunquit), *64*

Memorial Hall Museum (Deerfield), *139*

Menemsha Fishing Village (Martha's Vineyard), *164*

Meritage (Boston), *111*

Metropolis Café (Boston), *112*

The Metropolitan Club (Boston), *112*

The Mews Restaurant & Café (Provincetown), *194*

Miacomet Golf Course (Nantucket), *172*

Michael's Harborside (Newburyport), *182*

Mid-Winter New England Surfing Championship (Narragansett), *235*

Middlebury College Snow Bowl (Middlebury), *262*

Middlebury College (Middlebury), *261*

Miel (Boston), *112*

Mike's City Diner (Boston), *112*

Mill Street Inn (Newport), *241*

Millennium Bostonian Hotel (Boston), *99*

Millstone (New London), *226*

Mill's Tavern (Providence), *246*

Minute Man National Historical Park (Concord), *136*

Minuteman Commuter Bikeway (Boston), *87*

Mission House (Stockbridge), *202*

Mistral (Boston), *113*

MIT Museum (Cambridge), *128*

Moby Dick's (Wellfleet), *205*

Moffatt-Ladd House (Portsmouth), *229*

Mohawk Trail State Forest (North Adams), *184*

Mohegan Bluffs (Block Island), *231*

Mohegan Café (Block Island), *233*

Molly's (Hanover), *219*

Monhegan Lighthouse/Museum (Monhegan Island), *63*

Monomoy National Wildlife Refuge (Chatham), *133*

Montano's (Truro & North Truro), *204*

Monte Cristo Cottage (New London), *25*

Monument To Paul Bunyan (Bangor), *39*

Mooo Restaurant (Boston), *113*

Moosehead Marine Museum (Greenville), *54*

Morse Farm (Montpelier), *263*

Mother Church, The First Church Of Christ, Scientist Christian Science Center (Boston), *88*

Mount Ascutney State Park (Windsor), *275*

Mount Cranmore (North Conway), *226*

Mount Desert Oceanarium (Southwest Harbor), *75*

Mount Greylock State Reservation (North Adams), *184*

Mount Independence (Brandon), *252*

Mount Mansfield Gondola (Stowe), *270*

Mount Mansfield State Forest (Stowe), *270*

Mount Snow Ski Area (West Dover), *274*

Mount Washington Auto Road (Mount Washington), *224*

Mount Washington Hotel (Bretton Woods), *211*

Mount Washington Summit Museum (Mount Washington), *225*

Mountain Top Inn (Rutland), *268*

Munroe Tavern (Lexington), *159*

Murray's Toggery (Nantucket), *172*

Museum at The John Fitzgerald Kennedy Library (Boston), *88*

Museum of Afro American History (Boston), *88*

Museum of Art (Northampton), *186*

Museum Of Connecticut History (Hartford), *16*

Museum of Fine Arts (Boston), *88*

Museum of Natural History and Cormack Planetarium (Providence), *243*

Museum of New Hampshire History (Concord), *212*

Museum Of Science (Boston), *88*

Myers + Chang (Boston), *113*

Myles Standish State Forest (Plymouth), *190*

Mystic Aquarium (Mystic), *20*

Mystic Pizza (Mystic), *22*

Mystic Seaport (Mystic), *21*

Mytoi (Martha's Vineyard), *164*

N

Naked Oyster (Hyannis and Barnstable), *152*

Nantucket Arts Festival (Nantucket), *174*

Nantucket Film Festival (Nantucket), *174*

Nantucket Historical Association Whaling Museum (Nantucket), *172*

Nantucket Lobster Trap (Nantucket), *178*

Nantucket Maria Mitchell Association (Nantucket), *172*

Nantucket Town (Nantucket), *172*

Nantucket Wine Festival (Nantucket), *174*

Napi's (Provincetown), *194*

The Nashua House Hotel (Martha's Vineyard), *166*

Nathaniel Hempstead House (New London), *25*

National Heritage Museum (Lexington), *159*

National Monument to the Forefathers (Plymouth), *190*

Natural Bridge State Park (North Adams), *184*

Naumkeag (Stockbridge), *202*

Nauset Beach Club Restaurant (Orleans), *188*

Nauset Beach (Orleans), *187*

Neptune Oyster (Boston), *113*

New Bedford Whaling Museum (New Bedford), *180*

New England Air Museum (Windsor Locks), *34*

New England Aquarium Whale Watches (Boston), *89*

New England Aquarium (Boston), *89*

New England Fire & History Museum (Brewster), *123*

New England Maple Museum (Rutland), *267*

New England Patriots (Foxborough), *144*

New England Quilt Museum (Lowell), *160*

New England Revolution (Foxborough), *144*

New England Ski Museum (Franconia), *215-216*

New Harbor (Block Island), *232*

New Haven Green (New Haven), *23*

New Haven Symphony Orchestra (New Haven), *24*

New Rivers (Providence), *247*

New Year's Eve Portland (Portland), *69*

Newbury Guest House (Boston), *103*

Newbury Street (Boston), *88,*

Newcastle Inn (Damariscotta), *51*

The Newes from America (Martha's Vineyard), *169*

Newport Art Museum And Art Association (Newport), *238*

Newport Harbor Hotel and Marina (Newport), *241*

Newport Music Festival (Newport), *239*

Newport Winter Festival (Newport), *239*

Nichols House Museum (Boston), *89*

Nickerson State Park (Brewster), *123*

Nine Zero Hotel (Boston), *100*

No. 9 Park (Boston), *114*

No. Five-O (Ogunquit), *66*

Noah Webster Foundation and Historical Society (Hartford), *16*

Noden-Reed House & Barn (Windsor Locks), *34*

Nonantum Resort (Kennebunkport), *57*

Norman Rockwell Exhibition (Arlington), *249*

Norman Rockwell Museum (Rutland), *267*

Norman Rockwell Museum (Stockbridge), *202*

North Conway Grand Hotel (North Conway), *227*

North Hero House Inn (North Hero), *265*

North Hero House (North Hero), *266*

North Hero State Park (North Hero), *265*

North Light (Block Island), *232*

Norumbega Inn (Camden), *48*

Nunan's Lobster Hut (Kennebunkport), *59*

O

O Ya (Boston), *115*

Oak Bluffs (Martha's Vineyard), *164*

The Oak Room (Boston), *114*

Oarweed Cove (Ogunquit), *66*

Ocean Beach Park (New London), *25*

Ocean Edge Golf Course (Brewster), *124*

Ocean Edge Resort (Brewster), *124*

Oceanside Grille at The Brunswick (Old Orchard Beach), *67*

October Mountain State Forest (Lee), *154*

Ogunquit Lobster Pound (Ogunquit), *66*

Ogunquit Museum of American Art (Ogunquit), *64*

Ogunquit Playhouse (Ogunquit), *64*

Oktoberfest & Craft Show (West Dover), *274*

Old Burying Ground (Bennington), *251*

Old Castle (Rockport), *195*

Old First Church (Bennington), *251*

Old Fort Inn (Kennebunkport), *58*

Old Fort Western (Augusta), *37*

Old Gaol (York), *76*

Old Lyme Inn (Old Lyme), *28*

Old Man of the Mountain Historic Site (Franconia Notch State Park), *216*

Old Manse (Concord), *137*

Old Mill (Nantucket), *172*

Old Newfane Inn (Newfane), *265*

Old Newgate Prison (Windsor Locks), *34*

Old North Church (Boston), *89*

Old Port Festival (Portland), *69*

Old Sea Pines Inn (Brewster), *124*

Old South Church (Boston), *89*

Old South Meeting House (Boston), *89*

Old State House/Site of Boston Massacre (Boston), *90*

Old State House (Hartford), *16*

Old State House (Providence), *244*

Old Stone Mill (Newport), *238*

Old Tavern at Grafton (Grafton), *257*

Old Whaling Church (Martha's Vineyard), *164*

Old York Historical Society (York), *76*

Oleana (Cambridge), *132*

Olives (Boston), *114*

Omni New Haven Hotel (New Haven), *24*

Omni Parker House (Boston), *100*

Onyx Hotel (Boston), *100*

Oran Mor (Nantucket), *178*

Orchard House (Concord), *137*

The Orchards (Williamstown), *206*

Original Gourmet Brunch (Hyannis and Barnstable), *152*

Osterville Historical Society Museum (Hyannis and Barnstable), *150*

Otis Ridge (Great Barrington), *146*

Outermost Inn (Martha's Vineyard), *167*, 169

P

The Paddock (Hyannis and Barnstable), *152*

The Palmer House Inn (Falmouth), *143*

Pane E Vino (Providence), *247*

The Paper House (Rockport), *195*

Park Kitchen (Portland), *71*

Park Street Church (Boston), *90*

Park-Mccullough House Museum (Bennington), *251*

Parker House Inn (Woodstock), *278*

Parker River National Wildlife Refuge (Newburyport), *181*

Parker's (Boston), *115*

Patriot's Day Parade (Concord), *137*

Paul Revere House (Boston), *90*

Pauline's (Burlington), *255*

Peabody Museum & Essex Institute (Salem), *197*

Peabody Museum of Archaeology and Ethnology (Cambridge), *128*

Peabody Museum of Natural History (New Haven), *23*

Peabody Museum (Andover), *80*

The Pearl (Nantucket), *179*

Peirce-Nichols House (Salem), *197*

Pemaquid Point Lighthouse Park (Damariscotta), *50*

Peppercorn's Grill (Hartford), *17*

Phillips Andover Academy (Andover), *81*

Phillips Exeter Academy (Exeter), *214*

Pho Republique (Boston), *115*

Pico Alpine Slide And Scenic Chairlift (Killington), *257*

Pierce Manse (Concord), *212*

The Pier (Old Orchard Beach), *66*

Pigalle (Boston), *116*

Pilgrim Hall Museum (Plymouth), *191*

Pilgrim Monument & Museum (Provincetown), *192*

Pilgrims Inn (Deer Isle), *51*

Pioneer Village: Salem in 1630 (Salem), *197*

The Pitcher Inn (Warren), *273*

Pleasant Valley Wildlife Sanctuary (Lenox), *155*

Plimoth Plantation/Mayflower II (Plymouth), *191*

Plymouth Colony Winery (Plymouth), *191*

Point Judith (Narragansett), *234*

Polly's Pancake Parlor (Franconia), *216*

Pomegranate Inn (Portland), *70*

Pond Ridge Motel (Woodstock), *277*

Pops By The Sea (Hyannis and Barnstable), *151*

The Porches Inn (North Adams), *185*

The Port Inn (Portsmouth), *230*

Portland Harbor Hotel (Portland), *70*

Portland Head Lighthouse Museum (Portland), *68*

Portland Marriott at Sable Oaks (Portland), *70*

Portland Museum of Art (Portland), *68*

Portland Observatory (Portland), *68*

Portland Regency Hotel & Spa (Portland), *70*

Pot Au Feu (Providence), *247*

President Calvin Coolidge Homestead (Plymouth), *266*

Primo (Rockland), *74*

Prince and The Pauper (Woodstock), *279*

Providence Athenaeum Library (Providence), *244*

Providence Children's Museum (Providence), *244*

Provincetown Art Association & Museum (Provincetown), *192*

Provincetown Ferry (Plymouth), *191*

Provincetown Portuguese Festival (Provincetown), *193*

Putnam Cottage/Knapp Tavern (Greenwich), *13*

Q

Quality Inn & Suites (Augusta), *37*

Quechee Inn at Marshland Farm (Woodstock), *277*

R

Rackliffe Pottery (Blue Hill), *43*

Radcliffe College's Schlesinger Library Culinary Collection (Cambridge), *128*

Radisson Hotel Manchester (Manchester), *222*

Radisson Hotel New London (New London), *26*

Radisson Hotel Plymouth Harbor (Plymouth), *192*

Radisson Hotel Providence Airport (Warwick), *248*

Radisson Hotel Providence Harbor (Providence), *245*

Radisson Nashua Hotel (Nashua), *225*

Radius (Boston), *116*

Rafael Osona Auctions (Nantucket), *173*

Ralph Waldo Emerson House (Concord), *137*

Rangeley Inn (Rangeley), *72*

Rangeley Lake State Park (Rangeley), *72*

Reading Room (Bar Harbor), *42*

The Red Barn (Westport), *34*

Red Clover Inn (Killington), *258*

Red Clover (Killington), *258*

The Red Fez (Boston), *116*

Red Inn Restaurant (Provincetown), *194*

The Red Lion Inn (Stockbridge), *202*

The Red Lion (Stockbridge), *203*

Red Pheasant Inn (Dennis), *140*

Redwood Library And Athenaeum (Newport), *238*

Reenactment of The Battle Of Lexington and Concord (Lexington), *160*

The Regatta of Cotuit (Hyannis and Barnstable), *152*

Reluctant Panther Inn and Restaurant (Manchester), *260*

Renaissance Boston Waterfront Hotel (Boston), *100*

Rhode Island Quahog Company (Newport), *242*

Rhode Island School Of Design

(Providence), *244*

Rhode Island State House (Providence), *244*

Rialto (Cambridge), *132*

Ribollita (Portland), *71*

Richard Sparrow House (Plymouth), *191*

Ristorante Toscano (Boston), *117*

The Ritz-Carlton, Boston Common (Boston), *101*

Roberts House Inn (Nantucket), *176*

Rocca Kitchen & Bar (Boston), *117*

Rockport Chamber Music Festival (Rockport), *195*

Rockwell's at The Inn (New London), *226*

Roger Williams National Memorial (Providence), *244*

Roger Williams Park Zoo (Providence), *245*

Roger Williams Park (Providence), *244-245*

Rokeby Museum (Vergennes), *272*

The Roma Café (Portland), *72*

Rookwood Inn (Lenox), *157*

Roosevelt Campobello International Park (Lubec), *62*

Ropes Mansion and Garden (Salem), *197*

Rosecliff (Newport), *238*

Rotch-Jones-Duff House and Garden Museum (New Bedford), *180*

Route 66 (Bar Harbor), *42*

Rowantrees Pottery (Blue Hill), *43*

Royal Lippizan Stallions of Austria (North Hero), *265*

Royal Mohegan Burial Grounds (Norwich), *27*

Royal Sonesta Hotel Boston (Cambridge), *130*

Rubiners Cheesemongers & Grocers And Rubi's Café (Great Barrington), *146*

Rundlet-May House (Portsmouth), *229*

S

Sage American Bar & Grill (Essex), *11*

Sage (Boston), *117*

Sailfest (New London), *26*

Saint-Gaudens National Historic Site (Hanover), *218*

Salem Maritime National Historic Site (Salem), *197*

Salem Witch Museum (Salem), *197*

Salisbury Mansion (Worcester), *207*

Salts (Cambridge), *132*

Samoset Resort (Rockland), *74*

Samuel Adams Brewery (Boston), *90*

Samuel Whitehorne House (Newport), *238*

The Sandpiper Beach Inn (Harwich), *148*

Sandwich Glass Museum (Sandwich), *199*

Sandy Bay Historical Society & Museums (Rockport), *195*

Santarella (Lee), *154*

Sarah Orne Jewett House (Kittery), *61*

Sargent House Museum (Gloucester), *145*

Saybrook Point Inn and Spa (Old Saybrook), *29*

Sayward-Wheeler House (York), *77*

Scampo (Boston), *117*

Scargo Cafe (Dennis), *140*

School House (Kennebunkport), *56*

Schooner Days & North Atlantic Blues Festival (Rockland), *74*

Science Enrichment Encounters Museum (Manchester), *222*

Scott Covered Bridge (Newfane), *264*

Seamen's Bethel (New Bedford), *180*

Seamen's Inne (Mystic), *22*

Seaport Hotel (Boston), *101*

Seven Sea Street Inn (Nantucket), *176*

Shakespeare & Company (Lenox), *156*

Shaw Perkins Mansion (New London), *25*

Shelburne Farms (Shelburne), *268*

Shelburne Museum (Shelburne), *268*

Sheraton Boston Hotel (Boston), *101*

Sheraton Bradley Airport Hotel (Windsor Locks), *35*

Sheraton Braintree Hotel (Braintree), *122*

Sheraton Burlington Hotel and Conference Center (Burlington), *255*

Sheraton Commander Hotel (Cambridge), *130*

Sheraton Harborside Hotel Portsmouth (Portsmouth), *230*

Sheraton Hartford Hotel (Hartford), *17*

Sheraton Newton Hotel (Newton), *183*

Sheraton Springfield Monarch Place Hotel (Springfield), *201*

Sheraton Stamford Hotel (Stamford), *31*

Sherburne Inn (Nantucket), *176*

Ship's Knees Inn (Orleans), *187*

The Shire Riverview (Woodstock), *277*

The Shops at The Prudential Center (Boston), *90*

Shore Acres Inn (North Hero), *266*

Siasconset Village (Nantucket), *173*

Sidewalk Art Show (Portland), *69*

Sienna (Deerfield), *139*

Silks (Lowell), *161*

Silver Lake State Park (Nashua), *225*

Simon Pearce (Woodstock), *279*

Sir Cricket's Fish and Chips (Orleans), *188*

Ski Butternut (Great Barrington), *146*

Skipper Restaurant (Yarmouth), *209*

Sleepy Hollow Cemetery (Concord), *137*

Smith College (Northampton), *186*

Snug Cottage (Provincetown), *193*

Something Natural (Nantucket), *173*

Sonsie (Boston), *118*

Sorrelina (Boston), *118*

South County Museum (Narragansett), *234*

Spa at Mandarin Oriental (Boston), *121*

The Spa at Norwich Inn (Norwich), *27*

Spa at White Barn Inn (Kennebunkport), *59*

Spa By The Sea (Nantucket), *179*

Spencer's (Great Barrington), *147*

Spooner House (Plymouth), *191*

Spring Festival of Historic Houses (Providence), *245*

Spring House (Block Island), *232*

Springfield Armory National Historic Site (Springfield), *200*

Springfield Museums at The Quadrangle (Springfield), *200*

Spruce Point Inn (Boothbay Harbor), *45*

Squam Lakes Natural Science Center (Holderness), *219*

Stage Neck Inn (York), *77*

Stamford Marriott Hotel & Spa (Stamford), *31*

Stanley-Whitman House (Farmington), *12*

State Capitol (Hartford), *16*

State House (Augusta), *37*

State House (Boston), *90*

State House (Concord), *212*

State House (Montpelier), *263*

Steamship Authority (Hyannis and Barnstable), *150*

Stella (Boston), *118*

Stephen A. Douglas Birthplace (Brandon), *252*

Sterling and Francine Clark Art Institute (Williamstown), *205*

Stone Hill Inn (Stowe), *271*

Stonehedge Inn (Lowell), *161*

Stonehenge Inn (Ridgefield), *30*

Storrowton Village (Springfield), *200*

Stowe Mountain Resort (Stowe), *269-270*

Stoweflake Balloon Festival (Stowe), *270*

Stoweflake Mountain Resort & Spa (Stowe), *270*

The Straight Wharf (Nantucket),

173

Strawbery Banke Museum (Portsmouth), *229*

Street & Co. (Portland), *72*

Striped Bass & Bluefish Derby (Martha's Vineyard), *165*

Stripers (Kennebunkport), *59*

Strong Wings Summer Camp (Nantucket), *173*

Student Prince & Fort (Springfield), *201*

Suffolk Downs (Boston), *91*

Sugar Hill Inn (Franconia), *215*

Sugarbush Inn (Warren), *273*

Sugarbush Resort (Warren), *273*

Sugarloaf Inn (Kingfield), *60*

Sugarloaf/Usa Ski Area (Kingfield), *60*

Suicide Six Ski Area (Woodstock), *276*

Sullivan Station Restaurant (Lee), *155*

Summer House (Nantucket), *179*

Sunday River Ski Resort (Bethel), *42*

The Sunken Ship (Nantucket), *173*

Sunset Hill House-A Grand Inn (Franconia), *215*

Sweet Life Café (Martha's Vineyard), *169*

Swift House Inn (Middlebury), *262*

T

The Taggart House (Stockbridge), *203*

Taj Boston (Boston), *102*

Tanglewood (Lenox), *155*

Tantaquidgeon Indian Museum (Norwich), *27*

Tapeo (Boston), *119*

Tapping Reeve House (Litchfield), *18*

Taranta (Boston), *119*

Taste of Greater Danbury (Danbury), *9*

Tate House (Portland), *68*

Ten Center Street (Newburyport), *182*

Terra Ristorante Italiano (Greenwich), *14*

The Terrace by the Sea (Ogunquit), *64*

Terramia Ristorante (Boston), *119*

That Little Italian Restaurant (Greenwich), *15*

Theatre Workshop Of Nantucket (Nantucket), *173*

Thomas Henkelmann (Greenwich), *15*

Thomas Waterman Wood Art Gallery (Montpelier), *263*

Thorncroft Inn (Martha's Vineyard), *167*

Thornewood Inn & Restaurant (Great Barrington), *147*

Three-County Fair (Northampton), *186*

Top Of The Hub (Boston), *120*

Topnotch Resort and Spa (Stowe), *271*

Topper's (Nantucket), *179*

Topsmead State Forest (Litchfield), *18*

Toro (Boston), *120*

Touro Synagogue National Historic Site (Newport), *239*

The Towers (Narragansett), *235*

Townshend State Forest (Newfane), *264*

Trapp Family Lodge (Stowe), *271*

Tremont 647/Sister Sorel (Boston), *120*

Trinity Church (Boston), *91*

Trinity Church (Newport), *239*

Troquet (Boston), *120*

Truro Historical Society Museum (Truro & North Truro), *204*

Tuck Memorial Museum (Hampton Beach), *217*

Tucker Hill Inn (Waitsfield), *272*

Twenty-Eight Atlantic (Chatham), *135*

Twin Farms (Woodstock), *277*

Two Steps Downtown Grille (Danbury), *10*

U

Union Bar and Grille (Boston), *121*

Union Oyster House (Boston), *121*

University of Hartford (Hartford),

16

University of Massachusetts (Amherst), 80

University of Vermont (Burlington), 254

Upstairs on the Square (Cambridge), 133

US Coast Guard Academy (New London), 26

USS Constitution (Boston), 91

V

Valley Railroad (Essex), 10

Vanessa Noel Hotel (Nantucket), 176

Veranda House (Nantucket), 176

Vermont Historical Society Museum (Montpelier), 263

Vermont Institute of Natural Science (Woodstock), 276

Vermont Mozart Festival (Burlington), 254

Vermont State Craft Center at Frog Hollow (Middlebury), 262

Vermont State Craft Center at Windsor House (Windsor), 275

Vermont Teddy Bear Company (Shelburne), 269

Vermont Wildflower Farm (Shelburne), 269

Via Matta (Boston), 121

Victoria Mansion (Portland), 68

Village Restaurant (Litchfield), 18

Vincent House (Martha's Vineyard), 164

Vincent's (Camden), 48

Vineyard Haven and Edgartown Shopping (Martha's Vineyard), 164

Vineyard Museum (Martha's Vineyard), 165

W

Wadsworth Atheneum Museum of Art (Hartford), 16

Wadsworth-Longfellow House (Portland), 69

Walden Pond State Reservation (Concord), 137

Walking Tour of Historic

Apponaug Village (Warwick), 247

Wanton-Lyman-Hazard House (Newport), 239

Warner House (Portsmouth), 229

Warren's Lobster House (Kittery), 61

Warwick Heritage Festival (Warwick), 248

Water Street Grill (Williamstown), 206

Waterfire (Providence), 245

Waterfront (Camden), 49

Water's Edge Resort and Conference Center (Old Saybrook), 29

The Wauwinet (Nantucket), 175

Waybury Inn (Middlebury), 262

Wayside (Concord), 137

Webster Cottage (Hanover), 218

Wellfleet Bay Wildlife Sanctuary (Wellfleet), 205

Wellfleet Drive-In Theater (Wellfleet), 205

Wendell Gilley Museum (Southwest Harbor), 75

Wentworth Resort Hotel (Jackson), 221

Wentworth-Gardner House (Portsmouth), 229

Wequassett Resort and Golf Club (Chatham), 134

West Parish Meetinghouse (Hyannis and Barnstable), 150

Western Gateway Heritage State Park (North Adams), 185

Westin Boston Waterfront (Boston), 102

Westin Copley Place (Boston), 102

The Westin Providence (Providence), 246

Whale Watching (Provincetown), 192

Whaler's Inn (Mystic), 21

The Whalewalk Inn (Eastham), 141

Wheatleigh (Lenox), 156, 158

Whistler House Museum of Art (Lowell), 161

The White Barn Inn Restaurant (Kennebunkport), 59

The White Barn Inn

(Kennebunkport), *57*

White Elephant Resort (Nantucket), *175*

White Horse Tavern (Newport), *242*

White Mountain Hotel & Resort (North Conway), *227*

Whitehall Inn (Camden), *48*

Whitehall Museum House (Newport), *239*

Wildcat Inn & Tavern (Jackson), *221*

Wilhelm Reich Museum (Rangeley), *72*

Williams College Museum of Art (Williamstown), *205*

Williams College (Williamstown), *205*

Williamsville Inn (Stockbridge), *202*

Williamsville Inn Restauarant (Stockbridge), 203

Willowbend Children's Charity Pro-Am (Hyannis and Barnstable), *151*

Wilson Castle (Rutland), *267*

Windflower Inn (Great Barrington), *147*

Windham Hill Inn (Newfane), *264*

Windjammer Days (Boothbay Harbor), *44*

Windjammer Sailing (Camden), *46*

Windjammer Weekend (Camden), *46*

Windjammers (Rockland), *74*

Windswept Cranberry Bog (Nantucket), *173*

The Winnetu Inn & Resort (Martha's Vineyard), *166*

Winnipesaukee Scenic Railroad (Meredith), *223*

Winter Carnival (Middlebury), *262*

Witch Dungeon Museum (Salem), *197*

Witch House (Salem), *198*

Woodford State Park (Bennington), *251*

Woodlawn Museum (the Black House) (Northeast Harbor), *63*

Woodstock Country Club (Woodstock), *276*

Woodstock Historical Society (Woodstock), *277*

Woodstock Inn & Resort (Woodstock), *278*

Woodstock Inn (Woodstock), *280*

Woodstocker Bed and Breakfast (Woodstock), *279*

Worcester Art Museum (Worcester), *207*

The Wyndhurst Restaurant (Lenox), *158*

X

XV Beacon (Boston), *102*

Y

Yale Repertory Theater (New Haven), *24*

Yale University (New Haven), *23*

The Yard (Martha's Vineyard), *165*

York Harbor Inn (York), *78*

CONNECTICUT

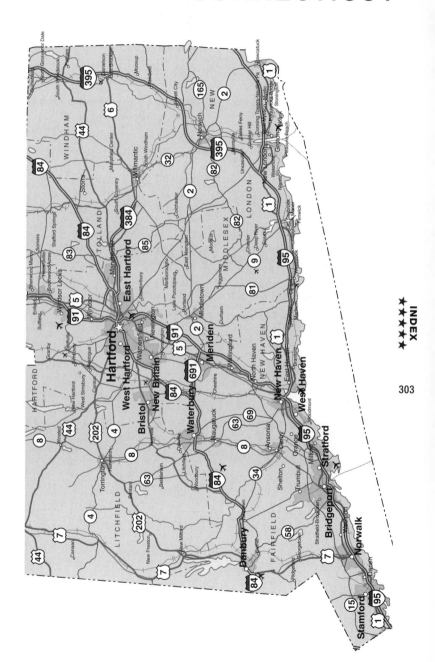

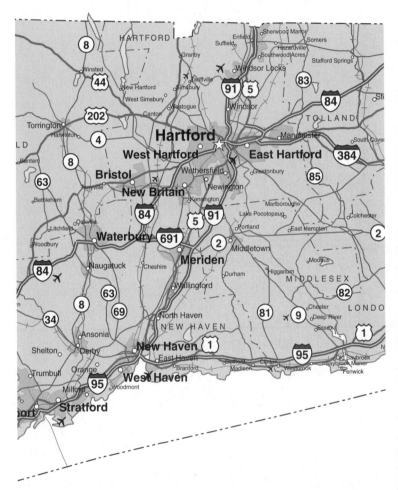

MAINE

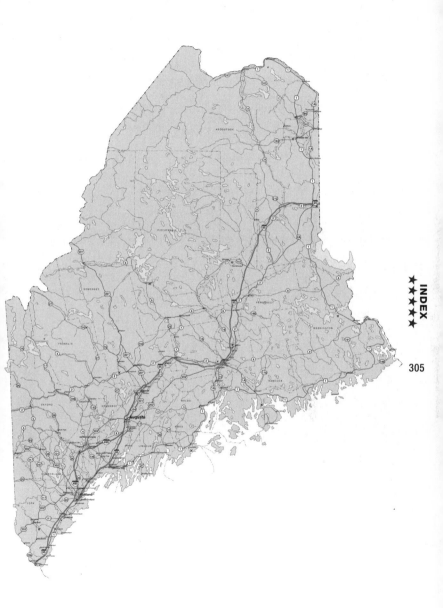

AUGUSTA AND PORTLAND

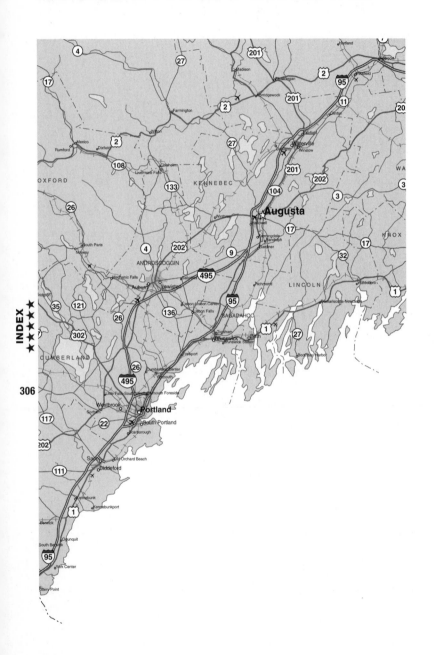

BOSTON AND THE CAPE

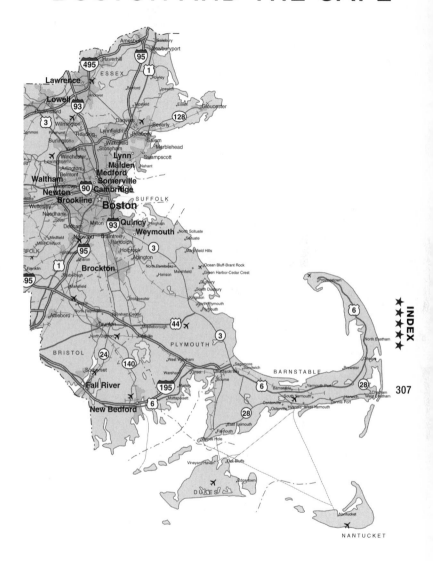

MASSACHUSETTS

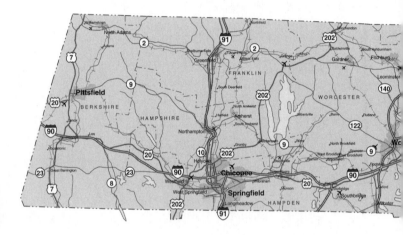

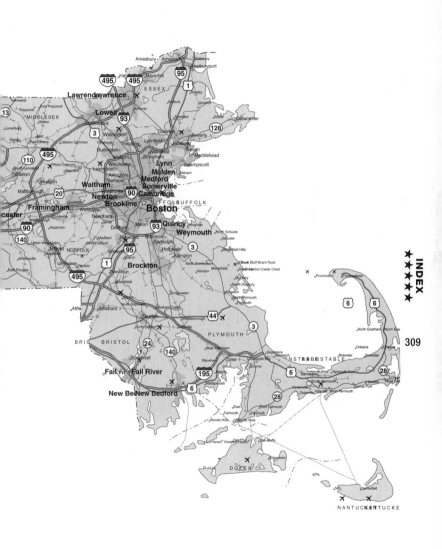

NEW HAMPSHIRE

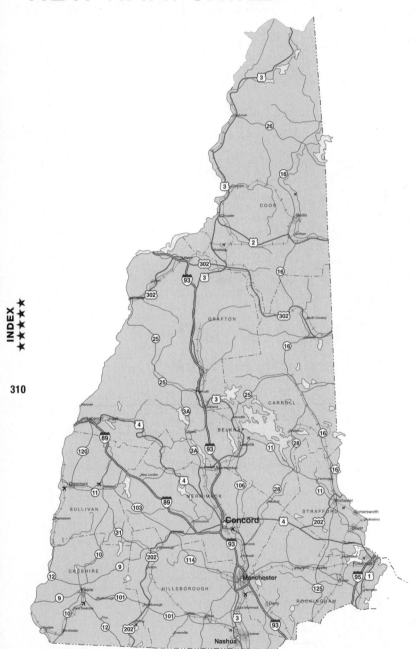

CONCORD

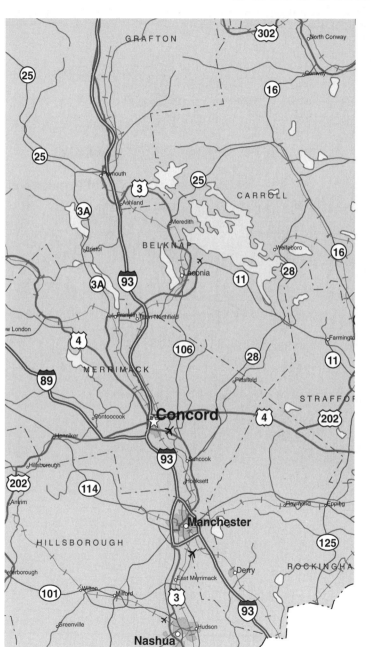

RHODE ISLAND

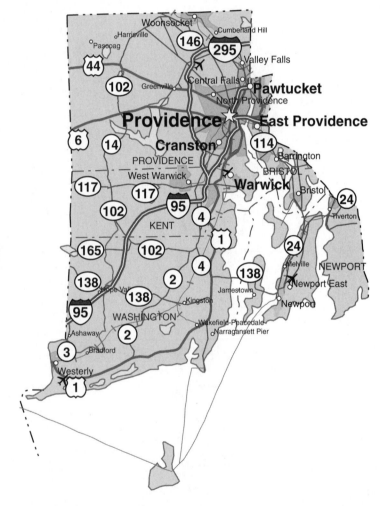

VERMONT

MONTPELIER

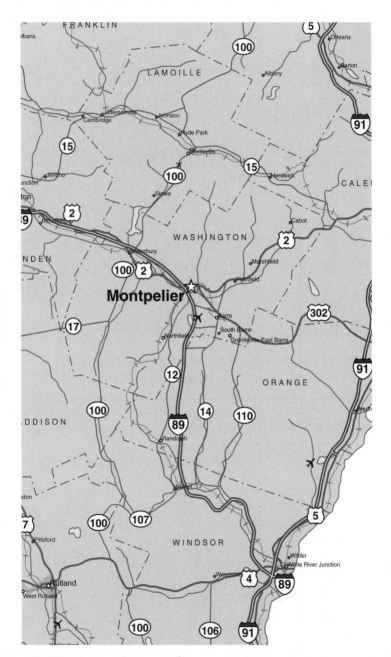

NOTES

NOTES

NOTES

NOTES